Asian Godfathers

Also by Joe Studwell

The China Dream

Asian Godfathers

Money and Power in Hong Kong and Southeast Asia

Joe Studwell

Grove Press
New York

First published in Great Britain in 2007 by
Profile Books, Ltd., London, England

Printed in the United States of America

Published simultaneously in Canada

ISBN-13: 978-0-8021-4391-4

Grove Press
an imprint of Grove/Atlantic, Inc.
841 Broadway
New York, NY 10003

Distributed by Publishers Group West

www.groveatlantic.com

11 12 13 14   10 9 8 7 6 5

For my father, Eric, who died unexpectedly while this book was being finished. We miss him.

Contents

SOUTH EAST ASIA IN 1900

CONTEMPORARY
SOUTH EAST ASIA

Introduction

Fitzgerald: *'You know, the rich are different than you and me.'*
Hemingway: *'Yes, they have more money.'*

An exchange Ernest Hemingway claimed to have had with F. Scott Fitzgerald[1]

This is a book about a small group of very rich men – the south-east Asian billionaires who, in the post-Second World War era, came to dominate the domestic economies of their region. For the purposes of what follows, south-east Asia is defined as the five original members of the Association of South-east Asian Nations (ASEAN) – Singapore, Malaysia, Thailand, Indonesia and the Philippines – plus Hong Kong, a place that traditionally swivels on an axis that allows it to be part of 'greater China' and south-east Asia as self-interest dictates. These six entities are the economic story of their region, the south-eastern contributors to what the World Bank dubbed in 1993 'the East Asian miracle'.[2] Five other states – Vietnam, Cambodia, Laos, Myanmar (Burma) and Brunei – describe themselves as south-east Asian, but they return a combined economic product little more than half that of Singapore (with a population of four million people) and are referred to only in passing.[3]

It is very unusual for a book about the south-east Asian region to attempt a thematic appraisal of half a dozen territories. Most academic scholars have limited themselves to one or two countries. A handful of generalist works have tended to feature different chapters on separate states. These self-determined limitations are not without merit in what is an extremely diverse region. Nevertheless, this book undertakes a broad sweep, because it aims to highlight the fact that the six territories discussed are linked by powerful, unifying themes – most importantly, similar historical legacies and a very particular relationship between political and economic power. These historical and structural similarities, and their significance, have been under-estimated and under-reported by academic and journalistic commentators who have focused on individual countries.[4] The states' tycoon businessmen demand attention because they are a common symptom of a common set of circumstances.

In 1996, the year before the start of the 'Asian financial crisis' that turned the region's economy on its head, *Forbes* magazine, in its annual ranking of richest individuals, listed eight south-east Asian businessmen among the top twenty-five in the world and thirteen among the top fifty.[5] A small region that, concurrently, could not boast a single non-state corporation among the global top 500 none the less accounted for a third of the wealthiest two dozen people on the planet. These were the vanguard of the Asian godfathers, each with more than four billion American dollars to his name – the likes of Li Ka-shing, Robert Kuok, Dhanin Chearavanont, Liem Sioe Liong, Tan Yu and Kwek Leng Beng; behind them came a phalanx of lesser tycoons, with one, two and three billion dollars of net worth.

In a region where US$500 a month is a very good wage, this embarrassment of riches of the few provides a remarkable contrast. So why have secretive tycoons come to rule the economies of south-east Asia? What have they contributed to the region's overall economic development? And, perhaps most important, why are they still so powerful, when the depth and potency of the Asian financial crisis – an event to whose origins they were central – appeared, to many observers, to be likely to emasculate them? It did not. As we shall see, the tycoons today are as entrenched as ever, with only a small minority of the weakest members of their class having succumbed to the corporate debt load that was brought into focus by the crisis. The quest for answers to the above three questions is the central task of this book.

In the search for answers, what follows uses the tycoons as a convenient vehicle for examining broader economic and political issues. This is a structural sleight for which no apology is offered: a straight historical narrative covering two entrepôt city states (as Hong Kong and Singapore are most usefully, if not politically correctly, considered) and four 'proper' countries – Malaysia, Thailand, Indonesia and the Philippines – would be unduly segmented and draining. A circuitous but more reader-friendly approach is preferred. In this respect, Lytton Strachey's celebrated tome *Eminent Victorians*, published in 1918, is something of an inspiration. When Strachey wanted to capture the cant and hypocrisy of Victorian England, he refused what he called 'the direct method of a scrupulous narration' and focused instead on the lives of a few 'eminent' people. It is hoped the tales of Asian tycoons might be half as illuminating. It is also hoped that an analysis of south-east Asia – once fingered for developed region status but more recently overtaken as the darling of international punditry by China and India – will provide useful input to the imperfect science that is developmental economics.

The Plot

There is a danger with a bottom-up (if this term can be used in reference to a few eminent people) approach to south-east Asia's recent history. It is that the reader may be drawn too deeply into the anecdotal detail of tycoons' sometimes bizarre and extraordinary lives, and lose track of the bigger economic and political picture. In order to minimise this risk, it is helpful to précis the book's main themes upfront.

These are, first and foremost, that the south-east Asian economy is the product of a relationship between political and economic power that developed in the colonial era and was sustained, with a different cast of characters, in the post-colonial era. In this relationship, a political élite grants to members of an economic élite monopoly concessions, normally in domestic service industries, that enable the latter to extract enormous amounts of wealth, without a requirement to generate the technological capabilities, branded corporations and productivity gains that drive sustainable economic development. During the colonial era, these arrangements were confined mostly to members of the colonial élite, and to a lesser extent to other outsider groups. In the post-colonial era it was expedient for new indigenous political leaderships to nurture their own dependent class of, typically, non-indigenous tycoons who could siphon off economic rents, give a share to their political masters, and not pose a threat to political power. The tycoon class served its political purpose, and generated enormous personal wealth, but did little to promote overall economic growth. Instead, growth came from a combination of small-scale entrepreneurs, many concentrated in and around manufacturing, and a policy of renting out the local labour force to efficient multinational exporters. The city states of Hong Kong and Singapore prospered as ports, financial processors and offshore centres in which to stash capital generated in the rest of the region. All these economic arrangements appeared to work acceptably well until the July 1997 onset of the financial crisis. At that point it became clear that south-east Asia had major failings of political and institutional development, which set the region up for an almighty crash. Most of those problems have not been tackled in the decade since the crisis broke and it remains unclear whether they will be. The political and economic élites continue to live high on the hog – and believe in their right to rule – and there is no way to predict whether they will undergo some kind of moral epiphany.[6]

Finally, something must be said about the title of this book. In dubbing the tycoons 'godfathers', the author is neither judging them as an entirely malevolent species nor suggesting that they are involved in running organised crime. As will become apparent, some of our Asian godfathers have been involved in smuggling – of soft and hard commodities and, less often, of people, drugs and weapons. A significant minority is also intimately connected with gambling. These activities frequently involve contact with Asia's criminal underworld – Chinese triads, Indonesian *preman*, and so on – and this is a fact of life that tycoons deal with. But it does not mean they are mafia bosses. Rather, most Asian organised crime inhabits a parallel, but connected, universe to that of the tycoons. It is also worth remembering that Asian politicians – British and Japanese colonists, the Chinese Communist Party, Suharto – have a long history of co-operating with organised crime groups when it is in their interest; in this respect they are not so different from their local business leaders as they might like to think. [7]

The use of the term godfather in this book aims to reflect traditions of paternalism, male power, aloofness and mystique that are absolutely part of the Asian tycoon story. The title is also more than a little tongue-in-cheek. Just as Mario Puzo, author of the original *Godfather*, always said his construct was an elaborate fantasy – 'a very romanticized myth', he called it[8] – so it is the contention of this work that another great mythology has grown up around south-east Asia's tycoons: one that makes them appear equally mysterious and untouchable. The Asian legend contains sub-myths about race, culture, genetics, entrepreneurialism and, indeed, the entire grounding of economic progress in the region since the end of colonialism. In this sense, *Asian Godfathers* is Mario Puzo in reverse – we already have a myth; the job in hand is to deconstruct it.

What the Plot is Not

In its attempt to peel back the layers of received but unsubstantiated opinion surrounding south-east Asian history, the narrative path of what follows does cross some rather fraught and dangerous terrain. This is the landscape of race, ethnicity and culture in one of the world's most disparate regions. The modern history of south-east Asia is one bound up with migrations – of Europeans and Americans (colonial rulers and otherwise), Chinese, Indians, Sri Lankans, diasporic Jews and Armenians and more – into what were previously pre-industrial, quasi-feudal societies. Moreover, the host populations were already ethnically and religiously extremely mixed – not to mention horizontally riven by distinctions of class and birthright that are readily intelligible to Europeans – creating an environment with at least as much fuel for ethnic and social conflict as Europe or Africa. In this sectarian maelstrom, racial stereotyping is still all too often the norm, while many people – as we shall see – have reason to pretend to be things they are not. This book tries to cut through some of the more egregious nonsense that is reported about matters cultural in south-east Asia; the author begs forgiveness at the outset for any unintended offence given in the process.

At the economic level, race-based interpretations of development have long formed the bedrock of analyses of south-east Asia. Every Asian school child knows that in the nineteenth and early twentieth centuries many colonials viewed their endeavours through the prism of what Rudyard Kipling termed 'the white man's burden'[9] – they were bringing their superior scientific, institutional and moral resources to bear on inferior Asian peoples, carrying them towards modernity. More intriguing is that in the post-independence era, racial interpretations have continued to predominate in discussion of the economic boom that followed the white man's departure. The chief reason is the commercial pre-eminence of the largest migrant group in the region, the Chinese. This has encouraged more nuanced, but none the less unmistakeably culture- and race-based readings of the development story of the past fifty years. Some see the Chinese as particularly brilliant, others see them as particularly parasitic; still others argue that they are culturally predestined in different ways (excellent family businessmen, cannot operate globally, guaranteed to remain sub-scale, and so on). This book takes issue with each of these stereotypes.

It is not difficult, however, to see how raw data recommend notions of Chinese exceptionalism. The ethnic Chinese share of listed equity in ASEAN stock markets has been estimated at between 50 per cent and 80 per cent, depending on the country in question;[10] this compares with an ethnic Chinese share of population of 2 per cent in the Philippines, 4 per cent in Indonesia, 10 per cent in Thailand, 29 per cent in Malaysia and 77 per cent in Singapore. Looking at it from another perspective, researchers in the 1990s estimated that 'Chinese' interests controlled 45 per cent of major firms in the Philippines, all but two of the twenty largest corporations in Indonesia, nine of the ten biggest businesses in Thailand, and twenty-four of the top sixty companies in Malaysia.[11] Most of Asia's godfathers are ethnic Chinese.

The boom years of the 1990s were an apogee for racial theorists and brought forth a slough of culture-based books about the economic prowess of the overseas Chinese. Among the more memorable and influential were S. Gordon Redding's *The Spirit of Chinese Capitalism* (1990), Sterling Seagrave's *Lords of the Rim* (1995), and Joel Kotkin's *Tribes: How Race, Religion and Identity Determine Success in the New Global Economy* (1992) – the latter including the overseas Chinese among a number of global 'tribes' predestined for commercial success. The expression 'bamboo network' came into fashion to describe perceived links between ethnic Chinese around the region that would explain their economic dynamism. In general, the media – serious and sensational – bought into this cultural analysis in a big way; its mystery and masonic undertones do make for strong stories. At the same time, academia produced a small but steady stream of economists more sceptical of Chinese exceptionalism; they were led by Japanese scholars, but their ranks broadened in the run-up to and aftermath of the financial crisis.[12]

The author would like to put his cards in the cultural determinism debate on the table straightaway. The experience of living for a decade in China, plus a long period of research for this book, has produced three fundamental objections to a culture-centred explanation of the economic contribution of ethnic Chinese in south-east Asia. The first is that notions of a cultural imperative ignore historical context. Most south-east Asian migration took place in a colonial era when different groups were channelled by colonial governments – with their 'superior' organisational capacity – towards different activities. Educated Indians and Sri Lankans (Ceylonese, as they then were) in the British Empire were recruited for government and professional positions. Hence an observer outside the high court in Singapore or Kuala Lumpur today will note that a disproportionate number of lawyers and judges are of subcontinental ancestry. This is not because Indians are genetically modified to be lawyers, it is the legacy of British colonial rule. When the Chinese arrived in south-east Asia, they were frequently barred from government service and from many professions, and often not permitted to own agricultural land or engage in farming; opportunities in trade and commerce, however, were largely untrammelled. Those who say that Chinese are 'born traders' are guilty of the same simplism as those who say Jews are 'born financiers'. It is omitted that in pre-nineteenth-century Europe Jews were excluded from guilds, from many areas of trade and from farming, while the Christian church proscribed its followers from lending money at interest (not unlike contemporary Islam). Most economic opportunities for Jews were circumscribed while those in banking were unnaturally ripe. A contemporary echo of this situation can be found in Russia, where almost all of the post-Cold War 'oligarchs' who dominate the country's economy – at the behest and whim of a more purely Slavic political élite – are Jewish.[13]

The second objection to culture-based theory is that it implies that the Chinese are homogenous and that the Chinese in south-east Asia are typical of the Chinese race in general. Yet the Chinese of the pre-1949 era of mass migration were particularly unhomogenous. This is most starkly apparent in the matter of spoken language. China remains a place where one need travel only fifty or sixty kilometres to find a new and entirely unintelligible dialect (a misleading word in the Chinese context, since in other countries a different dialect means relatively modest changes in pronunciation, vocabulary and grammar). The importance of the parochialism this engendered in Chinese history is disguised today by the fact that the post-1949 communist government successfully promoted the use of a national, standard Mandarin Chinese, as well as unprecedented levels of literacy. By 1949, however, almost all Chinese migration to south-east Asia was complete. When it took place, people left home not so much as 'Chinese', but as members of mutually unintelligible dialect groups, thrown into an alien melting pot. Many outside observers in the colonial era commented on the results. Victor Purcell, in *The Chinese in Malaya*, observed: 'Chinese tribes were brought into a proximity unexampled in their native country – tribes speaking different dialects regarded one another almost as foreigners.'[14] The adventurer George Windsor Earl noted as early as the 1830s that different Chinese speech groups in south-east Asia were 'strongly opposed to each other, as much so, indeed, as if they belonged to rival nations'.[15] These writers, however, failed to grasp the economic implications of their observations. The fragmentation of the Chinese 'tribes' meant that they competed fiercely – sometimes violently when effective government was absent – for economic opportunity. And there is nothing more fundamental to economic progress than competition. In this sense, the cultural determinism argument can only be sustained if one says that historically a big part of being overseas Chinese has been about not really being 'Chinese' at all. Such an argument would likely be difficult for contemporary Chinese eugenists, such as Singapore's Minister Mentor Lee Kuan Yew, to swallow.

The corollary issue of whether the south-east Asian Chinese in particular can be said to reflect 'norms' of Chinese-ness is also an historically subtle one. In general, it is probably fair to say that emigrants from any society – be they Irish or Italians who went to America, or Japanese who accepted transit to Brazil in the early twentieth century – outperform, in the aggregate, those they leave behind. Such migrants are a self-selecting group of individuals unusual in their willingness to take significant risks for the chance of a better future. In this sense it is a commonality of migration that the people who go are not a good match for the people who stay home, and one should therefore be wary of cultural extrapolations. But in south-east Asia, the story is more nuanced still. This is because, although the use of trickery, coercion and inequitable indentured labour contracts was not uncommon among Chinese who migrated, in south-east Asia they were much more likely to be free and self-selecting emigrants than the second-biggest group of arrivals – people from the Indian subcontinent. In the era of indentured labour (a 'liberal' replacement for slavery from the 1840s), Indian estate and mine labourers came from a British colony where recruitment systematically focused on low-caste, often 'untouchable' communities. These cowed serfs gave white plantation owners little trouble, but they were relatively less likely to become economic winners compared with the self-selecting Chinese.

The third, and final challenge to the notion of Chinese cultural supremacy in south-east Asia is that it conflates Chinese emigrants with the godfathers. This is deeply misleading. To begin with, although most overseas Chinese enjoy above-average incomes, in places like the north coast towns of Java and Sumatra or non-metropolitan Thailand there are myriad Chinese families that have lived for generations in poverty no less abject than that of other peoples. Ethnicity is not a guarantee of success. As the historian of the overseas Chinese, Lynn Pan, put it: 'The later typecasting of the overseas Chinese as successful entrepreneurs obscures the fact that failure was very much a part of the migrant's experience.'[16] If most billionaires are ethnically Chinese or part-Chinese, it should also be remembered that emigrants from China were prime movers in the creation of communist movements in south-east Asia, a reflection of their more commonly proletarian and downtrodden status. Chinese in south-east Asia do not inevitably identify themselves along ethnic lines and class is an entirely intelligible concept to them – even if, in the past half century, it has been made politically taboo to mention class in their part of the world.

As to the godfathers themselves, it is suggested that they are an atypical élite, an economic aristocracy of outsiders that works hand in glove with local political élites. Culturally, the godfathers are chameleons who tend to be well-educated, cosmopolitan, polylingual and thoroughly insulated from the humdrum cares of their supposed kinsmen. Moreover – and contrary to popular prejudice – the region's tycoons are far from all Chinese. Only a minority is pure Chinese with a strong cultural and linguistic affiliation to China. Other tycoons are pure Chinese but have lost much of their cultural affiliation and some or all of the ability to read and write Chinese (though this is often not admitted). Many are Eurasian, though the non-Chinese bloodline is sometimes seen as a source of embarrassment and played down, particularly in a Chinese setting. And then there are godfathers who are not Chinese at all. This book will show that the behaviour of the ethnic Chinese majority among the tycoon fraternity does not differ substantively from that of English or Scottish 'taipans' in Hong Kong, ethnic Spanish godfathers in the Philippines or the richest man in Malaysia, a Sri Lankan Tamil. They are defined by godfatherdom first, and by race second.

Despite all of the above, it would be overly dismissive to suggest that the reams of academic research published about 'Chinese capitalism' are a sham. The point is simply that cultural interpretations are overused and should be treated with scepticism, particularly when they shade off – as will be described – into crude racial theories. At the most general level, the relative economic success of the overseas Chinese makes it hard to argue that cultural factors – cohesive familism, the stress on prescribed roles, discipline and filial piety – are without influence at grass roots level. But the more abstract argument about a Confucian 'value system' driving a unique form of Chinese entrepreneurialism does not stand up. In particular, discussion of Confucianism fails to distinguish between the theory of a roster of vague moral precepts and the implementation of ideals so utopian as to be far more honoured in the breach than in the observance. What can be said with assurance in overwhelmingly Chinese societies like Singapore, Hong Kong and China itself, is that appeals to the Confucian ethic have traditionally been used by politicians – local and colonial – to justify all manner of decidedly un-idealistic social control.

Nurture over Nature

If the culture-tinged conclusions reached by most economic analyses of south-east Asia (in which ethnic Chinese tycoons – for better or for worse, depending on the writer -- are at the apex of the development process) are fundamentally flawed, what are the true reasons for the godfathers' rise and for their apparently unshakable grip on power – so strong that most weathered the turbulence of the Asian financial crisis unscathed? This book argues that these individuals are above all the economic products of the political environment in which they operate and that it is this same political environment that is preventing the region from achieving sustained economic progress. In a worst-case scenario, south-east Asia may be headed towards Latin America-style stagnation and inequality.

Centralised governments that under-regulate competition (in the sense of failing to ensure its presence) and over-regulate market access (through restrictive licensing and non-competitive tendering) guarantee that merchant capitalists – or asset traders, to use a more pejorative term – will rise to the top by arbitraging the economic inefficiencies created by the politicians. The trend is reinforced in south-east Asia by the widespread presence of what could be called 'manipulated democracy', either in the guise of predetermined-winner democracy (Singapore, Malaysia, Suharto's Indonesia) or else the scenario where business interests gain so close a control of the political system that they are almost unaffected by the changes of government that do occur (as in Thailand and the Philippines). In both instances, politicians spend huge sums to maintain a grip on power that has some semblance of legitimacy. This can only be financed through direct political ownership of big business or, more usually, contributions from nominally independent big business that is beholden to politicians. Whichever, the mechanism creates a not entirely unhappy dependence of élites between politicians and tycoons. And the most comfortable relationship is between the politician who is indigenous and the tycoon who is a politically unthreatening immigrant.

After fifteen years of looking at developing countries in Asia, the author's conviction is that systems are far more important than people in determining which societies climb the slippery slope to prosperity. It is not individuals but more efficient political and social institutions that have made countries as diverse as Japan, the United States and most of the members of the European Union rich. The fact that south-east Asia – excepting its two, extremely lucky city states – is still rather poor is a result of political failure, not because the region produces unusually rapacious businessmen; that political failure is not on the level of communist Vietnam or Laos or of the kleptocracies in Cambodia and Myanmar, but it is none the less failure. Politics and institutional life will have to change if the region is to move forward.

The Asian godfathers reflect rather than shape local economies, just like the early nineteenth-century European financial dynasties – the Warburgs, the Rothschilds, the Barings – or the turn-of-the-century American financiers and tycoons – Morgan, Vanderbilt, Carnegie, Rockefeller – were the products of a particular set of economic and political circumstances. The European bankers exploited an era of weak and sub-scale states where rulers without treasuries, central banks and adequate tax collection had no other channel through which to raise and invest capital. In turn-of-the-century America, financier J. Pierpont Morgan further leveraged the power of the middleman at a time when emergent corporations were poorly organised and short of cash, when minority shareholders could be abused with near-impunity and when the legislative overseeing of anti-competitive practices was in its infancy. (Some of this may sound familiar to Asians.) In this benign setting, oil, industrial and railroad tycoons were contented accomplices in stacking up giant oligopolies or 'trusts'.

The story of the middleman tycoon ended in Europe and America when states developed the capacity to manage their own finances, and the public, via its elected politicians, decided it had had enough of what a popular 1930s book dubbed 'robber barons'.[17] The American godfather was reined in by President Teddy Roosevelt's trust-busting Bureau of Corporations, a Federal Reserve Act that established a central bank independent of commercial actors, a rigorously enforced Securities Act with requirements for public disclosure of corporate information, and the well-known Glass–Steagall Bill, which forced the separation of retail banking from securities businesses and thereby cut off the broadest avenue to minority investor abuse.[18] All this took place around a series of debilitating financial crises – most notably the Panic of 1907 and the Wall Street Crash of 1929.

The United States political machine, despite suffering a significant degree of corruption at the time, reacted to these crises with the implementation of fundamental institutional reform. Two questions addressed in the latter stages of this book are who or what will tame the Asian godfathers and when might this happen? At the inception of this project the author thought – in the blissful ignorance of pre-research speculation – that the Asian financial crisis had been so severe, and exposed so many naked emperors, that the region would be compelled to make root-and-branch changes in pursuit of political and economic systems that can deliver sustainable development. As the air miles and interview notes piled up, however, it became apparent that south-east Asia is balanced in a much more precarious position. Each of the 'proper' countries we will follow has yet to make clear choices between a policy path that leads to developed nation status or a trajectory that circles endlessly around, Latin America-like, in the purgatory of what the World Bank calls 'lower middle-income economies'.[19] One reason for this, it is suggested, is that the Latin American scenario is not so unattractive to powerful élites that will continue to live well even while the dreams of the majority are shattered. Meanwhile, the city states of Hong Kong and Singapore have big -- and not so different as one might imagine -- political issues of their own to resolve.

Where Growth Really Came From

Asian godfathers exploit political inefficiency for gain. This much will soon be clear. But it is also important to establish the true measure of their contribution to regional development. The short answer is that this has been far less than is popularly believed. The godfathers have been much more the beneficiaries than the instigators of growth. One barometer of this is that their companies' performance in terms of productivity typically lags behind that of the overall economies in which they operate. And nothing is more fundamental to sustainable economic development than productivity gains. As one example, a recent study in Thailand showed that productivity increases in the past twenty years have been markedly higher in agriculture and manufacturing than in the services businesses in which tycoons predominate.[20] Equally, returns in listed companies controlled by the godfathers have been far from impressive, helping south-east Asia – contrary to the popular image of 'tiger economies' – to post the worst stock market performance of any emerging region over the past two decades; this sorry phenomenon will be discussed in some detail.

So, if not the men who adorn the covers of Asian business magazines, what has been the region's economic locomotive? The argument of this book – though not an orthodox economic analysis – is that it is smaller-scale local businesses and the hard work and thrift of ordinary south-east Asians that have driven development. This is true in an indirect way – through public saving – with collateral consequences that are sometimes unintentionally negative, and in a more purely positive direct manner – through small- and medium-scale business. Indirectly, much growth has been funded by investment made possible by working people's high propensity to save their income – usually defined in terms of the regional 'savings rate', or the portion of disposable household income that is squirreled away in banks and other savings instruments. A world-beating regional savings rate that peaked before the Asian financial crisis at close to 40 per cent would appear admirable, but it increasingly put too much cheap money, via financial systems, in the hands of politicians and their tycoon partners. We shall see how, in extreme cases in countries like Indonesia and the Philippines, godfathers turned commercial banks into personal piggy banks. In the run-up to the Asian financial crisis of 1997, so much investment was thereby diverted to projects of no commercial merit that a collapse became inevitable.

Directly, smaller-scale businesses – as suppliers and principals – and ordinary people drove south-east Asia's development because they are at the heart of the region's stunning export success. Nothing, over the span of the past forty-five years, has made a comparable contribution to sustainable growth. While heavy industrialisation and import substitution policies – often involving godfather corporations – have had poor results, the promotion of export manufacturing has been perennially successful. The dollar value of exports from the original ASEAN countries increased by between 11 and 15 per cent a year over the years from 1960 to 2005, and by much more in peak periods, such as that after the mid-1980s. This is not a book constructed around graphs, but it is worth committing to memory the message contained in Figure 1 (p.299) in the appendix. The figure shows the clear relationship between economic growth (nominal increases in Gross Domestic Product (GDP)) and exports since 1965 in the countries we are surveying. There is some divergence before the regional export economy took off at the start of the 1970s, but thereafter growth and exports move almost in lock-step. In short, without their exports, these economies do not shift.[21]

The great discovery of south-east Asian governments in the late 1960s was that their diverse populations (contrary to colonial myth) were rather uniformly hard-working and would happily toil through the day and night in factories making clothing, shoes, appliances and electronics. Government needed only to woo investment – most of it foreign – with full ownership rights for production facilities, tax breaks and central bank intervention to keep local currencies undervalued and hence exports cheap. The proposition was irresistible for cost-cutting multinationals and spawned globally competitive, but small-scale local businesses to provide components and contract manufacturing and support services: anything from making models for toy moulds to packaging semiconductors to cleaning multinationals' factories. For the most part – once import substitution policies were dismantled – the tycoons stayed out of the export processing game; it is one that must by definition be internationally competitive and is not therefore attractive to people whose comparative advantage lies in their ability to finesse deals, exploit bureaucratic loopholes and butter up politicians.

Small business and diligent individuals working in foreign factories – a majority of exports from Thailand, Malaysia, Indonesia, the Philippines and Singapore are made in foreign-owned businesses, while most Hong Kong manufacturers produce to order for multinational designers and retailers – became the relentless and largely unsung value-adders of the south-east Asian economy. Such was the scale of the foreign trade boom that Malaysia – the dollar value of whose exports increased 118-fold between 1960 and 2005[22] – posts annual export totals in excess of its gross domestic product. (This is possible because, unlike GDP, export numbers are not reported on a value-added basis and in countries like Malaysia include many imported components.) Singapore, whose exports went up 150 times in the same period, posts much the world's highest current account surplus – an astonishing average of 17 per cent of GDP since 1990 – reflecting its enormous, positive balance on trade in goods and services.[23]

Unfortunately, the export dependency model – more recently taken up by China – does have its drawbacks. Where too many exports are made by or for foreign companies, those buyers can be fickle friends. In the 1990s southeast Asian countries discovered this when foreign manufacturers began to relocate their operations to lower-cost sites, most obviously in China, but also in countries like Vietnam and Bangladesh. The process began well before the financial crisis but exacerbated its effects. It was no coincidence that 1996, the year before the meltdown, witnessed a sudden slowdown in export growth throughout the region. In Thailand, where the crisis began, exports contracted.[24] In subsequent years there has been a recovery in exports from south-east Asia, driven by shipments of commodities like timber, rubber and palm oil and some specialised manufactures, but the trend for lower value-added manufacturing exports is that the process of scaling back foreign production facilities has a way to run.

When the export engine stops humming in south-east Asia, the effect is to refocus attention on what else the region's economies have to offer. The answer, at present, is not enough. The big domestic businesses run by the Asian godfathers grew up on a diet of protected markets, cartels and non-competitive tenders for public works. The result is that, almost without exception – from Singaporean banks to Hong Kong supermarkets to Indonesian noodle makers – south-east Asia lacks globally competitive companies. Moreover, unlike in Japan, South Korea and Taiwan, there has been a heavy dependence on foreign providers of technology and project management because the godfathers are so concentrated on finessing deals in over-regulated markets that they leave technical execution to outsiders. This has led to what one of the earliest critics of the godfather economies, the Japanese scholar Yoshihara Kunio, termed 'technologyless industrialisation'. South-east Asia has all the trappings of a modern economy – high-tech factories, stunning high-rise buildings, contemporary transportation systems and utility providers – but no indigenous, large-scale companies producing world-class products and services. As a result, there are no global brands.[25] Real competitiveness is limited to relatively small-scale businesses because tycoons have plucked all the fat economic fruits for themselves. It is worth recalling what Mr Yoshihara said in his seminal work two decades ago: 'My real purpose ... is to call attention to the emergence of an inefficient, at best lacklustre, superlayer of the economy, and to invite thought about the problems it poses to economic development in the future.'[26]

Written ten years before the Asian financial crisis, those words were a prescient warning, as were others delivered in the early 1990s by the likes of the American economist Paul Krugman.[27] In the aftermath of the crisis, it did seem for a time that the political and economic structures that created that 'superlayer' to the south-east Asian economy would be swept away. There was much talk, and even some action, with respect to reform and deregulation. In

Indonesia there were democratic elections and in Thailand (yet) another new constitution. But expectations of a watershed were misplaced. Today, a part of the reason to take another tour of the godfather economies is to understand how south-east Asia's political and economic élites managed to protect their fiefdoms. Yet there is no need to be entirely pessimistic about the future. In Europe, the United States and Japan in the late nineteenth century, it was a slow but concerted popular challenge from below that moved political life – and, by association, big business – forward. Whether such momentum can be built in south-east Asia remains to be seen.

The Lovable Rich

It would be a mistake at the outset of our odyssey to think that the godfathers – despite their billions and their place at the centre of the Asian financial crisis – are a myopic bunch. Certainly, they are required by the region's political and economic architecture to bribe as well as to lobby, to threaten as well as to persuade, and to tell a good many lies. But they have risen to their exalted positions because of an unparalleled ability to understand the commercial angles of south-east Asia. We have much to learn from them. While – like those erstwhile godfathers in Europe and the United States – they do not readily throw open their doors to strangers, there are private moments when some will let down their guard. In so doing, this author's experience is that many tycoons regard the distortions in the south-east Asian economies as just as silly as an independent observer does. But their job, like that of any businessman, is to make as much money as possible, with as little fuss as possible, in the environment that prevails. They defend that environment, sometimes shamelessly, because it is part of their businesses' success.

It is also wrong to think that the tycoons conform to any personality stereotype. Their characters vary enormously – though most are utterly charming. (In the course of research it became the author's droll refrain that one could not wish to be expropriated by a nicer bunch of people.) What is true is that in public affairs the godfathers exhibit a high degree of élite consensus that is invariably pro-establishment. Businessmen everywhere are conservative, but this trend is reinforced in south-east Asia by the extremely diversified nature of the tycoons' businesses, which depend more on particularistic favours from governments and less on competitive specialisation. With everyone playing the same game, there is little to argue about in public; the open conflicts – as opposed to private backstabbing – that do occur, increasingly, are with end users of expensive godfather goods and services, like electricity or port facilities in Hong Kong. One of the region's very richest tycoons, in a quiet and candid chat at home, likened the region's economy to 'a nice bowl of fish soup', with plenty to go around for him and his peers. He questioned the motives for this book with the words: 'Why do you want to add lots of chillies?'

In response to that enquiry it should be stressed, emphatically, that it is not the author's desire to demean the tycoons. Discussion of them by academics and the media hitherto has oscillated between fawning admiration for some mythic Asian entrepreneurialism and an equally crude condemnation of perceived parasitic rent-seekers. This book will show that in reality the tycoons are just highly effective traders in rent-offering environments. The economic effect of this has been to make domestic goods and services – whether an apartment in Hong Kong or flour in Malaysia – more expensive than they would otherwise be and to limit the growth of globally competitive companies. But the blame for the resultant situation, in as much as it needs to be attributed, belongs with politicians not with businessmen. It is the politicians' job to defend society's interests. (The knotty problem that arises when Asian business people become politicians – rather than just being their accomplices – will be addressed in due course.) The job of the regular businessman is simply to make money.

It will soon be time to meet the godfathers. But first we must understand the basic facts of their provenance. Contemporary commentators on south-east Asia rarely elucidate historical context, and yet without this it is all but impossible to understand the region's economic story. Consequently, a short tour of pre-colonial and colonial south-east Asia must be undertaken. This concludes with Japan's revolutionary 1930s challenge to white colonialism, the profitable chaos of the Second World War and the Korean and Vietnam wars, and the struggles for independence. Thereafter, we will see how contemporary godfathers have filled their boots to overflowing.

Author's note

Asian languages have given rise to competing systems of romanisation, while confusion reigns in the styling of proper names, whether in Bahasa Indonesia, Thai or Chinese. This book follows whichever usage is likely to be most familiar to contemporary English language readers. With respect to Chinese names, where three major variants on romanised presentation are at work in south-east Asia, those given are the stylings most frequently employed in a person's place of residency. Hence in Hong Kong, where Chinese given names are hyphenated, we have Li Ka-shing. Elsewhere in south-east Asia, where three separate words are preferred, we find Liem Sioe Liong. Mainland Chinese, in the *pinyin* system, are defined by two words, as in Hu Jintao. People who mix Western and Chinese nomenclature are rendered as we know them – like Peter Woo. Of course, this being south-east Asia, many people – especially those from immigrant families – have several names: a Thai one, a Chinese one and an English one, for instance.

As much as possible, this book employs contemporary political and geographical terms familiar to readers. This is also the case in chapter 1, which deals with south-east Asian history as relevant to our story. The close detail of shifting legal definitions of different political entities and amendments to state names, especially in the transition from colonialism to independence, is passed over as a distraction. With respect to the particular complexities of Malaysia and Singapore, however, the following historical recap may be a helpful reference.

The British colonial presence in south-east Asia in the nineteenth century followed two basic legal forms. The island of Singapore, the island of Penang and adjacent province Wellesley in peninsular Malaysia, Malacca, and a few other small islands were taken as colonies, officially confirmed as such from 1867, and were referred to as the Straits Settlements. Other Malay states came under British 'protection', involving the appointment of resident advisers, in a series of agreements starting in 1874. The states of Perak, Selangor, Negri Sembilan and Pahang were then formed into an administrative federation known as the Federated Malay States. Four northern states whose suzerainty was ceded to Britain by Thailand in 1909, plus the important state of

Johore (bordering Singapore), were managed individually. Although the term 'Malaya' is often used, this had no formal legal basis before the Second World War. After the war, Singapore alone was reconstituted as a British Crown Colony, and from 1948 the Federation of Malaya grouped British interests on the peninsula as well as islands including Penang. In 1957 the Federation of Malaya gained independence and in 1963 Malaysia was formed with the inclusion of Singapore (already largely independent as the state of Singapore since 1959), Sarawak and British North Borneo (today the state of Sabah). Singapore left the union in 1965.

British rule in Malaysian territories only reinforced a local predilection for a convoluted system of honorary titles that persists to this day. Apart from the hereditary title Tengku (spelled Tunku in a small number of states), equivalent to 'prince', there are several federal honorifics granted on a non-hereditary basis by the elected head of the nine royal families of Malaysia (but typically on the advice of government), as well as more common state titles, which are used in this book:

Tun   A senior federal title held by no more than twenty-five living recipients
Tan Sri The second most senior federal title
Datuk   A more junior federal title
Dato'   A state title

Honorifics given in other south-east Asian territories are a little less complex and are explained in the text as they arise.

The expression 'overseas Chinese' is employed in this book. It is a common but problematic term. Overseas Chinese, or *huaqiao* – a composite of the words *hua*, meaning 'Chinese', and *qiaoju*, meaning 'a long-term resident' – is the name, historically, that the Chinese gave to their overseas migrants. It implies two things: that the people in question are Chinese by nationality, and that they will return to China when their sojourn is over. This reflected the view of most migrants: they set off for south-east Asia and elsewhere expecting to come back, having made their fortunes. In reality, most people did not come back; they settled down abroad, away from their dysfunctional and impoverished country of birth, had children, and became genuine immigrants of varying degrees of assimilation, acquiring in the process a new nationality. As a result, the term overseas Chinese is now inappropriate to the various Malaysian-Chinese, Thai-Chinese (and so on) people we will discuss. The expression, however, is still so frequently and loosely employed that this book overlooks its inaccuracy and, indeed, the semantic damage it does to relations between emigrants of Chinese ethnicity and the populations of the countries of which they are now nationals – implying, as it does, that the Chinese might up sticks and 'go home' if the fancy takes them. Ironically, there has in the past fifteen years developed a new global population of *huaqiao* to whom the term is more appropriate – hundreds of thousands of (often illegal) Chinese migrants who have travelled abroad, often to the European Union and the United States, expecting to make lots of money and then return to China. It remains to be seen how many will in the end stay away.

The term cartel is used frequently in this book. In its narrowly-defined, European origin, the word meant a collusive association set up by enterprises seeking to monopolise, and control the pricing of, a product or service. The Italian word *cartello*, derived from the term for a piece of paper, originally inferred a written agreement to these ends. A narrow European interpretation of the term cartel is not appropriate to this book – which is about south-east Asia – and is not intended. In south-east Asia, many, if not most, cartels are the product of government policy (and often the legacy of colonial government policy) to restrict market entry, usually by means of licensing. In such cases, businessmen are party to cartels, they benefit from cartel pricing opportunities and restricted competition, but they cannot be said to have concocted a cartel. It is a primary argument of this book that south-east Asian businessmen are a product of the political environment in which they operate, and this is a case in point. From time to time, the expression 'de facto cartel' is employed to remind the reader that cartel arrangements in south-east Asia often do not have the genesis implied by the narrow reading of the term.

Sums of money in this book are expressed in the text either in local currency or in US dollars, depending on what is more appropriate. In a few instances, local currency values are given with US dollar conversions in parentheses. These occur when a complex currency conversion – typically one over an extended period requiring an average exchange rate – is necessary. For simple conversions of other local currency values, the following table will be helpful. It shows US dollar exchange rates on 1 July 1997 (the day before the Asian financial crisis began), the lowest daily rate after the start of the crisis, and the rate at 1 April 2007. South-east Asian currencies were 'pegged' in different ways to the US dollar before the crisis, and so the 1 July 1997 rates are a rough guide to dollar values at all points from the mid-1980s to 1997.

South-east Asian Exchange Rates against the US Dollar

	1 July 1997	Lowest daily rate 1997–2007	1 April 2007
Hong Kong dollar (HK$)	7.75	n/a	7.82
Singapore dollar (SG$)	1.43	1.79 (12/01/1998)	1.52
Thai baht (THB)	24.8	55.8 (13/01/1998)	32.50
Malaysian ringgit (MYR)	2.52	4.66 (09/01/1998)	3.46
Indonesian rupiah (IDR)	2,433	16,475 (17/06/1998)	9,099
Philippine peso (PHP)	26.38	46.10 (06/01/1998)	48.23

n/a = not applicable. Hong Kong's currency board sets absolute trading limits; the limit in 1997 was 7.75 but this has recently been increased to a narrow trading band of 7.75 to 7.85, reflected in the 1 April 2007 value of 7.82.
Source: oanda.com. Rates are daily averages of inter-bank rates.

For those wishing to know more about the identities and backgrounds of any of the businessmen and politicians in this book, there is a substantial Cast of Characters section, on p241. All reasonable efforts have been made to ensure the accuracy of this reference, but it should be noted that relatively more of the information in the Cast is drawn from secondary (as opposed to primary) sources than in the main text of the book.

Part I
Godfathers of Yore

1

The context

'People are trapped in history and history is trapped in them.'

James Baldwin, *Notes of a Native Son* (1955)

The contemporary economic landscape of Thailand, Malaysia, Indonesia, the Philippines, Singapore and Hong Kong was shaped by the interaction of two historical forces: migration and colonialism. Migration came first. Long before European colonists arrived in south-east Asia, Arabs, Indians and Chinese were settling in the region. The latter, hailing from what was the world's biggest economy until the nineteenth century, were the most numerous.

The early history of these immigrants is sketchy at best.[1] What we know is that, landing in a patchwork of small, feudal states (where Thailand was the only unified state approximating to its current geographical footprint), the new arrivals engaged in much more than arm's-length trade.[2] In Thailand, where historical records are more complete than elsewhere in the region, immigrants were employed in a range of court-sanctioned roles from at least the sixteenth century. Persians and Chinese (the latter hailing from Thailand's main international trade partner) operated trading monopolies and tax farms – paying an agreed, fixed sum to the royal household for the right to collect a given tax in a given locale. As of the eighteenth century, Chinese are recorded working for the Thai court as administrators and accountants. In many cases – perhaps most – however, Persians, Arabs and people from the Indian subcontinent were preferred as administrators; the Bunnag clan, which is still prominent in the Thai civil service and politics[3], were Persian Muslim immigrants who from the late eighteenth century ran the entire greater Bangkok region. Chinese dominance in court-sanctioned commercial monopolies in Thailand became overwhelming in the nineteenth century. On the island of Java, in today's Indonesia, there is evidence that Chinese entrepreneurs entered into administrative and monopoly management arrangements with Javanese aristocrats before the arrival of Europeans in the sixteenth century.

What developed, in the early stages of state formation in south-east Asia, was a pattern that has never disappeared: a racial division of labour in which locals were the political entrepreneurs – focused on the maintenance of political power against indigenous rivals and, later, in partnership with European and American colonists – and outsiders who became economic, and as a corollary bureaucratic, entrepreneurs. Political power, of course, trumps all other power, and so the arrangement made perfect sense to indigenous aristocracies.

That immigrants know their place is attested by the direction of acculturation – the process of cultural adjustment. South-east Asian aristocracies did not become clones of their immigrant employees; instead, the immigrants acculturated to them. This was as true of Chinese as Persians, despite the reputation of the former as having an unbiddable cultural identity. Pre-modern Thai history, for example, is a story of Chinese who were successful in the country turning rapidly into Thais. The Thai kings encouraged this, ennobling their ethnic Chinese revenue farmers and officials. All Chinese were required to choose between a Thai and a Chinese identity on reaching adulthood; if they opted for the former they cut off their Manchu queues. The vast majority of families did so within two or three generations. The Thai élite was the place to be; it took a fat slice off the top of commercial profits for no risk, while unassimilated Chinese traders received a secondary cut in return for all the risk. It was hardly surprising that, given the choice, Chinese immigrants preferred to be political rather than economic entrepreneurs. A similar trajectory occurred in Java, where successful Chinese sought to marry into the Javanese aristocracy.

Despite the attention lavished by historians on the impact of Chinese culture throughout Asia, migration to the south-east of the region – Chinese, Persian, Arab and Indian – really highlighted a different lesson: that migration into existing societies is less about the export of a culture, and more about the migrants' willing approximation to dominant local forms. Moreover, the most rapid acculturation occurs among the most ambitious, go-ahead individuals who recognise that economic progress is all but impossible without integration into local élites. This was a lesson that proto-godfathers learned early, and it was not difficult to follow because south-east Asia was a broadly ecumenical and tolerant place with sparse populations that meant limited competition for resources. Put simply, in an agricultural era, south-east Asia was blessed with natural abundance, particularly when compared with China and India.

Out for a Burden

The arrival of European colonists, present from the sixteenth century but not aggressively expansionist until the nineteenth, both reinforced and realigned the tendencies that were already apparent. Reinforcement occurred because colonialism in the countries with which we are concerned was not backed by heavy allocations of personnel. As a result, the colonials sought to rule through existing élites, both political and economic. Realignment occurred because colonial power created triangular relationships where before there had been simpler bilateral ones. The Europeans now represented ultimate power and local political and economic leaders needed to have relations with them as well as with each other. This had profound effects. For ambitious migrants, it meant they began to acculturate towards the Europeans because they represented dominant power. The local political élite also moved some way towards European cultural norms, while its relationship of cultural superiority to immigrants – most notably the Chinese – was shattered. The exception was Thailand, which was not formally colonised. There, the process of Chinese turning into Thais continued apace until the early twentieth century, when a rapid increase in the pace of immigration (driven by economic and political breakdown in China and the availability of new passenger ship services), the arrival of more Chinese women and a surge of Thai nationalism temporarily interrupted the assimilation process.

It was the Dutch in Java, and subsequently the rest of Indonesia, who most ruthlessly built on the division between political and economic activities. Control of the bulk of the population was exercised through the local *priyayi* aristocracy, who continued to govern their provinces and districts, with small numbers of Dutch colonial 'residents' in the background. Key economic roles went to the Chinese. They were revenue farmers for all kinds of taxes and monopolies, ranging from fees on the slaughtering of animals to the right to operate licensed markets. The biggest revenue farm was that for the manufacture and sale of opium. It became a mainstay of government income in each of the territories we are concerned with, but it was particularly important in Indonesia because indigenous people were also big consumers; elsewhere opium smoking was largely a Chinese pastime.

As well as cementing the Chinese economic role, the Dutch exalted a small number of powerful Chinese community leaders (immigration from China increased markedly in the seventeenth century) who were loyal to them. These men became some of the region's original tycoon godfathers. The Dutch picked up on a tradition begun by the Portuguese – the first European power in south-east Asia – to give the foremost person in the Chinese community the military title of captain. This was expanded into a complete officer system of Majoor, Kapitan, Luitenant – a hierarchy that persisted for two centuries. The Chinese officers kept a Chinese census, levied Chinese taxes and fines, issued permits, and their opinions were important in court cases. They were extremely powerful and, simultaneously, usually held the big revenue farms and worked as *compradors* – intermediaries – for the Dutch. Moreover, ordinary Chinese were compelled to live in designated Chinese quarters of approved towns and travel only with permission. These restrictions did not apply to the Chinese élite and their revenue farm employees. The *cabang atas*, or 'highest branch', as the Chinese élite came to be known, had the run of the country at the same time that their compatriots – and potential competitors – were theoretically confined to urban ghettos. The pass laws were often ignored, but the officers had more than enough power, including quasi-legal authority, to make life deeply unpleasant for anyone who crossed them.

Chinese society at large continued its process of acculturation in Indonesia, with successive generations of immigrants losing command of their different Chinese languages and becoming habituated to local customs. But as the Dutch expanded their power through the archipelago there was less incentive for ambitious migrants to seek employment in the households of Javanese kings or marriage into the *priyayi* aristocracy. On the other hand, white northern European society would not tolerate intermarriage and assimilation to the Dutch group. Unlike Thailand, where complete integration with the ruling élite was possible, what happened was that a 'halfway house' identity developed. By the nineteenth century the Chinese who spoke Malay (the indigenous language of trade), followed a culture comprised of both southern Chinese and Javanese elements, while looking to the Dutch colonials for favour and advancement, were a large and definable group called *peranakan*. It was the leading *peranakan* who were the leaders of Chinese society: they worked with the Dutch as officers to keep the Chinese population in line; they tendered for revenue farms; and they worked with the local *priyayi* to protect their farms – which were often challenged by smugglers, especially in the case of opium. The most successful entrepreneurs were almost inevitably the least purely 'Chinese' ones. They required a position of cultural equilibrium between Dutch residents, *priyayi* aristocrats and an evolving mix of almost exclusively male Chinese immigrants.

A similar state of affairs developed in the Philippines, where the Spanish arrived from across the Pacific via their Latin American colonies in the late sixteenth century. Unlike Dutch and British colonists, who were represented by monopolistic trading corporations – the Dutch Vereenigte Oost-Indische Compagnie (VOC) and the British East India Company – the Spanish colonial mission was an overtly political and religious one. It sought to convert Filipinos to Catholic Christianity. In this respect the Chinese, who were already trading in the Manila region when the Spanish arrived, were irksome. The Spanish needed the Chinese to provision their garrisons and trade Chinese luxury goods; but the Chinese were initially resistant to Christianity. There followed an uneasy stand-off punctuated by a series of bloody pogroms in the course of the seventeenth century. At the same time, the Spanish rewarded Chinese who did convert to Christianity, and who married local women, with lower taxes, freedom of movement and an ability to join the local political élite. A process of acculturation began and by 1800 there were an estimated 120,000 Chinese *mestizos* – equivalent to the Indonesian *peranakan* – versus 7,000 Chinese and 4,000 *blancos*, or whites, in the Philippines; they accounted for around 5 per cent of the population. Strict controls on the number of pure Chinese who were allowed residence further encouraged the development of *mestizo* society.

The *mestizos* dominated internal trade in the islands and moved increasingly into landholding. The Spanish always feared they would lead the native *indios* in rebellion, but in reality the Chinese *mestizos* were at least as attached to the Philippine version of Spanish culture as were the urbanised *indios*, and gave up most attachment to Chinese culture. As in Indonesia and Malaysia, they acquired their own dress forms and customs that reflected a hybrid culture.

The Era of Mass Migration

From the mid-nineteenth century, the pattern of low-volume migration and a heavily assimilated resident Chinese population began to change. There were two reasons for this. First, the number of immigrants increased exponentially. And second, the objectives of the ruling colonial powers both changed and broadened.

Technology facilitated a migration boom. The first steamships came into use in the 1840s and were widely deployed on passenger routes in Asia by the 1860s. The so-called Opium Wars of 1839–42 and 1856–60 forced open the principal ports of the Chinese coast, particularly the traditional migrant centres of the south, and these were quickly connected by steamer link to the major ports of south-east Asia. Much migration was determined by nothing more complex than the destination of the local steamship link. The opening of a service from Haikou in Hainan island to Bangkok, for instance, is a key reason that there are lots of people of Hainanese ancestry in Thailand.

Best estimates suggest that by 1850 there were half a million people of Chinese extraction, mixed race and not, in the territories we are following. The largest concentrations were in Thailand and Indonesia, with Hong Kong, Singapore and Malaysia (not yet formally incorporated into the British Empire) just taking off. By the time of the First World War, there were 3–4 million ethnic Chinese in the region, the vast majority of them first generation. There was an increasingly long list of reasons for people to get out of China. The country came under serious population pressure from the eighteenth century. Rebellions occurred with increasing frequency, building up to four major conflagrations in the mid-nineteenth century: Muslim-led rebellions in the south-west and north-west of China, and the Nian and Taiping rebellions in the central provinces. The latter, led by a man who believed himself to be the younger brother of Jesus Christ and a deputy who claimed to be the Holy Ghost, was the most disruptive; it cost the lives of several tens of millions of people in the 1850s and 1860s.

With regular steamships to transport them from what one historian dubbed their 'grimly Malthusian setting',[4] the southern Chinese found south-east Asia's underpopulated and relatively peaceful destinations most attractive: labour rates were often a multiple of those at home.[5] In the mid-nineteenth century there were just 5 million people in Thailand, 2.5 million in Malaysia and 23 million in Indonesia (Java was the one place in south-east Asia that was relatively densely settled) – around one-tenth of today's levels. The more fortunate migrants were assisted, both financially and with job-seeking, by relatives or kinsmen who had already travelled abroad.

The rising tide of migrant workers coincided with the dawn of so-called 'high imperialism' from the middle of the nineteenth century, and a sustained, labour-intensive commodities boom that continued into the twentieth century. From the 1830s the monolithic Dutch and British trade monopolies were dismantled and the European states took over colonial management in south-east Asia. An agreement between Holland and Britain in 1824 to delineate their respective areas of interest in the region presaged a Dutch campaign to control the complete Indonesian archipelago and, later, the rolling-out of the British presence in peninsular Malaysia. Direct colonial control was sometimes the prerequisite for the development of vast new plantations or mines and sometimes – as in peninsular Malaya, where small Chinese mines were well established – it occurred after the fact. There was to an extent a contradictory political impetus in Europe – on the one hand to extend the limits of colonial power, on the other to deregulate many aspects of international trade and investment. In an era informed by the writings of David Ricardo and Adam

Smith, both Singapore (1819) and Hong Kong (1842) were established as free ports without restrictions or taxes on trade. (These colonial acquisitions also reflected the British imperial appetite to control strategic islands.)[6] A Hong Kong governor persuaded the Thais to deregulate trade with the eponymous Bowring Treaty in 1855. Even the Spanish Philippines moved in this direction, ending the trading monopolies of provincial governors in 1844 and opening up to foreign business; since the industrial revolution had passed Spain by, trade came to be dominated by British and American firms with little more than the flag to remind merchants that they were on Spanish soil.

By the second half of the nineteenth century, the pieces were in place for a globalisation-driven boom which in certain respects pre-figured the one that began in the 1990s. The demand impetus was the developed world's hunger for agricultural and mineral commodities which were either buried in the ground in south-east Asia or could be grown there; vast tracts of land were available for the establishment of plantations. Technological facilitation came with the opening of the Suez Canal in 1869 and the concurrent development of steamships that allowed for low-cost bulk shipping throughout the year.[7] The final component was abundant, cheap, imported Chinese and Indian labour.

As a general distinction, it is fair to say that the great majority of Indians were imported to work in estate agriculture in the British colonies and parts of Indonesia, with minority subsets of manual labour for public works projects and colonial civil servants; a tiny élite of Indian entrepreneurs – including Parsees, Sindhis and Chettiar – was spread around the region. Chinese immigrants dominated mining, but were also widely dispersed across trading, retailing, what would today be called logistics services, agriculture and more. This reflected the fact that the average Chinese had relatively greater freedom of choice in making migration decisions. The vast majority of Indian emigrants between 1850 and the First World War were indentured agricultural labourers, meaning that they signed contracts to work on plantations, were transported to those plantations and housed in barracks and – if they survived – were usually sent back to India.[8] The southern Chinese used credit ticket systems, which meant that migrants were bound to employers until they had paid off their passage, with interest, but subsequently they were relatively more likely to stay on in south-east Asia and merge into the established, mainly urban communities of overseas Chinese that had roots going back centuries. A United Nations report on migration published in 2004 makes a brave attempt to pull together historical records from India and concludes that 30 million Indians left for destinations around the world between 1834 and 1937, but 24 million came back.[9] We do not know the returnee proportion among Chinese because China has no state records comparable to those maintained by the British in India, but it was certainly much lower.[10]

This is an important point. There were huge numbers of Indians around in colonial south-east Asia but they did not become more important to local economies in the long run because most of them did not hang around long enough to become embedded in society.[11] They were also, relative to the Chinese, a more downtrodden and unhappy group of people. The Indian *arkatia* – or recruiters – who organised indentured labour for export focused much of their attention on minority groups at the bottom of the caste ladder (which has no sociological equivalent in China), like Tamils from the south or hill tribesmen from the north-east. These people suited plantation owners and colonial governments because – unlike the more uppity Chinese – they created no trouble. Sir Frederic Weld, governor of the Straits Settlements from 1880 to 1887, recommended an increase in the importation of Indians when leaving the job with the words: 'Indians are a peaceable and easily governed race.'[12] He probably did not realise he was used to a rather atypical cross-section of Indians.

The original agricultural produce that had drawn Europeans to south-east Asia was spices, used largely for curing meat in the era before artificial refrigeration. But the nineteenth century brought a host of other cash crops, among which sugar from the Philippines and Thailand was the most important. Then came tin, first mined by Chinese gangs in Indonesia but later found in far greater quantities in Malaysia and southern Thailand. At the turn of the century there was rubber – in whose production Indian labour was thoroughly dominant – which was an essential input in the dawning age of the automobile and for many other consumer products. There was also a rolling cycle of commodity booms in the region in which technological advances further increased the scale of trade. In mining, for example, new technologies transformed the activity from an essentially manual undertaking with mattocks to a large-scale mechanical one involving dredges.

Change, Change, Change

From the perspective of the established south-east Asian godfather the end of the nineteenth century was an era of both greater uncertainty and greater opportunity. Traditional assimilated Chinese Thai, Indonesian *peranakan*, Malaysian *baba*[13] and Philippines' *mestizo* élites were challenged by the arrival of wave after wave of hungry immigrants, who were not always easy to control. At the same time, as the Thai state and the different colonial regimes became stronger, they had less need of freelance revenue farmers and monopoly holders and gradually dismantled these arrangements, beginning in the 1880s. None the less, the economic pie was becoming much bigger. And the tripartite split between colonial power, indigenous political élite and economic élite of now overwhelmingly Chinese origin continued to reward the tycoon who could most effectively work his external relationships while maintaining authority within a burgeoning immigrant community. (Indian labour was usually imported direct by colonial plantation owners and hence threw up fewer Indian godfathers.) A look at the salient characteristics of stand-out tycoons at the turn of the century highlights this.

Oei Tiong Ham was the richest man in Indonesia. Based in Semarang in central Java, home to the island's dominant *peranakan* opium farmers in the nineteenth century, Oei was the son of an established merchant who had been appointed Majoor of the Semarang Chinese. The son, however, was able to multiply his father's already considerable wealth through cosmopolitan expansion from a traditional base. In the 1880s, when revenue farmers were hit by an economic downturn, he tendered for and won important tax farm concessions. He spoke no Dutch, but understood the language of colonial formality better than most Europeans. One of his daughters recalled in her autobiography: 'I used to stand on the wide veranda of our palace, waiting for the sight of Papa's carriage racing through the valley below ... By the time it swept through our entrance gates, a Malay servant had appeared from nowhere carrying a hot towel soaked in *eau de cologne* on a silver tray. Papa, impressively handsome in immaculate white trousers and a smart, Western-style white jacket, would wipe his hands and face with the scented towel before he stepped down from the carriage and approached me. It was like a ballet.'[14] Oei was a lavish entertainer and gift-giver to colonial officers. Like his father, he was Majoor of the local Chinese, but he lived on a large estate in the European quarter of town; he spoke Javanese and Malay better than any Chinese dialect.

In business, Oei followed a diversification strategy that became the hallmark of south-east Asian tycoons of the era. He obtained a steady source of cash flow from revenue farms, in particular opium, and used it to finance expansion into myriad other activities. He was most prominent in the sugar industry, developing plantations and constructing processing mills. The latter used imported European machinery maintained by Dutch technicians; Oei also employed Dutch accountants and administrators in key roles. He expanded into shipping and opened a bank in Semarang. At the time of the First World War, Oei relocated to Singapore, where he died in 1924. His was the one local business that could compete for scale with large Dutch companies.

Still more adaptable was Loke Yew, reckoned the richest Chinese on the Malaysian peninsula at the turn of the century. He built an early business provisioning rival Chinese mining gangs, and the triads that represented them, with food and weapons on the west coast. As the British took formal control of Malaya from 1874, he developed an open-cast tin mining empire employing thousands of Chinese labourers whom he also supplied with opium, liquor and gambling facilities under state revenue farm licences. Loke Yew worked closely with Chinese secret societies to import and manage his labourers; he was a member of the powerful Ghee Hin triad. British Residents in the key mining states relied on him both to control the Chinese populations and to contribute a large share of fiscal revenues. In turn, Loke Yew was at pains to put his colonial counterparties at ease. He acquired English manners, developed a friendship with the first Resident-general of the four Federated Malay States[15], Frank Swettenham, and was one of the main sponsors of the élite English language school in Kuala Lumpur, the Victoria Institution. He entered ventures with English and Scottish companies, as well as with the Tamil Indian tycoon Thamboosamy Pillay.[16] His negotiating power with the colonial rulers was considerable. When, for instance, the tin price fell in 1896, the Selangor state administration took the unprecedented step of giving him a reduction on the fixed fee he paid for the opium farm because he was deemed so important to state business. In 1898 he was offered a range of revenue farms in the Benteng area of Pahang state at nominal cost, and reduced taxes on the tin he mined, as an incentive to open up the area. Apart from mining, Loke Yew diversified into real estate, rubber plantations and more; he was given a British knighthood.

The strategy of integrating revenue farming operations with mining and plantation ventures was common to tycoons around the region. Most obviously, it reduced the cost of already cheap labour. Thio Thiau Siat, whose interests were truly regional, ran opium, liquor and tobacco farms on both sides of the Malacca Straits, in Sumatra, Malaya and Singapore, and conjoined these with a vast empire centred on plantations. The Khaw family developed an integrated tin mining and revenue farm business that stretched from Penang to south-west Thailand, and thereafter diversified. In Singapore it was the families that dominated pepper and gambier (used in tanning and dyeing) cultivation, the biggest employers there in the late nineteenth century, which held revenue farms – including the key opium farm – and contributed as much as half the government's annual revenues. Wherever there were revenue farms – which inferred a delegation of state powers of coercion

– there were also triad enforcers. But this was not a great concern to colonial governments that had long since recognised that accepting the presence of the secret societies was the easiest way to manage Chinese immigration. As the *Straits Observer* noted on 17 February 1899: 'Government has no direct means of communication with the lower class Chinese, and it is this work which the Secret Societies carry on.'

In the Philippines, the greatest of the *cabecillas* (literally 'headmen') was Don Carlos Palanca Chen Qianshan. He was a coolie broker, operator of a major opium monopoly and tax collector with general commercial interests ranging from textiles to sugar and rice trading to real estate. Arriving from China's Fujian province as a chain migrant with relatives already settled in Manila, he learned Spanish, converted to Catholicism and found a power-ful colonial mentor in Colonel Carlos Palanca y Gutierrez, whose name he adopted. At the same time, he was careful to establish his credentials with imperial Qing China, thereby shoring up his role as leader of the burgeon-ing Chinese community in the Philippines. Like many contemporaries, he purchased Mandarin titles and donned Mandarin robes for formal occasions. Chen Qianshan was instrumental in pressing the Qing government to open a consulate in Manila, which was located in buildings that also housed the *Gobernadorcillo de los Sangleyes* (as the Chinese leader was formally titled by the Spanish) – Chen sometimes held this post and sometimes merely influ-enced it – and the *Tribunal de los Sangleyes*, a court that Chen was repeatedly accused of manipulating. He and his son were consuls.

Chen died a very rich man in 1901. He had established perfect sociological equilibrium between the immigrant Chinese and colonial Spanish communi-ties, receiving honours from both states. As one historian of the Philippines, Andrew Wilson, observes: 'The Chinese experience of the late nineteenth century made it clear that social and economic power rested with those who not only controlled the institutions that defined Chinese identity in the colo-nial Philippines, but also had the greatest rapport with and institutional link-ages to external sources of authority.'[17]

Not everyone was admiring of the ability to fulfil these criteria. The novel-ist and Philippine nationalist José Rizal, himself of mixed-race Chinese origin, almost certainly used Chen Qianshan as the model for the obsequious, duplic-itous character Quiroga the Chinaman in his novel *El Filibusterismo* (1891). It was the hybrid nature of Quiroga's identity that Rizal found so objection-able – expressed, said the author, in the 'lamentable confusion' of styles in his house. Yet the ornamental Chinese gardens, Greek columns, Scottish ironwork and Italian marble floors favoured by south-east Asian godfathers also reflected their strengths.[18] Their work drove them to try to be all things to all men. In the process the curiosities they spawned were not merely architectural. Men such as Oei Tiong Ham, or key collaborators of the British colonial government in Hong Kong like Sir Kai Ho-kai,[19] set up by themselves and by colonisers as leaders of their communities, had only the shakiest grasp of any Chinese dialect. They were truly stuck in a cultural limbo.

Shaped by Circumstance

Brief sketches of these turn-of-the-century godfathers show the extent to which their activities were shaped by the environment in which they operated. They sought revenue farms because these were the easiest way to make a lot of money. The fattest margins were achieved in the middle of the nineteenth century by Chinese revenue farmers who knew much more about the value of their monopolies than the states that granted them. As states became stronger and better informed, rigged bids, late payment and the like became more difficult. Revenue farming was naturally combined with employment of immigrant Chinese labour, which was flooding into south-east Asia from the mid-nineteenth century and was a major consumer of the offerings of the vice farms. And management of labour was tied up with community leadership of the mutually hostile immigrant speech groups that were looking for work. Often backed by speech-group-specific triads, the tycoon could create a wondrous, circular business in which almost all money ended up in his hands: operate vice and other farms, employ dependent immigrants in labour-intensive businesses like mining and plantations, often in remote regions, and then sell vice products and services, and anything else required, to the workers in order to recover most of their income. On top of all this, the godfather provided the only form of political identity that emigrants had in their new homeland; he was the person who represented community interests before the holders of ultimate political authority.

But colonial power (and international economics in the first great era of globalisation) shaped the world of the aspirant godfather in more ways than simply by making him a revenue farmer and exploiter of his co-nationals. The period established an economic architecture in south-east Asia that would prove hard to change. The colonial powers had no dastardly master plan for the region, but they did institute the trading structure that was most favourable to them. This meant the import into the first world of commodities in return for the export to south-east Asia of finished manufactures to pay, at least in part, for those commodities. In the process, the commodity boom was accompanied by a regional rationalisation of output. Thailand was a rice economy with some tin mining in the south, Malaya did tin and rubber, the Philippines produced sugar and coconuts, Java was planted with sugar and coffee and from Sumatra came tobacco and rubber.[20] Finished consumer goods, construction materials and machinery were imported from Europe and the United States in a process facilitated by low import tariffs. This situation was even replicated in non-colonial Thailand,[21] which applied a minimal 3 per cent import duty on manufactured goods until 1926. When the United States took possession of the Philippines in 1898 after its war with Spain, Washington combined low import tariffs with a guaranteed export quota for Philippine sugar, further accentuating the bias towards the export of basic commodities and the import of more value-added manufactures in the south-east Asian economy.

The effect of all this was one that has never been thrown off. There was almost no incentive to invest in manufacturing in south-east Asia. Colonials preferred to sell goods made in their home markets while local entrepreneurs were not inspired to compete with imports that were either duty-free or lightly taxed. By contrast, rising commodity prices made the operation of plantations and mines, as well as related service businesses like shipping, attractive. Chinese and other Asian entrepreneurs did not become focused on the trade-based economy because they were 'born traders', but because manufacturing was more risky and more difficult. All the way to the Second World War, the macroeconomic story of south-east Asia was one of trade expansion – witness Singapore's boom period trade growth from an average S$67 million per year in 1871–3 to S$431 million in 1900–1902 – without any industrial take-off. The economic historian James Ingram described the experience in Thailand as succinctly as anyone:

We have seen many changes in the economy of Thailand in the last hundred years [1850 to 1950], but not much 'progress' in the sense of an increase in *per capita* income, and not much 'development' in the sense of utilisation of more capital, relative to labor, and of new techniques. The principal changes have been the spread of the use of money, increased specialisation and exchange based chiefly on world markets, and the growth of a racial division of labor. The rapidly growing population has been chiefly absorbed in the cultivation of more land in rice ... For the most part, economic changes have occurred in response to external stimuli. Thailand has been a sort of passive entity, adapting to changes and market influences originating in the world economy. Few innovations have originated within, and most of the adaptive response to external influence has taken place along traditional lines.[22]

The tycoons were merely fellow travellers in this experience, facilitators of a game in which they had no influence on the rules. They profited handsomely as individuals, but in the aggregate their earnings were nothing compared with those of the large European firms. As new technologies increased the need for higher capital investment in many businesses, the tycoons also came under pressure at the turn of the twentieth century because their traditional advantage had been to organise high-volume, low-cost immigrant labour. Tin mining, where Loke Yew prospered, was a typical example. He worked an army of more than 10,000 coolies, to whom he also provided everything from lodgings to food to opium. But the invention of steam-driven bucket dredges, which coincided with the exhaustion of the most easily accessible open-cast mining sites, changed the nature of the business from the second decade of the twentieth century. By 1920 there were twenty dredges able to work to a depth of sixty feet in operation in peninsular Malaysia, and by 1930 there were more than a hundred. The Chinese mining groups that pioneered open-cast excavation could not compete. Most could not harness the necessary investment for capital equipment and even those that could, like Loke Yew, lost their comparative advantage with the move away from the labour-intensive model.

The importance of access to large amounts of capital in twentieth-century business became apparent around the region. Chinese businessmen had competed effectively when agriculture was on a relatively small scale and junks required a relatively modest investment. But as the most profitable plantations multiplied in size, mining was mechanised and modern ships grew in both size and technological complexity, a new capital barrier to entry was raised. In general, would-be Asian tycoons were pushed back by their European competitors between the early twentieth century and the Second World War. In Thailand, for instance, European corporations came to dominate logging and saw milling where Chinese and Burmese interests had once dominated with small-scale activity; tin smelting where large plants became the norm; and steam shipping where Thai and Chinese sailing vessels had predominated. The only field successfully dominated by Chinese revenue farmers moving into new commercial ventures in the late nineteenth century was rice milling, primarily because the necessary capital equipment was relatively cheap and major consumers of the product were the Chinese populations of Malaya, Singapore and Hong Kong.

The dominant European banks – led by Hongkong and Shanghai Bank and Chartered Bank of India, Australia and China – confined almost all of their activity to the financing of trade. Large European and American companies raised their investment capital at home. The colonial banks also had an effective race bar when it came to dealing with most Asians. One octogenarian billionaire recalls of the pre-independence era: 'For a Chinese businessman to get to see decision makers in the British colonial banks was like seeking an audience with God.'[23] The Indian Chettiar and Sikh moneylenders who proliferated in the region offered credit lines to locals but charged rates of interest far higher than those enjoyed by Europeans. A number of Chinese banks did develop in the first two decades of the twentieth century, but they too were constrained by their operating environment. There were no central banks to act as lenders of last resort when commercial bankers needed temporary liquidity, while the fact that most south-east Asian territories operated currency boards further restricted lending. The effect of this system – which a few states around the world still operate today – is to tie the local monetary base directly to the supply of foreign exchange. If foreign exchange receipts from commodity exports fall, so does the supply of local currency. With commodity prices volatile and south-east Asian countries heavily dependent on just one or two exports, money supply tended to be equally volatile. The monetary base in Malaya fell by a half in the early 1920s, largely because of falling rubber prices. As a result of such fluctuations, local banks kept around half their deposits liquid, instead of lending them out; international banks had no such problems. And, despite their prudence, most Chinese banks in Malaya and the Philippines collapsed with the depression and commodities crisis of the 1930s.

Prior to the depression, the south-east Asian economy boomed – with odd blips – for forty years. This was fuel aplenty for would-be godfathers, but it could not disguise the fact that some aspects of the operating environment were beginning to work against them. The new capital intensity of big business coincided with the winding down of revenue farming, which had traditionally supplied the cash flow that carried powerful men into a range of regular commercial businesses. By the 1920s the farms were finished. At the same time, the colonial powers dispensed with their various 'headman' systems that automatically confirmed the tycoon as the head of his community. In Malaya, for example, the last headman to be designated was in the first decade of the twentieth century and the last one to step down was in the third. To a significant extent, the headman institution was replaced by the development of the local Chinese chamber of commerce, whose key players were the most powerful businessmen. But the old certainties of being a Majoor or 'captain China' and thereby identified by the ruling power as 'in charge' were gone.

In rare instances there did appear to be the beginnings of a transition to a less externally dependent form of entrepreneurial tycoon business in the final decades before the independence era. The two obvious cases occurred in Singapore in the form of Aw Boon Haw and Tan Kah Kee. These men, born in 1882 and 1874 respectively, built up large businesses without being *compradors* or operating revenue farms. Perhaps more tellingly, they moved into consumer goods rather than dealing solely in raw and semi-finished commodities. Aw Boon Haw's signature product was Tiger Balm, a cure-all ointment and muscle rub that is still widely sold. His Haw Par empire developed a range of over-the-counter pharmaceutical remedies for headaches, seasickness, sore throats and constipation. There were wholesale and retail operations in Hong Kong, mainland China, Java, Sumatra and Thailand. From medicines, Aw Boon Haw expanded into newspaper publishing around the region, mostly in the Chinese language.

Tan Kah Kee started out with plantations, but unlike other Asian producers who fitted into the colonial matrix as providers of raw commodities, he determined to manufacture with the rubber he grew. Tan had factories making tyres, rubber shoes and toys and opened retail operations to sell the output. His decision to take on European, Japanese and American manufacturers without tariff protection, however, only contributed to the downfall of his major business interests during the depression. His was a valiant attempt to buck the system, and it ended in failure.

Nationalism and Class, a Prelude

Tan was curiously, almost exceptionally, politically idealistic for an overseas Chinese business tycoon. Visits to pre-1949 China convinced him to support Mao Zedong's communists and in 1950 he left Singapore to spend the rest of his life in the People's Republic, where he died in 1961. This was not the norm in south-east Chinese Asian communities, where big-time success was traditionally linked to an ability to identify with local political power as a means to commercial ends. Tan Kah Kee's 'stand' was an almost unique event encouraged by an era when businessmen were no longer beholden to colonial grants of licences and revenue farms and one when nationalism was on the rise throughout the region. Nationalism, however, was very much a double-edged sword from the overseas Chinese perspective. Its rise in south-east Asian countries could only focus attention on the economic role of the Chinese. The concurrent growth of class consciousness further highlighted the more general dominance of élites in business and politics. None of this augured well for tycoons in the 1930s. Yet actual experience was that traditional structures of power would survive the challenges of political populism intact. The pre-Second World War test case for this came in Thailand.

Global recession, not least in the demand for commodities, helped precipitate a bloodless coup in Thailand in June 1932 that substituted constitutional for absolute monarchy. The People's Party came to power with an avowed agenda to govern in the interests of ordinary people. This agenda had a strong racial lilt. 'The Thai economy for Thai nationals' became a political rallying cry of the 1930s. In fact, Thai nationalism had been brewing for some time. King Rama VI, who reigned between 1910 and 1925, had been much taken with the racial theories popular in Europe at the time, translated William Shakespeare's anti-semitic *Merchant of Venice* (1594–7) into Thai and penned an essay about the Chinese in Asia entitled *The Jews of the East* (1914). What became apparent, however, as restrictive measures were implemented against the Chinese, was that the ethnic Chinese élite was in a position to adapt where ordinary people were not.

The immigrant mass was hit after 1932 with increases in the cost of immigration registration certificates and bans from a range of common occupations. Coming off the back of worldwide depression, this both curtailed immigration and expedited the return to China of many sojourning workers. The ethnic Chinese élite was confronted with a rolling nationalisation programme in businesses where it dominated, including salt, tobacco and rice. However, while political change finished off the economic ascendancy of old revenue farming families, it did not undermine the ascendancy of the broader Chinese business community. New families broke through from the ranks of Chinese traders to become active partners of the government in managing new 'state' businesses. Thai bureaucrats had no more intention of sullying their hands with trade than previously. The government leased and bought over Chinese-owned factories and mills in many sectors, but most of those businesses remained Chinese-managed, while state-led monopoly concentration often pushed up prices and profits. 'The Thai economy for the Thai people' did not mean an increase in social equity; it was a readjustment of the deal between the élites. As the economic historian Suehiro Akira notes: 'Whatever the original intent, "Thai people" later did not come to indicate either the common people or Thai farmers. Rather, it came to mean the government officials or a specific political group.'[24] Suehiro conducted an exhaustive survey of companies that were nationalised in the period and showed that most of the Thai shareholders and directors turned out to be members of the People's Party, or persons connected with it, while their partners were invariably the tycoon Chinese families. He concludes: 'At the level of Chinese business leaders, several groups were able to transform dexterously this state control into an instrument for expanding their enterprises ... In exchange for providing management skills and capital funds, Chinese business leaders obtained security as well as political patronage.'[25]

Where the tycoons were once freelance revenue collectors for the Thai court, they now became joint venture partners of the Thai bureaucracy. This set the pattern for the post-war era of military dictatorship that ran from 1947 to 1973. Under military rule, however, the scale of state involvement in the economy – in the form of businesses involving different army and police factions – and the level of collaboration with ethnic Chinese business leaders became far greater than under the pre-1947 civilian government. The military were not managers – their earnings were taken as shareholders and directors – but political muscle allowed them to define the terms of business activity. For major consumer items, for example, from tobacco to pork, distribution monopolies were established that meant Chinese-run cartels could reliably control pricing. In the 1950s the major areas of military–Chinese expansion were banking and insurance, with the military side providing protection and the Chinese side benefiting from the squeezing-out of foreign competition, access to state capital and a role providing finance to public works. The fundamental rule of the game, as Suehiro notes, was simple: 'No leading Chinese capitalist could survive or expand their business without alliances with the Thai ruling élite.'[26] This was a small price to pay if it also meant – as it would in other countries – an ability to keep European and American companies out of the market.

But First, a Beautiful War

Before the Thai generals took charge, however, there was the Second World War, the biggest agent of global political change in the twentieth century. In south-east Asia there was no exception. The war, which arrived with the invasion of Japanese troops in the region in December 1941, meant the end of the imperial game. Although the Japanese were defeated after three and a half years, too much changed in this time. On the one hand, the absence of British, Dutch and American administrators gave a major boost to nationalist politics; on the other, the situation provided fertile ground for aggressive businessmen. A new generation of tycoons made early fortunes from the opportunities for smuggling and speculation thrown up by the conflict and its aftermath. Much of this activity focused on Singapore and Hong Kong, the two key ports.

As one of the richest men in contemporary Asia recalls: 'It was a very corrupt time.' Although unforthcoming about details of his own family's smuggling activities during the war, he notes that a deal to supply fruit and vegetables to 80,000 Japanese prisoners after hostilities ended was a major break. Smuggling, war trading, the purchase and sale of surplus military equipment and post-war reconstruction contracts involving hefty kickbacks were the early making of many of today's godfathers. One of the very few who has ever said anything public about this era is Stanley Ho, the Macau casino magnate.[27] His tale is instructive of the possibilities that were available to the chameleons of the godfather class.

When the Japanese invaded Hong Kong, Stanley's great uncle, Sir Robert Ho Tung, the leading *comprador* tycoon of the era, had already made off to neutral Macau on a tip-off from the Japanese consul, who recognised that occupation would require godfather co-operation.[28] Stanley Ho, who was only eighteen years old, was enrolled by the British in Hong Kong as a telephone operator. When the colony fell, he threw away his uniform and took a boat to Macau (before he could get away, however, Japanese troops in Hong Kong stopped him because of his Eurasian appearance; but he could write Chinese fluently and so was not arrested as a prisoner-of-war). In Macau, which was now the smuggling epicentre of the Hong Kong–China region,[29] uncle Robert gave him a job. Soon Stanley found a more interesting position with the Macau Co-operative Co., set up as a three-way joint venture between the Japanese, local *über*-godfather Pedro Lobo and a group of Chinese businessmen.

Lobo, the lynchpin of the business, made Stanley Ho's chameleon credentials look thin. Ethnically Chinese–Portuguese–Dutch–Malay, he was born in Portuguese East Timor, raised in a Catholic seminary and went on to become simultaneously Macau's chief economic minister and its leading tycoon, with his own fleet of flying boats and a lock, together with his Chinese partners, on the lucrative local gold trade.[30] Stanley Ho was in excellent company and learned a great deal. The Macau Co-operative supplied tugs, lighters and other transport to Japanese troops based in Guangzhou, in return for rice, clothing and anything else in demand from Macau's exploding population (as well as from people in Hong Kong and elsewhere who were buying goods smuggled out of Macau).

As he learned the ropes, Stanley Ho started trading on his own account with the Japanese. He obtained enough money to open a small kerosene factory, which became a licence to print money after the Americans bombed Macau's gasoline terminal in the outer harbour. Stanley acquired political cover because he gave English lessons to Colonel Sawa, the local Japanese *Kempeitai* (secret police) chief, and the real political power in Macau.[31] Ho claims he only once called on Sawa to intervene on his behalf – when the local Japanese navy commander tried to wriggle out of a rice delivery he owed him in return for some machinery; Stanley got his rice. There were numerous hairy moments on Stanley's smuggling and trading trips up the Pearl River and its innumerable tributaries – including an attack by pirates – but Stanley survived and prospered. According to those who know him, he dealt in everything from gold to aeroplanes. At the end of the war envoys of the Chinese Nationalist Party attempted to have Stanley arrested as a collaborator but, Stanley says, the Macau police commissioner was convinced of his case and put the Nationalists' emissaries in jail instead. Stanley Ho was on his way to becoming very rich. As he cheerily told the historian Philip Snow in 1995: 'I made a lot of money out of the war.'[32]

The great thing about the war, from a business perspective, was that it never really ended. There was a chaotic, corrupt period of allied military administration following the official close of the Pacific war and then, in 1950, the Korean conflict started. In 1951 the United Nations imposed a trade embargo on China, which was allied with North Korea, creating a vast smuggling industry centred on both Macau and Hong Kong.[33] Stanley Ho carried on his smuggling operations, shipping corrugated iron, rubber tyres and, he says, vast quantities of Vaseline into China. His future partner in the Macau gaming monopoly, Henry Fok, became a sanctions-buster on a far greater scale, shipping huge quantities of petroleum products and pharmaceuticals and – though he always denied it – some weapons as well.[34] A *Time* magazine investigation in August 1951 found 'freighters on the Pearl [river] last week were laden with steel rails, zinc plate, asphalt, Indonesian rubber, Pakistan cotton, American trucks, steel piping, tubing'.[35] In Macau, oil pumping docks were operating day and night, hundreds of Hong Kong dock workers were being hired to meet the demand and 'air-conditioned opium dens were prospering'.

Apart from Stanley Ho and Henry Fok, rumours of involvement in smuggling surround several major business families in Hong Kong but – as in Singapore – local authorities never brought any significant prosecutions. The Hong Kong government was lambasted by Washington for its lack of action, and chided by the British government in London, but claimed the situation was beyond its control. In the end it was business, and that was what Hong Kong and Singapore did, although one or two participants were troubled by their consciences. John Cheung, the Chinese partner of the unscrupulous stock market manipulator and Wheelock-Marden boss George Marden in Hong Kong, was said to have sold so much suspect medicine during the world and Korean wars that he lived in fear for his life. Simon Murray, former chief executive of fellow Hong Kong-based conglomerate Hutchison, says he went to a meeting at Cheung's home to find him living in a windowless room with the bed pushed across the door.[36]

In Singapore, the veil of secrecy surrounding wartime smuggling is drawn still closer. The island, the logistical centre of a region split since the nineteenth century into economic units specialising in different agricultural and industrial commodities had at least as much potential for illicit trade as Hong Kong and Macau. The rewards were enormous for those who could surreptitiously move rice from food-abundant Thailand to starving Malaya or get industrial commodities out of Indonesia. A reticent, octogenarian confidante of the local tycoon fraternity is not keen to discuss the subject, but notes that the obelisk on the Singapore sea front raised by businessmen in memory of Chinese killed by the Japanese was 'mostly paid for by smugglers'. A friend of, among others, the Kwek family, whose current twin heads are billionaires Kwek Leng Beng and Quek Leng Chan,[37] the source says that wartime patriarch Kwek Hong Png 'never really denied' that much of his wealth stemmed from smuggling Indonesian rubber and trading with the Japanese.[38] In the Korean War, much of that rubber found its way to China, as *Time*'s journalists noted in 1951.

The end of the Second World War in Indonesia morphed into a nationalist war against the Dutch, who were attempting to retake control of their colony. This provided still more opportunities for Singapore-based smugglers. Many of the weapons used by Indonesian forces came from the Malay peninsula, where there was an abundant supply of Japanese and British arms. It was Chinese traders, usually operating between Singapore and Sumatra, who handled the movement of weapons, medicines and foodstuffs. Contemporary Dutch government reports show that barter prices for smuggled weapons were well established: one tonne of rubber, for instance, for thirty cartridges, two tonnes for a rifle.[39] The trade was enormously profitable and ships owned by major business concerns were involved. A vessel belonging to a subsidiary of Lee Rubber, controlled by Tan Kah Kee's son-in-law Lee Kong Chian, was found by Dutch authorities to be importing non-lethal military goods to Indonesia in August 1946. Chang Ming Thien, a Malaysian whose rise to regional godfatherdom was only interrupted by his premature death from a life of excess, made his early money as a big-time smuggler of Indonesian rubber. So did Ko Teck Kin, who in the late 1950s became president of the Chinese chamber of commerce in Singapore.[40] After the civil war ended, Mohamad 'Bob' Hasan was the partner of a then divisional army commander based in

Semarang called Suharto in a big sugar-smuggling operation in defiance of central government authority. Suharto, who had already been involved in opium running during the civil war, was lucky not to be cashiered.

Smuggling, however, was not the only way to make money out of conflict. In British colonies, the end of the war brought many months of British Military Administration (BMA), which saw tired and sometimes greedy officers with little or no business experience dispense valuable procurement and construction contracts. The concession to feed 80,000 prisoners-of-war, mentioned earlier, was decided in a couple of hours by two Commonwealth officers. When the time came in different territories to disband the local BMA, or in some instances later, there were auctions of military and civilian surplus equipment that also provided the first millions for new tycoons. Before he became an epic smuggler, Henry Fok was a prime beneficiary of auctions in Hong Kong.

The myth has grown up in Hong Kong that Fok was born on a sampan and received no formal schooling. In reality he won a scholarship to Hong Kong's élite King's College on Bonham Road where he learned the English that enabled him to read auction gazettes. Cheap deals at auction after the war were his first serious business. In Malaysia, casino magnate Lim Goh Tong admits in his official biography that he became adept at rigging the bidding in post-war auctions, by working with a group of friends.[41] He made his first fortune selling on bulldozers, cranes and similar equipment, or using it to kit out his own construction firm.

It was the educated, the well-heeled and the cosmopolitan who profited most readily from war. In Hong Kong members of the local Chinese élite made fortunes buying up 'duress notes' – Hong Kong dollars issued by local bankers under Japanese direction – just before the British resumed power. The notes were purchased at a fraction of their face value in the expectation that the returning colonial power could be persuaded to honour the currency as a means to restore 'economic stability'. In 1946, this turned out to be the case. The Hongkong Bank bought HK$119 million of duress notes at their full face value. One of the prime beneficiaries was said to be Sir Sik-nin Chau, a London- and Vienna-trained surgeon and businessman and son of Sir Shouson Chow, who had been the first Chinese appointed to Hong Kong's Executive Council.[42]

In addition to the short-term profits it generated, the Second World War presaged a seismic shift in the business landscape in south-east Asia, because it displaced European and American interests for an extended period. Until the end of the Pacific war in August 1945, foreign businessmen not killed in fighting were either interned or forced into exile, and those who returned to work in Asia usually did not do so until some time after the armistice. In the meantime Asian businessmen, typically the ethnic Chinese who were fitted by colonial structures into an intermediate role between local agrarian economies and Western big business, were presented with opportunities to change their status. In Thailand, for instance, fourteen banks and twenty-five insurance companies were set up between 1943 and 1952, most of them run by ethnic Chinese businessmen and fronted by senior Thai bureaucrats as chairmen and board members. The Japanese historian Suehiro Akira observes: 'When the Europeans returned to Thailand, they found that major industries, especially in the commercial and financial sectors, that they had previously controlled were now dominated by either the Chinese or Indians.'[43] The transition was not so acute in every country, but the war shook up the economic order in an unprecedented manner.

From world war and the Korean conflict, the region slipped into the Cold War and the US-led fight against communism. This had further, important ramifications for the territories we are following, because it caused a river of American money to flow into the region. In the Philippines, there were two major military bases after independence – Subic Bay naval station and Clark air base – and billions of dollars of aid money, much of it collected by the Marcos regime. In Thailand, US grants for military spending to shore up what was deemed a 'front line' anti-communist state underwrote the military regimes of the 1950s and 1960s. All pro-American states in the region benefited and, with them, local politicians and the businessmen they patronised.

An extreme example in Thailand concerned Phao Sriyanonda; he became deputy director-general of police after a military coup in 1947, and director-general in 1951. Phao used CIA-supplied military hardware to establish a police air force and maritime and armoured units that, in the course of the 1950s, became the biggest opium-smuggling syndicate in the country, while Thailand itself became the centre of the global heroin trade.[44] The key tycoon client of Phao, and his powerful father-in-law Marshal Phin Choonhavan, was Chin Sophonpanich, the developer of Bangkok Bank, the largest south-east Asian financial institution outside Hong Kong and – as we shall see – the financier of many of the post-war godfathers.

Nationalism and Class: the Main Non-event

If Thailand in the 1930s had suggested that ordinary men and women would not be major beneficiaries of political change and the end of colonialism, the rest of the region proved it after the war. The war was a powerful catalyst for nationalism and class consciousness throughout south-east Asia. Its end also coincided with the rise of new ideas about how governments could intervene in economies to produce outcomes that would meet popular expectations for social and ethnic justice. And at face value, this was an incendiary era. The 1950s witnessed powerful communist currents in the newly democratic countries of the region – the Malayan Emergency, an armed political insurrection, began in 1948; Sukarno, Indonesia's first post-independence leader, flirted heavily with the country's communist party. Anti-Chinese sentiment came to the fore and indigenous political leaders found that moves to legislate against perceived ethnic Chinese economic dominance were popular. Yet, despite all this, the pre-war Thai experience had shown that traditional working relationships between separate political and economic élites – ones that crossed the ethnic divide – were extremely durable; so it proved elsewhere in the region.

The experiments with democracy in the Philippines, Malaysia and Indonesia – and previously in Thailand – failed to overhaul traditional social structures. In the post-colonial states the colonisers disappeared, but the new indigenous political élites fell back, despite moments of sometimes violent racial and nationalist discrimination, on familiar ways. It is necessary to consider briefly how the challenges of popular politics were dealt with in different countries in order to understand how tycoon economics survived.

The *Balimbing* Convention

The Philippines had had a false start with nationalism long before Thailand's 1932 coup and transition to a constitutional monarchy. There was a revolutionary uprising against the Spanish in 1896. But the rebels were not united and their action had centrifugal tendencies – it seemed as likely to split the country up as to bring it together as an independent state. In the event, the uprising was superseded by a distant war in 1898 between the United States and Spain over Cuba, which put the Philippines in American hands. Washington decided to keep the archipelago. It first befriended the local revolutionaries, then fought a two-year campaign to suppress them; several important rebels were bought off with cash payments and consequently endorsed the new regime. Since the US was without colonial experience, the only practical way to run the Philippines was by co-operation with existing power brokers. As a result, Manila-based and regional élites were not just back in business, they were centre stage. The Americans did bring an element of political idealism with them, but it was insufficiently applied – a bastardised US political system was grafted on to the Philippines that left central government weak, while landed potentates from the regions dominated a new congress, controlling the requisite votes in their localities even as the franchise expanded. Whereas in Thailand or Indonesia the political élite controlled the bureaucracy and made deals with mostly ethnic Chinese businessmen in order to share economic rents, the system that developed in the Philippines saw regional interests working to control parliament and then plunder the central state. The ethnicity of the landed oligarchs – mostly Spanish and Chinese *mestizo* – was of little apparent consequence; they were all playing the same game. It is instructive that Paul Hutchcroft, the author of *Booty Capitalism* (1998), a major academic study of the expropriation of the Philippine state by the tycoon fraternity, hardly bothers to distinguish between who is and is not of Chinese ancestry.[45] What matters in the Philippines is whether you are a godfather or a member of the *masa* – the masses.

The model for so much of what was to come was established in 1916 with the setting-up of the Philippine National Bank (PNB). This occurred just as the US colonial power granted Filipino control over both houses of congress. PNB became the oligarchs' personal treasury, making loans to families in estate agriculture. The government was required to keep all its deposits with the bank, which could also issue currency. It took just five years for PNB to arrive at its first major crisis, by which time the bank had squandered its entire capital base, half the government's deposits and undermined the national currency. At the same time that oligarchs were being fed a steady supply of credit from PNB, they were assisted by US economic policy, which provided a guaranteed export quota and tariff protection for sugar and also supported the coconut industry. Sugar exports increased seven-fold between the US Payne–Aldrich tariff act of 1909 and the mid 1930s, becoming around half of total exports. It was a scenario guaranteed to throw up rent-seeking tycoons who were able to sell globally uncompetitive agricultural products into the US market while manipulating a political system that was ostensibly democratic. They were granted huge economic rents, and control of congress enabled them to prevent the two things that would damage their interests – land reform and increases in the effective rate of taxation. The only problem for the élite, as many commentators have noted, was that it had to call for Philippine independence in order to have a minimum of electoral credibility; in reality, US-era godfathers were terrified of the economic implications of independence. Enormous effort went into securing a bilateral trade agreement that preserved quota access to the American market before independence came on 4 July 1946.

With the spoils of the US relationship secured until 1974 by what became the Laurel–Langley tariff act, and many more dollars guaranteed by deals for post-war reconstruction aid and the hosting of US military bases, the Philippine government announced it had thrown off the colonial yoke. The electoral tradition of dividing up the requisites of power, whether in the form of the political appointment of all bureaucrats or the disbursement of public works budgets, grew and grew. Political ideologies were a liability in a system where politicians jumped back and forth between the two main parties, looking for the most generous terms; Filipinos refer to their congressmen as *balimbing*, a star-shaped fruit that looks the same from every side. The political trajectory was one that led, unsurprisingly, to the kleptocracy of Ferdinand Marcos in the 1960s. Along the way there were moments of heightened chauvinism in popular politics – most obviously the Retail Trade Nationalisation Act of 1954, which sought to force non-naturalised Chinese out of their traditional shop-keeping niche – but these in no way constituted an attack on the hyper-élite structure of society. The Chinese and Chinese *mestizo* godfathers identified with other godfathers, not with the kind of Chinese who ran shops.

An Absolute Bargain

Malaysia's journey to independence in 1957 produced an arrangement between its separate political and economic élites that was sufficiently explicit to become popularly known as 'the bargain'.[46] The traditional Malay political élite, aristocracy-based, faced a similar problem to the Philippine politician–tycoons as nationalism increased in potency: it was necessary to support the cause of independence without paying an economic price. Just as American colonialism underwrote the position of the Philippine landed class, so the British presence guaranteed the status of the Malay élite in a situation where, by the 1950s, the Malays were barely a majority because of massive immigration from China and India. With the advent of democracy, the party of the Malay ruling class – the United Malays National Organisation (UMNO) – needed a political accommodation with the Chinese economic élite that would guarantee everyone's interests. The means to this end was the race-based Malayan Chinese Association (MCA), a political party set up in 1949 and sponsored by leading Chinese businessmen. These included Lau Pak Khuan and H. S. Lee, major tin miners, and Tan Cheng Lock and his son Tan Siew Sin, members of a Malacca *baba* dynasty with extensive rubber interests. Tan Siew Sin was to become an important finance minister. The MCA and UMNO formed the Alliance, the pro-independence electoral vehicle driven by an unspoken élite consensus for Malay domination of the bureaucracy and no state attacks on the Chinese position in business. Edmund Terence Gomez, the leading scholar of business–state relations in Malaysia, characterises the arrangement as 'ethno-populism camouflaging class dominance'.[47] In the first general election in 1955, the Alliance swept 51 out of 52 parliamentary seats.

In the post-independence government, MCA leaders took key economic posts in finance, and trade and industry ministries, and leading Chinese businessmen were granted requests for banking and tariff-protected manufacturing licences. UMNO leaders held ultimate power and hence limitless possibilities for enrichment. The élites were happy. Through the 1960s, however, inequality increased within each of Malaysia's racial groups, and most particularly the Malay group. There were various projects to set up trust agencies and a policy bank to support indigenous *bumiputras*, but nothing substantial enough to head off race riots in Kuala Lumpur in May 1969.

The reaction to the violence was a stark reminder to the Chinese community of its lack of any real political power. In 1971 the government launched a New Economic Policy (NEP) with various targets – share of corporate equity, urban employment, university enrolment, and so forth – designed to enhance the position of ethnic Malays. While middle-class Chinese and their children were significantly affected by provisions of the NEP – because of exclusion from employment and educational opportunities – the increase in the indigenous share of corporate wealth was largely achieved by state buy-outs of foreign (mostly British) businesses, using 1970s petrodollars that conveniently became available. There was no rupture of the economic structure at the élite level. After the twenty-year term envisaged at the outset of the NEP expired in 1990, the Malay share of corporate equity in Malaysia had increased from almost nothing to around one-fifth, but the Chinese share had also doubled, from one-fifth to two-fifths. This reflected the fact that the tycoon fraternity was doing better than ever; the NEP had not ended deals between the ethnically separate political and economic élites.

Sukarno's Champagne Socialism

Indonesia was the post-independence country that most clearly threatened to upend the traditional social and economic structure. Sukarno, the country's first president, was from a privileged background, but he was also a firebrand nationalist who regarded himself as a revolutionary. The backing he extended to the Partai Komunis Indonesia (PKI), Indonesia's widely supported communist party, was at least in part motivated by a desire to rid the country of its stultifying feudal traditions. But in the end Sukarno, who himself lived a life of excess in the presidential palace, did no such thing. The structure and anti-commercial prejudices of Javanese culture remained intact. There was a long period of populist persecution of Chinese immigrants for allegedly robbing the indigenous population of its birthright, but this entrained no fundamental change in society. The so-called Benteng Programme, which from 1950 to 1957 allocated foreign exchange and import licences to indigenous traders to support their development, was subsumed in an orgy of corruption. This set a pattern not for the growth of competitive indigenous business but instead for a culture of kickbacks and political fixing. Efforts to curb the economic role of ethnic Chinese culminated in 1958 in the banning of aliens (covering about half the Chinese population that did not have citizenship) from engaging in retail trade in rural areas. Some areas of the countryside banned residence altogether for aliens. As in the Philippines and elsewhere in the region, it was less well-off Chinese who bore the brunt of the ethnic fury. In the Indonesian case, repression was such that in 1960 an estimated 130,000 people accepted an offer of free repatriation made by the People's Republic of China.

The Sukarno era was unpleasant for almost all ethnic Chinese – even Oei Tiong Ham's assets were taken over by the state. But nothing happened at a structural level to prevent a quick reversion to historical form when Sukarno was pushed out in the 1960s. In fact, quite the opposite. When, in 1957, Sukarno used a territorial dispute over Irian Jaya (western New Guinea) – which the Dutch clung on to until 1963 – to start nationalising Dutch, and later other foreign, businesses, he was opening up the economic space into which ethnic Chinese businessmen would subsequently move. The five biggest Dutch trading houses alone handled 60 per cent of foreign trade. In total, some 800 foreign enterprises came into state hands after 1958 and neither the government nor the army could run them effectively. Through the first half of the 1960s the condition of the economy deteriorated at a frightening pace while inflation raged. The stage was perfectly set for a rescue operation involving a return to a traditional division of political and economic labour.

That is what happened following an abortive coup in 1965 that saw Colonel Suharto begin a rise to power which ended with his replacement of Sukarno as president in 1967. Suharto was the 'normal' kind of petty Javanese aristocrat, content with the traditions of deference in local culture and committed, above all, to maintaining harmonious – which is to say, carefully regimented – societal relationships. He served in the army under the Dutch and Japanese, and learned to preserve stability through force. In short, unlike Sukarno, Suharto was a natural conservative, and much of the officer class – where many Javanese *priyayi* aristocrats wound up after independence – were just like him. Suharto was also a quartermaster familiar with doing business with Chinese traders. When he was running the Diponegoro Division, based in

Semarang, in the 1950s, he worked with Mohamad 'Bob' Hasan and others to make trading in essential commodities like sugar a military monopoly and thereby supplemented his official budget. Suharto was also involved in smuggling, for which then army commander A. H. Nasution censured him; he escaped a military tribunal in 1959 because of the support of his superior officer, General Gatot Subroto, who also happened to be Bob Hasan's adoptive father.[48] With ultimate power in his hands, in the 1960s Suharto could dole out concessions in a manner familiar to him – to people who would get a job done and who posed no political challenge to his authority.

These individuals tended to be Chinese immigrants of relatively recent arrival. Best known of them was Liem Sioe Liong, a petty trader who arrived in Java in 1938, with whom Suharto had also had commercial dealings in the 1950s. During the Second World War and the war against the Dutch, Liem had made some early money with his brother provisioning the republican army, which is how he became acquainted with key officers in Java, including Suharto. In 1968 he was granted a half share in a monopoly for importing cloves, the key ingredient of Indonesian *kretek* cigarettes; in 1969 that concession became a complete monopoly on the import, milling and distribution of flour, and in the 1970s a near-monopoly on cement production.[49] He also enjoyed protected positions in the trading of rubber, sugar and coffee. It was a return to the nested relationships between political power and Chinese traders that characterised the nineteenth century. As Edwin Soeryadjaya, the eldest son of William Soeryadjaya, one of Indonesia's wealthiest Suharto era tycoons, puts it: 'When Suharto came to power he wanted to be the king. So he did exactly what the Dutch did.'[50]

The Indonesians came up with the term *cukong* to describe the businessman who is politically beholden for his commercial success and has to cut politicians and the military in for a share of the returns. The Philippines in the 1960s gave birth to the expression 'crony capitalist'. In Malaysia, businesses fronted by ethnic Malays but actually run by Chinese became known as 'Ali Baba' operations, where Ali was the Malay and Baba the Chinese. Fred Riggs, an academic specialising in Thailand, coined the phrase 'pariah capitalist' – after a sub-group of Indian untouchables – to define businessmen who are outcasts in political terms but who are tolerated so long as they stick to their job – commerce. All these expressions point to the same thing – that the use by political power of a wealthy but dependent class of tycoons was too attractive to be ditched merely because of the end of colonialism. Only a bottom-up reordering of political life would have changed this pattern of activity, and such did not occur. Throughout south-east Asia, popular forces of nationalism and class were contained and constrained within the old social structures, whether governments were democratically elected or not.

Zeitgeist Economics

In terms of broad policy, a global intellectual influence acting on the region in the era of independence was economists' penchant for more planning and control. This was only a boon to the local structures of godfather business. Every era has its economic *zeitgeist* – its 'spirit'. In the early modern era in Europe, from 1500 to 1800, mercantilism was the unquestioned economic rationale. In the nineteenth century came the rise of free trade theories. By about 1930, as a result of global depression, the First World War and social-ist thinking, planning and control were in the ascendancy. This period of interventionist economics started under colonial management and continued through early independence, with its objectives shifting from imperial prefer-ence to domestic development as locally led governments took power.

In the mid-twentieth century, each of the south-east Asian economies we are following tried what was known as import substitution industrialisation (ISI). ISI was a reasoned response to the end of colonialism. Advocates pointed out that colonial powers had structured the economies they controlled to provide raw commodities and buy finished manufactures – most obviously through tariff policy – and this discouraged Asian manufacturing. The result was economic dependency in which south-east Asian countries were stuck in low value-added activities in agriculture and mining, and forced to export commodities to advanced industrial nations in order to import their relatively expensive manufactured goods. The only way to break out of the cycle, it was argued, was to increase import tariffs, subsidise industrial credit and micro-manage the supply of foreign exchange in order to support the development of native manufacturers.

The theory was sufficiently compelling that it had considerable support in international agencies like the World Bank and the International Monetary Fund (IMF). In practice, however, ISI went wrong in one country after the next – at least if judged by the intention to create internationally competitive domestic industry. The reason was that policy was undermined by the tradi-tional, dominant relationship between political and economic élites. Some of the experience has been alluded to in the preceding section, because it was very much tied up with the post-independence agenda of nationalist politics and the backlash against perceived historic Chinese dominance in matters economic. (The latter notion, of course, is a myth since it was really big Euro-pean and American companies that dominated in the colonial period.)

In Thailand, nationalisation began in the late 1930s, but ISI was mainly associated with the regime of Field Marshal Sarit Thanarat, who came to power in a coup in 1957. At every turn the ISI process in Thailand was built around civilian and military bureaucrats-turned-capitalists and a small number of ethnic Chinese tycoon collaborators. The tycoons were from trading backgrounds, and this defined their approach to manufacturing. They sought concessions from politicians and the army and then turned to foreign businesses – usually Japanese – to supply them with technology and production processes. Existing manufacturers in Thailand were usually not able to trade up in scale because government projects for import substitution in new industries involved requirements for minimum investment or minimum production capacity that were beyond their means. Instead of incumbent manufacturing firms being assisted by government policy to grow to competitive scale, what happened was that well-connected merchants monopolised deals for protected manufacturing.

The norm was for a product's importer to become its local assembler in an arrangement with the foreign supplier. One example is cars and motorcycles, where tariff protection gave rise to manufacturing joint ventures with Nissan, Toyota, Mitsubishi, Hino, Daihatsu, Isuzu and Honda, but no genuine domestic production. Import substitution produced large companies, but it did not achieve the objective of making Thai businesses originate internationally competitive manufactures. By the 1970s Thai industry was a series of big conglomerates dependent on foreign partners, started at different times by merchant tycoons responding to new import substitution policies: in auto assembly, electrical appliances, steel products, glass, chemicals and animal feedstock. Suehiro Akira, airing what has become the key Japanese critique of south-east Asia, observes: 'In Japan and in other industrialized countries, technical experts and factory owners frequently became significant contributors to domestic industrial development … in Thailand, there was no comparable development.'[51]

A pattern of the existing business élite grabbing the fruits of ISI policy was even more apparent in the Philippines. The difference there was that the local élite was rooted not just in trading but, as a result of colonial legacy, in agricultural land. This created powerful contradictions. Well-connected landowners went into manufacturing in the 1950s and 1960s – typically final-stage assembly of American products – because foreign exchange allocations, state loans, tax breaks and tariff protection meant windfall profits. But landed tycoons were also exporters of agricultural and mineral commodities who were forced to surrender their export earnings to the central bank to support the ISI programme. As a result they backed ISI in the early, high-return stages – when manufacturing growth was around 10 per cent a year in the 1950s – and then turned against it in the early 1960s. In 1962 exchange controls were lifted and the peso devalued by some 50 per cent. The legacy was tycoons whose interests spread across agriculture, mining, manufacturing and banking who had no particular commitment to any national development strategy – they simply sought concessions. The major landed families that spread into manufacturing and banking under ISI included the Aboitizs, Aranetas, Ayala-Zobels and Cojuangcos; the Gokongweis and Palancas came out of mining. The Philippines economist Temario Rivera writes of a social structure 'dominated by landed families whose pursuit of a self-contradictory set of interests weakened the constituency for a coherent strategy of industrial growth and development'.[52] In other words, ISI was hijacked by the usual suspects.

Indonesia, as discussed above, pursued the nationalist Benteng Programme in the 1950s which apportioned most foreign exchange to indigenous traders. The economic historian Richard Robison observes that it created 'not an indigenous merchant bourgeoisie but a group of licence brokers and political fixers'.[53] The same would be true in the 1970s when, suddenly flush with oil and gas money, as international prices soared, the government experimented with manufacturing ISI. Licences and support did not go to small- and medium-size manufacturers, but to well-connected *pribumi* and ethnic Chinese tycoons. Steel, cement, automotive, chemical and fertiliser plants were again constructed on the basis of merchant traders bringing in multinational firms to provide technology while they concentrated on finessing political deals. Adam Schwartz, a long time Indonesia specialist, author and journalist, writes of the bureaucratic maze that was created: 'While many private enterprises with strong political pull did well in this period, smaller firms, buried under an avalanche of credit ceilings and regulations covering production, investment and distribution, suffered.'[54]

This was the constant in the region: ISI did not nurture small local manufacturers into larger, internationally competitive manufacturers, it simply reinforced the position of the trading-based élite of the colonial era. In Malaysia, ISI policies in the period prior to the 1969 riots saw, for instance, Robert Kuok – from an established trading family – move successively into protected positions in sugar milling, flour milling and shipping through partnerships with Japanese technology providers. Many beneficiaries of ISI protection in Malaysian manufacturing were British companies whose interests in the market had been guaranteed by local politicians in return for an early grant of independence. Chinese merchants in the period obtained important licences to open banks and gaming operations. After 1969, ISI gave way to nationalisation of British and other foreign assets – using windfall oil and gas revenues – many of which were in turn later privatised into the hands of the godfather élite. Everywhere in the region import substitution industrialisation failed to create a tradition of industrial capitalism to complement the merchant capitalism that had been allowed to prosper in the colonial era. Instead, successful merchant capitalists acquired manufacturing interests in joint ventures or technology tie-ups with Western and Japanese industrialists. The pattern never subsequently changed.

The Hong Kong and Singapore Thing

One of the least helpfully discussed themes in Asian economic history is how Hong Kong and Singapore fit into the overall economic structure of southeast Asia and, since its policy of re-opening to the outside world after 1979, of China, too. This is unfortunate because the region is only properly understood if the special dynamic of these two cities is recognised. The product, as we have seen, of a British imperial and economic quest for self-contained, offshore island bases, the structural roles of Hong Kong and Singapore are remarkably similar. This fact is only obscured by the reflexive description of post-war Hong Kong as a bastion of free enterprise (which is not, with respect to its domestic economy, true) and Singapore as a statist behemoth. Singapore's description of itself as a 'country', while technically true, is also confusing from an economics perspective.

What is important about Hong Kong and Singapore is that they are archetypal city states – 'port city states' would be more precise. Since colonial inception they have offered tariff-free trade (with few or no questions asked about what is being traded) and have been places to park money (with few or no questions asked about where the money came from). As relatively easily managed city states, with highly motivated and purely immigrant populations,[55] Hong Kong and Singapore perform a simple economic trick: they arbitrage the relative economic inefficiency of their hinterlands. In other words, business comes to them because they perform certain tasks – principally services – a little better than surrounding countries. They are both natural deep ports and have long built on this advantage. Hong Kong's immediate hinterland is southern China, but the closing of the mainland to most trade between 1949 and 1979 made the city focus more than it otherwise would have done on business with south-east Asia. Singapore's dominant hinterland, contrary to the apparent geographic logic that suggests the Malay peninsula, has long been Indonesia. This is not to say that Malaysia has been unimportant, only that Indonesia has been more important, because it is a relatively much bigger economy. Singapore's trade with Indonesia (focused on Sumatra and Borneo) was greater than that with peninsular Malaysia in the late nineteenth century and this continued to be the case in the twentieth century. In the 1950s, for instance, almost half Singapore's exports were rubber and most of this came from Indonesia, often obtained by illegal barter exchange for manufactured goods. So dominant was Singapore as the ocean-going port for both Malaysia and Indonesia in the post-Second World War era that the Singaporean government suppressed much of its trade data in a largely successful bid to avoid unwanted publicity.[56]

Hong Kong and Singapore have long traditions as the regional centres of smuggling trade as well as of legal trade. For as long as surrounding countries have imposed tariffs or quotas on trade in their efforts to fund government, Hong Kong and Singapore have profited from circumventing those restrictions. As long ago as the 1860s the Hong Kong chamber of commerce and influential merchant houses like Jardine Matheson expressed outrage when Britain's Sir Robert Hart and his largely British staff took on the running of China's Maritime Customs Service and tried to help the weakened Chinese state raise essential taxes. When Hart began to clamp down on smuggling originating in Hong Kong, he found the Hong Kong government unwilling to co-operate.[57]

Hong Kong and Singapore have been at least as important historically as places to store capital, and this role has only increased in recent decades with the development of modern financial services. Ethnic outsider tycoons who have profited from business concessions in surrounding countries have always sought to keep funds offshore, fearing – with good reason – that they may one day be the victims of political change. The possibilities for tax evasion and transfer pricing between different south-east Asian jurisdictions have also produced vast funds in need of off-shore havens. Hong Kong and Singapore's banking secrecy, their willingness to bank the accounts of exotic shell companies with nominee directors, and Hong Kong's exemption of private companies from the need to produce public accounts, have offered the perfect, readily accessible refuge. It was said, for example, in the Marcos era that Hong Kong received a boost from the development of the private jet, simply because Marcos's family and cronies could pop over to their Hong Kong banks for the day; Imelda Marcos did a lot of shopping in the colony.

The regional offshore roles of Hong Kong and Singapore have been absolute constants since their founding, and show no sign of change. In the aftermath of the Asian financial crisis Michael Chambers, head of research in Indonesia for Credit Lyonnais Securities Asia (CLSA), estimated – based on information from banking sources – that some US$200 billion of Indonesian capital was sitting in Singaporean banks.[58] That compared with an Indonesian GDP of US$350 billion. Some money in city state banks is legitimate expatriated capital and some is ill-gotten gains; Hong Kong and Singapore show little interest in separating the two. Indeed, in recent years, as the European Union finally brought pressure to bear on Switzerland and other European private banking centres to block tax evasion and introduce withholding tax for some non-nationals, Singapore moved to fill a global – as well as its regional – niche. The city increased account secrecy provisions and changed trust laws in a manner designed to attract the kind of money Switzerland had dealt in; the number of foreign private banks in Singapore almost doubled between 2000 and 2006.[59] After Singapore hosted an IMF conference in September 2006, there was a rare and highly entertaining insight into how some – normally reticent – investment bankers really view the island state. Exasperated by the 'nauseating pleasantries' of the conference and a dinner with prime minister Lee Hsien Loong at which foreigners 'fawned [over] him like a prince', Morgan Stanley's chief economist in Asia, Andy Xie, fired off a missive to colleagues. People at the meeting, he said, 'were competing with each other to praise Singapore as the success story of globalization ... Actually, Singapore's success came mostly from being the money laundering centre for corrupt Indonesian businessmen and government officials ... To sustain its economy, Singapore is building casinos to attract corruption money from China.' When the email was leaked, a flustered Morgan Stanley spokeswoman said its content was 'aimed at stimulating internal debate' in the firm; Mr Xie resigned.[60]

Together with banking services in Hong Kong and Singapore go real estate, shopping and entertainment. The luxury housing markets of the city states have always been driven by outsiders – today it is mainland Chinese in Hong Kong; in Singapore it has always been Indonesians. The Hong Kong or Singapore bolthole has been a source of security and a reliable investment for tycoons from Thailand, Malaysia, Indonesia and the Philippines, whether in the nineteenth century or today. After the Asian financial crisis and anti-Chinese riots in Indonesia, the early Monday morning and Friday afternoon flights between Singapore and Jakarta became a tycoon express as ethnic Chinese Indonesia tycoons shuttled back and forth. They moved their families out of their Jakarta homes and into their Singapore ones. Hong Kong and Singapore also have long been the regional centres for luxury shops and fine cuisine, while Hong Kong has its horseracing and the nearby gambling and money laundering fleshpot that is Macau. Though many people expressed surprise, it was not one in terms of historical continuity when the authoritarian regime in Singapore decided in 2005 that it would license two huge casino resorts. The post-independence Singapore of Lee Kuan Yew and family has only evinced moral fervour when it does not interfere with the business of a city state. Hence the contrast between banking secrecy and long-tolerated prostitution – which largely serves visiting businessmen – on the one hand, and Singapore's fines for not flushing urinals or failing to shut the curtains while in a state of undress on the other. Prime Minister Lee Hsien Loong greeted the legalisation of gambling with the rhetorical question: 'If we don't change, where will we be in twenty years?' But in reality Singapore's casinos are just the latest chapter in its remaining the same.

Hong Kong and Singapore were destined to succeed. All they had to do was to be one degree more efficient, one degree more attractive to capital than surrounding countries and they would prosper. Smallness would be a virtue. This was not always apparent to Singapore's leadership, however. In 1963 the leaders of the newly independent state were obsessed with the idea that the place could not survive on its own and they took the city into the Federation of Malaysia, only to be bumped out two years later; premier Lee Kuan Yew wept in public. The episode perhaps gives succour to those who argue that Singapore's dominant post-independence politician never understood much about how business and businessmen really operate. If he had, he would have recognised that Singapore was always better off on its own. Under Mr Lee – who never much liked private businessmen – Singapore followed a statist model, with the government taking public control of most significant companies. Any absolute loss of efficiency from this form of development did not matter because the port and the banks in Singapore were still relatively more efficient, and secure, than those in Indonesia and Malaysia. Hong Kong pursued an apparently opposite free market model – though, as we will later see, its services were in reality always heavily cartelised – and had private port operators and many more privately held banks. At the end of the twentieth century the result of ostensibly diametrically opposite approaches to economic management was GDP *per capita* in the two cities that varied by less than US$1,000 – US$23,930 in Hong Kong and US$22,960 in Singapore. The lesson? That a city state with a strategic deep water port in a region that has relatively higher levels of mismanagement, corruption and political uncertainty will prosper with little reference to official economic philosophy.

In terms of their resident tycoons, Hong Kong and Singapore have always had two kinds – imports and locals. There has been a steady stream of godfathers who have migrated in from surrounding countries. A long line of Indonesian tycoons, from Oei Tiong Ham on, have settled as corporate and individual residents of Singapore; the only drawback for them is that this tends to upset the Indonesian government. Equally, there has been a long line of Malaysians, from Eu Tong-sen to Robert Kuok, who have ended up in Hong Kong. Some native Singaporean tycoon families – like that of Ng Teng Fong – have split themselves between Singapore and Hong Kong; Hong Kong tycoons do not migrate to Singapore, where the state crowds out a lot of private activity.

Local Hong Kong and Singapore godfathers divide in turn into two further sub-types: those based in land and those based in banking. Since land is structurally scarce in the city states, from the nineteenth century on real estate has always been expensive by regional and international standards, subject to considerable price volatility and productive of high speculative returns. Real estate has therefore been the root of most tycoon wealth. Banking has been the other billionaire mainstay, although in Hong Kong, where colonial government continued until 1997, two British banks – Hong Kong and Shanghai Banking Corporation and Standard Chartered (the successor to Chartered Bank of India, Australia and China) – were able to remain the dominant players; in Singapore, government banking left room for three sizeable local private banks. The one other thing to know about godfather wealth in Hong Kong is that there is a secondary structural connection to the smuggling and gambling riches of nearby Macau. The former Portuguese colony is a truly wondrous, corrupt and enthralling place that will be referenced as we proceed. To conclude our historical survey, however, we need to return to the world of macroeconomics.

The Last Word in Acronyms

Import substitution industrialisation (ISI), as we have seen, was both a part of global economic fashion and the natural post-war reaction to the manner in which colonial regimes structured south-east Asia as a provider of commodities and purchaser of manufactures. In the short-term ISI produced respectable growth rates in the region. But it was all too easily manipulated by a tycoon class that was raised on trading. Every effort to plan industrial development was another arbitrage opportunity for the politically well-connected. Usually, the procedure was for a tycoon to obtain the necessary licence, bring in a foreign partner to provide a manufacturing process that was reduced to kit assembly (with most parts and components imported), and then hide behind tariff barriers selling goods that were unsaleable internationally. The result was profits, but minimal progress in constructing a sustainable domestic manufacturing base. The level of abuse varied from project to project and from country to country, but by the late 1960s it was clear that ISI was not a panacea for economic development. Moreover, countries in north-east Asia – Japan, South Korea and Taiwan – were developing more quickly and sustainably than south-east Asia on a model based on manufactured exports. South Korea and Taiwan, for instance, overtook the Philippines – second only to Japan among countries in the region by GDP *per capita* at independence – on almost all economic measures by the end of the 1950s.

Thus began the great acronym transition in south-east Asia, from ISI to what economists call export oriented industrialisation, or EOI. This was encouraged by the World Bank, the IMF and, in particular, the US government. The story started in Singapore, which itself had a flirtation with ISI from the mid 1950s, building steel rolling capacity and vehicle assembly plants. The experience was short-lived. Singapore's planners switched trains. By the mid 1960s the Jurong Industrial Estate on the west side of Singapore island was reclaimed from swamp land and the government set out to woo export-oriented foreign investors to fill it up. Early success came with American semiconductor manufacturers like Texas Instruments and Fairchild, and Singapore's role as an electronics outsourcing centre was primed. By the early 1970s, with multinational companies experiencing huge cost savings from the use of Asian labour and the Singaporean government doing everything in its power to accommodate them, most of the world's offshore processing of semiconductors – comprising the lower value-added finishing processes – had relocated to Singapore. In 1973 the value of manufactured exports exceeded commodities for the first time. Over the long run, Japanese investment proved to be more significant than American. Multinationals from Japan moved a full range of export-oriented investments to Singapore, including heavy industrial projects in ship repair and shipbuilding in the 1960s and early 1970s, and a vast chemicals complex established by Sumitomo. The yen was appreciating against other major currencies in the 1970s, and this encouraged the exodus offshore. Matsushita led the charge of the household goods manufacturers to Singapore, setting up a first refrigerator compressor plant in 1972.

What began in Singapore, and expanded so impressively, spread around the region. Governments signalled their change of tack with new legislation. The Philippines, for instance, passed an Investment Incentives Act in 1967, while Malaysia followed suit with an act of the same name in 1968. Governments were also quick to curtail worker rights in order to reassure foreign investors.

The Sarit regime in Thailand repealed legislation granting workers employ-ment rights and banned unions as early as 1958. In Singapore the People's Action Party (PAP) of Lee Kuan Yew, which had come to power on the back of an alliance with workers' groups, established government control over unions and deliberately suppressed wages in the 1970s via a National Wages Council. The pace of implementation of foreigner-friendly investment regimes varied, and governments continued to protect domestic businesses with tariffs and other measures, but the direction of economic policy changed fundamentally. EOI met the requirement for economic growth, generated lots of foreign exchange and was also much better than ISI at creating employment, some-thing essential as post-war population growth picked up dramatically.

From the 1970s, south-east Asia's development was defined by EOI. In Malaysia, as one example, manufacturing's share of exports increased from 12 per cent in 1970 to 74 per cent in 1993. Exports grew to a point where they actually exceeded gross domestic product. South-east Asian EOI was very much driven by assembly operations using imported components. The most important phase of the export boom came from the mid 1980s. During the 1970s, governments in Malaysia, Indonesia and Thailand had consider-able room for policy manoeuvre as oil and gas price rises made their income from these commodities rocket. But after a debt-fuelled recession in the mid 1980s, it became necessary to court foreign investment more assiduously. This coincided with a big increase in multinationals' focus on the benefits of offshore manufacturing and led to powerful export growth throughout the region for a decade from 1987.

EOI brought growth and jobs, but it was not a mirror image of the north-east Asian experience. In Japan, South Korea and Taiwan, exports were developed by indigenous companies while governments blocked foreign investment. The sustainability of the model came from firms' rising ability to manage research and development of new products, and slowly build international brands. Import substitution industrialisation failed to achieve these objectives in south-east Asia, instead creating assembly operations beholden to foreign partners and suppliers. And EOI did not solve the problem either. What it did, instead, was to rent out south-east Asia's cheap labour to multinational com-panies, which outsourced manufacturing processes while keeping research and development activities in more developed countries. There is an argument that this created a new form of dependency, albeit one over which indepen-dent governments – in contrast to the colonial commodities-for-manufactures structure – had ultimate control. Whether or not the argument has merit, the impact of EOI was still enormous. By 1990 in Singapore, where the model first took hold, almost nine-tenths of direct exports came from foreign-invested enterprises using the city state as a manufacturing platform.

The reaction of local business to the multinational exporters, welcomed back so soon after foreign enterprises that grew up in the colonial era had been kicked or bought out, is telling. Small firms found innumerable opportunities supplying parts and components and services to multinational investors. But their ability to move up the value chain was inhibited by a lack of scale that left them without resources for research and development. Tycoons, on the other hand, had scale and access to capital, but were rarely interested in working in the export sector. The reason is simple. Exporting is a globally competitive business. Where the godfathers outperformed was in trading on the inefficiencies of south-east Asia's domestic economies, whether in the form of politicians' willingness to disburse monopolistic concessions on the basis of personal relations or through the profits to be made when governments tried to micromanage industrial development. For tycoons, the benefit of EOI was significant but indirect: the growth it produced underwrote the continued relationship between political and economic élites and eased pressure for effective deregulation of domestic economies. Public works projects without tenders, and privatisations decided behind closed doors, were politically much more feasible when exports were driving the south-east Asian economy. This was the real, macroeconomic background to the hubris of the late 1980s and 1990s, when tycoons congratulated themselves at conferences and in the media for making south-east Asia prosperous while (mostly) female assembly line workers in export processing factories really did make south-east Asia prosperous. The graph on every godfather's wall ought to be the one on page 299; unfortunately, like most people, they demonstrate a limited capacity for self-analysis. As Stephen Brown, the veteran head of research at Kim Eng Securities in Hong Kong, puts it: 'They honestly believe that: "If I wasn't the business genius I am, you would all be out of a job."'[61]

Part II
How to be a Post-war Godfather

2

How to be a Godfather, #1: Get in character

'We are so accustomed to disguise ourselves to others that in the end we become disguised to ourselves.'

La Rochefoucauld

The post-Second World War, post-independence environment described in the previous chapter was one of great turbulence. But the enduring interdependence of separate political and economic élites was not broken. Certainly the era of rising class consciousness and aggressive nationalism in the 1950s and 1960s (and earlier in Thailand) was threatening to the overseas Chinese and Indian communities. But the people who really suffered were shopkeepers, small businessmen and labourers, not the godfather class. As organised labour and nationalism were reined in by a new group of authoritarian leaders, it was striking how they not only fell back on colonial era modes of interaction with ethnic minority businessmen, but in many instances reinforced them. The challenge to the godfathers therefore came not from any structural shift in society, but in coping with the struggle for power among indigenous political élites once the colonials had exited. In this respect the tycoons' ability to get into, and change, character was more important than ever.

In Thailand, Field Marshal Sarit's 1957–63 regime stabilised relations with Chinese and Indian trading élites based on the military as their passive business partners. Although the country's post-1932 political history is superficially chaotic – Sarit's is only one of eighteen coups to have taken place, the most recent being the ouster of Thaksin Shinawatra in 2006 – after 1957 it was rare for incoming juntas and governments to move against incumbent tycoons. Instead, the godfathers became adept at backing all factions. As Sarasin Viraphol, Dhanin Chearavanont's top executive at his sprawling chickens-to-telecoms CP group, says, it is a matter of money and good house-keeping: 'We back everyone … And you would always have a portrait of the military leader on the wall. That was general practice. And of the commander of police, the commissioner for metropolitan Bangkok …'[1] Even Chin Sophon-panich, who was so tight with Sarit rivals and heroin traffickers Phao Sriya-nonda and Field Marshal Phin Choonhavan that he skipped town to Hong Kong when Sarit took power in 1957, was allowed to continue building Bangkok Bank into Thailand's largest financial institution from exile. It was, says Sarasin, a 'gentleman's game' of coups.

There was greater godfather discontinuity in Indonesia in the 1960s than there was in Thailand after Sarit put an end to populist nationalism. Follow-ing Sukarno's chaotic nationalisation of foreign business in the 1950s, the repatriation of tens of thousands of Chinese in 1960 and the anti-communist blood bath of 1965, Suharto turned reflexively to the Chinese businessmen he was familiar with after he seized power. This meant a handful of rela-tively unknown business people being catapulted to the top of the godfather pile. The most important were long-time associate Mohamad 'Bob' Hasan, an ethnic Chinese convert to Islam, and Liem Sioe Liong, also known as Sudono Salim, who rose from petty trader to the nation's leading businessman in a few years. The precariousness of Suharto's position – or at least his percep-tion of it – as he shored up his power in the late 1960s made the relationship between him, as the Javanese political insider, and his business cronies, as unthreatening ethnic Chinese outsiders, all the more important. Through-out his reign, Suharto was said by confidantes in Jakarta to complain that *pribumi* businessmen could not be 'trusted';[2] the Chinese could. In time a small number of ethnic Indian and Sri Lankan businessmen also became key dependents. The best-known of these was the Sri Lankan Tamil Marimutu Sinivasan, a long-term conduit for political slush funds for Suharto's Golkar party. Sinivasan's Texmaco Group was able, on Suharto's authority, to secure US$900 million in hard currency from the central bank at the height of the Asian financial crisis and, after the dictator fell, was said by the Indonesian government to be its biggest delinquent creditor, owing US$2 billion.[3]

In the Philippines another usurper, Ferdinand Marcos, demonstrated a similar response to Suharto's with respect to the possibilities of godfather relationships. After winning two presidential terms in (distinctly dirty) elec-tions, Marcos circumvented his country's two-term presidential limit by declaring martial law in 1972. Like Suharto, he also looked beyond the estab-lished godfather élite – in the Philippines, traditional Spanish and Chinese *mestizo* families – to find some of his key business proxies. The archetype was

Lucio Tan, a first-generation immigrant and one-time janitor who became, under Marcos' patronage, the Philippines' leading tobacco vendor, as well as having interests in everything from banking to real estate. It is probable that – as with Liem Sioe Liong, who knew Suharto from the latter's military postings in central Java – Tan and Marcos knew each other from Ilocos, the president's home region where Tan had his first, small cigarette factory.[4]

Both Suharto and Marcos signalled regime change by promoting new, non-indigenous outsiders to godfather roles. Tan was a clear break in the ethnically more mixed and integrated Philippines because he represented the so-called 'one-syllable Chinese' – those who had not assimilated and adopted local surnames. The promotion of new outsiders achieved two useful things for the dictators: it provided ultra-dependent, ultra-loyal sources of future finance for them and their families; and it served as a warning to the established, more integrated economic élite that it was not indispensable. In the pre-Marcos Philippines, businessmen of every ethnic make-up had been increasingly successful in overrunning and manipulating a weak parliamentary system and thereby obviating the need to make deals with ultimate political power. Ferdy reversed this trend, though it remains a latent tendency in both the Philippines and Thailand whenever central leadership is weakened.

Malaysia's chronology ran later than those of surrounding nations, but still observed a pattern of rising populist class consciousness and nationalism followed by a return to nested relationships between political and economic élites. Colonial rule did not end until 1957 and its last decade was bound up with a fight against a significant communist insurgency, led by the largely ethnic Chinese (with a few Indians) Communist Party of Malaya (CPM). The departure of the British gave way to an era of somewhat phoney independence in as much as the colonial economic architecture was left almost untouched; this was agreed to by the Malay aristocrats who assumed power. Nationalism eventually arrived with the 1969 riots, leading to the New Economic Policy (NEP).

The promise of pro-*bumiputra* affirmative action, however, could never disguise the persistence of what came to be known in Malaysia as 'political business' at the élite level. Affirmative action in education and employment targeted ordinary Chinese and Indians – the latter were big losers because they were turfed out of the civil service – while financial sector policies benefited upper-class *bumiputras*. Rural *bumiputras* remained poor, while Chinese and Indian godfathers became richer than ever. Racial ghettoisation was sustained, not least because the rising political star of the 1970s, Mahathir Mohamad, saw it as all but inevitable. Mahathir set out his unabashedly race-based views on the roots of economic success in his book *The Malay Dilemma*, published in 1970 while he was briefly expelled from the ruling United Malays National Organisation (UMNO), and banned in Malaysia. It is indicative of Mahathir's thinking that one solution he proposed for Malays' perceived genetic handicap was intermarriage with other races. He himself had an Indian Malayali father from Kerala and a Malay mother, a fact that is never publicly mentioned in Malaysia.[5] In popular politics, Mahathir's racial arguments were used to justify affirmative action. But in terms of personal conduct his own prejudices shone through. After becoming prime minister in 1981, he patronised a small group of ethnic Chinese and Sri Lankan Tamil businessmen whom he deemed the people most likely to carry forward his vision of a thoroughly modernised Malaysia. It was left to his long-time political ally Daim Zainuddin to try to nurture *bumiputra* winners. South-east Asia's four major post-war autocrats – Mahathir, Lee Kuan Yew, Suharto and Marcos – all had a fundamentally racist view of life, and this was good news for godfathers.

Meanwhile, in Town …

When Lee Kuan Yew became prime minister of Singapore in 1959, local godfathers did have one problem: that he did not much like private businessmen. Lee had no personal experience of business; he was a political organiser brought up in an anglicised environment and influenced by both the radical statist schools of the 1930s – communism and fascism.[6] As the Singaporean state expanded its economic reach, opportunities to acquire private shares in cartels or monopolies were reduced; they went to the government. On the other hand, Lee – a super-élitist – was not about to let the boorish proletariat upset his or the godfathers' lifestyle. He suppressed dissent, tamed unions and started to construct the world's leading nanny state. Some incumbent tycoons – usually ones, like Lee, who were more 'sophisticated' and formerly closer to the colonial establishment, such as bankers Lee Kong Chian and Wee Cho Yaw – got on okay with the new leader. Others, like the rougher-at-the-edges smuggler and speculator Kwek Hong Png, were less palatable. But Kwek also owned a lot of assets, especially real estate, in Singapore, and Lee Kuan Yew was not in the business of forcible expropriation. There was room enough for the odd Kwek type to prosper in tandem with a *dirigiste* city state.

In Hong Kong, there were particularly vociferous calls after the Second World War for the cancellation of knighthoods, for investigations and even for trials of tycoons who were perceived to have co-operated all too willingly with the Japanese. But the British had no replacement for the anglicised Chinese and mixed-race Eurasian élite who facilitated their rule, and they were swiftly restored. Local newspaper editors were told to leave stories about collaboration with the enemy alone.[7] In the aftermath of the war, the tycoon group, along with its British peers in the form of the leaders of the major colonial conglomerates, or *hongs*, was instrumental in blocking tentative British plans for democracy; that was the end of the local class threat for half a century.[8] Instead came the expanded, but largely impotent, Legislative Council (Legco). Big business played out its political role through its members and lobbyists appointed to the Legco. This pseudo-oligarchical system was preserved by the British for the Chinese in 1985 – when the Joint Declaration on resumption of Chinese sovereignty in 1997 was agreed – by the creation of 'functional' constituencies, which allowed godfather interests in banking, real estate, insurance and the like to place more lobbyists inside the Legco. Separately, the Chinese set up their own 'advisory committee' on the colony's return, whose membership was dominated by tycoons. The main point, however, is a simple one: whether Hong Kong has been ruled by British colonialism, Japanese imperialism or Chinese communism, it has always been managed through the same group of people.

Despite Hong Kong's claim to be a city of free trade, there has long been plenty to play for in terms of tycoons' political activities. Information is always valuable, as seen in 1946 when several establishment godfathers made millions from speculation in Hong Kong dollars issued by the Japanese that were redeemed by the returning British. A connection to political power was also essential to the tycoons' ability to present themselves as community leaders who 'understood' the best interests of the population at large. But more than anything in the post-war era, political influence was about maintaining a heavily cartelised domestic economy which provided generous economic rents to a small number of businessmen. Chinese tycoons, as we shall see, already had a solid position in what was a closely rigged real estate market. From the 1970s, local godfathers began to wrest control of large parts of other cartels from the British-controlled conglomerates that had developed them. It would have been most unedifying if, in the transition of ownership, there had been politically inspired moves to introduce more competition into the local economy.

Political activity remained extremely important to the aspirant Hong Kong tycoon. He served his own interests, and those of the colonial government, simultaneously, and called his work 'community leadership'. During widespread strikes in the 1920s, then senior godfather Sir Robert Ho Tung had mediated a seamen's dispute. Robert Kotewall and Shouson Chow, two other leading figures who went on to receive knighthoods, helped organise street orators to harangue Chinese labourers against joining strikes and ran a force of heavies to protect those staying on their jobs from pro-strike agitators.[9] When the proles raised their heads again in the late 1960s, in response to China's cultural revolution, the tycoons were on hand to lend the government support and urge the population to resist overtures from the Communist Party of China. As Leo Goodstadt, a former chief policy adviser to the Hong Kong government, puts it: 'The political violence of 1967, in particular, appeared to make the survival of British rule more dependent than ever on the élite.'[10] The British Foreign Office and the godfathers saw off the lower classes, and the former's Hong Kong governors were grateful enough to prove highly resistant to liberal political and social ideas emanating from London in the 1960s and 1970s. Hong Kong's government and tycoons boasted instead to the world that they had created a great *laissez faire* society; no one seemed to notice that this was simply not the case in the domestic service sector and construction parts of the economy occupied by the godfathers.

On the Couch, Please

When the dust settled on post-colonial south-east Asia, the godfathers were back where they had always been – managing shifting political relationships in order to profit from particularistic favours and government-induced economic distortions. So what kind of people, up close, are the post-war godfathers?

Only one really compelling piece of empirical research has been completed about the social and cultural backgrounds of south-east Asian tycoons in the past half century.[10] It limited itself to the ethnic Chinese godfathers of Thailand, but none the less contains results that resonate for other immigrant groups and other societies. In the mid 1950s, an American scholar, G. William Skinner, achieved an extraordinary level of access to Thailand's tycoon fraternity. He enlisted the help of two Chinese bank *compradors* and other well-informed sources to identify the 135 most powerful ethnic Chinese businessmen in Thailand and he succeeded in interviewing 130 of them. He was equipped with fluency in both Thai and Mandarin Chinese, and knowledge of southern Chinese dialects, as well as astonishing tenacity. No academic or journalist has produced a survey of such quality since.

The results pointed unequivocally to a group of men stuck in a cultural middle ground between a Chinese immigrant population they sought to represent as community leaders and a Thai political élite to which they acculturated as a means of gaining concessions and advancement in business. A major finding was that most of the businessmen were less 'Chinese' – in terms of language, customs, education – than was expected. With respect to the relationship of the tycoons to the core Chinese community, Skinner proposed a concept of 'leadership from the periphery' to capture the fact that the godfathers were leading their communities by dint of wealth and influence, despite being culturally distant from them. 'One of the major theses of the present study,' he wrote, '[is] that a significant number of the most influential Chinese leaders are, almost inevitably, leaders from the periphery of Chinese society and culture – men whose ethnic orientation and loyalties are mixed.'[12]

Skinner's research highlighted all kinds of complexities in the identities of his godfather subjects that are brushed over by normal stereotypes of the 'Chinese tycoon'. There emerged a broad correlation that the more wealthy and influential a 'Chinese' tycoon was, the less demonstrably Chinese he turned out to be. Skinner developed tables that plotted wealth and prestige (as assessed by peers) against the degree of assimilation to Thai culture among his subjects. There was no doubt that success was to do with moving away from 'Chinese-ness' and towards the culturally Thai identity of political power. At the same time, there was a requisite amount of Chinese-ness for remaining a leader of the ethnic Chinese community that also supplied the key personnel in tycoons' businesses.

Herein, possibly, lie the contradictory forces that have informed the identities of godfathers around the region. Without an empirical study like Skinner's across different states, such a thesis cannot be demonstrated scientifically. But the anecdotal evidence gathered for this book supports the proposition that godfather personalities are stretched and confused. A relative of Henry Fok – a man who early in his career was close to the British establishment in Hong Kong before becoming close enough to the communist establishment in Beijing to be appointed vice chairman of the Chinese People's Political Consultative Conference – says tycoon behaviour should be viewed through the prism of Eric Berne's 1960s bestseller *The Games People Play*, adding: 'They all want a shrink ... to get it off their chest.'[13] Berne developed a branch of psychotherapy called Transactional Analysis, which highlights the malleability of identity. Henry Fok, who died in a Beijing hospital in October 2006, knew all about multiple identities. He underwent anglicisation on a British government scholarship to an élite school in Hong Kong, becoming an accomplished tennis and soccer player, and continued his family's acculturation by sending his sons to the English public school Millfield. But as parts of the British establishment spurned him because of his huge smuggling operations in the Korean War, and Beijing rewarded him with monopoly trading concessions for the same activity, he was reborn as a rabid Chinese nationalist. *Forbes* magazine tried for years to set up an interview with Fok, who only cared to speak with mainland Chinese journalists he knew would publish official encomia. When he finally agreed to a meeting in Zhuhai, he got out of his car long enough to make the following statement: 'Once old countries go down – like India, Egypt, even Britain – they never come up again. But China will come up again.' He then jumped back into his car and sped off, leaving *Forbes* very short of copy.[14]

The role-playing that is part and parcel of the godfathers' lives may explain the insecurity that appears to afflict them. One facet of this is an obsession with status. Asian godfathers collect and display gongs – honorary titles, doctorates, and so on – with a hunger that puts Western billionaires to shame. Stanley Ho, for instance, insists that underlings refer to him at all times as 'Dr Ho'; Henry Fok used to insist on 'Dr Fok'. This is incongruous for gambling tycoons; as one of Stanley's assistants announces on the telephone, in English, 'Dr Ho's office', one can frequently hear Cantonese yelling and the sound of his tribe of bodyguards in the background. In Malaysia, the senior billionaires combine the various titles that federal and state authorities give them with those from academia, and style themselves with triple honorifics. As an example, Khoo Kay Peng of Malaysia United Industries (MUI) is 'Tan Sri Dato Dr Khoo Kay Peng'. Observing the same tendency in Thailand, where outsider tycoons have long craved titles bestowed by the royal family, Skinner highlighted research into social psychology. Work on minority group situations, he noted, shows that people who undergo a high degree of assimilation are particularly driven to acquire the full set of prerogatives available to the group to which they have assimilated. 'The most influential Chinese leaders, in point of fact,' wrote Skinner, 'are more susceptible than other Chinese to pressures toward further assimilation.'[15] The symbols of recognition that constitute official titles therefore become terribly important.

But the godfather crisis of identity goes beyond honorifics (and a weakness for outsize penthouse offices – they like to be literally on top). One controversial theme is the frequency with which the tycoons are attracted to evangelical Christianity. Thomas and Raymond Kwok of Sun Hung Kai and Ronnie Chan of the Hang Lung group in Hong Kong, Khoo Kay Peng of MUI and the Yeoh family of the YTL group in Malaysia, the Riadys of the Lippo group and the Soeryadjayas who controlled Astra in Indonesia are just some of the region's many born-again Christian billionaires. Among the most aggressively proselytising is Khoo Kay Peng, a friend and business partner of US televangelist Pat Robertson, who bought a disused Kuala Lumpur theatre to serve as a chapel and started a Businessmen for Christ group. The Riadys built a private chapel in Hong Kong's Lippo Centre office tower, to which they have invited potential converts; a long-time family friend says he lives in fear of being hauled in there.[16] Some of those who know the Christian tycoons are cynical about their religious beliefs, but this does not answer the question as to why a substantial section of the tycoon fraternity is drawn to evangelical religion.[17] YTL's Francis Yeoh himself says that Christianity counters the excessive individualism inherent in Chinese culture; the Chinese, he complains, are like, 'amoeba'.[18] In Indonesia Edwin Soeryadjaya, eldest son of family patriarch William, says of Christianity's attraction: 'One reason could be there is no certainty in this country. So who do you put your faith in?'[19] What no godfather believer suggests, but what may also be true, is that evangelical Christianity allows them to have a strongly held belief where their daily lives are all about expressing no belief at all unless given a cue by political power. It is also possible to believe in religion without upsetting Asian politicians, whereas to have independent political or social views is disastrous.

One more thing that appears to be an expression of insecurity among Chinese godfathers is an obsession with demonstrated 'Chinese-ness' and with eugenics; this has only become more apparent recently as China has re-emerged as a regional power. The best-known case study is Lee Kuan Yew, a tycoon of sorts by virtue of the fact that he nationalised and ran much of Singapore's economy after 1959. Lee had an English education,[20] attending the élite Raffles Institution and Raffles College in Singapore as well as Cambridge University (institutions that educated various Malaysian and Singaporean tycoons-to-be, including Robert Kuok and Quek Leng Chan). Back then he was called Harry Lee. In 1967 he told an audience in the United States: 'I am no more a Chinese than President Kennedy was an Irishman.'[21]

But as Singapore became prosperous and China began to open up in the 1980s, Lee became ever more exercised in explaining his city state's success in terms of Confucian culture and 'Asian' values. He had learned Mandarin and Hokkien Chinese in the late 1950s and early 1960s as he framed his popular political persona, and the identity of Harry Lee was buried. In its place came the Lee Kuan Yew who warned Singaporean students in 1986 that they must never lose 'their Confucian tendencies to coalesce around the middle ground, that day we become just another Third World society'.[22] As the historian of the overseas Chinese Lynn Pan has written: 'The remaking of Singapore in the Confucian image is in some ways a larger embodiment of a personal *enracinement*.'[23] Lee's identity odyssey has seen him become increasingly enamoured of the kind of racist eugenic theories that were popular in Edwardian England. He set up a state matchmaking agency in Singapore, the Social Development Unit, to help pair off mates of similar intelligence, and argued for a return to the upper-class polygamy of traditional Chinese society. Lynn Pan refers to journalist T. J. S. George's observation that 'he detected in Lee the insecurity of a man alienated from his Chinese moorings, a man who, because he does not quite belong anywhere, has had to remake Singapore in his own image to compensate for his own alienation'.[24]

It is not difficult to understand the psychological pressure that goes with being caught between different cultures. The typical godfather needs to be a polyglot who can play out more than one cultural identity to succeed: a big-time Chinese tycoon will speak two or three regional Chinese languages – Cantonese, plus a couple more – as well as Mandarin Chinese, English, a native south-east Asian language like Thai or Bahasa Indonesia, and probably some Japanese picked up in the war. There is a perpetual stress that goes with this, related to what one's 'real' identity is.

Lee is still hung up on the fact that his Chinese is not as good as his English. This is a condition that affects many Chinese educated in the British system. David Li of Hong Kong's Bank of East Asia, who was sent away to an English public school, is sensitive about the fact that his grasp of written Chinese is far from complete. Budi Hartono, ethnic Chinese CEO of the Djarum tobacco empire and one of the richest tycoons in Indonesia, was schooled by Dutch colonists and still reads and writes Dutch better than he does Bahasa Indonesia; he speaks no Chinese. Conversely Dhanin Chearavanont, the ethnic Chinese patriarch of Thailand's CP group, is perpetually embarrassed that his Thai is still heavily accented with Chinese even though his family has been operating in Thailand since the 1920s.

On top of this discomfort is the racial prejudice that men of the senior godfathers' generation suffered in the colonial era. The patronising attitude of the British colonial administration in Singapore cannot have been easy to endure for a man of Lee Kuan Yew's ego. Robert Kuok, who has become well-known to associates for his genetic theories and strident racial views, was sent to a convent school as a child where nuns told him his family's visits to Buddhist shrines were a form of devil worship. Both his élite British education – English College in Malaysia's Johor Baru and Raffles College in Singapore[25] – and his emergence as a 'born-again Chinese' in the independence era, mirror the trajectory of Lee Kuan Yew. Kuok became a major sponsor of overseas Chinese 'conferences' in the 1990s; he signalled the purity of his second marriage (the first was to a Eurasian woman) by giving their children only Chinese names; and he became ever more forthright in proposing the genetic basis of the economic success of the overseas Chinese.

Where cold analysis of the success of men like Lee Yuan Kew, Robert Kuok and Henry Fok finds its roots in their cosmopolitan-ness – their ability to work in different languages and cultures – they themselves have sought a monocultural explanation. This can be uncomfortable for godfather children, many of whom – befitting the cross-cultural environments they grew up in – are married to non-Chinese. An in-law of Robert Kuok describes him as the 'biggest racial bigot I've ever met'.[26]

The larger point, however, is that the godfathers are engaging in a double self-deception. The first is to pretend that the south-east Asian economic development story is a Chinese one where it is an immigrant one. The second is to avoid the fact that they – the tycoons – usually had the kind of practical advantages among their immigrant peer group that assist success the world over. Returning to Skinner's work on Thai tycoons, it is obvious what those advantages are. Skinner's subjects were better-educated than popularly believed: 'With regard to educational attainment, the leaders unquestionably form a privileged group within Bangkok Chinese society,' he writes.[27] And only a fifth of them could be described as 'self-made from scratch'. The fact of such widespread advantage of birth is the context of the godfathers' most striking dissemblance – their determination to demonstrate a rags-to-riches genesis.

We of Humble Origin

Tycoons have long been at pains to establish their status as self-made men of humble origin. As seen above, the regimes of Suharto and Marcos did produce genuine working-class-to-billionaire stories as the dictators reached for unknown outsiders to become their trusty accomplices in divvying up the economic spoils of power. But this was not the norm in more settled political climes. If there is a class stereotype for south-east Asian godfatherdom, it would be that of a rapid-cycling economic aristocracy.

A well-known Chinese proverb refers to three-generation wealth, in which one generation makes a fortune, the next holds on to it and the next loses it. Actual experience in the past hundred years points to a four-generation sequence, in which the first generation establishes a kernel of capital that a second generation, with improved ties to political power, leverages into a serious fortune. A third generation then tries to hold on to an extremely diversified range of assets that reflect the unique personality and relationships of the father. By the fourth generation a lack of application to this task, the decay of the original relationships on which the empire was built, and the inherent weakness of businesses based on family rather than professional management bring the edifice down.

One-generation, rags-to-riches stories are exceptional. The domestic economies of south-east Asia are far too closely controlled by governments to make such a thing likely. As Adrian Zecha, a Chinese–Dutch–Malay–Czech–Thai–German–Indonesian luxury hotelier[28] and socialite who knows most of the contemporary tycoons, says of the path to godfatherdom: 'In one generation it is very difficult because it is not an open economic society. You get that in America. To a lesser extent in the UK. To a lesser extent still in continental Europe.'[29] Wang Gungwu, a prolific writer on the overseas Chinese based at the National University of Singapore, concurs: 'I have yet to find a businessman who started as a coolie.'[30]

Despite this, there is a long tycoon tradition of mythologising a humble background and a struggle to escape the clutches of poverty. A classic example is Thailand's richest businessman, and recent premier, Thaksin Shinawatra. In speeches and official publications Thaksin relates tales of a hard-scrabble upbringing and underfunded schools with broken equipment. He proclaimed in a speech in Manila in 2003: 'Through my modest family background … I learned the hardship of poverty in the rural areas. I learned the importance of earning rewards by working hard.' In reality, Thaksin's family is a well-established dynasty from Chiang Mai that was involved in tax farming before 1932, and moved into the silk business as well as finance, construction and real estate thereafter. Thaksin himself went through the best local schools and military academies and married a general's daughter.[31] His rise through the ranks of the Thai police force and access to state concessions were very much an insider's story.

In Hong Kong, Asia's richest tycoon, Li Ka-shing, revels in his reputation as the son of a schoolteacher who arrived in Hong Kong penniless in 1940. The official website of his Cheung Kong Holdings instead states: 'Shouldering the responsibility of looking after the livelihood of the family, Mr Li was forced to leave school before the age of 15 and found a job in a plastics trading company where he labored 16 hours a day. By 1950, his hard work, prudence and his pursuit of excellence had enabled him to start his own company, Cheung Kong Industries.' In reality, Li went to school for a couple of years and then started working for a wealthy uncle (from the family that owns Hong Kong's Chung Nam Watch Co.).[32] Subsequently he became part of an important subcategory of tycoons who got ahead, in part, by marrying the boss's daughter. Li's late wife, Amy Chong Yuet-ming, was a first cousin – the wealthy uncle's daughter. The business where Li worked in fact belonged to his father-in-law; and what Li did was to build the operation up. According to a long-time intimate of Li's, his mother-in-law also gave him additional financial backing.[33]

Marrying the boss's daughter is not uncommon in godfather development. One well-known example is Singapore's Lee Kong Chian, who in 1920 married Tan Kah Kee's daughter and prospered for the next seven years as treasurer of the old man's business before breaking out on his own. C. Y. Tung, founder of the shipping company Orient Overseas Line and father of Hong Kong's first post-colonial chief executive, Tung Chee-hwa, married into money in the form of Shanghai's wealthy Koo family.[34]Among the current generation, Cheng Yu-tung of the New World group married into Hong Kong's ubiquitous Chow Tai-fook jewellery business; the company remains his key private vehicle. For the would-be godfather who cannot rely on his father's wealth to prime a career in business, the recourse has been the wealth of a wife's family.

There should be no great surprise about this given the social-élitism of south-east Asian societies. Yet it is curious how bound up tycoons are with the rags-to-riches myth. Sir David Li, billionaire head of the Bank of East Asia family in Hong Kong and normally an astute observer of the world around him, is adamant that many tycoons are self-made. Reaching for examples, he cites the film and television magnate Sir Run Run Shaw, Lee Shau-kee of Henderson Land and Henry Fok. But Run Run Shaw and his brothers are sons of a Shanghai textile magnate, Lee Shau-kee comes from a wealthy banking and gold trading family from Shuntak county in Guangdong province, and Henry Fok – though from a genuinely working-class background – was set apart by a British government scholarship to an élite school. Without a Marcos or a Suharto to shake things up, Asian godfathers are not the products of great social mobility. The notion that they are, however, is part and parcel of the tycoons' self-image. It is important to their personal sense of pride and it is critical to the maintenance of authoritarian political structures and unfree markets in the region which constrain opportunities for many other talented entrepreneurs.

Selective Frugality

Something that further confuses the popular image of the tycoons is their reputation for thrift. Part of this is justified and another part is very much for public consumption. The genuine thrift is that which reflects an entrepreneur's instinctive desire to preserve capital. As one lifelong Asian investment banker and tycoon intimate observes: 'They are better at denying themselves immediate earthly rewards than your average investment banker.'[35] As an example, Robert Kuok bought a mansion on Hong Kong's Deep Water Bay Road (a sort of Tycoon Alley close to a nine-hole golf course favoured by the godfathers for their early morning rounds) during the Asian financial crisis for the knock-down price of HK$80 million. He tried living in the house but, according to family members, became obsessed with the notion that the property was excessive, even for a man worth several billion dollars. Eventually he knocked the house down, built five modest townhouses in its place, took one for himself, two for his family and rented out two more. Kuok lives in the kind of house that in Europe or the United States would be associated with a modestly successful bank manager.

Godfathers are also keen to telegraph useful messages to employees and service providers. An investment banker in Malaysia recalls a meeting in London in 1999 with Lim Kok Thay, son of gaming billionaire Lim Goh Tong, to seal the US$2 billion acquisition of Norwegian Cruise Line. Leaving the lawyers' office in the City, Kok Thay hailed a taxi which the banker assumed would take them to Heathrow airport for a flight they were due to catch to Norway. After half a mile, however, the billionaire heir ordered the cab to stop and ushered the party into an entrance to the London Underground. He saved a few pounds by riding the train to the airport. Once at Heathrow, the nonplussed investment banker found the group were booked into economy-class seats for the flight to Oslo.[36] K. S. Li (as Li Ka-shing is often known in Hong Kong) likes to point to his modest appetites by reminding people about the cheap Seiko and Citizen brand watches he has worn over the years – 'that fucking watch', as one of his executives who has heard the reference once too often remembers.[37] A cheap timepiece has become his symbol. In a rare interview with *Fortune* magazine, Li inevitably wheeled out the watch theme: 'Yours is more luxurious,' he pointed out to the interviewer. 'Mine is cheaper, less than US$50.'[38]

Apart from the instinct to preserve capital, and the sensible business tactic of displaying thrift to employees, however, there is a good deal of cant about the supposedly modest lifestyle of the average godfather. Another source of public pride for Li Ka-shing is the fact that he draws tiny salaries from his public companies – just HK$10,000 from his flagship Cheung Kong Holdings in 2005. It is never mentioned that in Hong Kong there is tax on salaries but not dividends, so there is a tax-avoidance incentive for tycoons to live off the latter. Peter Churchouse, a former managing director at Morgan Stanley in Hong Kong, points to the case of one of K. S. Li's peers: 'Lee Shau-kee,' he says, 'has been taking US$150 million to US$300 million in dividends just from [flagship company] Henderson [Land] for twenty years.'[39] Among other things, Lee has used the money to buy 30,000 apartments in the United States. These are not, in the final analysis, men living off small incomes.

The real, secret profligacy of the tycoon fraternity is their high-stakes gambling. Most members of the tycoon fraternity claim that all other members (not themselves, naturally) are at it all the time. 'They're all big gamblers,' says one Hong Kong-based billionaire. 'The only ones who are not big gamblers are [gambling godfathers] Stanley Ho and Henry Fok.'[40] Investment bankers in Hong Kong and Singapore trade endless rumours of golf games played for US$1 million a hole. Or vast losses accumulated on gaming trips to Australia and the US. Of course, nothing makes it into the media because tycoons do not make bets in public. But the rumours are legion and suggest a form of gambling that echoes that of Middle Eastern potentates – vast sums of money blown away by people who do not know its real value because they have not really earned it.

Big Daddy

What is incontrovertibly true about the godfathers is that they hold to male-dominant, patriarchal traditions of the family with a vengeance. In running family businesses they demand total obedience from relatives and use a variety of tactics to secure it. Among the most effective is to keep children and other relatives loyal with the prospect of vast inheritances, while simul-taneously keeping them cash-poor. Ng Teng Fong, Singapore's biggest private landlord and multibillionaire, is not untypical. His eldest son Robert runs Sino Land, the Hong Kong end of the family operation and itself one of the half dozen biggest developers in the territory. Robert, educated at an English boarding school and now in his fifties, still lives in an apartment rented from the company and owns only about US$1 million of Sino Land equity.[41] Mean-while his father telephones each day to check on the business's cash balances. Younger brother Philip is kept on a similarly tight leash in Singapore.

Michael Vatikiotis, former editor of the *Far Eastern Economic Review* and the journalist who gained closest access to Thailand's reclusive Chearavanont family, recalls having dinner with the patriarch and his middle-aged sons, who were not allowed to speak. An investment banker who has worked with the Chearavanonts paints a similar picture, in which the sons find 'they have to beg for a new car'.[42] Another factor that ensures patriarch power in Chinese families is that there are no rules as to who will take over what part of the family fortune. It is a common misperception that there is some form of primogeniture at work. In reality, an eldest son is only a business heir if he is deemed worthy of the position. It is quite normal to pick a different sibling, although males always come before females. Malaysian casino magnate Lim Goh Tong, for instance, chose Lim Kok Thay over his elder brother. Indonesia's Liem Sioe Liong bypassed his eldest son Albert when he designated Anthony

Salim as heir. Henry Fok sidelined his eldest son Timothy in favour of his sibling Ian. Younger sons are less likely to disappear when they know they are not necessarily out of the running to become the big boss.

The culture of the family business can be stifling, and is often a recipe for much unhappiness, but it is almost never challenged. Moreover this cuts across all kinds of sociologies, unaffected, for instance, by whether a family is mixed-race or whether the godfather went to a colonial school. The patriarch is always king.[43] On the outside this manifests itself in what Helmut Sohmen, the Austrian son-in-law of the late shipping magnate Y. K. Pao, calls 'the love of pre-eminence'.[44] The same notion is captured in K. S. Li's frequent description of himself as 'the friendly lion'.[45] In this respect, the south-east Asian tycoon aspires to benign godfather status. But while this may be possible in terms of public perception, actual authority within families – and often companies – is all too often wielded by mundane bullying. The middle-aged children of major tycoons like K. S. Li and Robert Kuok live in fear of their fathers' outbursts. An executive of Li's recalls his eldest son Victor dozing off in a meeting to be awoken as if by electric shock by his screaming father.[46] Board members at the *South China Morning Post*, controlled by Robert Kuok, were not sure where to look at an infamous February 2003 board meeting when the patriarch lost his temper with son Ean, then aged 48, bawling him out in front of a room full of directors. Another Hong Kong-based multi-billionaire, meanwhile, has been seeking to control his outbursts with the help of a behavioural therapist.[47]

Billionaires are by definition busy people and it is expecting a lot of them that they should achieve what has become known as a 'work–life' balance. But the unbridled, unquestioned power of the patriarch is a corrupting influence on family relationships. K. S. Li's younger son Richard has been a rare example of semi-active rebellion. He was sent away to boarding school aged twelve and his mother is widely believed in Hong Kong to have committed suicide.[48] An unauthorised Chinese-language biography published in 2004,[49] which can only have been informed by Richard Li's inner circle, dwells on his close relationship with his mother, the process by which he set up his own company and then took over Hong Kong Telecom without informing his father, and the fact that he describes Lee Kuan Yew – not Li Ka-shing – as his hero. The message to a Chinese audience is extremely clear: that father and son do not fit the harmonious cultural stereotype. Tim Fok, eldest son of Henry Fok, gives away something of the nature of tycoon family life when he describes the bizarre experience of coming home from English public school for the holidays aged sixteen and being sent off by his father to buy the first Hitachi jetfoils for the Hong Kong–Macau ferry route. It is difficult not to sense that there is an element of bitterness when he concludes: 'I think my father was more interested in going to nightclubs.'[50]

Nothing defines the godfather's power within the family as much as his licence to indulge his sexual appetite at will. Henry Fok, who died in 2006, and Stanley Ho both took several wives – polygamy was not outlawed in Hong Kong until the Marriage Reform Ordinance of 1971. Many tycoons enjoy multiple mistresses and copious amounts of extramarital sex. One of the richest men in Asia is remarkably candid in saying that in the godfather lifestyle sexual liaisons are the main punctuation between periods of time spent at the office: 'It's all business,' he says. 'None of these people has social friends. They fuck a girl, shake off their horniness and then it's back to work.'[51] Of course he is not quite candid enough to admit the observation applies to him as well, though a member of his family assures that it does: 'If they don't have a woman a day they can't function,' the person says of the tycoon fraternity.[52] It would be unduly prurient to dwell on the mechanics of how seventy- and eighty-year-old men organise a constant supply of fresh sexual activity, but suffice it to say that billionaires who own entire blocks of apartments, hotel chains and gin palace yachts have plenty of private space away from home.

There is a long tradition of the godfather-as-stud. Pre-war Indonesian tycoon Oei Tiong Ham's daughter wrote of her father: 'All his life he had great interest in women and sex. He had eighteen acknowledged concubines and a total of forty-two children by them.'[53] Today's peer group is somewhat more modest, though Indonesia's Eka Tjipta Widjaya is associated with at least thirty children. Stanley Ho has only seventeen acknowledged children. None the less, the Asian tycoon still enjoys unusual sexual licence. As one veteran Hong Kong investment banker puts it: 'Sexual rapaciousness is endemic to their culture ... the fact that their wives say nothing about it sets them apart from Western billionaires'.[54] This does not mean, however, that children are unaffected. What is noticeable in several godfather families is how resentful and affected male children have become because of their father's sexual profligacy and its effect on their mothers. What is equally noticeable is that those male children have grown up to be sexual profligates themselves.

Power without Accountability

The final component of the standard godfather make-up is secrecy. This is almost invariably presented as a reflection of Asian and Chinese culture, not least by the tycoons themselves. A 1991 Robert Kuok letter to the *Far Eastern Economic Review* refusing an interview is typical. 'The average Chinese,' wrote Kuok, 'is publicity shy for various reasons, is averse to indulging in washing linen in public and, consequently, also averse to dealing with the media.'[55] But behind the recourse to cultural defences by thoroughly cosmopolitan men like Robert Kuok lies a larger truth: that dealmakers such as him and secrecy go hand in hand in any society. It is worth remembering how the old private banks that dominated international finance in London and New York at the end of the nineteenth century – Warburg, Rothschild, Morgan and others – did not even put nameplates outside their headquarters. The main office of J. P. Morgan & Company at the corner of Broad and Wall in Lower Manhattan had nothing more than the number 23 on the door.

Men like J. Pierpont Morgan lived in a world where business was determined by relationships and insider information. As a result, as Morgan's biographer Ron Chernow writes: 'The old Wall Street felt under no obligation to explain itself either to small investors or the citizenry at large.'[56] Such is the case in south-east Asia. Most deals involve some element of government licensing or concession, things that both parties prefer to keep private. Domestic markets are heavily cartelised and it is rare that a non-participating business will make a public challenge to a cartel as part of a campaign to break into its activity; Asia's diversified conglomerates all benefit from cartels and so are dissuaded from complaining in public about specific arrangements that irk them. And it is only since the Asian financial crisis that there has been the beginning of a movement of shareholder activism in the region. In sum, tycoons have been able to maintain a low profile because they have not had to fight for markets – only concessions – and their shareholders have traditionally been passive.

Secrecy, of course, is myth-compounding. Someone like Malaysia's Quek Leng Chan is, in his hazy public image, the archetypal inscrutable Chinese tycoon, hidden away in a penthouse on the top of his Hong Leong office tower in Kuala Lumpur. But Quek is also a cigar-chomping barrister who was called to the bar at Middle Temple, one of London's four Inns of Court. His family is now thoroughly anglicised. Cousin Kwek Leng Beng, a hotel and real estate tycoon based in Singapore, also read law in the UK, graduating from the University of London. Kwek can be even more secretive than his cousin. He is infamous at shareholder meetings for refusing to take questions and reading only prepared statements. But is this because he, like his cousin, is ethnic Chinese, or because they are both extremely cosmopolitan but can get away with behaviour that would not be tolerated in US or European markets?

Perhaps the most powerful argument against notions of inherent tycoon modesty in Asia is that their relationship to publicity is far more subtle than their simply wanting to avoid the media. When one does gain access to godfathers, it is striking how often the big boss's corporate waiting area is filled with literature of the most narcissistic kind. In the course of interviews for this book, copies of *Fortune*, *Forbes* and the *Far Eastern Economic Review* in the era when it was a Dow Jones weekly[57] – and featured endless fawning lists of 'outperforming' Asian companies – were much the most common literature on display. Titles like *Fortune* and *Forbes* are also those to which the tycoons are prone to grant their rare and not terribly searching public interviews. The notion of the egoless Asian godfather is difficult to sustain. It is telling that the first thing Li Ka-shing, master of the image of public reticence, does when he arrives at the office in the morning is to read the papers – those in Chinese directly, with those in English having been translated into Chinese for him. His office keeps copies of articles about him and he is partial to the use of a high-lighter pen and margin notes when confronted with those who would criticise him. According to managers of Hong Kong newspapers, anything Mr Li takes serious exception to translates into curtailment of advertising expenditure by his companies. Li businesses stopped advertising with *Next* magazine and its sister publication *Apple Daily* after investigations into the circumstances sur-rounding the death of his wife. But less speculative reporting can produce the same results. A mention of Li's 1986 censure for insider trading, for instance, in the *South China Morning Post* in November 2003 – almost two decades later – led to an immediate drop-off in Li company advertisements placed with the paper.[58]

There is one, undeniably good, reason for Asian godfathers to stay out of public view: there has for several decades in south-east Asia been a problem with the kidnapping of businessmen – usually ones with some Chinese eth-nicity, and often with the involvement of Chinese criminal gangs. The Philip-pines has the biggest problem. John Gokongwei, a pure Chinese tycoon who runs the eponymous J. G. Summit conglomerate, had his daughter Robina kidnapped in 1981, and in 1997 lost his son-in-law, Ignacio Earl Ong, when police fired hundreds of rounds into a car in which he was being seques-tered. The Philippines averages more than one hundred kidnappings a year. Elsewhere the threat is less acute, but not to be underestimated. A cousin of Robert Kwok's – who looks not unlike him – was kidnapped in Malaysia in a case of mistaken identity; in a tale that is probably apocryphal, friends of the family say that Robert Kwok paid the ransom and then asked his cousin to pay him back.

In the mid 1990s kidnapping took a spectacular turn in Hong Kong with the arrival of mainland Chinese triad-connected gangs. The group of 'Big Spender' Cheung Tze-keung in 1996 grabbed Walter Kwok of the Sun Hung Kai real estate family and kept him in what Walter has privately described as a 'box' for five days, until he was ransomed. The experience strained relations with Walter's two brothers, whom he perhaps suspected of spending too much time haggling over the price. In 1997, Big Spender and colleagues seized Li Ka-shing's eldest son Victor, demanding HK$1 billion for his return. According to persons close to the Li household, there ensued an experience that would have been comic had it not also been very dangerous. Like the Kwoks, the Li family decided not to tell the police.[59] Instead, K. S. Li turned to trusted colleagues and employees to withdraw HK$1 billion from Hong Kong banks at short notice, which is not an easy thing to do. Big Spender, an extremely reckless individual, then turned up at Li's home above Deep Water Bay to collect the swag. He had not reckoned, however, with the physical volume of the money. He could not fit it all in his car and so took one lot, then came back a second time for the rest. The last laugh, none the less, was on the kidnapper. He was picked up with many of his followers across the border in China, was tried behind closed doors and executed in December 1998. Rumour was rife in Hong Kong that K. S. Li and his private security personnel – headed by a former commissioner of the Hong Kong police – had wanted Big Spender arrested in China proper so that he could be executed. The Hong Kong government – which does not impose the death penalty – made no effort to seek extradition over what were crimes committed in its jurisdiction. Tycoon chief executive Tung Chee-hwa said Big Spender was being tried for crimes 'planned' in China. Few people in Hong Kong were sympathetic to the dead man, and his kidnappings are a reminder that godfather families do have reason to think about their security. But the kidnap threat does not go far in explaining the broader culture of secrecy among the tycoons.[60]

In Conclusion

The history of Asian godfathers has always been one of men who could adjust their identities in chameleon fashion. The ethnic division of political and economic power required this. Colonialism required this. And most recently, for ethnic Chinese tycoons, the re-emergence of China, with its manipulative appeals for 'patriotic' overseas Chinese, required this. The tycoon has long been habituated to 'get in character' as needs dictate.

At one level this is part of the 'game' of Asian business to which the tycoon set, conscious or unconscious of the full import of the metaphor, frequently refers. Henry Fok's eldest son Tim, for instance, encapsulates his father's career as follows: 'It's not about money,' he says. 'It's a game.'[61] A member of Robert Kuok's family, explaining the futility of the 83-year-old tycoon's three attempts to retire over the past fifteen years, observes: 'Why stop doing business and start playing golf? It's only another game.'[62] And Helmut Sohmen sums up the motivation of his late father-in-law Y. K. Pao in the same terms: 'He liked the game, he liked the work.'[63]

The game is indeed a lot of fun when a concession is won or a deal comes off. But the contortions of identity to which the godfathers have traditionally submitted themselves have not made for peace of mind. There is no shortage of circumstantial evidence – from the craving for titles and official rank to the recourse to evangelical Christianity – that many of the tycoons are in search of their true identity. This is particularly apparent to the large number of outsiders who have married into ethnic Chinese godfather families in the past half century. Helmut Sohmen, the Austrian who married the eldest of Y. K. Pao's four daughters, Anna, remarks wryly of the identity struggle: 'Give it another generation and maybe people will stop thinking about what it means to be Chinese.'[64] For now the struggle goes on, leaving some curious impressions. In one instance, the author visited the office of a truculently Chinese billionaire in Hong Kong to find it, unsurprisingly, filled with the most stereotypical pictorial and furniture trappings of 'Chinese-ness'. Unexpectedly invited back to the godfather's home, however, what was striking was that there were almost no Chinese cultural 'markers' to be found: the walls were decorated with nondescript European art; one rather bad painting, bizarrely, still had the sales label on the front. Still more perplexing was an outburst from the tycoon – a man reputed to follow Chinese superstitions in an almost comicbook manner when making business decisions – as he berated one of his children for wasting time with a Chinese medical therapy. 'I don't believe in it,' he snapped.[65] Does this mean the man's life is a deliberate sham? Almost certainly not. What it points to is a billionaire living with a mixed cultural identity and far from at ease with himself.

The godfather state of mind is not helped by the fact that they are usually completely out of touch with what is known as the real world. In this respect the rags-to-riches fable is particularly misleading because it implies the average godfather has experience of ordinary life. In reality the Hong Kong or Singapore billionaire knows no more about life on the cities' public housing estates than the Malaysian billionaire cocooned in Kuala Lumpur knows of life in the Malay *kampong*, or village. Bernard Chan, a grandson of Chin Sophonpanich from the Hong Kong side of the Bangkok Bank family, has – for a tycoon-heir – a highly unusual interest in social policy. He tells of a perhaps unique expedition he organised to introduce a group of older godfathers to the poverty that is widespread among the city's elderly. He took them far from their own mansions on Hong Kong island and into the estates beyond the Kowloon peninsula. 'Each one of them was shocked,' Chan says, as they met people who rent bunk beds by the night.[66] They were oblivious to the fact that such poverty exists in Hong Kong. But the point of the story is the reaction of one of the wealthiest men in Hong Kong. In an attempt to provide helpful policy advice,[67] he suggested that the poor be relocated to mainland China where their limited spending power would go further. There was no consideration of whether social or medical services in mainland China would be adequate, or whether people were willing to go. Bernard Chan refuses to confirm who the tycoon was; another person party to the trip says it was one of the born-again Kwok brothers. A manager who has spent many years working for Hong Kong godfathers says of their relationship to everyday life: 'The perception is that tycoons know what it is like. They have no idea.'[68]

3

How to be a Godfather, #2: Core cash flow

At the heart of the average godfather's empire is a concession or licence that gives rise to a monopoly or oligopoly activity. In the instances this is not the case, a structural economic anomaly created by government leads to an environment where a cartel of godfathers can flourish or competition is artificially suppressed. This is the basic reality of tycoon business in southeast Asia. Every rising godfather is on the look-out for this non-competitive core cash flow, the river of molten gold that will keep him going through good times and bad, ensuring that even the most sprawling business empire is difficult to topple.

The source of core cash flow can be extremely simple. Half a dozen of the richest men in Hong Kong and Malaysia depend on money from gaming monopolies to fund expansion of their business conglomerates. Stanley Ho, who obtained the Macau monopoly on all forms of gaming in 1961 and was able to renew it for fifteen years in 1986, is well-known for this. But behind Stanley Ho was Henry Fok, who funded a similar equity share in Sociedade de Turismo e Diversões de Macau (STDM), the private firm set up to run gambling in the former Portuguese colony. These two men were joined by a third tycoon-to-be, Cheng Yu-tung, in bidding for what was to become by the 1970s the third-largest gaming centre in the world after Las Vegas and Atlantic City.[1] While Fok has been popularly viewed as a major real estate developer in Hong Kong and mainland China, and Cheng developed a stable of listed companies under the New World name, it was casino earnings that underwrote their expansion. (Fok, who helped China circumvent the United Nations embargo during and after the Korean War, obtained a second cash-churning monopoly on the importation of mainland sand to Hong Kong during the post-war construction boom.)[2] The exact shareholdings in STDM have never been confirmed, but company directors over the years have suggested that

Ho and Fok held 25–30 per cent each and Cheng around 10 per cent. Despite Cheng Yu-tung's limited stake, it is speculated in Hong Kong financial circles that his STDM shares generated more cash than his controlling position in publicly traded flagship New World Development.

Ananda Krishnan, Malaysia's richest resident since Robert Kuok relocated to Hong Kong in the 1970s, is seen as a real estate, telecommunications and media magnate who built what were briefly the tallest buildings in the world, the Petronas Twin Towers in Kuala Lumpur. But for almost twenty years, Krishnan has been able to rely on a steady supply of cash from a monopoly franchise on Malaysia's racetrack betting.[3] Another Malaysian billionaire, Vincent Tan, relies on cash from the sale of formerly state-controlled gaming activities in the 1980s. In 1985 Tan acquired control of Malaysia's Sports Toto lottery in a 'privatisation' that involved no prior announcement of the sale and no public tender. Billionaire Lim Goh Tong was the original post-independence beneficiary of the kind of private gambling franchise that echoed the old colonial vice farms. In 1969 he obtained a three-month, renewable licence to operate Malaysia's only legal casino. The licence has been active ever since. Lim's partner was Mohammad Noah Omar, father-in-law to not one but two Malaysian prime ministers – Abdul Razak (1971–6) and Hussein Onn (1976–81). Lim's Genting group subsequently diversified into plantations, real estate, power generation, paper making and cruise ships, but its vast casino continues to produce most of the earnings.

The earliest government-sanctioned monopolies and cartels after independence in south-east Asia were those for importing and trading foodstuffs. The creation of licences was not simply designed to line the pockets of a godfather class. It aimed to curb speculation and stabilise prices for what were deemed essential commodities. But ultimately the suppression of competition led to guaranteed cash flows that fed tycoons for decades. One of the biggest beneficiaries of import monopolies was Indonesia's Liem Sioe Liong. After Suharto came to power in 1965, Liem was granted a monopoly on the import of cloves in concert with Suharto's half-brother Probosutedjo. Separately he was granted a monopoly on flour manufacturing, which in turn made him the noodle king in a noodle-eating country. Here was the core cash flow that allowed Liem to move into everything from real estate to textiles to rubber to logging to steel to cement. Along the way, he could afford to make considerable mistakes given the scale of the economic rents he had been granted. In Malaysia, Robert Kuok was the prime beneficiary of policies restricting imports of refined sugar and flour. A soft commodity trader by background, he also partnered Liem in Indonesia in his sugar and flour businesses. Kuok remains the controlling shareholder in three of Malaysia's four sugar refineries and is allocated the bulk of a government-set quota for the import of raw sugar. The arrangement is justified on the grounds that Kuok has kept sugar and flour prices stable in the face of international market fluctuation. But, as in Indonesia until the import monopolies were scrapped after Suharto's 1998 ouster, the other reality is that consumers pay, on average, more than they would in a free market. When Kuok was lobbying for full tariff protection and sugar refining licences immediately after independence, his main co-investors were two other tycoons-in-the-making, Khoo Kay Peng and Quek Leng Chan. The attractions of monopoly were not hard to spot.

In the Philippines a tradition of political allocation of state offices and government largesse built up from the 1920s, under American colonial rule, until it reached its logical conclusion under Ferdinand Marcos. There were trading monopolies for major foodstuff imports, and marketing monopolies for the key local crops – sugar and coconuts. Eduardo 'Danding' Cojuangco was one of the leading Marcos monopolists. (It is a reminder of the small and élitist world in which money and power resides in south-east Asia that Danding is from the same landed family as Cory Aquino, whose 'people power' movement overthrew Marcos in 1986.) Danding, a Marcos favourite, benefited from a new levy on coconut production that funded the development of United Coconut Planters Bank. He was made president of the bank, which in turn bought up most of the Philippines' coconut milling facilities. Danding's coconut cash flows were strong enough to buy up much more besides. He became known as Mr Pacman, after the video game character that eats everything in its path. Marcos monopolies set new standards in the powers they conferred. Lucio Tan's Fortune Tobacco Co., which was given tax, customs, financing and regulatory breaks that were tantamount to a domestic monopoly on cigarette making, wrote a new cigarette tax code that Marcos signed into law.[4] In the same period Tan is alleged to have printed his own internal revenue stamps to paste on cigarette packets. The cash flow from tobacco propelled him into chemicals, farming, textiles, brewing, real estate, hotels and banking. After Marcos fled to Hawaii in 1986, Tan wrote an open letter to new president Cory Aquino in which he asserted: 'We can proudly say that we have never depended on dole-outs, government assistance or monopoly protection throughout our history.'[5]

Cartels, Cartels Everywhere

The crudeness of the monopolies handed out by Marcos and Suharto tends to obscure the almost universal presence of monopolies, cartels and controlled markets in south-east Asia. Hong Kong is a case in point, not least because it is regularly voted one of the freest economies in the world. The right-wing American think tank the Heritage Foundation has ranked Hong Kong first (and Singapore second) in its Index of Economic Freedom for the past fourteen years. The Nobel Laureate economist Milton Friedman lauded Hong Kong for decades as a bastion of the free market; a week after the territory's return to Chinese sovereignty in 1997, he lamented: 'If only the United States were as free as Hong Kong.'[6] Such assertions reflect a focus on Hong Kong's status as a free port with tariff- and exchange control-free international trade. But Hong Kong's domestic economy, where the godfathers operate, is a different story. It has long been a patchwork of de facto cartels.

The origin of the cartels lies in the colonial era. The best known of them dominates the territory's real estate market and is the core source of wealth of every Hong Kong billionaire. The British administration set the scene for real estate oligopoly because it chose to depend heavily on land sales – all land was deemed 'Crown land' until sold – to fund its budget. As Hong Kong grew in the post-Second World War era, the government auctioned off development land in ever more expensive chunks: US$1 billion a pop for large plots by the mid 1990s. Anyone who acquired land in the secondary market that was not designated for building – agricultural acreage in the New Territories was targeted by the tycoon families behind Sun Hung Kai and Henderson in the 1970s and 1980s – had to pay a hefty upfront conversion premium before construction could begin. The effect was to rule out small players and persons without good connections to the large British banks. A government-commissioned 1996 report by Hong Kong's Consumer Council found that three-quarters of new private residential housing was supplied by only ten developers between 1991 and 1994, and 55 per cent came from the four biggest developers. A separate look at profitability considered thirteen large residential developments. Margins were extraordinary, especially where conversion fees had been set by private tender on large lots of agricultural land. In such cases, the lowest return the Consumer Council found – as a percentage of total estimated development costs, including land – was 77 per cent. The highest was 364 per cent.[7]

Such high levels of concentration in the real estate market are, at the level of economic theory, bound to be anti-competitive. Rumours of bid-rigging are a traditional source of Hong Kong discourse. 'The property guys used to do a bit of bidding. Then one guy gets it. Then a tea party where it's all divided up,' remarks Sir William Purves, former chief executive of HSBC, matter-of-factly.[8] So long as land revenues flowed in and budgets were balanced, colonial governments (and the always-influential HSBC, the biggest mortgage lender and developer financier) were not unhappy with the real estate arrangements. The system was simple and low maintenance. As one of the real estate tycoons puts it: 'British capitalism as practised in Hong Kong has always favoured the big boys.'[9] Middle class Hong Kongers, meanwhile, paid low nominal taxes but some of the world's highest rents, or mortgage repayments, and apartment management fees equivalent to 13–15 per cent of rents.

The Hong Kong colonial tradition of working with a small number of 'big boys' – originally these were the British *hongs* which ran cartels in everything from air-conditioners to elevators – echoed the indigenous south-east Asian autocrat's need for trusted commercial lieutenants. An interesting example of this came in the 1950s and 1960s when the Hong Kong government successfully negotiated the world's largest textile export quotas for local manufacturing industry. It was admirable behaviour by a colonial administration since it went against the best interests of British textile producers. But when it came to distributing quotas, the government showed little impartiality. Instead of auctioning the right to export to the highest bidder or finding some other formula to identify the most efficient producers, bureaucrats simply gave away the enormously valuable quotas to the largest manufacturers and export houses. Many of these were run by former Shanghai textile magnates, who had moved to Hong Kong in 1949, and were close to the colonial establishment. There then developed a secondary market in quotas whereby those receiving them for free became rentier capitalists and sold the export rights on.[10]

Hong Kong has no competition law and its godfathers, Chinese, British and otherwise, extract hefty tolls on local services. The port, the busiest in the world, is perhaps the source of greatest chagrin. Hong Kong's container terminal handling charges are also the highest in the world, despite labour costs far below those in countries with comparable *per capita* GDP.[11] The typically small manufacturing firms across the mainland border that use Hong Kong's port have campaigned against the port oligopoly for years, as have shippers, but without success. The shareholders that dominate the container terminal operating companies are the big tycoon real estate players: Hutchison, New World, Sun Hung Kai, Jardine's Hongkong Land and Wharf. Li Ka-shing's Hutchison is the undisputed leader of the pack, with current control of fourteen of twenty-four berths.[12] It is cash flow from his port operations that has allowed K. S. Li to take huge speculative bets in the real estate market over the years; investment bankers believe he would have been bankrupted during a mid-1980s property crash but for the Hutchison port revenues.

Other Hong Kong de facto cartels include supermarkets, where K. S. Li's PARKnSHOP and Jardine's Wellcome control about 70 per cent of the groceries trade, and drug stores where Li's Watson's and Jardine's Mannings are similarly dominant. Efforts to break the multibillion dollar groceries duopoly by French retailer Carrefour and a well-funded local start-up, Admart, during the past decade, foundered. The incumbents, with their big property arms, own key retailing sites around Hong Kong and make clear to suppliers that their business will be cut if they work with new competitors. According to Mark Simon, who shut down the Admart business after losses of US$120 million, the company's delivery trucks were not allowed into residential and office buildings controlled by K. S. Li.[13] Li also has half of Hong Kong's electricity-generating duopoly, in which the other half is held by the Iraqi Jewish Kadoorie family's China Light and Power. A government regulatory scheme links the profit the companies are allowed to make to capital expenditure, creating an incentive to over-invest in fixed assets with long depreciation periods. The side effect is higher electricity prices. Other important cartels include ones in buses, petrol, ready-mix concrete and professional services.

It is telling that almost every major Hong Kong business in which K. S. Li operates has cartel characteristics – real estate, ports, power, cement, concrete, asphalt and chain retailing. As Simon Murray, who ran Hutchison for Li from 1984 to 1993,observes: 'Hong Kong is a cartel environment ... If the government's going to give you a monopoly, grab it.'[14] Among Murray's major deals was the takeover of Hongkong Electric. One former cartel and one monopoly that operated in Hong Kong have been dismantled in recent years. An interest rate cartel was employed by the territory's banks from 1964 for more than three decades, with managers meeting every Friday to set rates (government also employed *ad hoc* measures to restrain the entry of foreign banks and thereby helped keep HSBC and sister bank Hang Seng's share of deposits around 50 per cent).[15] But the biggest attack on a Hong Kong monopoly came with the deregulation of the telecommunications industry under the last governor, Chris Patten. Interestingly, it led to a frenzied rush by tycoon-controlled conglomerates to enter the telecommunications business, destroying profit for all comers.[16] The message seemed to be that the tycoons were unused to operating in conditions of genuine competition.

One of the earliest substantive actions of the first post-colonial government, led by shipping tycoon Tung Chee-hwa, was to reject the Hong Kong Consumer Council's call for a general competition law. The position has not substantively altered under Tung's successor as Hong Kong chief executive, career bureaucrat Donald Tsang, although popular demands for a curb on cartels continue to rise. International bodies including the World Trade Organisation, the Organisation for Economic Co-operation and Development, and the European Parliament have criticised Hong Kong's failure to enhance competition in its domestic economy. As Professor Richard Schmalensee, dean of the MIT Sloan Management School, put it: 'The fact that Hong Kong doesn't have a law against price fixing and basic cartel behaviour is fairly amazing.'[17] Yet, somehow, the influence of big business on government is such that this remains the case.

Until recently, Singapore was the only other developed economy in the world without a competition law. The more southerly city state passed a Competition Act in 2004, which started to come into force in 2006. However, vast swathes of the domestic economy – electricity, gas, water, sewage, telecommunications, media, postal services, ports and some banking services – that are controlled by public companies are exempt from the legislation. It is far from clear that local competition in Singapore will become any freer than it is in Hong Kong. The contrast between globally competitive external economies – those of the export manufacturers – and cosseted domestic economies – those of the tycoons – is equally apparent in both cities. In Hong Kong and Singapore, for instance, banks can happily force retail and small business customers to queue for an hour before hitting them with charges that are unknown in other developed economies.[18] Hong Kong banks charge shopkeepers to provide them change for their businesses. Singapore banks monopolise the sale of mutual funds and staff often know little of what they are selling. Customer experience is not what one would expect when walking into the sleek skyscrapers that dominate these cities.

Rentiers Then, Rentiers Now

The pursuit of core cash flow is about obtaining monopolistic or oligopoly licences, wherever a godfather operates in south-east Asia. The main difference between locales is that these rights were distributed afresh by post-colonial era governments in Thailand, Malaysia, Indonesia and the Philippines; they were – with the exception of some banking and real estate entitlements – grabbed by the government in Singapore; and they were gradually transferred in Hong Kong as local tycoons began to challenge and take over the established British *hongs* starting in the 1970s. Fundamentally, however, everywhere has witnessed a process of evolution that echoes the colonial carve-up of economic rights. An unnamed commentator in a 1991 profile of

Robert Kuok – perhaps the region's most accomplished transnational tycoon – put it as succinctly as is possible: 'Robert Kuok,' he said, 'modernised the rentier system in south-east Asia.' And that is what other godfathers did.

Along the way, tycoons have greased plenty of palms. The author did something of a double-take when one of the region's leading billionaires, in an off-the-record conversation, nonchalantly described bribing a prime minister in order to obtain an important licence that was extended soon after one nation's independence. Of course, he said, he always referred to the bribe as a loan, recalling the precise amount half a century later.[19] An ethnic Chinese tycoon with businesses in several south-east Asian countries is scathing about what he regards as a graft-seeking culture among indigenous politicians: 'They're broke every week,' he says. 'Feed your mouth, feed your prick. That is how they think.'[20] But the same person is not much less damning of the iniquity of the colonial regimes he dealt with. He refers to 'unseemly practices' in Hong Kong, senior civil servants and Hongkong Bank executives holding court in private boxes at the races, and the cosy relationship that British big business enjoyed with the colonial regime. As an example he recalls John Bremridge, who transitioned from running British *hong* Swire in Hong Kong to being Hong Kong's Financial Secretary, in which post he stood before the Legislative Council and announced the territory would not license more than one airline. The incumbent, Cathay Pacific, was and is one of Swire's principal businesses. Bremridge left government in 1986 to return to a job at Swire's headquarters in London.[21] A similar trajectory was followed by Baroness Lydia Dunn, who joined the Swire group in 1963, became the senior member of Hong Kong's Executive Council, and then returned to London with Swire.

In Hong Kong and Singapore, relations between businessmen and political power have long been carefully choreographed to avert any appearance of overt collusion. In Hong Kong there are the Leglislative and Executive Councils to provide a patina of representative government, despite the fact that they are packed with the unelected representatives of big business. In Singapore, the relationship between establishment political power and tycoons is shrouded in greater mystery. One correlation that may be apparent and which dates back to the colonial era, is that favoured families show their appreciation through the works of a local charity, hence the Shaw Foundation (set up by the Shaw brothers in 1957) and the Lee Foundation (set up by the family of Lee Kong Chian in 1952). This tradition continues. Those tycoons who survived or prospered despite the British, or their successor Lee Kuan Yew do not bother with high profile charitable activities. Kwek Hong Png, rubber-smuggler-made-good, and son Kwek Leng Beng, who sought and were denied the core cash flow of a Singaporean banking licence, have not thrown money at a foundation.

Elsewhere the business–politics nexus is much cruder. Suharto used charitable foundations – *yayasan* – controlled by himself and his family as vehicles to collect billions of dollars in bribes. But the calculation for the godfather who wants to survive is much more complicated than hitching his cart to a leading politician and paying him off. There is a long list of tycoons who paid the price for putting all their eggs in one political basket. Liem Sioe Liong was the inevitable primary target of the backlash against what Indonesians dubbed 'KKN' ('*korupsi, kolusi dan nepotisme*' – 'corruption, collusion and nepotism') during the Asian financial crisis. Rioters made a beeline to his north Jakarta home, looting it and painting the words 'Suharto's dog' on the gate. In Thailand, Chin Sophonpanich fled to Hong Kong for several years after Marshall Sarit's 1957 coup because of fears his closeness to the ousted regime would put his life at risk. In Malaysia, whole cliques of businessmen had their fortunes irreparably damaged because they were too close to former finance minister Tengku Razaleigh Hamzah when he challenged Mahathir for the leadership of UMNO in 1987,[22] or to Anwar Ibrahim when Mahathir decided to terminate the deputy premier's political career a decade later. When a Malaysian tycoon has been described as one of 'Anwar's boys' or 'Daim's boys' – after finance minister Daim Zainuddin – it has usually turned out to be a sign he was headed for a fall.[23] The truly great godfather never allows himself to be identified with only one side of a potential political argument.

It is no coincidence, then, that the two richest Malaysians, Robert Kuok and Ananda Krishnan, are masters of being all things to all politicians. Kuok's relationships are impeccable partly by virtue of longevity. His father played *mah jong* with Onn bin Jaafar, aristocrat and founder president of UMNO, when Robert Kuok was growing up in Johore state. Robert attended school with Onn bin Jaafar's son and Malaysia's third prime minister, Hussein Onn, and was a contemporary at Raffles College of Malaysia's second prime minster, Abdul Razak, as well as Harry Lee Kuan Yew.[24] It was all but inevitable he would know the entire evolving establishments of independent Malaysia and Singapore. Despite sometimes strained relations with Lee Kuan Yew and Mahathir, Kuok never put himself in a position where his investments in Singapore or, remarkably, his still-functioning soft commodity monopolies in Malaysia, came under threat.

Krishnan is still more remarkable. In the 1960s and 1970s he was an intimate business partner and friend of Razaleigh, and advised the finance minister on the creation of Petronas, the national oil company, and the nationalisation of tin mining. When Mahathir became premier in 1981, Krishnan continued to find favour, being appointed a director of the central bank in 1982 and a director of Petronas in 1984. As relations between Razaleigh and Mahathir soured, Krishnan remained close to each of them, taking holidays with both men and looking after the children of the latter when they were abroad. Other tycoons close to Razaleigh, like Khoo Kay Peng, found themselves out in the cold after their patron's defeat in the 1987 UMNO election, but not Krishnan. He had covered every angle. When a reconciliation of sorts was effected between Razaleigh and Mahathir in 1996, the meeting took place at Krishnan's home.[25]

Few Asian godfathers play politicians so well. The deal for which Krishnan is best known – the 88-storey Petronas Twin Towers that define the Kuala Lumpur skyline – was a master class in the art of gentle manipulation. The man who had already nailed his core cash flow with Malaysia's off-course betting monopoly then identified the 39-hectare site of the Selangor Turf Club in downtown Kuala Lumpur for a gargantuan real estate development. He went to the Argentinian–American architect César Pelli with a remit that Mahathir would find irresistible – the tallest buildings in the world, commensurate with the premier's Vision 2020 to make Malaysia a developed nation by that year, with a design that incorporates elements of Islamic architecture.[26] Mahathir was sold, and to this day retains a vast, fishbowl-shaped private office at the top of one of the towers.[27] According to documents filed with Malaysia's Registry of Companies, Krishnan obtained the project site at a total cost of MYR378 million. But private appraisers immediately valued the site at over MYR1 billion (about US$385 million at the time). Krishnan was able to borrow against the independent valuations and, with Mahathir's support, bring in Petronas as a cash investor and anchor tenant. The upshot was that the godfather obtained 48 per cent of a real estate development that was capitalised at MYR1.3 billion without having to use his own money. He then called in Japanese and Korean construction companies – to put up a monument to Malaysia.[28]

Krishnan repeated the trick with media and telecommunications, pandering to Mahathir's fantasies about developing an Asian media industry. Assisted by government subsidies, he put Malaysia's first satellites into orbit. He set up production companies to make wholesome Malay-language programming devoid of 'Western' influence. But mixed in with these high-tech, morally wholesome undertakings were businesses yielding great profits. Krishnan obtained exclusive licences that made him the pre-eminent player in cellular telephony. He cornered the only bit of the satellite television market that is seriously profitable – supplying imported Chinese-language programming, wholesome and otherwise, to Malaysia's Chinese population. And he received further cash investments from government companies; state investment agency Khazanah Nasional put up US$260 million for 15 per cent of his satellite television business. Like other godfathers, he bought in whatever technology and content he required on a turn-key basis.

The Real Home of *Guanxi*

The Chinese word *guanxi*, meaning a connection or relationship, is used a great deal in Asia as shorthand for the role that personal ties to holders of political power play in facilitating business. *Guanxi* carries with it the implication that bribes might be paid and accepted. With respect to China, the term is much overused. This is not because China is short on corruption. It is instead because the size and complexity of China are at odds with the simplicity suggested by the concept of finding the right person, greasing his palm and closing a deal. Foreign businessmen who fail to understand this spend vast amounts of time in Beijing sucking up to national politicians who are usually powerless to deliver the concessions and deals they want. South-east Asia is different; it is much more like the world of *guanxi* is supposed to be. A deal made by a Suharto, a Marcos or a Mahathir sticks. Hence the pursuit of good *guanxi* with such people is a rational business choice (Lee Kuan Yew, whose probity is beyond question, discovered the contrast with China, to the Singaporean tax payer's considerable cost, when his government invested billions of dollars in building an industrial town in China's Suzhou; despite Lee's unparalleled *guanxi* in Beijing, the local government took against the Singaporean project, promoting an alternative development zone, and quickly undermined it[29]).

It is colonial legacy and the traditional separation between indigenous political élites (aristocratic and anti-business by prejudice) and outsider economic élites that guarantee that south-east Asia is the real home of the *guanxi* merchant. The godfathers are entertainers and gift givers on a grand scale. When political leaders – or their families – travel abroad, the tycoons' homes, hotels and staff are at their disposal. Ananda Krishnan, whose attention to the private lives of politicians and their children is legendary, maintains a private jet, a huge yacht and homes in Switzerland, Australia and London. There is also no shortage of remunerated directorships for those who need to be kept happy. In Malaysia, for instance, it is the norm to both reward families from the ruling UMNO party and persons from the state royal households with shareholdings and directorships. Lim Goh Tong's casino empire keeps its Malay shareholders under very close wraps since gambling is an anathema to Islam; almost all the large shareholders in his main listed vehicles are nominee companies. But Lim cannot hide his dependence on close relationships with Malaysia's powerful police force. Retired officers take many jobs at his giant casino, while directors and executives of Genting, his main company, have included a former inspector general and deputy inspector general of the national police force. Tycoon Quek Leng Chan has used Malaysian royalty, a brother-in-law of Mahathir and children and siblings of former premiers, deputy premiers and ministers as directors. Sometimes, long-term investments in well-connected persons pay tycoons back. When Mahathir unexpectedly gave way to Abdullah Badawi in November 2003, Robert Kuok was able to push to the fore an executive, Lim Chee Wah, who had been building relations with Badawi ever since they attended the University of Malaya together. When other businessmen tried to challenge Kuok's near-monopoly in Malaysian sugar under the new regime, the government rebuffed calls for reform.

Mostly, however, directorships, free or underpriced share distributions and straightforward hand-outs are just a cost of business. Businessmen need political favour and those with power expect to be rewarded for their own investment in political entrepreneurship. As one of Badawi's political secretaries observes of the system in Malaysia: 'The *template* is corruption.'[30] None the less, while the south-east Asian system is corrupt, it is more efficient than ones that pertain in societies where holders of power also seek to be exploiters of business rents. South-east Asia is not comparable with the kleptocracies that have ruined many African countries. In most cases south-east Asian politicians sell public resources and economic rights to private businessmen and do not interfere in the running of the businesses. When Asian despots do behave more like African kleptocrats – as with the increasingly uncontrolled indulgence of Suharto's children in the last decade of his rule – the results are more similar.

The normalcy of political pay-offs in the region leads, from time to time, to unexpected admissions. The billionaire's casual recollection of bribing a prime minister, cited above, has an echo in the description by one of Chin Sophonpanich's sons of the process of paying off Thai politicians and generals as being 'gentlemanly'.[31] This is not a word that an outsider would naturally reach for, but it is employed by the great Thai tycoon's son without irony. Long before Thaksin Shinawatra became Thailand's prime minister, the Thai historians and authors Pasuk Phongpaichit and Chris Baker asked him what the standard kickback was on government-linked projects in the country. He replied without equivocation that 10 per cent was the norm, but that this might fall to 3–5 per cent on very large projects.[32] In the same way, businessmen spoke of rack rates of fees payable on business deals entered into under the Suharto regime in Indonesia; his wife, Madame Tien, was known in business circles as Madame Tien Per Cent. Sudarpo Sastrosatomo, owner of Indonesia's largest shipping company, describes the foundations Suharto used to collect kickbacks as a 'parallel tax system.'[33]

South-east Asia's centralised states, with their class-based social structures, make the region the Asian capital of *guanxi*. It was notable that when John McBeth, a veteran *Far Eastern Economic Review* correspondent in Indonesia, surveyed the country's leading luminaries as to what had gone wrong between independence and the Asian financial crisis, they pointed not to Sukarno or Suharto but to enduring feudal traditions. Roeslan Abdulgani, a respected political figure from the birth of the republic and a foreign minister under Sukarno, lamented: 'The upper classes in these structures were only looking for tribute.'[34] In Indonesia and Malaysia, the habit of selling concessions and licences transitioned through independence without interruption. Under the Dutch, Indonesia's *priyayi* aristocracy had always had saleable rents, assets and power. This was still more the case in Malaysia, most of which was not a formal British colony, thereby leaving land and many other valuable economic rights in the hands of the different royal families. Robert Kuok's big early real estate deals, for instance, were not based on transactions with the British, but with the Johore royal family. When the colonials departed, the concessions in their gift simply added to economic rents already in the hands of local political élites. In Thailand, there was a seamless continuation of rent-offering practices across the 1932 revolution that ended absolute monarchy; all that occurred was that a share of the spoils passed to the civilian bureaucracy and the military. In the Philippines, the corrupting of an ostensibly democratic political system was a work in progress under American colonial rule, as Washington gradually devolved power to Manila; the corruption was simply perfected after independence. Crude political corruption was not of the same order in Singapore and Hong Kong – although both cities had widespread bribe-taking cultures until the 1970s[35] – since their ability to attract regional capital depends on being relatively 'clean' and 'stable' compared to their hinterlands. But the amount of collusion between private business and government in both cities is none the less far greater than is popularly imagined.

Guanxi Does Not a Bamboo Network Make

Relationships are important in south-east Asia because they yield results. But while tycoons run around honing their *guanxi* with politicians, a considerable mythology has grown up about the manner in which the godfathers work with one another. This is the mythology of the 'bamboo network' that supposedly exists among the ethnic Chinese tycoons, providing them with a region-wide web of co-operation that is unique to their culture. The evidence that is held up to support this is the fact that Chinese godfathers invest together, which is undeniable. Asian business magazines and some academic tomes routinely feature diagrammatic illustrations of their co-investments. However, the bamboo network theory is misleading. The reality is that tycoons are typically forced to invest together because of the nature of the environment in which they operate. Licence-based economies require investors who cross borders to find politically influential partners; cartels also require co-operation. The partners will often be ethnic Chinese because of the pre-eminent economic role of Chinese emigrants in the region. But Chinese tycoons co-invest and co-operate with non-Chinese partners as well. Almost all of them operate joint ventures with multinational companies to obtain technology and management skills. They work with godfathers of other ethnicities too. The bamboo network is both an undue simplification and a romanticisation. While in the era of massive, first-generation migration, working-class Chinese depended on networks that were defined by dialect and were certainly a bamboo network, cosmopolitan godfathers have never been so circumscribed. They co-operate where they have to, but most of the time they compete – most obviously for political favour. Up close they are anything but the mutual assistance club that the notion of a bamboo network suggests.

The relationship between Indonesia's Liem Sioe Liong and Malaysia's Robert Kuok, two of the region's best-known tycoons of the past half century, is a good illustration. Kuok has been the dominant, licence-protected player in agricultural commodities – including sugar and flour – in Malaysia since the late 1950s. When he wanted to move into Indonesia, a major sugar producer, he turned naturally to his nearest equivalent in that country. Liem's influence with Suharto was unrivalled, and Suharto had made sugar trading a military monopoly, running much of the business through Liem. Kuok encouraged Liem to also lobby Suharto for an import monopoly on wheat, for flour milling, to be shared with the military. Kuok and Liem became co-investors in wheat and sugar trading businesses, and sugar cultivation, for three decades. The men were frequently hailed in the media as key network allies, whose families hailed from towns in China's Fujian province that are only forty kilometres apart. In reality, Liem and Kuok were partners in a forced marriage of convenience, like those of myriad other tycoons. In the mid 1990s, Kuok sold out of Bogosari, the Indonesian wheat importing and flour milling monopolist, convinced that Liem and the military were cheating him of his fair share of the profits. When the Asian financial crisis engulfed Liem's empire, Kuok returned the favour – along with many other Liem 'friends' – by refusing to loan him money. As Philip Purnama, a senior executive working with Liem's son Anthony to try to rebuild the family business, remarks: 'During the crisis when Anthony needed money this so-called network was asking him for 70 per cent interest.'[36]

The point about the real nature of tycoon co-operation was further clarified for the author at a breakfast meeting with one of Asia's very richest men. Perhaps because of an unexpectedly enjoyable godfather party the night before – he had slept only five hours – the tycoon was surprisingly unguarded in discussion of other billionaires with whom he was said by outsiders to be particularly close. He began with a man he had invested with for half a century, whom he dismissed as 'very uncouth' and 'unsophisticated', describing his conversion to Christianity as nothing more than an effort to ingratiate himself with white people. Another long-time business partner was 'a rascal' who cooks the books in their joint ventures. The interviewee said he once invented a sob story about having lost US$100 million in a shipping deal as a means to bargain with the fellow tycoon for a more equitable pay-out on one of their joint ventures; he received what he thought was an additional US$5 million, but then found it was deducted from his next dividend. A third long-time business partner received a racial lashing for the perceived shortcomings of his Chinese dialect group – which was deemed to be 'a mafia' – and was also condemned for his sexual lasciviousness. This was at least kinder than remarks reserved for the billionaire's direct competitors. One was 'a baby-faced killer'. Another, described as 'a cobra', recently sent a box of chocolates to one of the godfather's sons. The tycoon advised his heir to first feed a chocolate to his dog and, if the animal was still alive after a couple of hours, 'to try one on his wife'.[37]

Simon Murray, recruited by K. S. Li to run Hutchison after Hong Kong's top tycoon acquired the former British *hong*, recalls his own learning curve about the relationships between godfathers. Not long after his appointment, Murray received an invitation from Cheng Yu-tung, billionaire head of the New World group, to meet him for a chat. Since Cheng and Li are renowned as golfing and card-playing buddies, this seemed quite natural. When Murray mentioned Cheng's contact to Li, however, he was surprised by the reaction. He recalls that Li warned him quite sternly: 'Be very careful with these people. They are almost as smart as we are.' Murray notes: 'The theory was they were friends.'[38]

Looked at another way, the real nature of the relationship between tycoons is conveyed in the outcomes when they have attempted to proactively co-operate as groups in business. This is not the same as the more passive co-operation required to maintain a cartel or divide up an economic rent. A well-known example in Malaysia was the setting up under the auspices of the Malaysian Chinese Association (MCA), the main Chinese political party, of Multi-Purpose Holdings (MPH) in the mid 1970s. MPH was a collaborative investment vehicle that promised to defend Chinese commercial interests in the face of the government's pro-Malay affirmative action programmes. Although the company attracted around 30,000 mostly Chinese investors, few tycoons would have anything to do with it, preferring to seek out their own accommodations, direct with government leaders. The prominent business-men who were involved with MPH oversaw a disaster. By the mid 1980s the conglomerate was posting the biggest losses in Malaysian corporate history and its chief executive, Tan Koon Swan – a former senior manager at Lim Goh Tong's Genting – went to jail in both Singapore and Malaysia for fraud. He had siphoned off MPH funds to one of his own companies. A less dramatic but similar tale of failed tycoon co-operation, was the setting-up in Hong Kong in the early 1990s of a China-focused investment group in which Li Ka-shing, Stanley Ho, the Riady family of Indonesia and the Singapore Trade Develop-ment Board were among the partners. The New China Hong Kong Group achieved precisely nothing, because its plutocrat backers were unwilling and unable to work together.

Relationships, as the luxury hotelier Adrian Zecha observes, are critical in south-east Asia because societies are so élite-driven. 'If you are a developer,' he says, 'the chances are the planning guy was at school with you.'[39] It is cer-tainly true that a tiny number of educational establishments, usually colonial in origin, are the common provenance of élites from Hong Kong to Malaysia to Singapore. But the importance of relationships should not be confused with notions of co-operative networks. Asian business is a dog-eat-dog world in which aspirant godfathers compete for a finite supply of political patron-age. It is this which defines the tycoon as a thoroughly charming, individual-istic and ruthlessly pragmatic species.

Core Cash, Vertical Integration, Random Diversification

Bamboo networks do not make Asian godfathers rich; core cash flows derived from unfree markets do. Those cash flows also mask a good many business failings. Shortly after the richest man in the region, Li Ka-shing, acquired his dominant interest in Hong Kong's de facto port cartel, its perennial cash flows came to his rescue. In 1982–3, a global recession combined with a local political crisis, as negotiations for Hong Kong's return to Chinese sovereignty began. The property market went into freefall, and with it earnings at Li's core real estate company, Cheung Kong. Worse, Li was widely rumoured to be exposed to heavy losses via private companies that made property purchases on which he guaranteed minimum returns. Not to matter. In March 1984 Hutchison, the former British *hong* through which Li's port interests are held, poured out some of its cash through a special US$256 million dividend, the main chunk of which went to Li. (The dividend was paid only on preference shares – of which Li owned a great many – not ordinary stock). He was saved. Although K. S. Li has regularly been referred to in the Hong Kong press as 'superman', his investment career has been dotted with mistimed business deals and acquisitions that took a painfully long time to bear fruit. In the early 1990s, he soaked up considerable losses on early mobile telephony and paging investments in the UK, Australia and various Asian countries. He then made a vast windfall profit with Orange in the late 1990s, before plunging into 3G, which is still burning through unprecedented amounts of money. His 1987 move into Canada's Husky oil, and subsequent increases in his equity, brought years of losses and write-downs. All through these investments, core cash flow from ports, retail, electricity and other Hong Kong cartels underwrote Li's expansion. The experience of one of the region's best investors is a good guide to what has kept lesser rivals afloat.

Core cash flow is a godfather's insurance policy. It also encourages two other traits common to tycoon businesses. The first is vertical integration of activities that surround a monopoly or oligopoly. When Henry Fok acquired the monopoly to import mainland Chinese sand to Hong Kong in the 1950s, he soon bought up the barges with which to transport it and the warehouses in which to store it. Other monopolists go much further. To return to the example of sugar, discussed earlier, Robert Kuok has companies that grow sugar, that refine sugar, that make the bags in which the sugar is put, that trade sugar, that market sugar, as well as ships that transport sugar. Since Kuok has an effective monopoly on the distribution of sugar in Malaysia there is a natural temptation to invest in related activities. Vertical integration is also attractive because it gives tycoons considerable discretion over how much income shows up in profit and loss accounts at a particular stage of a business. Freight charges, for instance, might be increased to divert earnings into shipping, which is an offshore, tax-free activity. In Hong Kong, the families behind the publicly listed real estate companies that operate in an effective cartel all own private construction firms. This, in theory, provides an excellent mechanism to drain profit from the listed developers. The construction firms, being private, do not have to publish accounts under Hong Kong law.

The second impact of monopoly cash flows is somewhat counter-intuitive. Around the vertically integrated cartel businesses that generate most of their cash, the godfathers indulge in random diversification. Almost every one of them runs a conglomerate. It is quite normal for a top-tier tycoon to control three or four hundred private companies and up to twenty listed vehicles. In part this reflects the mentality of a licence-based operating environment in which competition is limited by the state and so any new business opportunity is to be grabbed at. There is also, as we shall see in chapter 4, the relatively weak influence of minority shareholders who would prefer more focused public companies with maximised earnings. And there is the impetus to own many different assets, in many different jurisdictions, in case the political winds in a godfather's home state blow from a different direction. But more than anything, diversification is the product of too much easy cash and too much easy credit. As elsewhere in the world, tycoons in south-east Asia are inclined to try lots of different things when they have cash geysers. This is true across the ethnic divide. Malaysia's ethnic Chinese Quek Leng Chan, with his nineteen listed companies in activities from banking and air-conditioners to semiconductors and real estate, is not much different from ethnic Tamil Ananda Krishnan, who turns his hand variously to animation, telecommunications, electricity generating, gaming, oil and gas exploration, and real estate. And neither is far removed from the world of the ethnic British Swire family that is engaged in businesses that include running a monopoly airline, shipping, retailing, soft drinks and a respectable, second-tier position in the Hong Kong real estate cartel. Ultimately, monopoly encourages monopolists to spread their money around.

4

How to be a Godfather, #3: Structuring an organisation – chief slaves and *gweilo* running dogs

'When a man tells you that he got rich through hard work, ask him: "Whose?"'

Don Marquis

How hard does a godfather work? This is an intriguing question. Received opinion is that they work hours that mere mortals would be incapable of. Tung Chee-hwa, the shipping magnate's son who became Hong Kong's first chief executive, frequently made public reference to his marathon shifts, eventually claiming that the effect on his health of a lifetime of 16–18-hour working days forced his resignation from the top government post. Tycoons from Y. K. Pao to Li Ka-shing have been defined by their pre-dawn waking hours and contempt for the notion of 'holidays'.

There is no doubt that godfathers put in the hours. But the nature of their working day is not that of a regular executive. As the chief financial officer to a Singaporean tycoon, and former executive of a major Indonesian family, reflects: 'Do they work hard? They work their relationships ...'[1] This is an important distinction. In Western management terms, godfathers are commonly perceived as chief executives. But in reality their activities are more like those of supercharged chairmen: setting strategy, deal making, hobnobbing, but ultimately leaving others to execute the substance as well as the detail of what they put in train. An operating environment in which *guanxi*, political favour and licences are relatively more important than the inherent efficiency and global competitiveness of a business make this inevitable. Godfathers, and their immediate support staff, spend inordinate amounts of time making sure photographs of the tycoons with ascendant politicians are on display in their offices (and that images of out-of-favour politicians are taken down), organising golf games, putting tycoon homes, yachts and hotels at the disposal of persons who need to be ingratiated, resolving the problems of politicians' wayward children and sending gifts around the world.

Golf is the base ingredient of this social–business mix. Almost without exception, godfathers play the game. In Hong Kong, for instance, the top tycoon rank – K. S. Li, Robert Kuok, the Kwok brothers, Lee Shau-kee, Cheng Yu-tung – are all long-time players and several of them own their own courses (over the border in mainland China) at which to host their guests in private. Asian dictators, too, have been big golf *aficionados*. Suharto played weekly, while Marcos claimed to have the lowest handicap of any world leader (his bodyguards stand accused of kicking his mis-hit shots out of the rough; playing partners said he never had a bad lie).[2] Golf, more than any other activity, is the social lubricant of Asian big business. As a result, golf is part of work. As is attending weddings and funerals of business associates and politicians – what Hong Kongers dub 'doing red and white': red being the colour of Chinese weddings, white that of funerals. As is conducting business while eating; godfathers are rarely seen at home for meals. And as is throwing endless parties and receptions.

The average godfather day is consequently long but social. On a typical day in the life of Li Ka-shing, Asia's richest tycoon, Li will be up before 6 a.m. and off down the hill from his home on Deep Water Bay Road, on the south side of Hong Kong island, to the nine-hole golf course next to the bay in time for a tee-off before 7 a.m. He might play with one or more of the ghetto of other billionaires who have homes close to the Hong Kong Golf Club, with one of his senior executives, or with a new business contact he wants to size up. Li arrives at the office at 10 a.m. Since the completion of the 70-storey Cheung Kong Centre that dominates the eastern side of the Central business district, this is located at the top of the chrome and glass tower, replete with a swimming pool whose roof retracts.[3] Li's first job is to check the press for anything that relates to himself or his companies. He speaks English, but prefers to read Chinese, so relevant parts of the English language papers are translated before his arrival. Li also pays close attention to what brokerage reports say about his companies. Those who provoke his ire can expect a call from one of Li's lieutenants or a letter from his lawyers; as mentioned previously, Li has frequently had his companies withhold advertising from newspapers that upset him. When papers and correspondence are in hand, Li might pick up the phone and speak with or summon one or more senior managers. The phone system alerts them that it is the Big Boss calling. At 11.30 a.m. Li is ready for a massage. Thereafter, there is time for further administrative tasks before a 1p.m. lunch, inevitably of the working variety. After lunch, Li puts in another couple of hours at the office before heading home at 4 p.m. At 5 p.m. he will likely take another massage and then, perhaps, a game of cards with business associates at 6.30 p.m. Finally, a business dinner before he retires at 10 p.m. and the cycle begins again.[4]

Since everything counts as work, Li and other godfathers can claim to put in sixteen hours a day. But the task of actually running their businesses, and putting deals cut over golf or lunch into practice, falls to managers. There are many of these, but in most tycoon businesses there is a clearly identifiable person who might be called 'the chief slave'. This is the first person who gets called when the godfather wants something done. In Li's case it is Canning Fok, the somewhat overweight executive with a greying, pudding-bowl hair cut who can occasionally be seen in public handing Li a mobile telephone with both hands – the ingratiating Asian gesture normally reserved for name cards. Fok undertakes tasks great and small. On the one hand he has overseen the investment of more than US$20 billion in Li's third-generation mobile telephony business. On the other, it can fall to him to bawl out equity analysts who have put a sell call on a Li company. Paul Mackenzie, a long-time analyst at brokerage CLSA who has had the Fok treatment, marvels that Fok can find the time. 'You'd think Canning Fok had better things to do,' he says.[5] The job of the chief slave, however, is to follow the boss's whim and act as his enforcer. Canning Fok is particularly prone to bullying. One Hong Kong source recalls listening to Fok talk about a business deal over lunch, before Li's man said of the counter-party: 'They are going to play ball on this and if they don't we will crush them.' It really was, the person says, 'like a scene from *The Godfather*'.[6]

The chief slave is the one who puts in the hard hours. They are well-remunerated – Canning Fok may be the best-paid executive outside the United States, earning around US$15 million a year – but they do nothing but serve and obey their master, every day. Fok is rarely in bed before 2 a.m. and back in the office hours before Li. The chief slave of Lee Shau-kee, K. S. Li's closest rival in wealth in Hong Kong, is Henderson Land vice-chairman Colin Lam. Lam owns, by Hong Kong standards, an enormous house in the territory's Repulse Bay. But he almost never gets to live there because he spends most nights in a flat he owns on May Road on the other side of Hong Kong island. The reason he does this is to be closer to his boss, who might summon him at any moment. Indeed, serious physical impairment through overwork is a common hazard of the chief slave position. Malaysian tycoon Ananda Krishnan's *über*-lackey, ethnic Indian Ralph Marshall, soldiers on despite major heart surgery in recent years. An investment banker who knows Krishnan describes his treatment of Marshall as that of 'serial bully'. As a typical example, the source recalls Krishnan in Europe deciding to telephone Marshall over the most trivial matter. On being reminded that it was 3 a.m. in Kuala Lumpur, Krishnan responded that this was unimportant and made the call to the sleeping aide.[7] When Marshall himself tells the author, 'I'm just an office boy', he is only half joking.[8] Robert Kuok's chief slave Richard Liu, who was on occasion reduced to tears by the stress of his work, dropped dead at Kuala Lumpur International Airport on Chinese New Year's day 2002. Liu's death forced Kuok back into day-to-day management.

Those closely acquainted with chief slave characters say it is not just their salaries, but the sense of power and proximity to the godfather that motivates them. The *frisson* of power is that much greater than in an impersonal multinational business, particularly since the tycoons' position is more directly bound up with their political access and favour. Ultimately, however, the chief slave's status is a mirage. He may receive share options but control of the business will never pass to him; rather it will go to the next generation of the tycoon's family. In this sense he suffers the whim of a capricious employer for nothing.

The Outsiders' Outsiders

The chief slave is, almost by definition, Asian. He is from the same ethnic group as the tycoon, able to speak the same languages and interact fully with the family. Another stock character in the modern godfather management cadre stands in stark contrast. This is the ethnic outsider, often a European or an American. There is a certain historical symmetry in the retention of such people. In the colonial era, Western banks and trading houses depended on *compradors* to intermediate business with the local population. It was an enormously profitable position, pregnant with possibilities for bribes as well as legitimate commissions. Stanley Ho's great uncle, Sir Robert Ho Tung, was the greatest *comprador* of them all (for Jardine, Matheson) and the first Chinese allowed to live on Hong Kong's Peak. Sir David Li's maternal grandfather was a *comprador* for Swire. The contemporary godfather is nothing like so dependent on outsiders as the colonials were on their *compradors* – he is far more cosmopolitan, often having studied abroad and typically speaking English – yet the outsider is still an important component of big business success in south-east Asia. He may be required for some specialist, technical ability or to overcome the political problems that go with family business.

In the late nineteenth century, tycoons like Indonesia's Oei Tiong Ham were already employing European engineers to help them run imported machinery. But in the post-independence era, the godfathers' needs became more complex. Suddenly they were the ones in league with political power, holding exclusive licences and in a position to buy out or muscle out old colonial commercial interests. As their power grew, they needed to know about global markets and global capital. In this context the stage was set for the rise of what might be called the *gweilo* running dog (*gweilo*, from the Cantonese meaning 'ghost man', is a common euphemism in the region for a foreigner; running dog comes from the Mandarin Chinese *zou gou*, meaning a servile follower). Some of the godfathers' running dogs brought nothing more than their professional management ability; others were, and are, less wholesome characters ready to engage in all manner of unseemly activities. Rodney Ward, the seasoned head of Swiss investment bank UBS in Asia, suggests that with respect to unprincipled business in the post-independence era: 'The *gweilos* led the way not only in terms of degree of avarice but also in denying it had anything to do with them.'[9]

One of the earliest *gweilo* running dogs was Charles Letts, a buccaneering British expatriate who had fought alongside a communist group in the Spanish civil war and later with Thai communists during the Second World War. A Thai speaker, he was captured by the Japanese and imprisoned. After the war, he took a job with Jardine, Matheson based in Singapore and Malaysia. But in the independence era Letts was increasingly frustrated that the British *hong*, and its aloof *taipan* family the Keswicks, would not adjust to the new business environment; he suggested bringing the rising stars of the local business scene on to the board but was quickly rebuffed. Letts was friends with emerging south-east Asian tycoons like Robert Kuok and Kwek Leng Beng. In the 1960s he became one of the first expatriate deal makers to cross the racial rubicon. He teamed up with Lee Loy Seng, son of a successful Malayan-Chinese tin miner, who was moving into the plantation business. After Malaysian independence in 1957, British companies began to sell off agricultural estates, a process much expedited by the arrival of the New Economic Policy (NEP) in 1970. Although designed to further the economic interests of ethnic Malays, the NEP was in fact more readily directed against the commercial interests of the former colonial power. Letts and Lee Loy Seng made an effective partnership, with Lee indentifying businesses and land he wished to acquire and Letts travelling to London to negotiate terms. Lee Loy

Seng became the biggest private plantation owner in Malaysia, concentrating on rubber and, later, palm oil. Letts, not surprisingly, became a suspect character among the expatriate establishment. Now in his late eighties, he still goes to his Singapore office each day and serves on the board of the private Lee family holding company.

As the imperial order crumbled, then, it was only natural that southeast Asia's ascendant godfathers would find foreign talent at their disposal. Among advisers and key personnel whom Robert Kuok picked up were Jacob Ballas, an Iraqi Jew who became chairman of the Singapore stock exchange, Paul Bush, a senior British accountant with Coopers and Lybrand (now PricewaterhouseCoopers) in Malaysia, and Piet Yap, a westernised Sumatran Chinese who had worked for big Dutch trading companies in colonial Indonesia and became a key manager of Kuok's burgeoning interests in the country. The only limit to the advantage that could be gained from hiring from a multiethnic talent pool was a tycoon's capacity to trust outsiders. In most cases this proved a constraint. Family-based businesses were naturally suspicious of outsiders, and particularly *gweilos*. After all, the average tycoon had a lot of secrets that needed keeping. But one godfather, more than all others, realised that a well-paid *gweilo* was just as trustworthy as an Asian. That tycoon was Li Ka-shing, who became the ultimate employer of the *gweilo* running dog. As Simon Murray, who ran Hutchison for Li for a decade, observes: 'K. S. is totally non-racist. He looks at people and sees the value.'[10]

Quite a Kennel

Li began to forge critical alliances with British expatriates in the 1970s. After he took control of the formerly British *hong* Hutchison in 1979, he recruited senior European and North American managers to his staff. Y. K. Pao, Li's forerunner as Hong Kong's pre-eminent tycoon, had what Murray calls 'invisible *gweilos*', but Li took internationalisation to a new level. While he himself operated his original real estate business, Cheung Kong, 'Hutchison was run, over there, as "*gweilo* country"', says Murray.[11] The *gweilos* were a mix of the unctuous, the greedy and the professional – but they were all useful.

One of Li's earliest and most enduring relationships was with Philip Tose, a man whose name is now synonymous with the collapse of the Peregrine group, until 1998 the largest Asian investment bank and brokerage outside Japan. It went down with around US$4 billion of liabilities and Tose was barred from holding company directorships in Hong Kong for four years for governance failures that contributed to Peregrine's downfall. He had arrived in Hong Kong in 1972, sent out by his stockbroker father to get rid of expensive British expatriates and localize the staff of Vickers da Costa, then one of the largest British-owned brokers. At a time when the local broking industry was in its infancy, he wrote what he claims was the first report on a Hong Kong Chinese company by an international brokerage.[12] The business in question was Li Ka-shing's Cheung Kong. Tose subsequently told Peregrine staffers that, prior to public distribution, he sent a copy of the report to Cheung Kong. When a Li minion telephoned to point out a minor error, Tose had the entire report reprinted.[13] It was the beginning of a three-decade-long working relationship with K. S. Li, whom Tose has described publicly as 'a very close personal friend'.[14] When Tose set up Peregrine in 1988, Li was one of his investors.

Tose's stockbroking persona was that of Hong Kong's, and Asia's, raging bull. Prominent on the social circuit, he was a sucker for tycoons. In the early 1980s he enthused about the fraud-based business empire of George Tan, publishing a gushing special review of his Carrian group in November 1981 and affirming a new buy recommendation from Vickers shortly before Carrian went under in the biggest corruption scandal in Hong Kong corporate history.[15]

There were periodic allegations that Tose's relationships with tycoons were closer than appropriate. In 1982 Hong Kong's first insider trading tribunal revealed Tose instructed his dealers to buy as many Hutchison shares as possible in the twenty-four hours before Li Ka-shing announced his takeover of the company; a portion of the shares was for Tose's personal family accounts. He denied trading on insider information and, supported by Li's testimony, was exonerated. In early 1991, former Peregrine analysts say Tose intervened to stop a 'sell' recommendation being put out on Hutchison in a research report. 'Philip Tose came down to the research department and rewrote it himself,' says a former staffer.[16] There is no allegation that the change in the report was linked to an investment banking deal, but it is indicative of the way Tose worked. He declines to discuss the incident.[17]

In early 1996 the Hong Kong bourse was filled with rumours of market manipulation when Peregrine did put out a sell call on Hutchison. The share price dropped around 13 per cent and K. S. Li stepped in to buy up large volumes of his own stock.[18] Might Peregrine have helped Li acquire his own stock cheaply? Until Peregrine imploded in 1998, Hong Kong's notoriously hands-off Securities and Futures Commission had little to say about the firm. Peregrine was censured once, in 1993, for farming out trading orders to other brokerages in a manner that made stocks it had taken to market appear more actively traded than they were.

The end of Peregrine was like the end of any un-hedged bull-market operator. The firm could not survive an economic downturn. As the Asian financial crisis unravelled in late 1997, Peregrine was caught with three-quarters of its capital lent out to just two of the more scrofulous companies in Indonesia – a Jakarta taxi firm called Steady Safe that was linked to the Suharto family and Asia Pulp & Paper, the vehicle of godfather Eka Tjipta Widjaya and the region's biggest delinquent debtor. The money did not come back, Peregrine could not meet its obligations, and so folded, in January 1998. Li Ka-shing did not open his wallet to save Peregrine, but he did show his trademark loyalty to a trusted lieutenant. Despite all the negative publicity surrounding the Peregrine debacle and Tose's court-sanctioned ban from running a business, he was put on the Li payroll as an adviser to Hutchison. There he remains, squirreled away on the top-most floor of Hutchison House in Hong Kong's Central, and surrounded by paintings of his youthful incarnation as a 1960s Formula 3 racing driver. A crash which left him in hospital for four months put paid to that career. Christopher Wood, the well-known Asian equity strategist who started as an analyst at Peregrine, observes of Tose's life: 'He doesn't know how to go round corners.'[19]

Another early *gweilo* recruit to the K. S. Li circle was Alan Johnson-Hill, who worked for him as his 'general assistant' in the late 1970s. Johnson-Hill was a former executive at Jim Slater's Slater Walker Securities, which went on an acquisition spree in Asia in the early 1970s that included Haw Par, the business founded by Singaporean tycoon Aw Boon Haw. Slater Walker was another aggressive investment firm that went bust, involving an investigation by the Singapore government. Much of this focused on Spydar Securities, whose shareholders were senior Haw Par executives (of whom Alan Johnson-Hill was one), set up to make parallel trades on Haw Par acquisitions, and other deals, for their personal benefit. One Haw Par manager, Richard Tarling, was sentenced to prison in Singapore in November 1979. Johnson-Hill was among those who were not charged. However, suspicion of securities malfeasance did not leave him. Working for K. S. Li, he was also named by Hong Kong's first insider trading tribunal as a purchaser of Hutchison stock – 170,000 shares – immediately before the tycoon announced his acquisition of a controlling share in the company. Johnson-Hill said he made the purchase several hours before Li told him about the deal. By the time the tribunal – to which he provided written statements but at which he did not offer himself for cross-examination – decided he had no case to answer, Johnson-Hill had returned to Europe, where he bought a vineyard in France. Hong Kong wags refer to its output as Château Cheung Kong.

The Haw Par connection continued with K. S. Li's recruitment of George Magnus, a British manager hired to run Haw Par in Singapore after the government began its criminal investigation. Haw Par had purchased a 20 per cent interest in K. S. Li's Cheung Kong as an investment, a stake that made Li's company a takeover target if it fell into the wrong hands.[20] A couple of weeks after Magnus resigned as Haw Par chief executive in 1978, it was announced the Cheung Kong stake had been sold to Li. Magnus subsequently resurfaced as an executive director of Cheung Kong, going on to become deputy chairman, as well as a director of other Li companies. He was with Li for more than twenty-five years before retiring to an island off Vancouver; he remains a non-executive director of Cheung Kong. In 1986 Li, Magnus and other Cheung Kong directors were found to be 'involved in culpable insider dealing' in Hong Kong's second insider trading tribunal.[21] The guilty verdict concerned trading in shares in International City Holdings, a Li company, and led merely to a symbolic censure, since insider trading was not made a criminal offence in Hong Kong until after the Asian financial crisis in 1997.

In 1984, Li hired Simon Murray, a former Jardine, Matheson manager who had set up his own trading business, to be Hutchison's chief executive. Murray, well liked and respected in Hong Kong business circles, was seen by some observers as an example of another use to which a *gweilo* might be put. K. S. Li had recently steamrollered Hutchison's board into paying out a special US$256-million dividend, the biggest chunk of which went to Li's Cheung Kong, which was severely cash-strapped by the early 1980s real-estate crash.[22] The payout occurred despite a public promise from Li's previous chief executive at Hutchison that the company would not be used as a cash dispenser. It was also the time when Li was coming under suspicion for insider trading with respect to International City Holdings. In this context, Murray brought much-needed credibility that the interests of minority shareholders at Hutchison would be defended.[23] He went on to run the company until 1993, when a number of differences – over everything from strategy to political views about Hong Kong's future – led to his departure. Li, true to form, was careful to ensure the split with Murray involved a gentle let-down. He kept him on the board at Hutchison and Cheung Kong, and backed Murray to start his own private equity business. In similar vein, Li's Hutchison had paid out nearly US$3 million in 1984 – a considerable sum in those days – to the three senior executives who were pushed out after the special dividend; they had not been happy with Li's behaviour, but left quietly.[24]

As Li's businesses expanded, more of the foreigners he brought in were employed for narrower professional tasks. Today, two Britons run, respectively, his ports and retail businesses. A Canadian holds the key role of chief financial officer at Hutchison. Whatever the *gweilos* do, Li's use of them is unmatched among other tycoons. He is the ultimate embodiment of the god-father as cosmopolitan manipulator. His self-taught English is not perfectly fluent, but it is more than adequate for communicating with his *gweilo* lieu-tenants. Yet Li never uses English at shareholders' meetings or on the rare occasions when the press pack surrounds him. At those times his identity is thoroughly Cantonese (albeit with a distinct Chiu Chow accent). The local press in Hong Kong lionised him for three decades – dubbing Li *chui yan*, or 'Superman', for taking on and beating colonial big business. Li made time for favoured Cantonese reporters. The foreign and English-language press, which showed less reverence, has rarely gained access to him. More usually, it has been the recipient of threatening letters from his lawyers. Three months before Li was among the first group of people to be named insider traders in Hong Kong in March 1986, he had secured damages, under threat of litiga-tion, from the *South China Morning Post* for alleging he was exactly that.

K. S. Li is the great puppet master – though Robert Kuok is more adept at blending in to different élite cultures around the region. Li is the outstand-ing *gweilo* handler. Whether obtaining dispensations from the colonial Hong Kong government or managing a critical relationship with the Hongkong Bank (see chapter 5), and whether recruiting an amoral running dog or hiring a technical specialist, Li has done so without any apparent racial hang-ups. This is not the norm in a region where a history of colonial racial prejudice and notions of Chinese exceptionalism create all manner of ethnic neuroses. As Chris Patten, the last governor of Hong Kong, observes: 'He didn't allow the advantages, which were stacked up in favour of the *hongs*, to make him bitter.' Li simply concentrated on what, in the long run, would make him the winner. Patten adds: 'He's one of the few businessmen I've met who is clearly a sort of genius.'[25]

But Why Modernise?

Li's people-handling skills have helped make him, by most estimates, the richest godfather. While some peers keep nothing more than a token company *gweilo*, almost as a racial reminder of who is in charge (one such lone running dog in Hong Kong, employed by a major regional family, is suf-ficiently underemployed to maintain an entertaining daily blog of his activi-ties),[26] Li has dotted his empire with executives recruited from international business. However, the role that monopoly and cartels play in creating all godfather wealth must not be forgotten. In Hong Kong, some investment bankers speculate that the other two leading beneficiaries of local land policy and the real estate cartel – Lee Shau-kee of Henderson and the Kwok family of Sun Hung Kai – might be just as wealthy, if not more so, than Li if all their assets could be counted. No one disputes that there is not much net worth difference between the three. This is despite the fact that Lee and the Kwoks have done nothing more with most of their earnings than recycle them into passive investments, often overseas. For all Li Ka-shing's perspiration in trying to build a global conglomerate with a global workforce, those who have remained focused on milking one unfree market are almost as well off.

In general, the godfathers have little to contribute to the corporate science of human resource management. They pay their chief slaves and *gweilo* running dogs well, because such people come from a globally traded management cadre. But the bulk of the personnel in their sprawling organisations is little more than corporate cannon fodder, with wages additionally constrained by south-east Asia's long-time suppression of union activity and importation of cheaper foreign labour when big business demands it (Indonesians to Singapore, mainland Chinese to Hong Kong, and so on). Godfather businesses are about obtaining a share of a monopoly and then cutting costs, rather than hiring the best people in order to make a challenge in a free market. Compared with multinational companies, management systems are relatively few and relatively arcane. What matters is the will of the Big Boss. At the heart of every tycoon business is a battery of secretaries, a chief slave and a phalanx of nervous executives awaiting the next instruction of one unpredictable individual.

5

How to be a Godfather, #4: Banks, piggy banks and the joy of capital markets

'I believe that banking institutions are more dangerous to our liberties than standing armies.'

Thomas Jefferson, letter to the US Secretary of the Treasury, 1802

There is, in addition to oligopolistic licences and concessions, a second resource which the south-east Asian godfather cannot do without: access to capital. In the post-colonial era, capital became readily available for the first time to local entrepreneurs because of three developments. The first was changes in the lending practices of existing banks. The second was the obtaining by well-connected tycoons of licences to open their own banks, which typically became akin to personal piggy banks, albeit ones filled with other people's money. The third development was the growth of the region's capital markets.

Few things constrained local businessmen so much under colonial rule as the difficulty of obtaining loans at reasonable interest. European and American banks were little concerned with lending to Asian businesses – their preferred activity was financing international trade with letters of credit and other support – and when they did lend to locals their *compradors* were rapacious in demanding kickbacks. There was a number of small ethnic Chinese- and Thai-controlled banks in the region, but they were extremely conservative in their lending practices. Most local businessmen turned to the traditional Indian moneylenders with their punishing rates of interest. Starting in the 1950s, however, more aggressive, entrepreneurial management at two Asia-based banks began to change this situation. The banks in question were Bangkok Bank, headquartered in Thailand, and the Hongkong and Shanghai Bank, based in Hong Kong.

The trail blazer was Bangkok Bank, led by Chin Sophonpanich, son of a Teochiu father and a Thai mother. A skilled trader and wartime black marketeer, Chin was brought in at the end of the Second World War to what was a failing institution set up under the aegis of the Thai royal family; he was employed first as *comprador* and subsequently as general manager. In the years that followed, Chin built out the most strongly politically-connected business in post-war Thailand, with Bangkok Bank at its centre. After the military coup of 1947, he co-opted the leadership families of Field Marshal Phin Choonhavan and police director-general Phao Siriyanon as shareholders and directors of his companies and restructured the bank to make the government its biggest shareholder. In return, he obtained a large injection of state capital, near-monopolies of gold and foreign exchange trading and the handling of overseas remittances by ethnic Chinese workers, protection from competition and an unrivalled client base. Like all the most successful godfathers, Chin also rose above the dialect differences of the Chinese community, recruiting the cream of Thai–Chinese graduates (pure Thais almost always preferred civil service careers to business) from the élite Thammasat University. One of the most important was Boonchu Rojanasathien, a Hainanese,[1] who saved Chin's bacon after Field Marshal Sarit Thanarat staged a coup in 1957. Chin quickly made Sarit an adviser and appointed his interior minister, Field Marshal Prapass Charusathiara, chairman of Bangkok Bank, but his links to the ousted Phin and Phao made him too nervous to remain personally in Bangkok. He went into exile in Hong Kong until Sarit died in 1963. In his absence, Boonchu ran the bank, backed by the most adeptly chosen management cadre in Thailand. A sense of how effectively the executives straddled the worlds of business and politics is given by the fact that, as of 1980, Bangkok Bank's board had produced three deputy premiers and two speakers of the Thai parliament.[2] But the executives were also entrepreneurial businessmen; they introduced time deposits (long-term saving) and rural credit to Thailand.

Chin Sophonpanich created the largest bank in south-east Asia and one that was extremely profitable. A report by the International Monetary Fund in 1973 claimed that Bangkok Bank's privileged position allowed it to make returns on its capital in excess of 100 per cent a year (a claim denounced by Chin's lieutenants).[3] What was not in dispute was that the bank's bulging deposit base could not be lent out at optimum rates in Thailand alone. This is where Chin revolutionised the south-east Asian banking scene. He personally travelled between Hong Kong, Singapore, Kuala Lumpur and Jakarta, identifying and courting the new generation of putative post-colonial tycoons. One multibillionaire remembers looking for money in the late 1950s to fund an import substitution deal for which he had obtained a licence. Having heard about Chin, he offered to come and see him. Chin's response was that there was no need – he would come to the client. 'For the Chinese businessmen of south-east Asia there was a major moment with Chin Sophonpanich,' says the tycoon. 'He broke what was then the highly conservative, highly colonialistic banking system.'[4]

Chin banked the key godfathers outside Hong Kong – Robert Kuok in Malaysia, Liem Sioe Liong in Indonesia, the Chearavanonts in Thailand – as well as various other players in Singapore and Hong Kong. In the mid 1970s, two-fifths of his bank's earnings came from more than a dozen branches outside Thailand. Chin is remembered fondly by the tycoon fraternity. 'He was absolutely charming – he had about six mistresses,'[5] reminisces one billionaire who knew Chin well during his sojourn in Hong Kong. Another calls him 'a chunk of granite'.[6] Chin was also a typically amoral tycoon. He was closely linked to the Thai heroin trade through his role as personal financier to the narcotics kingpin Phao Siriyanon, and to other politicians involved in running the drugs business; his private investments, according to a friend, included quite a few girlie bars.

Tycoons are money machines, and no one sought to pass judgement on Chin. From the early 1980s, however, his star – and that of Bangkok Bank – began to fade. Chin suffered a long illness before his death in 1988, exacerbated by his fondness for alcohol (particularly brandy) as well as women. At the same time he failed to take Bangkok Bank beyond its incarnation as a regional financier of upcoming ethnic Chinese tycoons. In the 1950s and 1960s this was revolutionary, but it was not enough to sustain Bangkok Bank's ascent. Chin was cosmopolitan enough to be banker to all Chinese, but not sufficiently so to create a truly Asian and then global institution. And when he died, management of Bangkok Bank was dominated by his children rather than the managers he had nurtured. Chin departed this world as another brilliant social chameleon. His assimilation and 'Thai-ness' were such that he was cremated in the Thai manner (the Chinese tradition is burial) and the pyre lit by the king himself. Yet, at his peak, he had promised so much more.

Where HSBC Came From …

It was left to a colonial firm to continue the financial revolution. The Hongkong and Shanghai Banking Corporation (HSBC) had given up its core operation in Shanghai and retreated to Hong Kong in 1949, following the communist victory in the Chinese civil war. What locals came to know as the Hongkong

Bank financed many Shanghai manufacturers who fled the mainland to restart their businesses in Hong Kong. None the less it remained an inherently colonial institution. Until the 1960s the bank still employed a *comprador*, who guaranteed the borrowings of local businessmen. The several hundred expatriate managers who ran the business rarely met with Chinese entrepreneurs and did not directly assess their creditworthiness. Expatriates dealt with the banking needs of other expatriates.

Unlike the family-controlled British *hongs*, however, ownership of the Hongkong Bank was widely dispersed – no individual was allowed to own more than 1 per cent of the shares – and its managers could rise all the way to the top of the business. It was perhaps this that led key executives of the post-war era to take a closer interest in a new generation of Chinese tycoons as their rising wealth became apparent, and to back them in takeovers of weakened colonial businesses. Racial prejudice went out of the window once it was clear the local godfathers were the key to the bank's development as Hong Kong's biggest business. As Leo Goodstadt, head of the Hong Kong government's Central Policy Unit in the 1990s, wrote: 'It [the bank] presided over an orderly and highly profitable transfer of economic control from British to Chinese companies.'[7] This does not mean the Hongkong Bank was a committed free marketeer. Its relationship to the colonial administration was second to none, and allowed it to defend a uniquely privileged position. Until the mid 1990s, and the setting up of the Hong Kong Monetary Authority, it was a *de facto* central bank,[8] issuing notes, acting as a clearing house, enjoying interest-free use of the banking system's surpluses, acting as banker to the government and knowing much of what went on in other banks. Protected by a moratorium on bank licences from the mid 1960s to 1978, an interest rate cartel that persisted into the 1990s, and a government-supported takeover of a major local bank, Hang Seng, in 1965, Hongkong Bank built up a roughly 50 per cent share of the Hong Kong deposit base. Its pre-eminence was even greater than that of Chin Sophonpanich's Bangkok Bank in Thailand and, like Chin, it used its capital to invest in its clients' businesses as well as lending out its vast deposits. In this way the Hongkong Bank became the kingmaker among the Hong Kong godfathers.

The two dominant Hong Kong tycoons of the post-war era – Y. K. Pao, who died in 1991, and K. S. Li – were both catapulted above the ranks of their peers by the Hongkong Bank. In the first case, it was the bank's decision to enter into shipping investments with Pao, and to finance them, that allowed him to become the world's leading private ship owner. Pao was from a prosperous mainland family and had considerable experience in manufacturing, insurance and banking before arriving with his family in Hong Kong in 1949. The Paos managed to bring a good portion of their wealth with them. In the early 1950s, Y. K. Pao built a successful import–export business in the colony – assisted by the Korean War boom – before buying his first cargo ship in 1955. It was this foray into shipping that gradually alerted him to what looked like an unusually good investment proposition. The Japanese government was supporting its shipbuilding industry by issuing export credits – loans – to foreign buyers to cover up to 80 per cent of the cost of vessels at fixed interest for terms around eight years. At the same time the post-war boom meant that Japan's large trading companies, the *sogo shosha*, were willing to sign long-term ship charters, typically running for more than a decade, to secure foreign-owned vessels that used cheap foreign crews. Critically, it was possible to get the trading companies' banks to issue letters of guarantee of the performance of the charterer, making a lease rock solid. When these pieces were put together, they added up to a rather extraordinary deal. Pao could build ships in Japan, pay for most of them with Japanese government money and charter them long-term to Japanese companies whose payments were guaranteed by Japanese banks. At the end of the charter a ship was his, fully written off. As his Austrian son-in-law Helmut Sohmen, who married Pao's eldest daughter and runs the Bergesen WorldWide shipping group,[9] observes: 'It was a banker's mind that saw the possibility to exploit a government's generosity.'[10]

Pao's problem was that he did not have a bank. He could put down the 20 per cent he needed to front up on a few ships, but in order to take real advantage of the opportunity he required much more money. Hongkong Bank's decision to back him was critical. It was driven by Jake Saunders and Guy Sayer, who were both to become chairmen of the bank in subsequent years, and were aware of Y. K. Pao from their work at the bank's trade finance department. It was far from normal for expatriate managers to deal direct with Chinese businessmen – 'There was still a colour bar,' says Sohmen[11] – but the fact that Pao taught himself English, had a background in banking and was already rich made a difference. So did the no-lose nature of the Japanese investments. Hongkong Bank went on to finance Y. K. Pao for ship purchases he made individually and became an equal partner in three joint-venture shipping investment companies.[12] By 1979 Pao controlled 202 ships totalling more than 20 million deadweight tonnes – the largest fleet in the world, far larger than the Greek Onassis and Niarchos fleets combined. Hongkong Bank profited handsomely from its relationship with Pao. In 1971 it brought him on to the company's board, and he went on to become bank vice-chairman. Pao was the bank's first Chinese director, his appointment signalling the beginning of a trend to fill up its board room with rising Chinese tycoons.

It was only when Hongkong Bank assisted Pao's assaults on other British-controlled businesses, however, that it really rocked the Hong Kong establishment. In the late 1970s Pao sold off a large chunk of his fleet, amassing cash for other investments. One of these was a gradually rising stake in Hong Kong and Kowloon Wharf and Godown Co., a company linked to Jardine, Matheson. When Jardine decided to see off Pao with a takeover bid in 1980, he trumped its offer with credit from Hongkong Bank and was advised by its investment banking unit, Wardley. A few years earlier it would have been unthinkable that a Chinese businessman could take anything away from Jardine. But with Hongkong Bank's support, Pao did so. An exemption by the stock exchange from having to make a general offer for Wharf shares he did not own showed Pao was now a real insider. In 1985 he went on to take control of another British *hong*, Wheelock Marden. Jardine, Matheson – once untouchable – was terrified by Hongkong Bank's alliances with Chinese tycoons and spent much of the 1980s engaged in costly restructuring exercises to defend against further raids on its interests.

The so-called princely *hong* was right to be scared, for Hongkong Bank was entering the most aggressive period of its development. In the mid 1970s the bank was using its own capital to be a significant player in Pao's shipping business, as well as owning a quarter of the Swire *hong*'s key asset, the airline Cathay Pacific, and a fifth of another, troubled British *hong*, Hutchison Whampoa. It was in dealing with this last investment that the bank forged a godfather relationship even more important than the Y. K. Pao one.

It happened on the watch of the most flamboyant and controversial of the Hongkong Bank's post-war chief executives, Michael Sandberg, chairman from 1977 to 1986. A leader with more of a trading and deal-making background than his predecessors, Sandberg was flash by Hongkong Bank's staid standards and, many said, greedy to boot. He left his physical mark on the bank with the construction of its current Hong Kong headquarters, a no-expenses-spared Norman Foster design that cost four times as much as the nearby, larger Bank of China building. Sandberg was still more lavish in refurbishing his own bank-provided home, Sky High, on Hong Kong's Peak. At a strategic level, he began the globalisation of Hongkong Bank with the acquisition of Marine Midland in upstate New York in 1980. He also bought two London merchant banks and tried but failed to buy Britain's Royal Bank of Scotland. But it is for his relationship with Li Ka-shing that Sandberg is remembered in Hong Kong. Sandberg confirmed Li as Y. K. Pao's successor as chief godfather when he put in his hands, by way of an untendered sale, a controlling stake in Hutchison Whampoa.

The bank owned the stake as a result of a bail-out of Hutchison and its former subsidiary Hongkong and Whampoa Dock Company in the early 1970s. Like Peregrine twenty-five years later, Hutchison foundered on the rocks of risky business in Indonesia, in its case leasing activities. Hongkong Bank refinanced what became Hutchison Whampoa in return for 22 per cent of its equity, putting in an Australian manager, Bill Wyllie, to nurse it back to health. Two years after Sandberg became Hongkong Bank chairman, he decided to sell the revived business. He did so, however, without offering it around to obvious potential purchasers – the two dominant British *hongs*, Jardine and Swire, or Y. K. Pao, the bank's existing Chinese tycoon partner. Instead, a deal was struck with Li Ka-shing on terms that appear extremely generous. Bill Wyllie calculated that the HK$639-million price agreed was less than half the net asset value of Hutchison's constituent businesses, and says he had buyers lined up who would have paid much more. 'For Li, it was a brilliant deal,' Wyllie recalled more than two decades later. 'The breakup value of the company was more than double the amount he paid.'[13] Moreover, Li was given a deferred payment option, further reducing the effective price.

An untendered sale at a very low price begs many questions. At a strategic level, however, the decision to sell to Li was no wild punt. By 1979, when the Hutchison deal was done, K. S. Li's Cheung Kong was already Hong Kong's number two property company after Jardine's Hong Kong Land. Thereafter, the prime Hutchison assets guaranteed Li's ascent to the top of the tycoon pile. He acquired a leading position in the container port cartel, a share in the retailing duopoly in supermarkets and pharmacies with PARKnSHOP and Watsons (the other player was Jardine), and valuable land on Hong Kong island. In short, Li joined the cosy colonial commercial stitch-up that was Hong Kong's domestic economy. He was already banking with Hongkong Bank, but in the 1980s and 1990s would put vast amounts of business their way. 'K. S.'s present back was to do all his business through the bank,' observes a senior Li executive.[14] He was made non-executive deputy chairman of Hongkong Bank, succeeding Y. K. Pao, as the trend to fill up non-executive positions on the board with Chinese tycoons accelerated. This sent out the message to other godfathers that the bank was ready to finance them.

Sandberg developed close relationships with other major players, such as New World's Cheng Yu-tung. Everyone (except the Keswicks at Jardine, Matheson) was happy. Hongkong Bank cemented its position as the totally dominant provider of capital in south-east Asia's leading financial centre;

Chinese tycoons were allowed to fulfil their potential and muscle in on colonial business; and the basic cartel structure of the local economy remained intact. When Sandberg retired in 1986, K. S. Li made clear the closeness of their relationship by giving him, as a leaving gift, a gold reproduction, around a metre high, of the new Hongkong Bank headquarters. A select group of guests at a dinner held at Li's Hilton hotel was awestruck when the immodest token of affection was revealed.[15] One of those present quips that the statue has doubtless since been 'melted down' at Sandberg's English estate.

Playing kingmaker to the new tycoons guaranteed that Hongkong Bank's pre-eminent position in the city state endured through the post-war era. All the big boys – even someone like Henry Fok, whose links to the Communist Party of China in theory ended his links to the British establishment – had major banking relationships with what was known in Hong Kong simply as 'the bank'. Of course, the ability to pick winners was not entirely foolproof. Under Sandberg, there was the spectacle of the bank chairman falling for the outstanding con artist of the era, George Tan Soon-gin. Tan was a Singapore bankrupt, born in Malaysia, who arrived in Hong Kong in 1972 and overstayed his visa by eleven years. With borrowed money, lots of bribes and limitless *chutzpah*, he fashioned Hong Kong's 'hottest' investment company of the early 1980s, the Carrian Group. Tan's mode of operation was reflected in an opulent wood-panelled office stuffed with expensive art and thick-pile oriental carpets. He employed a phalanx of *gweilo* running dog executives that further made him look the godfather part. His biggest line of finance came from the Hong Kong subsidiary of the Malaysian government's Bank Bumiputra. But Tan's key local backer was the man he called 'Uncle Mike'. Sandberg fell for George Tan hook, line and sinker. He entertained him in his box at the Hong Kong races and introduced him to key businessmen in the colony. Hongkong Bank made substantial loans to Tan – Sandberg, questioned by journalists, said publicly the total was less than US$200 million. At least as important, Sandberg's and the bank's endorsement of Tan encouraged a roster of European and American banks to back him as well. When Carrian collapsed, amid a falling Hong Kong property market, it had debts of US$1.3 billion – Hong Kong's biggest ever bankruptcy. The affair was powerful testimony to the power of Hongkong Bank, both direct and indirect, in the allocation of capital in the colony.

Sandberg retired in 1986 to an English peerage and a Hampshire estate, untouched by the criminal investigations surrounding George Tan's demise.[16] Nonetheless, the bank's reputation 'suffered a bit towards the end of his sojourn', concedes a former senior colleague.[17] Sandberg's close relationships with George Tan and the Australian Alan Bond, another would-be Asian tycoon who went to jail, as well as his appetite for business gifts, had begun to embarrass some of his peers.[18] 'He collected funny watches. From time to time people gave him watches,' recalls the colleague, alluding to Sandberg's vast horology collection.[19] Sandberg sold his set of timepieces at auction in 2001 for just over US$13 million and set tongues wagging once more. Whatever his personal foibles, and whatever the case for selling Hutchison in a no-bid deal to Li Ka-shing, however, Sandberg concluded the economic transition in Hong Kong that began when the bank backed Y. K. Pao. Henceforth, two surviving British *hongs* – Swire and a much-weakened Jardine – would share power in the domestic economy with a group of Chinese tycoons. It was the result of decisions made by the supreme arbiter of capital allocation in Hong Kong, the Hongkong Bank.

Banks that Always Say Yes

Singapore had some echoes of the Hong Kong experience, with four large banks determining most access to capital. The difference was that behind those four banks, directly and indirectly, was one family, the Lees. The government stopped issuing full banking licences in 1973, restricted the business foreign banks could conduct and made local banks apply for permission to enter new product lines and launch takeovers. The biggest of the local banks is state-owned Development Bank of Singapore (DBS). The other major players – Oversea-Chinese Banking Corporation (OCBC) and United Overseas Bank (UOB) (which took over a third large private bank, Overseas Union Bank (OUB) in 2002) – are run by anglicised families whose heads have similar élite backgrounds, and are on cordial terms with, Lee Kuan Yew. The result is that local non-banking godfathers have been, if not beholden to, then extremely conscious of the need to stay on the right side of the Lee family in order to keep their credit lines open. When a family like that of Ng Teng Fong, for instance, is invited to a gathering organised by the Lees, father, son Philip (based in Singapore) and son Robert (based in Hong Kong) will drop whatever they are doing and attend in unison. Lee Kuan Yew well understood the value of controlling Singapore's purse strings after independence, as well as its political ones.

Elsewhere in the region, the fight for access to capital played out differently. Instead of being hostage to a dominant third-party banking institution, as in Hong Kong, or a banking system under the thumb of a ruling dynasty, as in Singapore, leading tycoons prevailed on their political sponsors to let them run their own banks. This was a recipe for financial disaster, but one which governments none the less signed off on. Part of the reason was the very poor long-term performance of state banks, which always seemed to fall victim to corrupt manipulation. It was a curiosity that policy makers thought godfather banks might be better than widely owned private ones. Of course, the allocation of bank licences was the source of some of the fattest bribes in the region. The pace setter in bank mismanagement was the Philippines.

The studied abuse of the banking system by Filipino tycoons was first practised in the era of rule by the United States. The Americans, who were to some extent accidental colonists following their victory in the Spanish-American war of 1898, devolved considerable power to the local élite at the time of the First World War. From 1916, Filipinos controlled both houses of congress and directed much of the national administration, with limited oversight from an American governor-general. At the same time, the US set up the Philippine National Bank (PNB) as a well-capitalised state development bank to support modernisation; it held government deposits, issued notes and traded foreign exchange. Unfortunately, a combination of devolved political power, a weak bureaucracy unable to restrain businessmen-turned-politicians, and a large bank stuffed full of money proved to be a poor combination. From the outset, PNB's loan book grew on the basis of political favours extracted by powerful agricultural families. Directors of the bank, and their associates, were among the biggest borrowers. When local government deposits and foreign reserves held in New York ran out as a source of loans, PNB – as a quasi-central bank – was able to print money to fund further lending. By 1921, after only five years of devolution, local godfathers had not only reduced Philippine National Bank to insolvency, they had undermined the currency and left the central government on the edge of bankruptcy.

It was an impressive start by the tycoons and a harbinger of things to come after independence in 1946. In this era, the emphasis in the financial sector switched to the creation of new private banks, concurrent with legal constraints on the activities of foreign institutions. The number of private commercial banks increased from one in the late 1940s to thirty-three in 1965. Paul Hutchcroft, the leading academic specialist on the Philippine financial system, observes: 'Nearly every major family diversified into banking.'[20] Government, which became the plaything of the business oligarchy, supported the new banks with low requirements for capital, state deposits, central bank relending and guaranteed foreign exchange swaps. The families behind the banks, meanwhile, took the money in them and lent it to their own companies and those of their friends. As former central bank governor Gregorio Licaros told the *Far Eastern Economic Review* in 1978: 'The average Filipino banker is in banking not for banking profits; he uses his bank for allied businesses.'[21]

No one has ever been successfully prosecuted for illegal related-party lending in the Philippines and yet every bank crisis has involved it. The crises began in the mid 1960s and never stopped. A run on Republic Bank, the third-largest private institution, in 1964 set the tone. The politically well-connected bank's loan portfolio was able to grow fast because half its deposit base was made up of government money. Huge loans were extended with insufficient or no collateral, and about half of these went to members of the bank's board. When a run on the bank pushed it to the brink of insolvency, the central bank ordered a takeover by PNB. But Republic Bank's controlling shareholder, liquor and lumber tycoon Pablo R. Roman, had other ideas. He was elected to a seat in congress at the 1965 election, became chairman of the House Committee on Banks, Currency and Corporations, and sued the central bank for its treatment of Republic Bank. He won a series of cases on the basis that the central bank was 'arbitrary' in its behaviour, and he was restored as president of his bank in 1968. Similarly, the supreme court annulled the liquidation order of Overseas Bank of Manila, run by tycoon Emerito Ramos, after it was taken over by the central bank in 1967 because of massive insider lending and other regulatory infringements.

In the Marcos martial law era, the abuse of banks became worse. After promising to rid the country of 'an oligarchy that appropriated for itself all power and bounty',[22] he and his inner circle of godfathers obtained control of a dozen banks. Lucio Tan, the supreme Filipino godfather who has survived ever since, gained contol of Allied Bank out of the ashes of General Bank and Trust Co. (Genbank), which was stricken by runs in 1976 after it lent out much of its money to its principal shareholders. Tan, who often co-invested with Marcos, and associates 'bought' Genbank in a 1977 auction that was held with only three days' notice. In 1990, the Philippine Commission on Good Government alleged he paid a sum that was less than 1 per cent of Genbank's estimated value at the time.[23] Tan was then granted an entirely new bank licence and Genbank became Allied Bank, which went on to benefit from a stream of central bank loans and central bank guarantees of foreign borrowing; in two years it was the third-biggest bank in the country.

Tan had at least proven himself in business before, unlike most Marcos cronies. Roberto S. Benedicto, Marcos's classmate at the Philippines Law School, favourite golf partner and frequent business front, was first handed the chairmanship of the Philippine National Bank and later allowed to take over two private banks. He and his friends plundered them all; one of the institutions, Republic Planters' Bank, was able to fund half its lending with central bank funds.[24] Herminio Disini, who married Imelda Marcos's first cousin, was also given control of two banks; the money in them saw him expand from an office with one secretary and a messenger in 1969 to a 50-company conglomerate ranging from petrochemicals to nuclear power by the mid 1970s.[25]

Such antics caught up with the Philippines in the early 1980s, when the debt-laden regime defaulted on its foreign borrowings and several banks failed.[26] After the departure of Marcos in 1986, however, the government of Cory Aquino bailed out the banking system by issuing high-yielding government bonds and providing additional, cheap government deposits. The cost of this action became apparent in 1993 when the old central bank was closed down with a US$12-billion write-off to be born by the treasury, and hence taxpayers. The annual cost of servicing this debt in the mid 1990s was more than the Philippines' health budget.[27] Those tycoons who did not, like Benedicto and Disini, flee with Marcos, and survived the Philippine Commission on Good Government, found their banks revived with public money and able to enforce cartel pricing that in the late 1990s gave them the best banking margins in Asia. Despite all the trading and production cartels and monopolies sanctioned by Marcos and others in the Philippines, Paul Hutchcroft concludes that the banking sector has always been 'the country's most heavily fortified bastion of privilege and profits'.[28]

Bank Galaxy

Indonesia's variation on the theme of bank plunder stands out because of the sheer number of banks that were allowed to operate prior to the Asian financial crisis – no fewer than 240. By the mid 1990s every major business in the country, and many lesser ones, had a captive bank, leading to an orgy of related-party lending that teed up the financial system meltdown of 1997–8. Not only did regular godfathers have banks, Suharto's children had banks, Suharto's bribe-gathering foundations owned banks and different factions of the military had banks.

As with many bad ideas, Indonesia's galaxy of banks had its origins in a well-meaning effort to resolve a perennial problem. Like the Philippines and Malaysia, post-independence Indonesia had a long-running issue with state banks that were manipulated by godfathers and corrupt politicians to fund investment projects that did not merit loans. By the late 1980s, the proportion of loans in state banks on which interest or principal, or both, was not being repaid was around one-fifth, and the situation was set to deteriorate further in the 1990s.[29] The way forward, government technocrats decided, was to deregulate the financial system and introduce more private banks that would be profit-oriented. Unfortunately, deregulation was implemented without a strong regulatory framework and, more important, the rules that were written were frequently not enforced. The paid-in capital requirement for a new bank was set at just US$12 million. Most banks quickly recouped this investment and raised more capital by listing a minority interest on the Jakarta stock exchange. Between 1988 and the mid 1990s, around 120 new banks were opened. Instead of seeking to maximise returns for their shareholders, however, they became sources of cheap funds for the godfathers who controlled them. Limits on related-party lending were never enforced by the central bank, which also failed to regulate effectively borrowing from overseas. In the wake of the Asian financial crisis, investigators revealed extraordinary levels of exposure to sister companies among the banks of the major godfathers. At Liem Sioe Liong's Bank Central Asia, loans to affiliates were around 60 per cent,[30] versus a maximum legal threshold of 20 per cent. At another of the biggest private banks, Sjamsul Nursalim's Bank Dagang Negara Indonesia (BDNI), affiliates accounted for more than 90 per cent of lending. It was Nursalim's wife who, rather taken by I. M. Pei's Bank of China skyscraper in Hong Kong, asked the Chinese-American architect to build two of them, side by side, in Jakarta for BDNI. The first part of their superstructures can still be seen, a pair of concrete stubs sticking up like giant cigarette ends.

There was no shortage of clues as to where the Indonesian banking sector was headed in the 1990s. It took Edward, the eldest son of the country's second-richest tycoon, William Soeryadjaya, only three years to create one of the ten biggest banks in Indonesia, lend himself most of its money and blow it on projects around south-east Asia. The collapse of Bank Summa in early 1993, with liabilities of around US$700 million, should have served as a powerful warning.[31] Edward Soeryadjaya cost his family control of Indonesia's main automotive company, Astra, and dropped his father way down the tycoon rankings. But other godfathers bought up the Soeryadjaya assets, the central bank took another debt on to its books and life went on.[32] In 1994, one of the big seven state banks, Bapindo, collapsed under the weight of politically directed lending. In 1995 Bank Pacific, a mid-size private bank controlled by the family of former state oil chief Ibnu Sutowo, became insolvent after guaranteeing US$1 billion of high-yield offshore commercial paper, largely to fund investments by other family businesses. The central bank bailed Bank Pacific out, at the taxpayer's expense.

With the benefit of hindsight, it should have been no surprise when, in 1997, there was a systemic crisis in Indonesia's financial system. Greg Sirois, who ran a leasing business for Bank Summa before it went bust, says of the tycoon fraternity: 'Everyone had a bank or two and they were catapulted into a position they were not equipped to deal with.'[33] Kevin O'Rourke, a former Jakarta securities trader and author of a major work on the financial crisis, takes a longer view: 'By revealing the true state of Indonesia's banking system, the crisis triggered, in effect, a one-off reckoning for decades' worth of wrongdoing.'[34] As in the Philippines, however, godfathers with banks, especially large ones, were protected by the fact that the government dared not let them fail. As the crisis deepened in Indonesia from November 1997, the big tycoon bankers asked for and received central bank loans to cover demand for withdrawals. At least two-thirds of the loans went to the banks of four godfathers: Liem Sioe Liong, Sjamsul Nursalim, Mohamad 'Bob' Hasan and Usman Atmadjaya.[35] Auditors subsequently discovered that central bank loans totalling IDR45 trillion (then about US$14 billion) were around three times the value of bank withdrawals in the period when they were disbursed. The likely explanation is that the godfathers used much of the balance of the central bank credits to buy foreign exchange (helping drive the rupiah exchange rate down at the height of the crisis) in order to shift their wealth offshore, particularly to Singapore. There is no doubt the godfathers would rather that the crisis had never happened, but when it did their involvement in banking provided an insurance policy for their interests. When the dust settled, the Indonesian Bank Restructuring Agency (IBRA) was left trying to recoup the government and central bank's money by accepting tycoon assets whose value was often suspect. One of the most high-profile instances was when Nursalim handed over a vast shrimp farm and processing plant, which American investment bank Lehman Brothers valued at US$1.8 billion; two years later IBRA assessors wrote down its value to US$100 million. The total write-off by IBRA when it ended its efforts to clean up the financial crisis in 2004 was US$56 billion; the judiciary refused to accept almost all cases it put forward against debtors.

Where the Money Is

The line attributed to the famous American bank robber Willy Sutton – 'I rob banks because that's where the money is' – would not be an inaccurate job description for a good many Asian godfathers. The havoc that tycoons wrought through their abuse of private and public banks was accentuated by the region's unusually heavy dependence on bank finance. Before the financial crisis, bank lending accounted for between half and four-fifths of all financial assets in south-east Asian countries, compared with one-fifth in the United States. Lending in these countries in the decade before the crisis was fuelled by an average annual increase in domestic bank deposits of more than 20 per cent, as household savings rates increased. The metric was simple: ordinary people put their money in banks and godfathers took it out to finance their investments, driving a six-fold lending increase across Thailand, Malaysia, Indonesia and the Philippines between 1986 and 1996.

The financial system would have been much safer if it had been diversified across banks, equities, bonds, leasing and other instruments in a manner more similar to Europe and America. As will be seen below, equity markets in the region were expanding fast from the 1980s, but they were still relatively small and heavily manipulated by insiders. Bond markets were about one-tenth as important, in relative terms, as in developed countries. There are many reasons for this, but the simplest one is that it was just too easy for south-east Asia's economic aristocracy to get money out of banks. Everywhere in the world, commercial banks are problematic – Nobel Prize-winning economist Merton Miller dubbed banking 'a disaster-prone nineteenth-century technology'[36] – but in the context of south-east Asia, banks were a disaster guaranteed to happen.

Perhaps the most refined and gentlemanly exponent of bank plunder was the venerable Singapore-based godfather Khoo Teck Puat, who died in 2004. He was a typical tycoon in most respects, born into a wealthy family, the son of Khoo Yang Thin, an investor in several Singapore Hokkien banks that were merged into Oversea-Chinese Banking Corporation (OCBC) in 1933. He was constantly at pains to demonstrate his simple tastes – wearing cheap clothes and buying his lunch from market stalls – while he also kept a fleet of Rolls-Royces, Mercedes and BMWs. Khoo began working at OCBC and rose to the position of deputy general manager. However, he never had control of the business. In 1959 he left and started Kuala Lumpur-based Malayan Banking Corporation, which expanded extremely rapidly, opening a hundred branches across Malaysia and Singapore in only six years. A good portion of the funds were lent out for Khoo investments, particularly in real estate, including the beginning of his large hotel portfolio in Singapore. Rumours about the scale of Khoo's lending to himself, however, precipitated a run on the bank in 1966 and the Malaysian government forced him to give up control.

Khoo's next bank venture was in Brunei. He persuaded the then sultan, Omar Ali Saifuddien III (father of the current sultan), to let him establish the National Bank of Brunei in 1965. Various members of the royal family were involved as minority shareholders of the bank, which was the only one domiciled in the tiny state and subject to minimal prudential oversight. Khoo was soon making large loans to himself to expand his real estate holdings in Singapore, Australia and elsewhere. The arrangement endured for two decades until Sultan Omar died, in 1986, and his son hired American investigators to examine the National Bank's books. The loan exposure to Khoo companies was overwhelming and the new sultan shut the bank down. Khoo managed to avoid arrest, probably because he scrambled to sell assets and reached a settlement with the Brunei treasury. His son Khoo Ban Hock, who had been bank chairman, served two years in prison. The great irony of Khoo's bank adventures was that the same year that the National Bank of Brunei went down he invested US$300 million in Britain's Standard Chartered. That investment in a properly regulated bank was worth US$2.7 billion when Khoo died, his key asset. He also retained most of his Singapore property interests, including the Goodwood, York, Omni Marco Polo, Orchard Parade and Holiday Inn hotels.

And Then There Were Stock Markets

South-east Asia's high savings rates, most of which flowed into bank deposits, lent themselves to outsize banking systems, which invited godfather abuse. There is, in turn, a pretty direct line from the insider manipulation of regional banks to the Asian financial crisis. The 'over-banked' nature of south-east Asia also helps explain a conundrum that has occupied some of the region's equity investors: why, despite heady economic growth, have long-term stock market returns in south-east Asia been so poor? Since 1993, when a flood of foreign money increased capitalisation in regional markets by around 2.5 times in one calendar year,[37] dollar-denominated returns with dividends reinvested (what investors call 'total' returns) in every regional market have been lower than those in the mature markets of New York and London, and a fraction of those in other emerging markets in eastern Europe and Latin America.[38] Between the beginning of 1993 and the end of 2006, dollar returns in Thailand and the Philippines were actually negative; their stock markets destroyed capital. Returns in Malaysia and Indonesia were worse than leaving money in a high street bank account in an era of unusually low interest rates.[39] Singapore produced less than half the gain of London or New York. Only Hong Kong approached developed market returns, but managed half those in Latin America and one-third of those in eastern Europe. Stock market performance was better in the late 1980s, but this was of little consequence to most investors because south-east Asian exchanges were so small at the time that they had almost no asset allocation from international money managers. Even if one goes back to the end of 1987, when the most commonly used Morgan Stanley Capital International (MSCI) indices for Asian emerging markets were established, every south-east Asian bourse except Hong Kong has underperformed the equity markets of the United States and the United Kingdom.[40]

A part of the explanation for the disappointing returns in south-east Asia's stock markets is almost certainly the collateral impact of the region's super-abundance of savings that are kept in banks. This pushes down borrowers' cost of funds – particularly when the borrower controls the bank – and reduces general returns on capital. The whole of Asia suffers from the perverse curse of high savings rates and bloated banks, which have depressed stock market returns throughout the region. Long-term returns on equities have also been poor in developing north-east Asia, in Taiwan and South Korea,[41] but south-east Asia has been worse. There the impact of high private savings concentrated in banks combined with the weakest prudential supervision of banks to create minimal pressure on capital markets to offer decent returns. Looked at another way, why work hard to increase a company's stock price and pay dividends when all the capital you need is available at a real interest rate close to zero per cent from a bank whose board you control? It should be no surprise that the best stock market returns in south-east Asia come from Hong Kong which – even if Y. K. Pao and K. S. Li were critically beholden for their success to their relationships with a heavily protected Hongkong Bank – has much the most commercially driven banking system in the region. As mentioned above, no one stockholder was allowed to own more than 1 per cent of Hongkong Bank's equity, which probably explains why HSBC is the only global bank to have grown out of south-east Asia.

When reflecting on the region's high growth and low stock market returns it is also helpful to remember that here the universe of listed companies does not reflect the real economy. This is unusual. Japan, South Korea and Taiwan – not to mention London and New York – have branded, technology-developing export companies that are traded on their bourses alongside banks, insurance companies, retailers and the rest. But the export sector which propelled the economic lift-off in south-east Asia was dominated by multinational companies that do not have listings in their host countries; and nor do the global retailers that profited handsomely from the region's ability to cut manufacturing costs. Instead, south-east Asian markets are dominated by a few big players in services and construction – to wit, our godfathers. This is even the case in Hong Kong, which does at least boast a few globally competitive businesses (like HSBC). If ten mainland Chinese businesses are stripped out of Hong Kong's Hang Seng index, eight of the remaining twenty-four companies are tycoon real estate companies,[42] while four are tycoon-controlled utilities. Several other companies are godfather businesses – the family of K. S. Li alone controls five Hang Seng constituent stocks. In other words, buying equities in south-east Asia is fundamentally about buying into the godfather business model; it does not allow the investor to access the foreign trade and globalisation story that has driven the region's economies. This is another reason why south-east Asian stock markets are always likely to underperform expectations.

Finally, south-east Asia's godfathers have not been shy about expropriating minority shareholders. Stock markets provide an excellent stage for the talents of tycoons – complex financial engineering, opaque interplay between public and private companies and the potential to ramp and bludgeon individual stocks by the timely release of insider information. Ever since the first London brokers arrived in Hong Kong in the early 1970s, triggering the first great speculative bubble in the region, it has been clear that the combination of an ill-informed public, the godfathers and a supply of scrofulous foreigners is a bad one for the minority investor. The standard for a generation of regional stock market disappointment was set by that original Hong Kong bust. In 1973, the Hang Seng index was ramped up and up to a March peak of 1,775 points before freefalling to 150. Simon Murray, then a neophyte greedy expatriate manager working for Jardine, Matheson, recalls he was punting £60,000 in the market – most of it borrowed – at a time when his salary was £2,000. He went skiing as the market hit its peak. Out on the slopes one day he suddenly realised that a cryptic telex he had received – 'BS156' – referred to his Butterfield and Swire stock,[43] whose price had increased nine times. He crossed his skiis, he says, and wiped out, thinking of all the money. Unfortunately, the index dropped to 820 before he finished his holiday, and to 420 before his plane landed in Hong Kong. 'That was my last visit to the stock market for quite a long time,' he recalls.[44]

Sir William Purves who, unlike Michael Sandberg, is not the speculative type, remembers the era for the piles of initial public offering (IPO) prospectuses and related paperwork that impeded the normal functioning of the Hongkong Bank. 'It was shambolic,' he says. 'There was so much physical paper that people could not get into the bank on IPO days.' Purves attempted to hire Hong Kong island's Cathedral Hall as an IPO processing centre to keep the investor frenzy out of his bank, but the Anglican church refused to have Mammon in its building. Instead, he obtained the use of the St John Ambulance station up Hong Kong island's Garden Road 'in the hope the climb would put people off', which of course it did not.[45]

Behind the droll anecdotes, however, is the standard south-east Asian tale of godfather manipulation, ordinary folk losing their shirts and the shameless behaviour of *gweilo* running dogs. The defining characteristic of the 1973 bust was that, in the words of Purves, 'The boom was pushed along to a great extent by London brokers.'[46] Post-crash, the prices of many well-known stocks that listed in early 1973 – such as Cheung Kong and New World – dropped to a tenth or less of their IPO levels. First and foremost among the London brokers was Vickers da Costa. It is surely telling that three of the senior executives at the London house that led market making activities in Hong Kong at the time would subsequently end up on the wrong side of trading-related court cases. Philip Tose – 'Tosey' to his public schoolboy followers – was eventually banned from Hong Kong directorships for his part in the downfall of Peregrine (which in many respects was a 1990s reincarnation of Vickers da Costa, employing many of its former personnel). The second person was Ewan Launder, a Vickers director who went on to be managing director of HSBC's investment bank, Wardley, which began its life as a joint venture with Vickers with Michael Sandberg responsible for setting it up and for approving senior management. Ewan Launder fled Hong Kong when it became clear he would be prosecuted for receiving large payments from Sandberg's friend George Tan, after the collapse of his Carrian group in 1983; Launder spent a decade on the run before being arrested in Britain. He was eventually found guilty of accepting HK$4.5 million in return for granting Tan loans and sentenced to five years in prison, only to get off on appeal; Hong Kong's Court of Final Appeal cited grammatical errors in the charges that had been laid. The third person, Geoffrey Collier, was one of Philip Tose's original research analysts at Vickers in Hong Kong, who rose quickly through the ranks and went on to work for Morgan Grenfell in London, as joint global head of equities. That was a mistake. Under a more rigorous UK judiciary, Collier became the first person in Britain to be convicted of the newly criminalised offence of insider trading, in 1987.[47] He made the insider trades for which he was convicted through old friends at Vickers. The school for scandal theme at Vickers did not end there. In the course of the 1990s, several more directors from the 1980s were censured or convicted for insider dealing and other offences.[48] The obvious point is that before we deconstruct the godfathers' listed businesses to see how they have shafted the minority investor, it is important to bear in mind that the foreign broking and investment banking communities have frequently been hewn from the same moral block.

Welcome to the Web

The basic mechanism for the expropriation of minority shareholders in southeast Asia is the conglomerate web, through which a godfather exercises enormous but opaque power over myriad different companies. Regular businesses – a General Electric, a Tesco, even an HSBC – have a single listed vehicle. But a godfather business has fifteen or even twenty listed vehicles that can be readily identified, with minority positions in many other listed firms that are harder to spot. As a typical example, Quek Leng Chan, Kuala Lumpur-based billionaire nephew of the late Kwek Hong Png and cousin of the Singapore-based billionaire Kwek Leng Beng,[49] has nineteen clearly identifiable listed subsidiaries. These are engaged in activities ranging from banking to air-conditioner manufacturing to real estate. Quek is then also present as a small but significant investor in other listed vehicles where his ownership is harder to detect and, separately, owns scores – probably hundreds – of private companies. It is the interplay between these declared public subsidiaries, untrumpeted listed companies in which the godfather has an interest, and private companies – which in most Asian jurisdictions file no public records[50] – that defines much tycoon activity. Another multi-billionaire godfather, who reckons to control somewhere between 300 and 400 companies – including about a score that are acknowledged public subsidiaries – observes: 'We sometimes set up fifteen companies in a month.'[51]

After the Asian financial crisis, the World Bank commissioned a group of economists and researchers at the Chinese University of Hong Kong to review ownership data on more than 2,500 Asian public companies – spanning Japan and South Korea as well as south-east Asia (but not China) – in order to better understand the region's corporate webs.[52] The results, if they are to be believed, are stunning. The researchers concluded that the eight largest conglomerates in the region exercise effective control over a quarter of all listed companies, while the top twenty-two conglomerates control one-third of listed vehicles. The identity of the top eight conglomerates was not made public at the time, but can be revealed here: six of the eight were big Japanese industrial conglomerates (or *keiretsu*) – as would be expected given Japan's industrial cross-holding tradition – and two were south-east Asian. These last two were the groups of Li Ka-shing and Malaysia's Sime Darby, the latter connected with several powerful overseas Chinese families, as well as the Malaysian government.[53] Each of the eight groups was determined by researchers to have more than twenty affiliate listed companies at the level of 10-20 per cent ownership, in addition to their more transparent public subsidiaries.[54] The main aim of the researchers was to analyse the structure of the relationships in the conglomerate webs in order to understand how they work. What they discovered, again and again, is that control is exercised through pyramid arrangements that deliver levels of control disproportionate to equity ownership. For example, a company at the apex of a conglomerate pyramid (there may be several different pyramids within the overall corporate web) might own 50 per cent of listed company X, which in turn owns 40 per cent of listed company Y, which in turn owns 30 per cent of listed company Z. As a result, the conglomerate has 6 per cent ownership rights in company Z, but it still has 30 per cent voting rights – enough to call the shots. The researchers used analysis of dividend payouts, which have to be given to all investors equally, to prove that minority investors are systematically expropriated at the bottom of pyramids. This usually occurs at a level of 10-20 per cent ownership where a conglomerate's stockholding is not widely noted but where it can still exercise control. The principals of the research project wrote a seminal paper for the *American Economic Review* in which their assertions were, by academic standards, bold: 'We document,' they stated, 'that the problems of East Asian corporate governance are, if anything, more severe and intractable than suggested by commentators at the height of the financial crisis.' The authors concluded: 'The concentration of expropriation within a few groups large enough to manipulate a nation's political system means that the critical issue is the political will to enforce laws and regulations on the books.'[55]

This last point is critical. A detailed review of what goes on within the big conglomerates reveals that, historically, a failure by politicians to enforce regulatory norms has been at least as important as a shortage of laws in allowing godfathers to get away with their behaviour. In a country like Malaysia, where exemptions from stock market rules are granted without media comment and information about untendered privatisations is subject to official secrecy laws, this is hardly surprising. But the observation also applies in a market like Hong Kong's. Ever since he hooked up with the Hongkong Bank in 1979 and became part of the economic establishment, the career of Li Ka-shing, the paragon of godfathers, has been one long series of often inexplicable exemptions from stock market rules. When Hutchison took over Hongkong Electric in 1985, Li was exempted from a general offer despite exceeding the 35 per cent ownership trigger. When Hutchison increased its stake in another Li web company, Cavendish, from 23 per cent to 52 per cent in 1987, he was exempted from a general offer. Similar exemptions were granted in the same year when Li increased his personal stake in Cheung Kong above 35 per cent and Cheung Kong increased its stake in Hutchison above 35 per cent; in these instances Hong Kong's financial secretary contradicted and overruled the stock exchange's takeover committee. In the 1990s, Li caused jaws to drop when he secured a series of extraordinary exemptions for his internet subsidiary, Tom.com, allowing it to issue new shares within six months of its IPO, to give staff options up to 50 per cent of the value of the firm's capital base (10 per cent is the rule), and to allow major shareholders to sell down their stakes after six months rather than the statutory two years. The Tom.com experience turned Li's reputed paramour, Solina Chau Hoi-shuen, into an overnight US dollar billionaire – at least on paper.[56] The bigger point is that stock market regulations appear not to apply to major godfathers, even in Hong Kong.

The indulgence shown to Li Ka-shing's listed companies over the years draws attention to some of his key working relationships. The link to Hong-kong Bank, whose chairman in the colonial era was always said to be more powerful than the governor, has been established. Almost as important has been the link with Charles Lee Yeh-kwong, one of the principals of the law firm Woo, Kwan, Lee & Lo,[57] who is both K. S. Li's lawyer and key adviser. As well as legal work on investment deals, Woo, Kwan, Lee & Lo does much of the conveyancing for the property arms of Cheung Kong and Hutchison. 'Imagine 2 per cent of all that,' drools a senior K. S. Li executive.[58] At the same time Charles Lee, who bears a passing resemblance to Toad of Toad Hall, was chairman of Hong Kong Exchanges and Clearing Limited, which runs the Hong Kong stock and futures markets, in 1992–4 and 2004–6; he is still an Executive Councilor. Another long-time K. S. Li associate, contractor and Li company director, the former real estate and construction functional constituency legislator[59] turned Executive Councilor Ronald Arculli, took over as chairman of the exchanges in April 2006. That same year, he was made chairman of the Hong Kong government's focus group for financial services reform, whose theoretical aim is to improve markets' functioning in the interests of general investors. Elsewhere, these palpable conflicts of interest would cause a political storm; in Hong Kong they barely register.

Don't Rock the Boat

The political cover given to godfathers around the region is both proactive and reactive. The first kind occurs when deals and favours are given to the tycoons. But the second kind, when politicians step in to defend the nexus between the political and economic élites that has existed for generations, may be just as important. Again, it also applies in Hong Kong.

A classic example occurred in 1987 when a young, brash Robert Ng, son of Singapore billionaire Ng Teng Fong, was speculating wildly in the Hong Kong futures market just as the market crashed in October that year. He had 12,000 long futures contracts, leaving him with a paper liability of just over HK$1 billion. Robert was punting the market through two Panamanian-registered companies and initially sought to deny responsibility for the debts on the basis of limited liability. Hong Kong's Commercial Crime Bureau (CCB), however, found *prima facie* evidence that there was collusion between Ng and one of the firms broking the futures contracts, which allowed him to avoid paying in margin as the market declined. This would be illegal.

The CCB unearthed a high-quality informant and armed itself with warrants to search more than twenty addresses. Senior officers were convinced that, for the first time, they were about to nail a major godfather. It never happened. At a series of meetings of minister-level government officials, culminating in an encounter at the governor's country residence at Fanling, it was decided that taking on Robert Ng posed a risk to the stability of the overall market; why this should be was never explained, publicly or privately.[60] The police were devastated. One of the senior officers recalls: '[Chief of staff of the CCB] Russ Mason came back and said: "That's it boys. Not in the public interest."'[61] Instead of an investigation, Robert Ng was cut a deal that allowed him to repay around 60 per cent of what he owed over eight years (equivalent to an immediate repayment of about half). The rest of the tab was picked up by foreign brokerages, which were strong-armed into making contributions by the Hong Kong government, and local taxpayers.

Interestingly, the person the police were allowed to pursue was Ronald Li, who was running the stock exchange at the time of the 1987 crash. Li made his fortune by requiring personal allocations of stock when approving IPOs and ran the exchange as a personal fiefdom. But it was his decision to shut the bourse down for a week in 1987, which caused great damage to Hong Kong's international reputation in money markets as well as undermining futures contracts, that saw the colonial power turn on him. Li was tried over share allocations in the listings of Cathay Pacific Airways and Novel Enterprises – even though it meant pointing up in public the collusion of Hongkong Bank subsidiary Wardley in the share allocations – and was sentenced to four years in jail. He was made a rare example. The policeman quoted above observes: '[Former New York Attorney General] Eliot Spitzer[62] would have a field day here. They'd all be going to jail. One after the other.'

Thankfully for the godfathers, south-east Asia is not New York and brazen treatment of minority investors and the general public passes for regular business. It was notable when Tung Chee-hwa became Hong Kong's first post-colonial chief executive that his own history of shocking corporate governance elicited barely a murmur. The media was interested in the fact that Henry Fok had engineered a bail-out of Tung's main company in the 1980s because it provided circumstantial evidence that Tung was beholden to Beijing, whose state banks provided most of the financing. But the deeper story was that Tung, the less gifted son of the late billionaire shipping tycoon C. Y. Tung, was in trouble in the first place because he engaged in exactly the same abuse of listed companies that other godfathers go in for. In the early 1980s, after Tung Chee-hwa took over the family empire, he authorised and maintained hundreds of millions of US dollars of loans from his main listed vehicle, Orient Overseas (Holdings) Ltd (OOHL), to what he called the Tung Private Group, a euphemism for more than 200 private companies he controlled. These loans, which no sane minority investor in OOHL would have wanted to make, were frittered away and otherwise blown on bad investments whose returns – had their been any – would have accrued to the Tung family alone. When OOHL was restructured in late 1986, the public company wrote off US$156 million of the loans it had made to the Tungs' private businesses. The crop-haired godfather sent a personal note to investors on 10 November that read: 'In the course of 1985 the OOHL Group's financial position seriously worsened prin-cipally as a consequence of the rapid deterioration in the financial position of the Tung Private Group, with which the OOHL Group is closely associated and from whom substantial amounts were owing.' Needless to say, there was no apology for the misuse of shareholder funds.[63]

The Art of the Kill

Tung-the-son is in fact not clever enough to skewer and execute minority investors with true godfather aplomb – as if they were bulls to ritual slaugh-ter in a Spanish ring. The real matadors can abuse other investors in a public company a hundred ways before they even notice and then, with a poker face, proceed to the perfect *denouement* – an offer to take a lacerated public business back into private hands for a fraction of the value of its assets. When the game is played properly there are no bail-outs or embarrassing, forced restructurings. It is an art form in which the godfather is always in charge. Robert Kuok, whose listed businesses have a long track record of underper-forming the broad indices of the markets in which they are traded, is a master. For many years he had a Singapore-listed dry bulk shipping company called Pacific Carriers Ltd (PCL), whose price and dividend performance were so appalling that the counter became known to traders as Please Cut Losses.[64] In 2001 Kuok took PCL private at a hefty discount to its net asset value (NAV – or the book value of the company's assets). Hardly had the wounds of minority investors in the Singapore market healed when the tycoon announced, in October 2003, that he was launching an IPO of a PCL subsidiary, Malaysian Bulk Carriers (MBC), up the road on the Kuala Lumpur exchange. Kuok had already sold 30 per cent of MBC to the Malaysian government at a healthy price and his local investment bank, run by the deputy premier's brother[65], ensured the IPO was an aggressively valued success. Kuok then sought to relieve long-suffering investors in his Hong Kong property arm, Kerry Properties, with an April 2003 privatisation offer at a discount of 53 per cent to net asset value. He bawled out his chief financial officer when minority investors failed to bite. In recent years Lee Shau-kee has attempted three privatisations at discounts of around 40 per cent to NAV; Y. K. Pao's son-in-law Peter Woo made an offer for a listed retail subsidiary that one analyst estimated to be a 100 per cent discount to NAV – and, after a modest increase in the offer, succeeded; Cheng Yu-tung sought to buy back his New World TMT for a few cents on the dollar; and K. S. Li's son Richard made a brilliantly devious attempt to privatise his Sunday mobile phone business on the cheap.[66] As Peter Churchouse, former managing director of Morgan Stanley in Asia, says of these businessmen: 'They make investment bankers look like school boys.'[67]

Of course, a listed business has to be weakened before it can be bought back cheap. Peter Woo's Lane Crawford department store, held in his listed vehicle pyramid through apex company Wheelock, posted US$72 million in losses in the five years prior to its 1999 privatisation; the firm did not even deliver earnings in the boom that surrounded Hong Kong's 1997 reversion to Chinese rule, allowing it to be bought back for no more than the value of its own stock portfolio and real estate. The Wheelock web of companies, in fact, was used as a case study of investor-unfriendly practices by the World Bank-funded researchers at the Chinese University of Hong Kong (CUHK). They showed how smaller businesses at the base of Wheelock's ownership pyramid are used to provide cash to their corporate owners and to take on disproportionate risk in joint investment projects.

A quintessential example of a south-east Asian listed company project occurred in 1997 when Wheelock, its first-tier listed subsidiary Wharf, two second-tier listed subsidiaries, New Asia and Harbour Centre, and a third-tier subsidiary, Realty Development, each took a 20 per cent interest in a real estate development above a public rail station called MTRC Kowloon Station Package Two. The researchers showed how funding for the project came from Wheelock's subsidiaries and that in many cases the loans were interest-free. Wheelock itself was the only net borrower in the inter-company joint venture; with cheap financing and minimal risk but an equal share in any upside, the company closest to Peter Woo could hardly lose. In 1999, the three least-owned subsidiaries in the Wheelock pyramid were lending the equivalent of between 60 per cent and 160 per cent of their market capitalisations to the joint venture project. The CUHK professor of finance Larry Lang described them as 'automated teller machines' controlled by Wheelock. At the same time, because the real estate development was a joint venture, it was not subject to normal reporting requirements. Hong Kong listing rules apply only to listed companies and their subsidiaries; everything else – which is a lot – is off the radar screen. It should come as no surprise that the stock market performance of New Asia, Harbour Centre and Realty Development has been lousy. In February 2003 Peter Woo privatised Realty Development back into New Asia at an unusually generous 19 per cent discount to NAV.

The listed company joint venture scam is an old Asian favourite, particularly in Hong Kong. The reason that K. S. Li's Cheung Kong mothership owns 49.9 per cent of Hutchison and not more is that this means joint ventures between the two businesses, which are many and large, are not subject to regular reporting requirements. Management contracts, supply deals and other asset trades do not face transparent scrutiny. The true debt, asset and liability positions of joint ventures cannot be reviewed by outsiders. A vast K. S. Li project that demonstrated this occurred in the early 1990s when Hutchison subsidiary Hongkong Electric vacated its old power station and oil depot at Ap Lei Chau, on the south side of Hong Kong island. The best way for Hongkong Electric to maximise the value of its vast site, connected by a bridge to a prime residential area, would have been to tender it for development among different property developers. Instead, Hongkong Electric was pulled into the inevitable joint venture with Cheung Kong and Hutchison. Together they put up thirty-four towers and two shopping malls without ever having to provide Hongkong Electric shareholders with detailed accounts of the project's costs and management. One can only guess what average returns in the Hong Kong stock market – which have been far better than elsewhere in south-east Asia – would have been if minority shareholder interests were treated on a par with those of the tycoons.

This does not happen, and what investors see again and again is that really good deals go to godfathers' private companies, while outsiders are left with the rest. Or as Li Ka-shing's former manager Simon Murray puts it: 'Would anybody put crap in their own company when they can sell it to the public?'[68] The difference is captured by the unbelievable rubbish – senseless new media projects, infrastructure dog-ends, mainland China mistakes – to be found in the listed businesses of New World group's Cheng Yu-tung versus the cash-generating beasts he owns privately. The best known of the latter is his long-time interest in Stanley Ho and Henry Fok's Macau gambling franchise. A typical recent addition came in 2001 when Cheng and tycoon pals the Lau brothers saw an opportunity to acquire Japanese department store Sogo's Hong Kong operation. It was a good business with a great location, but carried a lot of debt and was mired in Hong Kong's worst retail recession in a decade. Cheng and the Laus used their private companies to buy Sogo, pay off part of its debts and secure cheaper bank funding. At the time of acquisition, the rental yield on the Sogo building was already a healthy 9-10 per cent, but Cheng's and the Laus' listed businesses did not get a sniff of the deal. The new owners undertook some ruthless cost cutting and then, as the mainland Chinese economy heated up in 2003, announced a second Sogo project above the new subway on Shanghai's key retail thoroughfare, Nanjing Road. In April 2004, the Sogo stores were listed in a Hong Kong initial public offering and Chow Tai Fook, the private Cook islands-registered company that Cheng Yu-tung inherited from his wife's family, booked an enormous profit. At that point shares in Cheng's listed flagship, New World Development, were worth less than they were in 1986. The late Gary Coull, co-founder of Credit Lyonnais Securities Asia (CLSA), was close to Cheng, helped him list companies and served on the board of New World Infrastructure and New World TMT.[69] In the end the stockbroker admitted: 'He [Cheng] made a lot more money in private companies … Investors who have invested in New World at the macro level have been pummelled.'[70]

Since the first significant foreign money arrived in south-east Asia's capital markets in 1993, that has been a pretty good rule of thumb for investments in godfather businesses. Once again, however, it must be stressed that this is not a racial point about investing in ethnic Chinese tycoons. The point transcends race. When Sri Lankan Tamil Ananda Krishnan bought the valuable Chinese movie back catalogue of Celestial Films, he did exactly what Robert Kuok would have done. He purchased it with a private company and then sold it at what one of his investment bankers calls 'a fat profit' to his listed media business, Astro.[71] If one seeks the worst record of corporate governance in the region over the past thirty years, a serious contender has to be Jardine, Matheson, the original white godfather business. On a fully adjusted basis, shares in Jardine Matheson Holdings (JMH), the apex company in the group, were worth more in 1973 than they were in 2003. The Keswick family, who claim to be descended from William Jardine's niece, have treated minority investors in a manner that would make many godfathers blush. In the mid 1980s they created a corporate cross-holding structure within their listed company web that allows the family to run the group despite owning less than 7 per cent of JMH. At the same time they were pioneers in buying back stock on the cheap from subsidiaries they had run into the ground. The cross-holdings themselves were made possible by reincorporation and relisting in Bermuda, where the government of the British-controlled tax haven was prevailed on to write takeover laws that applied only to five Jardine companies and which help the Keswicks hold on to their inheritance. None of this, of course, did anything for minority investors, who may be forgiven when they refer to Jardine's Hong Kong headquarters, with its distinctive little round windows, as the Tower of a Thousand Arseholes.[72]

Bank, Banks, then Markets

In the aggregate, despite the pyrotechnics of the capital markets, south-east Asia's banks have been much more important to the godfathers' access to capital story. With such a high proportion of the region's savings mediated by banking systems, this is macroeconomic inevitability. The relationships between Hongkong Bank and Y. K. Pao and K. S. Li, Bangkok Bank and a who's who of Thai, Malaysian and Indonesian godfathers, Filipino and Indonesian banks and the kleptocrat tycoons that those island chains have spawned, and so on, are the underlying plot. As a rule of thumb, the greater the control that godfathers have exercised over banks, the greater has been the collateral damage they have inflicted on their fellow citizens. Widely held Hongkong Bank, for all that can be said against its long-term quasi-monopoly position, has never come close to a crisis; it is also one of the few listed businesses in south-east Asia to have given stockholders the kind of long-term returns that textbooks suggest they should expect in emerging economies. The systematic plunder of banks in the Philippines and Indonesia, on the other hand, has not only fleeced minority investors, it has crippled entire economies.

Stock markets came later than banks, and played a lesser role. Despite popular perceptions to the contrary, less than 15 per cent of adults in most south-east Asian territories own shares directly, even today; the proportion in Hong Kong, the leading share owning society, is 28 per cent.[73] None the less, the rather shocking returns in south-east Asian markets since the early 1990s – blame excess savings if you are a macroeconomist, blame the godfathers if you think individuals determine life's outcomes – do have a secondary impact. This is because Asia, and particularly south-east Asia, are the global capitals of forced public saving. Malaysia, Singapore and the Philippines have mandatory provident funds that date from the colonial era[74]. Indonesia started a mandatory pension fund for company employees in the 1970s, and Hong Kong added its Mandatory Provident Fund in December 2000. Thailand plans such a fund. As more forced Asian saving is directed into regional stock markets it will, unless the trend of low long-term returns changes, make ordinary people more exposed to the markets' poor performance.

This subject, however, is a tricky one to assess for two reasons. The first is that south-east Asians are already habituated to poor returns on forced savings. By the calculations of one academic, in Singapore in the period 1987–97, when the Central Provident Fund was overwhelmingly invested in government bonds, the annual return was close to zero.[75] The second issue is that south-east Asian governments are so secretive about what happens to forced savings that it is impossible to identify any trends with certainty. Singapore's Government Investment Corporation (GIC), which is one of the ultimate investors of Central Provident Fund balances, only revealed the composition of its board of directors in 2001. Harry Lee Kuan Yew, who chairs the board, claimed in 2006 that the average annual real return over twenty-five years at the GIC had been a healthy 5.3 per cent. Other information revealed at the time suggests the gains are a function of the fact that the GIC invested three-quarters of its money in the United States, Europe and Japan; Singaporeans must hope this asset allocation is maintained.[76] Both the International Monetary Fund and credit rating agencies like Standard & Poor's continue to criticise Singapore's unwillingness to provide detailed information on its management of public money. In Malaysia, the allocation and management of forced savings is still more of a black box, with critics alleging that short-term payouts from the Employees Provident Fund (EPF) have only been maintained by raiding its capital base and using transfers from other public sources, such as the Malaysian government's investment vehicle, Permodalan Nasional Berhad. The only sure thing is that, as elsewhere in the region, there is no reliable set of accounts available to the public.

Part III
Godfathers Today:
Defending the precious

6

The 1990s:
Ecstasy and reckoning

'The good thing about Confucianism is it makes Asian people willing to suffer pain …'

Hong Kong tycoon Ronnie Chan, *FinanceAsia* magazine (2002)

The decade of the 1990s – as in 'Remember the nineties' or 'What if it turns out like the nineties?' – is already historical shorthand in Asia for what can go wrong in developing economies. But to fully understand what happened, we must return briefly to the 1980s. Moreover, we must leave our friends the godfathers alone for a moment and consider what was happening in the aggregate, or macro, economy. For it remains the contention of this book that the godfathers are a symptom of south-east Asia's condition as much as they are a cause. Speak it in a whisper, but reality is more than the sum of the tycoons.

The macro story that led up to the Asian financial crisis was defined by four powerful and mutually reinforcing trends. The first of these was that by the 1980s governments of the 'proper' countries we are following emulated the examples of Singapore and Hong Kong and settled, in terms of their external economies, on a policy that delivered incontrovertible benefits. Export-oriented industrialisation (EOI) replaced import-substitution industrialisation (ISI) – which became mired in a bog of godfather arbitrage and corruption – as the prevailing orthodoxy. This coincided with the first major birth pangs of the contemporary globalisation era. By the 1980s there was no shortage of multinational companies looking to gain by relocating basic manufacturing operations to developing countries. Just when political south-east Asia was ready to rent out its cheap labour, so Western big capital was keen to lease it. Global foreign direct investment flows began to pick up significantly in the 1980s and by the mid 1990s, one year of worldwide cross-border investment was worth what had previously occurred in a decade. The knock-on effect was starkly evident in the expansion of south-east Asian exports. In the twenty-six years from 1960 to 1985, exports from Thailand, Malaysia, the Philippines and Indonesia rose an average 10–15 per cent a year. These were healthy gains, driven heavily by a commodities boom in the 1970s.[1] None the less, the increments came from low bases. When processed manufacturing exports kicked in from the mid 1980s – off a more substantial foundation – growth rates increased considerably. In the decade from 1986 to 1995, average export growth in Thailand, Malaysia and the Philippines increased by between 4 and 10 percentage points per year.[2] Over a decade, this uptick had a big impact. Thailand's exports jumped from US$9 billion in 1986 to US$57 billion in 1995.

The boom in labour-intensive manufacturing that filled up huge factory parks in the suburbs of capital cities and other specialist export centres like Penang coincided with a second force for accelerated growth: demographics. South-east Asian population growth peaked in the immediate post-Second World War decades, and by the 1980s hoardes of young people were looking for cash-based employment. Fertility rates remained high while infant mortality rates fell in each of Thailand, Malaysia, the Philippines and Indonesia in the 1950–80 period, and populations more than doubled in thirty years. Human capital is an economic input whose increase drives growth like any other.[3] Multinational business found itself in a halcyon era where labour had relatively low bargaining power (there was too much of it) and productivity increases comfortably outstripped wage hikes.[4]

The third trend was rising savings rates. Greatly increased numbers of people entered the labour force and earned wages – rather than working for little or no cash in agriculture – and they saved an increasing proportion of their income. Governments, which rarely ran budget deficits, saved, too. The result was that domestic savings as a proportion of GDP pushed up to between 30 per cent in Hong Kong or Indonesia, and more than 45 per cent in Singapore. In the mid 1960s, the savings rate in south-east Asia was on par with that in Latin America; by the early 1990s, it was around 20 percentage points higher. Here was the money that filled state and godfather banks to bursting point. From a macroeconomist's perspective, however, a deep pool of savings is a wholly good thing for a developing economy because it makes possible a high level of investment, and hence the infrastructure and productive capacity that are necessary to long-term growth. Investment is essential to early-stage economic development, the only caveat being that the expenditure needs to be, in the aggregate, productive and not a destroyer of capital.

In the mid 1990s, domestic savings were also supplemented by large inflows of foreign money as a source of investment. Later, in the post-mortem of the financial crisis, there would be a heated – and often low-quality – debate among politicians and economists about the degree to which this short-term foreign capital contributed to the meltdown.

Finally, in the pre-crisis era, south-east Asia seemed to be enjoying a form of psychological advantage that can be observed in fast-growing emerging economies in their early stages. The phenomenon might be described as the 'developmental honeymoon'. What happens in this period is that populations are unusually willing to trust authority and their leaders' promises to deliver continuous improvements in standards of living. When south-east Asians were told that free association of labour was antithetical to growth – a curiosity given unionisation's failure to prevent the emergence of the United States, Europe, Japan and South Korea – and that constraints on individual freedom and the media are part of Asian culture, they acquiesced. People went to their jobs and, in general, worked extraordinarily hard, believing it was a matter of only two or three more decades before their countries would emerge as developed nations in which everyone would enjoy a share in the spoils. Many people focused on their children's futures. With the average GDP growth rates from 1986 to 1995 picking up to 8-10 per cent a year in Malaysia, Thailand and Indonesia, versus 6-8 per cent in the period after 1960, they trusted politicians and waited for the bourgeois nirvana that would release them from the shackles of economic need.

Both Feet Off the Ground

Macro forces provided the context for a period of increasing, and ultimately monumental, delusion. The boom in foreign-invested exporting contributed to growth and provided lots of employment, but it did not change south-east Asia's inability to create globally competitive companies. The demographic spike drove growth, but it also clouded the fact that this growth came from increased inputs of labour as well as from productivity gains. The rising savings rate translated into more investment, but that investment was mostly mediated by state- and tycoon-owned banks that were not run on commercial lines. In the mid 1990s, stock markets fell precipitously from the peaks they hit in late 1993 and early 1994 as corporate earnings failed to keep up with investor expectations, but the banks just kept on lending. The meek deference of south-east Asian populations, meanwhile, both increased the region's reputation for industrious stability and stoked the narcissistic hubris of their leaders.

A fantasy world began to take shape, in which everyone believed in their version of the fantasy. Mahathir Mohamad, the Malaysian premier, spent more and more time refining a vision of how his country would achieve developed status within a quarter century; he called it 'Vision 2020'. Mahathir approved projects for vast dams, new airports and rail links. In 1995, he decided to move the federal administrative capital to a new site in the jungle, and connect it to Kuala Lumpur with a Multimedia Super Corridor dedicated to high technology;[5] much of the money for the infrastructure came from oil and gas revenues. The diminutive doctor moved into a vast new prime minister's palace with commanding views; he kept a close eye on surrounding construction sites and telephoned project managers daily demanding to know what was going on.[6] Mahathir's closest tycoon friend, Ananda Krishnan, began construction of his Petronas Twin Towers in the centre of Kuala Lumpur, which would be the tallest in the world when completed at the onset of the financial crisis.

In neighbouring Singapore, Harry Lee Kuan Yew was ever more vociferous about his 'Asian values' and Chinese racial theories of what was driving growth. He lectured the post-Marcos leaders of the Philippines, Corazon Aquino and Fidel Ramos, on the need for discipline before democracy in their society, apparently dismissing the possibility that the country's laggard performance in the 1990s might be related to the debt load from the highly disciplined, undemocratic kleptocracy run by Ferdinand Marcos until 1986. Aquino, herself one-quarter Chinese, labelled Harry 'an arrogant bastard' after an encounter with him.[7] The British queen's equestrian-obsessed daughter Princess Anne was made to listen to Lee's genetic theories before observing pointedly: 'It doesn't work with horses.'[8] With his neo-Confucian city state posting double-digit growth in 1993 and 1994, few people dared argue with Harry Lee.

In Indonesia, despite the 1996 death of his beloved wife and confidante, Madame Tien,[9] Suharto concluded that only he could be trusted to run a country growing at 8 per cent a year. At the age of 76, he would in 1998 seek a seventh five-year term as president, taking as his vice president Jusuf Habibie, a widely ridiculed minister who was spending billions of dollars trying to create an aircraft manufacturing industry in what was still a third world country.

In Thailand, the sense of excess and unreality were if anything more palpable. In May 1992, around fifty people had lost their lives in demonstrations that reversed a 1991 military coup. But within a couple of years it was not just business and politics as normal, it was surreally 'normal'. With the economy

growing at over 9 per cent, Banharn Silpa-archa, known for his political largesse as 'the walking ATM', won a 1995 election with a vow to cover the
country in six-lane highways. A year later former commander-in-chief Chavalit
Yongchaiyudh withdrew his support for Banharn, spent an estimated US$800
million on an election, and grabbed the top job for himself.[10]

Even in Hong Kong there was a tendency to assume that the good times
were built on rock-solid foundations. Chris Patten, despatched from London
with a mandate to exit the colony in 1997 in unusually principled fashion,
built his political strategy entirely around an expansion of the electoral franchise. With the exception of the deregulation of the British-operated telecommunications monopoly, there was no substantive move to address the
cartels filling local tycoons' pockets. A series of well-meaning but toothless
competition reports by the Hong Kong Consumer Council merely set the
trend for years of idle discussion about what to do with a self-evidently anti-
competitive domestic economy.[11]

Should Have Known Better?

Of course, politicians are always saying silly things and the behaviour of south-
east Asia's more self-aggrandising leaders in the 1990s was regarded by most
folk as somewhere between eccentric and tedious. What is really important
is what hard economic evidence there was – anecdotal and analytical – in the
period that a financial crisis was brewing. As a corollary to this, there is also
the question of how well the International Monetary Fund and the World
Bank performed their tasks of surveillance and advice. At an anecdotal level,
there were three patterns to be discerned in the mid 1990s. The first was that
greed, corruption and excess were spiralling out of control. The second was
that asset trading was replacing productive business as the core activity of
many corporations. And the third was that some financial institutions were
already beginning to crack under the strain.

A good example of where greed was leading was the affair of the phantom
Busang gold mine in Indonesia. It began in 1996, when a Canadian company
announced it had made a massive gold find in Borneo. It was also the year
that Suharto's wife, Madame Tien died. She was the one person who could
keep Suharto's kleptocratic children in check. What followed the Busang
announcement was a shocking public free-for-all as eldest son Sigit Harjoju-
danto and eldest daughter Siti Hardijanti Rukmana (known as Tutut) squared
off with rival international mining consortia to demand Suharto give them the
mining rights. Suharto, at a loss as to what to do, called in his godfather golf
partner, 'Uncle' Bob Hasan, to mediate between the siblings; Bob cut a deal

giving companies controlled by him and different members of the first family a 30 per cent stake in the prospective mine, with the details to be fought out in private. All this was reported in the international media, and the Suhartos had never looked so brazen or so greedy. The show ended in 1997 when it transpired that the original gold samples were fakes, there were no deposits and events had been driven by fraudsters ramping their mining company shares in Calgary.

Blind, unthinking greed also played a decisive role in the investment bank Peregrine's fatal misadventure in Indonesia. It was always reported in the media that the firm's US$270-million bridging loan to a Jakarta taxi company called Steady Safe was part of its drive to build an Asian junk bond business. It was true. But on this deal, Peregrine was not simply funding Steady Safe to buy some toll road assets from the ubiquitous Tutut Suharto; it was funding Tutut to cash out of those assets at a good price. Peregrine bankers wanted to lead the planned privatisation of Indonesian toll road operator Jasa Marga, over which Tutut had a pre-eminent influence. It was also rumoured that she would take over from her father if he did not complete a seventh presidential term. So Peregrine bet one-third of its capital base on a political maybe, when a regular bank would be hesitant to risk 5 per cent of its capital on an economic near-certainty. Sooner or later, huge unhedged bets like this were bound to end in tears. Philip Tose always refused to say if he personally sanctioned the Steady Safe deal.

'These companies don't have strategies. They do deals,' observed Michael Porter, the Harvard Business School management professor, of south-east Asian companies at the time. It was a moot point. Asset trading had come to define south-east Asian business. The trajectory of one of the region's brashest new tycoons, Vincent Tan Chee Yioun, bears this out. Tan began to ascend Malaysia's greasy corporate pole in the 1980s in the traditional manner. He constructed his links to Mahathir and the Malaysian political élite. He formed a close relationship with Mahathir's favourite nephew, Ahmad Mustapha bin Mohamad Hassan, and brought him on to several company boards; Tan and his brother Danny were also involved in a car trading business with a brother-in-law of Mahathir. In 1984, Vincent Tan obtained his first untendered privatisation, buying a small industrial company from state investment agency PERNAS. A year later came his core cash flow, in the form of a lottery privatisation, again untendered. Tan then went on an acquisition spree, building a stable of seven listed businesses involved in everything from consumer durables to infrastructure to media to hotels to logging to stockbroking. But what was most striking about his sea of corporations – he had an airline, too

– was how little operating profit was produced. Almost all income came from buying and selling assets, often between Tan's own listed companies. He had a textile firm that became a logging business; he had a logging business that became a financial services conglomerate; his lottery franchise was sold out from under the noses of his gaming company investors, only to reappear via a reverse takeover a year later. From 1989 to the mid 1990s, exceptional gains from asset trading constituted between two-thirds and all of Tan's holding company's profits in any given year. Net operating profit as a share of revenues was sometimes less than 1 per cent. By 1995, minority investors had figured out what was going on and were marking down shares in his companies; but the banks kept backing him. Vincent Tan and those like him were a calling card for business running off the rails.[12]

The financial crisis did not come completely out of the blue; banks were beginning to fail in the lead-up to it. As already recounted, in Indonesia, Bank Summa went bust in 1993, a major state bank, Bapindo, in 1994, and Bank Pacific in 1995. In Thailand, the collapse of Bangkok Bank of Commerce (BBC) in 1996 is held up as a powerful warning of the carnage to come. It was. But the fact that central banks in south-east Asia, which are directed by politicians, always bailed out failing commercial banks, made warnings painless and easy to ignore. From 1983 to 1991, the Thai state bailed out no less than thirty financial institutions.[13] Even as the horror of BBC's loan portfolio began to be made public in summer 1996, the central bank was secretly spending another US$20 billion (BBC needed around US$2 billion) to shore up scores of other financial institutions, mostly finance companies. This was only revealed in testimony by the central bank governor, Chaiyawat Wibulswasdi, after the crisis broke. In sum, bank crises were reaching a new peak, but south-east Asia always had bank crises and governments previously managed to deal with them behind closed doors.

Shoot the Economists

The analytical record of macroeconomists prior to the crisis was not good. The only timely reality check came from work by Alwyn Young at the Massachusetts Institute of Technology, and a team of fellow growth accountants, that was popularised by Paul Krugman in a *Foreign Affairs* article in November 1994. Krugman's 'The Myth of Asia's Miracle' was a direct riposte to a triumphalist World Bank report, 'The East Asian Miracle', published a year earlier. Krugman presented an analysis that showed most of Asia's growth was coming from increased inputs of capital and labour and that productivity gains lagged behind those of the mature US economy. Much of the data focused on Singapore and left Harry Lee apoplectic. Research since the crisis suggests that long-term productivity gains in south-east Asia have been better than Krugman's article indicated, but the basic point that the contemporary economic trajectory was unsustainable was as correct as it was contrary to received opinion. Young and Krugman, however, forecast a slowdown rather than a meltdown.

The World Bank, by comparison, was in the mid 1990s living in a dream world whose paradigm was neatly captured by its widely quoted 'East Asian Miracle' report, published in 1993.[14] The Bank had some excellent staff in the region, and over the years had produced some sharp, critical analysis. In Indonesia, for instance, it condemned the industrial licensing regime unequivocally in research published in 1981. In the early 1990s it warned about rising external debt. But as time went on the Bank, which ran substantial offices in south-east Asian countries, appeared to suffer more and more from being too closely embedded with local regimes. To continue the Indonesian example, foreign correspondents in Jakarta were astounded in 1996 when Bank staff lauded the government's issue of new telecommunications licences, stating that the sale of the licences was carried out with 'full transparency and strict adherence to clearly defined rules'.[15] In fact the whole telecommunications industry was carved up in the most opaque and corrupt manner among Suharto's children and cronies. The Bank, as the *Far Eastern Economic Review*'s veteran reporter Adam Schwarz wrote, 'spectacularly misunderstood the ravaging effect of corruption on Indonesia's economy'.[16] The World Bank's management showed almost no interest in questions of institutional governance. Only token protests were made about the siphoning off of billions of dollars of development funding. When an American academic, Jeffrey Winters, estimated that up to one-third of Bank funds were being lost to corruption, the resident representative in Jakarta dismissed the claim even as an internal Bank review was showing that up to 30 per cent of money was indeed going missing.[17] Much of the problem was that Asia, when set against Africa and Latin America, was the World Bank's star performer and staffers were loath to do anything that would embarrass their class favourites.[18]

The IMF, which is relatively more centralised than the World Bank, did not have a problem with being over-embedded in south-east Asia. In many respects, the institution's failing was the opposite: it paid insufficient attention to how policies it promoted were enacted on the ground. The IMF also omitted to question long-run theoretical assumptions in a changing environment until it was too late. As Jonathan Anderson, an IMF staffer based in Beijing during the crisis, observes: 'There's no question. The Fund was caught napping.'[19] The IMF's twin yardsticks of progress through the 1980s and early 1990s were privatisation and deregulation. But when privatisations were almost invariably conducted without tenders, and deregulation merely substituted godfather cartels for state monopolies, the agency failed to sound the alarm. It was as if the rhetoric of privatisation mattered more than the practice. This turned out not to be the case. The 'deregulation' of financial services had a particularly malign impact. Thailand and Indonesia spawned hundreds of new banks and non-bank financial institutions, operated by god-fathers, and lending most of their funds to related godfather businesses.

The IMF's failure to question long-run assumptions was most damaging with respect to its view on south-east Asian exchange rate policies. Beginning in the early 1980s, each of the governments we are interested in had decided to peg its national currency to the American dollar. The decisions to do this followed a series of banking crises in the early 1980s and recessions in the middle of the decade. The biggest attraction of pegged currencies – the tech-nical means by which this was done varied from one place to another – was that they reassured foreign investors about the future international value of their investments and exporters about the international competitiveness of their products. After fifteen years of heavy foreign direct investment flows and burgeoning exports, it was natural by the mid 1990s to see exchange rate pegs as a good and proven thing. Anything that is fixed, however, can change its character if the world around it changes. That is what happened in the 1990s as short-term flows of international money increased exponentially, the American dollar began to appreciate and investment bankers and Asian godfathers figured out the arbitrage opportunities with pegged exchange rate regimes. Mexico, another country with a dollar-pegged currency, expe-rienced a major financial crisis in 1995, but very few people saw this as a harbinger for Asia. Again, economists at institutions like the IMF had long-run assumptions that were hard to shift. Mexico's crisis was the Latin American sort, provoked by a government flirting with insolvency, and revolving around state bonds. South-east Asian governments, by contrast, ran budget surpluses and had manageable debt loads. In the region's two-track political economy, with largely separate political and economic élites, it was the private busi-ness sector that took on most debt. And private business did not behave as irresponsibly as governments. Or so it was thought. As Jonathan Anderson recalls: 'The Asian crisis was an entirely new kind of crisis that no one inside the IMF was even thinking about.'[20]

This is not to say that IMF employees were without concerns. They could see that Mahathir privatisations were not best practice, or that there were doubts about Indonesian bank data on related-party lending. But without thinking far outside their quotidian box – something almost impossibly difficult in the face of the hubris of the era – they were never likely to see what was coming. The IMF began to react to the looming crisis only when its spreadsheets said it should – when 1995 and 1996 data on current account deficits and stalling foreign trade suggested unsustainable economic imbalances. The Fund then, as one example, recommended that the Thai government de-peg its currency and devalue on several occasions before this actually happened.[21] It is a reminder of the limits to what international institutions can do that Thai officials, for their part, were already in 1995 and 1996 lying brazenly to the IMF and everyone else about what the real state of their foreign exchange reserves was.

The Trigger and the Gun

Much post-crisis analysis in Asia focused on the roles of international exchange rate movements, short-term capital flows and offshore corporate borrowing in undermining the region's pegged currencies. These subjects are all important and must be dealt with. However, as should be clear by now, the Asian financial crisis was about much more than short-term imbalances. Some economists argue that with better macro policies, and without interference from international institutions, there would have been no crisis. Milton Friedman went so far as to say that the IMF's bail-out of Mexico in 1995 created such widespread belief that international speculation is insured by the Fund – so-called moral hazard – that it caused the Asian crisis. Friedman, however, was wrong when he declared Hong Kong's economy to be the freest in the world, and he was also wrong on this count. Without pegged exchange rates and the IMF the timing and shape of the crisis might have been different, but it was a reckoning waiting to happen.[22] Financial meltdowns afflict countries with political manipulation of the economy, abusive banking systems, cartelisation and restrictions on free enterprise. Even in a globalised world, these internal imbalances are much more important than external ones. To say otherwise is to confuse the gun with the trigger. The key point is that by the mid 1990s south-east Asia had built itself a big gun, and it was ready to be fired.

The question of what was the trigger is not only secondary, it can never be satisfactorily answered because in a regional financial crisis there is more than one trigger. In this sense the gun metaphor breaks down. It is, however, important to set out what is known about the lead-up to the crisis. The first point is that investment rates increased most powerfully from the mid 1980s to the mid 1990s in Thailand (the country where the crisis broke) and Malaysia (a country damaged by the crisis, but less dramatically than Thailand). As a proportion of GDP, investment in these countries leapt from around 25 per cent to over 40 per cent. In the city states of Singapore and Hong Kong, the investment rate increased about 8 percentage points over the same period. In Indonesia, the country that would be most completely wrecked by the crisis, the increase in the investment rate was not so acute, trending up between the mid 1980s and mid 1990s from around 23 per cent of GDP to 30 per cent. The Philippine investment rate was crushed in the post-Marcos misery of the mid 1980s and only recovered to one quarter of GDP by the time of the Asian crisis. The increase in investment rates, though it is never mentioned, was therefore a less than perfect guide to what was going to happen and who would suffer most. Excluding the Philippines, with its Marcos-driven chronology, a better leading indicator was the relative level of abuse and corruption in the banking systems. From worst to best: Indonesia, Thailand, Malaysia, Singapore, Hong Kong.

Until the early 1990s, investment in south-east Asia was being funded overwhelmingly from domestic savings. The world-beating savings rates in the region would always tend to push down the cost of capital, and real interest rates in the early 1990s were either negative or low in most states. This meant that inflation and interest costs were roughly equal and domestic investors could reasonably expect the value of investments that are not internationally traded – real estate being the classic example – to at least keep pace with the nominal cost of money. Hong Kong, for instance, had negative real interest rates from the end of 1990 to the start of 1995. Gary Coull, the late co-founder of CLSA, said he understood what the 1990s was about when K. S. Lo, the real estate tycoon and elder brother of Vincent Lo, told him he would buy any property in Hong Kong sight unseen.[23] That was how clever godfathers were thinking and it was a pointer to the forcefulness of the investment trend. In Thailand, Malaysia, Indonesia and the Philippines, one-fifth to one-quarter of all lending in the run-up to the crisis was going to real estate projects.

The infamous foreign capital flows became significant only in the last few years before the crisis. If we take Thailand (which had the strongest foreign capital inflows) as an example, 93 per cent of investment in the 1987–96 period was funded by household savings. However, government finances – the traditional 'Asian difference' – weakened markedly in the 1990s and the Thai government over this period ran budget deficits that soaked up more than 10 per cent of domestic savings. It was the resulting shortfall of about 20 per cent of aggregate investment that was made up by foreign money, most of it short-term.[24]

The rush of foreign money into south-east Asian stock markets in 1993 has already been discussed. Other capital was attracted by high nominal interest rates. Where domestic investors wanted to borrow because of low real rates, foreigners wanted to lend for high nominal rates since they would later repatriate their money to places where inflation was lower. This somewhat unintuitive state of affairs was predicated on the fact that almost everyone expected the currency pegs to endure, so there was no risk that currency movements would spoil the trades. A lot of paper and hot air has been expended arguing whether foreign banks were aggressively pushing foreign exchange into south-east Asia, or whether local borrowers – principally our godfathers and their banks – were blindly seeking it out. The answer is both: everyone was looking for a deal, which is the nature of business. In Thailand, the situation was made worse by the fact that the government was actively encouraging foreign banks to lend foreign exchange from offshore as a stepping stone to deregulation and their entry into the domestic market; licences were expected to go to those who showed most commitment by lending the most money.[25]

The final ingredient in the pre-crisis mix was what was happening in international currency markets to the US dollar, to which south-east Asian currencies were pegged, and to the Japanese yen. The yen was important because Japan was the region's dominant provider of long-term investment for its export manufacturing sector. When the yen was strong relative to regional currencies, the textile, petrochemical, electronic and automotive exports that Japanese companies processed in the region were more attractively priced than when the yen was weak. This is obvious. In the aftermath of the crisis, however, there was a tendency to intimate that the weakening of the yen-to-dollar exchange rate in the run-up to 1997 was somehow an international knife in the back of south-east Asia. In reality, local export processing economies had had an unusually good ride from a very weak American dollar, and hence stronger yen, in the early 1990s – the result of a US recession and those familiar trade deficits. No one commented that that period was abnormal, yet many people after the Asian crisis said that the resurgence of the US dollar in the mid 1990s – it appreciated 30 per cent against the yen in eighteen months, starting in spring 1995 – was unusual. In reality, south-east Asian economies by this point were too fragile to prosper in the real world. A stronger dollar and a weaker yen made a portion of regional exports uncompetitive – low-end export processors were already moving to China in droves – and aggregate export growth collapsed. The export processing economy was still the only globally competitive part of the broad south-east Asian economy, but it could no longer deliver surpluses that would compensate for serial domestic weaknesses.

Fireworks

And then it started. By June 1997, the Thai central bank was almost out of foreign reserves. Amnuay Viravan, a former head of Chin Sophonpanich's Bangkok Bank, who as finance minister led the way in trying to bail out Thailand's banking cartel while keeping the IMF in the dark about the depletion of foreign reserves, resigned in the middle of the month. Two weeks later, on 2 July, the government gave up the dollar peg and let the currency float. The Asian financial crisis had begun. The baht promptly headed from 25 to the US dollar towards 50, an exchange rate that, by year end, would double the local cost of servicing foreign debt. The IMF was called in and, by mid-August, agreed a package of major structural reforms in return for US$17.2 billion of multilateral support, to be disbursed as changes were made. But Chavalit's coalition, and the godfather-run banking cartel, were not keen to take the IMF's medicine. In October Prime Minister Chavalit backtracked on tax reforms, another finance minister resigned (soon to reappear, as we shall see, as an employee of Thaksin Shinawatra) and street protests started in Bangkok. Chavalit failed to get military support to declare martial law and stepped down on 3 November, to be replaced by an administration under Chuan Leekpai.

Meanwhile, from the moment the Thai peg was broken, other regional currencies started to come under pressure. Foreign fund managers wanted some of their money out of local stock markets; foreign banks wanted to limit their lending exposure by calling in their short-term loans; local banks and corporates scrambled to buy dollars to cover their borrowing positions; godfathers started to move money offshore; and speculators, local and foreign, began to borrow and sell Asian currencies in the expectation of buying them back more cheaply in the future – what is called 'short selling'. For the first time in more than a decade, everyone in the region was focused on the implications of currency realignments against the US dollar. In this new environment, central bankers quickly succumbed to the inevitability of having to give up their dollar pegs, and within three months the pegs in Indonesia, the Philippines and Malaysia were abandoned. The Indonesian rupiah – local corporates had foreign exchange borrowings of around US$80 billion versus central bank reserves of US$20 billion – slid from 2,500 to the US dollar to 3,000 by the end of August, while the Jakarta stock market dropped 35 per cent. The Philippine peso drifted lower and the Manila government – already the region's IMF junky – immediately called in the Fund. The Malaysian ringgit dropped from 2.5 to the US dollar to 3 by mid-September. This was just the beginning.

In September Mahathir used the annual meeting of the IMF, which happened to be taking place in Hong Kong, to blame the unfolding 'manipulated crisis'[26] on a Jewish-led Western conspiracy to keep Asians poor. 'We are Muslims and the Jews are not happy to see Muslims progress,' he said, adding disingenuously: 'We may suspect that they have an agenda but we do not want to accuse them.' Mahathir banned short selling on the Kuala Lumpur market, but the index kept falling anyway. An IMF enquiry after the crisis found little evidence that hedge funds and other leveraged investors played a significant role. There was widespread anecdotal evidence in the region of massive capital flight orchestrated by local tycoons; but Singaporean and Hong Kong banking secrecy is such that this is impossible to quantify. On 8 October – by which time the rupiah was trading at 3,700 to the US dollar – Suharto called in the IMF and began negotiations. On 23 October, attention shifted to the biggest financial market in the region – Hong Kong. The Hang Seng index plunged 10 per cent in a day. Speculators had sought to attack the Hong Kong dollar, but, given the territory's rigid currency board system (meaning, essentially, that Hong Kong dollars in circulation are fully backed by US dollar reserves), this led not to a breaking of the peg but to an increase in interest rates; speculative demand for Hong Kong dollars for short selling just put up the price of borrowing them. However, the currency board was no panacea because high interest rates sent the stock market into a tailspin. Between early August and the end of October, the Hong Kong market lost half its capitalisation. Real estate prices also began a precipitous decline.

New Year 1998 saw an acceleration of the sell-off of south-east Asian currencies. In January the Thai baht collapsed to 56 to the dollar, the Indonesian rupiah to 15,000, the Malaysian ringgit to 4.8 and the Philippine peso to 44, representing falls of 45–85 per cent in a few months. These exchange rates were all close to the lowest levels experienced during the crisis. Over this period, Suharto's endgame began to play out in Indonesia. On 31 October 1997, the Indonesian government signed a first letter of intent with the IMF for a US$43-billion rescue package. But disbursement of the money was conditioned on dismantling 'Uncle' Bob Hasan's plywood cartel,[27] Liem Sioe Liong's Bogosari flour milling monopoly, Tommy Suharto's clove import monopoly for kretek cigarettes,[28] and much more. The IMF also demanded the closure of sixteen insolvent banks, including Ibnu Sutowo's Bank Pacific,[29] Bambang Suharto's Bank Andromeda and a bank controlled by Suharto's half-brother, Probosutedjo.

The bank closures, in November, may have been an error because they caused increased panic and withdrawals by depositors, and exacerbated capital flight – estimated at US$8 billion and rising in the fourth quarter of 1997. But more important was the fact that IMF money was not disbursed, because Suharto said one thing and did another. Even before agreeing the first letter of intent with the IMF, he instructed the central bank to lend funds – known as Bank Indonesia Liquidity Support (or BLBI, the Bahasa Indonesia acronym) – to cash-strapped private banks. In November, finance minister Mar'ie Muhammad pointedly refused to answer rumours that the central bank had already lent out IDR8 trillion in contravention of the tight money policy the IMF wanted to protect the currency. Bambang Suharto was allowed to transfer the assets and liabilities of Bank Andromeda to a Liem Sioe Liong-controlled bank. In December, Suharto fired four out of the seven managing directors of the central bank and BLBI credits spiralled out of control.[30] By the end of January, IDR85 trillion had been pumped into the banking system, a figure that would rise to IDR145 trillion. Of this only IDR50 trillion was withdrawn by the public; much of the rest was used by godfathers to buy up foreign exchange (and hence wreck the rupiah). It would also later transpire that Suharto's Tamil Sri Lankan crony Marimutu Sinivasan, head of the Texmaco group, availed himself of an astonishing US$900 million of the central bank's dwindling foreign exchange reserves in early 1998. Suharto told the central bank his friend needed the money.

The plunging rupiah never had a chance. Cash in circulation increased 50 per cent in the three months to the end of January. Indonesia was heading beyond crisis into chaos. One after another, world leaders telephoned Suharto and demanded he heed the IMF. In January, an IMF team returned and signed a second agreement, which gave rise to one of the enduring images of the era – IMF managing director Michel Camdessus standing over Suharto with arms folded as the old man put pen to paper. But Suharto was no more committed to this deal than the first one. In February his armed forces began reacting to student protests with extra-judicial abductions.[31] In early March he secured re-election as president and named the least credible cabinet in Indonesian history, starring Tutut Suharto as minister for social services and Bob Hasan as minister of trade and industry. On his second day in the job, Bob gave his view on monopolies: 'If they serve the needs of the people, then there's no problem,' he opined.[32]

Inflation was soaring, real wages plummeting, and protests spreading. Violence and rioting took hold in May in Jakarta, Yogyakarta, Bogor and Medan. Then events turned weird. The IMF made another agreement in April, one element of which was modest increases in fuel prices. On 5 May, Suharto instead put up fuel prices by 70 per cent and bus fares by a similar amount. On 9 May, Suharto held a rare press conference at which he said he sympathised with people's suffering because he himself used to be poor, and left the country on a 10-day trip. Fatal clashes with security forces began around Indonesia soon after, and the great Jakarta riots broke out on 14 May. Over three days mobs of *preman* – Indonesia's underworld answer to triads – and other looters pillaged, raped and murdered. More than 1,200 people died; the Chinese quarter of north Jakarta was heavily targeted. Security forces colluded with the *preman*, though under whose direction and to what ends remain matters of conjecture. If the military backed Suharto, violence might have suited his purpose; but if the military turned against Suharto – which was already happening in the case of senior commander and future presidential candidate General Wiranto – violence could also justify the military's management of his succession. In the end, the loser in the game of Encourage Turmoil and Present Yourself as Saviour turned out to be Suharto. Returning to Jakarta, he found the military and Wiranto decisively against him, and agreed to step down on 20 May. It was, however, a managed defeat since the military agreed that vice-president Jusuf Habibie would be Suharto's replacement.

Thus it was that Indonesia set most of the benchmarks – whether violent deaths or economic distress – in the Asian financial crisis. In the second quarter of 1998, official data showed the economy was 16.5 per cent smaller than the year before, while prices rose over 50 per cent in the first six months of the year. The ouster of Suharto made it possible to deal somewhat more seriously with the IMF, but it was not until January 1999 that laws were passed enabling more democratic elections later in the year that put an end to Habibie's tenure. There followed a short-lived government of blind cleric Abdurrahman Wahid, followed by another false start under the presidency of Sukarno's daughter, Megawati Sukarnoputri.[33] Both administrations were plagued with corruption and sectarian violence. Like most effective authoritarians, Suharto left behind him a political and institutional vacuum in which there was little of substance to replace him.

To Russia and Back

Just as Suharto was losing the presidency in summer 1998 amidst the worst violence in Indonesia for three decades, the Asian financial crisis spread out of the region to Russia. Despite IMF support in July, the rouble was devalued in August and government debt repayments were suspended. In reality the Russian crisis had little in common with what was going on in south-east Asia, but it added mightily to the sense of international malaise. In Kuala Lumpur, Mahathir decided he had seen enough of the IMF and that Malaysia's solution to its problems would be a unilateral one. He imposed capital controls on 1 September, having already recalled his old ally Daim Zainuddin to the cabinet. By this point capital that wanted to flee had had plenty of time to do so, but the two-fingers gesture to the IMF and the fact that Daim announced a US$2.7-billion bail-out for UMNO's long-time corporate vehicle, the conglomerate Renong, encouraged a final round of selling of other Asian currencies. Mahathir's deputy Anwar Ibrahim, a former student activist who had been co-opted by the UMNO political élite, was dumped out of his job and arrested on charges of corruption and, subsequently, sodomy. His real mistake was to disagree with his boss. Kuala Lumpur has by regional standards long enjoyed a relatively open and tolerant gay scene, but when he needed an excuse to destroy his deputy, Mahathir threw on the robes of moral outrage. Anwar denied all charges; he was subjected to beating and a farcical show trial. It was vintage south-east Asian cant.

Just as Mahathir was making ready to put Malaysia's markets on a tight leash in August, Hong Kong authorities suffered their own fit of acute paranoia. Joseph Yam, chief executive of the Hong Kong Monetary Authority (the local variant on a central bank), announced that the territory faced a 'severe conspiracy' by speculators. Yam would subsequently claim that: 'Speculators launched coordinated and well-planned attacks across our markets.'[34] In reality, the notion of an international conspiracy was fanciful, but individual speculators – as is their wont – were proving resourceful. They were amassing Hong Kong dollars by means such as short-term bond issues in order to have them ready to sell in tandem with short positions in the stock market. This made the currency board, which jacked up interest rates when Hong Kong dollars were borrowed through the banking system, less effective in heading off speculation against the peg. But rather than reach for regulatory adjustments – for instance, tightening settlement terms on short selling – the bureaucrats decided to go to war with the market. On 28 August the government poured US$15 billion of its reserves into the local bourse, buying up 10 per cent of large capitalisation (mainly godfather) stocks as a hammer blow to short sellers. It was instructive that Joseph Yam and his colleagues described this move, and the implicit threat of others, in terms of 'victory' and 'defeat' in a battle against speculation. There was no suggestion that Hong Kong's plight reflected systemic weaknesses in its economy, no references to deregulation, the need to break up cartels or ensure greater competition. The huge share purchase itself was fortuitously timed and would prove profitable.

But, in hindsight, the wider significance of the act was that it signalled a move towards more proactive, Singapore-style intervention in the economy. Six months later Donald Tsang would announce that the government was handing over the last prime residential development site on Hong Kong island to Li Ka-shing's son Richard in an untendered, deferred-payment arrangement to build what it called a 'cyberport'. This turned out to be a luxury residential development with a bit of extra wiring. Hong Kong had never been the free economy that British colonials claimed, but now it was heading further in the wrong direction.

The irony of these late summer antics was that south-east Asia's economies were already stabilising. The Thai baht, Indonesian rupiah, Philippine peso, Singapore dollar and the Malaysian ringgit were no longer highly volatile currencies by the autumn and strengthened, modestly, from September. The rhetoric was about currency crises and craven speculation, but a big piece of the reality was that the market had simply adjusted currencies to levels commensurate with economic fundamentals. In particular, currencies had fallen to points at which south-east Asian export sectors – which were always kept in reasonable shape because they produced internationally traded goods – were once more competitive. It was to be no surprise that recovery in the region would be led not by godfather conglomerates, but by exporters. While a slow and patchy recovery took hold, however, there was a long period in which it was far from clear what the permanent impact of the crisis on domestic business structures would be. With the benefit of a decade's knowledge, we can now speak with greater – but far from conclusive – authority.

A Nasty Crisis, for Some

The Asian financial crisis did two things to large-scale domestic business in south-east Asia. First, it culled or emasculated some of the least competitive, most value-destroying godfathers of the 1990s. Second, it brought about considerable regulatory change, although some of this proved superficial. As a corollary, foreign direct investment, and hence competitive pressure, in 'sensitive' sectors previously closed to outside investment – such as financial services – increased, and had a positive impact. However – and this is the big reservation – the crisis did not change the fundamental political–economic structure of the region. Local economies are still godfather economies, and the smartest, slickest godfathers were actually strengthened by the crisis. Until the system that creates tycoon economies changes, most godfathers will remain untouchable – just as their American equivalents were at the start of the twentieth century. Moreover, as we shall see, new godfathers will be created.

Among the very weakest godfathers were ones who had been promoted for what might be called sociological purposes. These were the showcase indigenous – *bumiputra* and *pribumi* – tycoons of Malaysia and Indonesia. The Philippines had a group of super-coddled godfathers under Marcos in the form of people given business empires for no better reason than they had been at university with the president or were friendly with his wife; those people were wiped out in the Philippine crisis of the early and mid 1980s.

In Malaysia and Indonesia, ethnic Chinese or mixed race citizens some-times claim *bumiputra* and *pribumi* tycoons failed in the late 1990s because they were culturally, even racially, unadapted to business. In reality, the people in question had never been filtered in the way outsider godfathers are; their families never had to make their own first millions in order to get into the godfather game. In Malaysia, they were literally picked off the street (this is not meant to suggest working-class streets); in Indonesia they were most obviously the children of Suharto, and their friends. Moreover, these people were not tycoons in the regular sense. A large part of their role was as reposi-tories of political wealth – assets and funding connected to the United Malays National Organisation in Malaysia and the ruling family and its Golkar political machine in Indonesia. In Malaysia, the highest profile *bumiputra* godfathers also lacked the core cash flows of their peers – monopolies on soft com-modities and gaming licences – that provided insurance against bad times. Muslims could not be seen to be running gambling operations and, by the time many indigenous players got into business, the most juicy monopolies were already sewn up. In short, the indigenous poster boys were acutely exposed to the crisis, but not for reasons of genetics.

Malaysia's *bumiputra* figurehead was Halim Saad, a man with expensive tastes in suits and office furniture, brought on by finance minister and UMNO treasurer Daim Zainuddin. Halim was introduced into the big time in 1990 when control of Malaysia's North–South Highway, then directly owned by UMNO, was passed to him;[35] he swapped the asset for control of a moribund listed company called Renong. This vehicle was then stuffed full of untendered privatisations and government contracts to the point where, in 1997, it had eleven listed subsidiaries involved in everything from banking and telecom-munications to infrastructure and oil and gas. Despite such largesse, Renong had a history of liquidity crises, made little money and by 1997 was MYR25 billion in debt – the largest debt in the country, accounting for about 5 per cent of outstanding loans in the banking system. When recession and devalu-ation hit, there was no way Renong could service its borrowings. The gov-ernment's solution was a bail-out that set a new standard of shamelessness.

Daim, returning to the cabinet in 1997, authorised one of Renong's less lever-aged listed subsidiaries, United Engineers Malaysia (UEM), to borrow MYR2 billion and use the loan, plus cash reserves, to buy 32 per cent of its parent without having to make a general offer. It was a royal shafting of UEM minor-ity shareholders – forced to buy a failing company – in order to save Renong. It did not work because the public outcry was such that Halim Saad was forced to promise to buy back Renong's equity within three years.[36]

But he had no way of doing this. He spent the time dreaming up a MYR17-billion bond issue that would somehow be honoured seven years hence with a one-off payment. The market was not interested. In 2001 the government was forced to use public funds to privatise UEM, and did the same with Renong in 2003. The cost to taxpayers, net of asset disposals, was at least MYR10 billion. Halim Saad, who in 1997 laid claim to a US$2-billion personal fortune, departed the corporate scene. Mahathir cut him loose after a fall-out with Daim in 2001 – the reasons are murky, but Mahathir is in the habit of falling out with a lot of people – and in 2006 Halim faced the indignity of being on the wrong side of a court judgement for criminal breach of trust.

The demise of another Daim protégé and former employee, Tajudin Ramli, followed a similar pattern. A well-born *bumiputra* like Halim, Tajudin was given a five-year monopoly on mobile telephony in the late 1980s and then, in 1992, received the biggest personal bank loan in Malaysian history to enable him to take control of national carrier Malaysian Airline System (MAS). When the financial crisis cut passenger traffic, MAS posted huge losses. The Malay-sian taxpayer, through the agency of Daim Zainuddin, came to the rescue in February 2001 by buying back Tajudin's equity at MYR8 a share when the market price was a little over MYR3 (around the same time, the Philippine government bailed out Marcos crony Lucio Tan, who had taken over Philip-pine Airlines). Tajudin used the money to shore up his phone business. Unfor-tunately, evidence emerged that he may have siphoned off a very large sum of money from MAS, much of it via air cargo handling contracts in Germany with a private company in which Tajudin held an undeclared but sizeable stake. MAS filed a claim against Tajudin Ramli in the Malaysian high court in 2006.

Among ethnic Chinese Malaysians, a few egregious miscreants were put to the sword. Joseph Chong, a former senior politician and Mahathir ally, con-structed a typical corporate Christmas tree in the 1990s with Sabah shipyard, a shipbuilder, large real estate projects and odd manufacturing businesses among its decorations. The biggest bauble was the Philippines' National Steel, part of a Mahathir scheme to export Malaysian industrial 'expertise' around the region. The Mindanao-based steel plant was already in deep trouble by 1996 and the government prevailed on Halim Saad, through a private company, to buy it over for MYR3 billion. The Malaysian debt financing for Halim left no claim on the physical assets in the Philippines – these were already pledged to local creditors – and Malaysian taxpayers picked up most of the tab after National Steel suspended production in November 1999. Joseph Chong, meanwhile, posted hundreds of millions of dollars of losses in his other businesses and was the first businessman to seek court protection from creditors when the financial crisis broke. He exited corporate life.

For Multi-Purpose Holdings (MPH), which went spectacularly bankrupt in the 1980s after being marketed as a co-operative godfather-led investment vehicle for the Chinese community, there was a *déjà vu* moment. MPH had been sold, after its former boss was jailed, to Lim Thian Kiat (known as T. K. Lim), a politically well-connected would-be godfather with links to Anwar Ibrahim. In the 1990s, Lim reprised MPH's folly, going on an acquisition binge and availing his businesses of nearly US$1 billion of debt. MPH had core cash flow – in the form of the Magnum gaming franchise – but Lim still managed to bankrupt it again. His association with Anwar meant he had no friends in power after the deputy prime minister's imprisonment in 1998.

In Indonesia, the fall of Suharto meant there had to be some modest reckoning with the most brazenly and publicly corrupt tycoons. The former first family, despite occasional political rhetoric to the contrary, were all but untouchable. Suharto knew too much about the sins of the rest of the political elite,[37] senior generals did not want him tried and his successors – especially Habibie, Wahid and Megawati – had almost no inclination to tackle the fallen king. Moreover, Suharto was old, claimed to have suffered a series of strokes after the crisis, and there were plenty of doctors ready to attest that he was unfit to face interrogation or trial. Charges were laid relating to fraud at the foundations his family controlled, but these were never seriously pursued and were dropped in May 2006. Various estimates were made of the wealth that the Suhartos had amassed during their time in power. A *Time* magazine investigation in 1999 said US$15 billion. Transparency International, a Berlin-based graft watchdog, reckoned somewhere in the region of US$15–35 billion. David Backman, an academic, listed 1,247 companies in which the family held equity.[38] In the face of extreme public anger, most of Suharto's children kept a sensibly low profile after the crisis; they quietly sold off assets, including luxury properties that highlighted their wealth;[39] in April 2002, Bambang divested his controlling interest in key family holding company Bimantara.

The problem was Tommy, whose supercilious contempt for the institutions of government and provocative public remarks made him a particular hate figure. At the end of 1998, then-president Habibie, desperate to distance himself from the first family before elections took place in 1999, allowed the attorney general to proceed with one small corruption case against Tommy.[40] He appeared in court in April 1999 before a gallery packed (by Tommy's henchmen) with supportive young women while Suharto's youngest son grinned arrogantly at the press. There followed an Indonesian judicial pantomime in which Tommy was twice cleared of all charges in the lower courts before being found guilty on appeal under the Wahid government in September 2000. Wahid's reason for appealing the acquittals may not have been so much the original, relatively minor offence, but the fact that every time Tommy or his brother Bambang was summoned by the state a bomb went off somewhere in Jakarta.[41] It began to look like Tommy and associates might be resorting to terror and, following a 13 September bombing of the Jakarta stock exchange in which fifteen people died, Wahid wanted him out of circulation. Tommy was sentenced to eighteen months and offered a special, luxury cell. He declined and went on the run. The following July the head of the three-member supreme court panel who had sentenced Tommy was assassinated, and two months after that another supreme court panel overturned Tommy's jail sentence even while he was still a fugitive from justice. Following a national and international outcry, Indonesia's police chief was sacked in November 2001 and, one day later, police miraculously found Tommy. He was brought to Jakarta police headquarters where the local police chief, perhaps forgetting the scene was being broadcast on live television, greeted him with a hug.[42] In July 2002, Tommy was sentenced to fifteen years on convictions including ordering the murder of a supreme court judge; prosecutors asked for an unusually light sentence, which was further reduced on appeal, and Tommy left prison in October 2006.

The second high-profile figure given a spell inside was Mohamad 'Bob' Hasan. His trial followed the pattern originally set out for Tommy, before Suharto's youngest son started killing people. Hasan was charged with two counts of fraud, relating to his timber concessions, and convicted on one, in February 2001. He was initially allowed to serve out his time under house arrest but, following another wave of public outrage, he was sent to the island prison of Pulau Nusakambangan, where thousands of Suharto's political prisoners had died. This looked like an impressive gesture, but it subsequently transpired that Bob was given a special cell and treated more as a guest than a prisoner; he left on parole in February 2004.

Other godfathers who were threatened with a little jail time followed the

Suharto route and became ill. Sjamsul Nursalim, of shrimp farm fame, was arrested in April 2001 on suspicion of fraud. He said he had a heart condition, was released, and fled to Singapore via Japan. Suharto's half-brother Probosutedjo, convicted of defrauding reforestation programmes in 2003 and sentenced to four years, became ill in Indonesia. In a surprise move in 2005, he was dragged out of an executive suite in a private hospital in Jakarta and taken to prison. Sinivasan Marimutu, the Texmaco boss who loaded up on the country's foreign exchange reserves during the financial crisis, decided to leave the country after ignoring several police summonses for questioning; his lawyer said he needed medical treatment. An international warrant remains out for his arrest and his profile still appears on Interpol's website.[43]

A Pinch of Deregulation

Far easier than taking down godfathers, and prosecuting corruption through judiciaries that have learned to respond to the highest bidder, was to pass new laws and allow some modest deregulation of south-east Asian economies. This was the second impact of the financial crisis. The initial driver in Indonesia and Thailand was the IMF bail-outs, which were conditioned on – for the IMF – an unprecedented number of structural reforms.[44] In Indonesia, structural changes included an end to restrictive marketing arrangements – cartels – for products including cement, paper and plywood, the end of public subsidy for Habibie's aircraft manufacturing venture, the elimination of Tommy Suharto's Clove Marketing Board, a reduction of support for the national car programme and the end of a compulsory 2 per cent after-tax contribution to charity foundations (that had previously been controlled by Suharto). This list of targets focused squarely on the Suhartos and their senior godfathers. The IMF has serious problems ensuring compliance to its conditions in developing countries, but these high-profile changes were mostly implemented.

The most important IMF demands, however, related to banks, and here results were better for quantitative targets than for qualitative ones. Across south-east Asia, governments forced the closure and merger of their smallest and weakest financial institutions, and increased requirements for paid-in capital to keep future bank numbers under control. Thailand and Malaysia went furthest among the 'proper' countries; in the latter, which did not participate in an IMF programme but where bank regulators kept a close eye on what the Fund was recommending, more than fifty banks were squeezed down to ten. Indonesia, where godfather banking was completely out of control in the run-up to the crisis, still had 131 banks in late 2006, but was persevering in a slow process of mergers that had been ongoing since 1997. What is harder to find is evidence of a qualitative change in the relationship between political power and banking. The IMF asked for legislated independent central banks, but the bank-led bail-outs mandated by Daim Zainuddin in Malaysia after the crisis broke, more politically sanctioned lending at state banks in Indonesia in recent years, and repeated efforts by Thaksin Shinawatra in Thailand to direct central bank policy suggest nothing of the sort is in prospect.

Central bank liquidity injections into banks in Indonesia and Thailand during the crisis, which were swapped for equity, made the local governments the owners of about half the shares in their banking systems (although this was followed by some privatisations). Given that state banks performed even worse than godfather-run private ones in terms of non-performing loans during the crisis, the expansion of state ownership, combined with the failure to create truly independent bank regulation, bodes ill. The crisis left a smaller number of banks in the hands of families and a larger number in the hands of the state.[45] It did not produce any banks with the kind of diversified private ownership, wholly separated from management, that has been the comparative structural advantage of the Hongkong Bank.

Foreign investors, often intra-regional ones, were presented by the crisis with opportunities that had not been available to them before 1997; in part, this reflected IMF conditions demanding increases in foreign equity allowed in a range of businesses. The biggest buyer was Singapore, which ever since the crisis has exported its huge current account surplus via overseas investments. State corporations bought banks in Indonesia – as did private banks UOB and OCBC – as well as telecommunications businesses in Thailand and much more. Malaysian state businesses and government agencies invested in plantations and banks in Indonesia. European, American and Japanese companies increased their equity in existing joint ventures in manufacturing, telecommunications, petrochemicals and insurance and in some cases, where allowed, bought out their partners entirely. There was a modest number of new acquisitions of manufacturing businesses and banks by multinationals and private equity firms. All this has had a positive impact on business efficiency, although globally competitive performance is still not necessary in most domestic south-east Asian businesses because their output is not traded across borders.

Hong Kong and Singapore did not face pressure for major adjustments to their banking systems because solid, well-capitalised banks have long been at the heart of their role as the region's offshore financial centres; large amounts of flight capital headed into the cities' banks during the crisis. Banking excess in Hong Kong was reined in by regulators after bank collapses in the early 1980s, and in Singapore by conservative state ownership of the largest institutions and an onerous regulatory regime.[46] Despite this, the Hong Kong Monetary Authority further increased requirements for financial disclosure by banks, while Singapore fired a shot across the bows of its more entrepreneurial private banks with an aggressive prosecution of UOB in 2000 over discrepancies in the listing of a non-core subsidiary.[47]

Much less responsive to the crisis in Hong Kong were the political leaders and the Securities and Futures Commission (SFC). The politicians, led from 1997 to 2005 by tycoon chief executive Tung Chee-hwa, resisted all calls for the creation of a monopolies regulator such as exists in every other developed state. The official position was opened up for long-winded discussion under Tung's successor, Donald Tsang, but did not substantively change. The SFC, whose board has long been dominated by godfathers and their proxies, showed no interest in the fundamental reforms most popular with minority investors;[48] instead, the agency contented itself with some tightening of existing rules. A survey published by CLSA Markets in April 2001 showed that only 5 per cent of listed Hong Kong companies had an independent chairman, less than 20 per cent had genuinely independent 'independent directors', while in four-fifths of businesses the board and management were substantially the same people.[49]

What did happen in Hong Kong after the crisis, however, was that an organised minority investor lobby developed in a manner that is unique in the region. In part this reflects the greater size and internationalisation of the local market, with more hedge fund and institutional investors unwilling to play the cosy, manipulative games that traditionally satisfied the needs of godfathers and their investment banks. The leading light in this bottom-up struggle was David Webb, a former investment banker and employee of local godfather Peter Woo, who founded the Hong Kong Association of Minority Shareholders (HAMS). HAMS' proposal that it become a properly resourced watchdog, with an elected board, funded by a 0.005 per cent levy on stock market transactions, was supported by many investors, but was inevitably shot down by the government, in 2002. None the less, Webb and HAMS' website acquired a roster of 14,000 registered subscribers and David Webb was elected a non-executive director of Hong Kong Exchange and Clearing, the company that operates the stock market, as well as a member of the Takeover and Mergers Panel. In these capacities he led campaigns for a range of reforms, built a database of cases of minority investor abuse and was at the forefront of moves that blocked some of the low-ball privatisation offers after the financial crisis by godfathers like Robert Kuok, Lee Shau-kee and Cheng Yu-tung.[50] As Webb says: 'It is feasible to achieve change here. I don't get physically threatened in Hong Kong whereas I wouldn't have tried this in Jakarta or Manila.'[51]

Singapore's reaction to corporate governance issues raised by the crisis was a perfect illustration of that city state's approach to business. On the one hand, regulators put in place much tougher corporate governance requirements than Hong Kong, with major amendments to the Companies Act in 2000[52] and a new Securities and Futures Act thereafter. On the other hand, Singapore retained its traditional bolt-hole role for the Indonesian godfather class. During the crisis the city became the base of operations for godfathers like Liem Sioe Liong and his son Anthony, while they waited for the security situation to improve in Jakarta and for confirmation that they would not face prosecution for the many illegal actions by their companies.[53] Sjamsul Nursalim, wanted for questioning in Indonesia on suspicion of fraud since 2001, also set up shop in Singapore, from where he continues to run his businesses. The Widjaya family's Asia Pulp & Paper (APP), which defaulted on US$14 billion of debt, and was then – as we shall see in the next section – the subject of an extraordinary subterfuge as the Widjayas attempted to buy back control of the company on the cheap, is incorporated in and run from Singapore; patriarch Eka Tjipta Widjaya has been based in Singapore since the crisis. Local authorities have never found cause to investigate APP or any other large Indonesian godfather business.

The crisis highlighted Singapore's true colours: a squeaky clean regulatory machine that stands in stark contrast to some distinctly unsavoury businesses and businessmen. During the crisis, the city state was also amending regulations that have helped it draw offshore financial work away from Switzerland, which is under pressure from the European Union to assist it in clamping down on tax evasion and money laundering. Meanwhile, the moralistic Lee family decided to authorise and tender two vast gambling resorts which – despite the importance of 'Asian values' – were suddenly deemed essential to growth and employment.

Elsewhere in the region, progress on regulation of corporate governance was characterised by the traditional dichotomy between theory and practice. The Malaysian stock exchange introduced a voluntary code on corporate governance in 2000, and made changes to the listing rules that include a ban on (previously much-favoured) loans to unlisted holding companies and other third parties. While these modest changes were being introduced, however, the government was busy bailing out politically connected companies like Renong and Malaysian Airline System. In the Philippines there was almost no statutory change, and the presidency of Joseph Estrada confirmed a case of stock markets as usual. One of the contributing factors in Estrada's fall in 2001 was a stock manipulation scandal in which Estrada was trying to block investigating authorities.[54] Lucio Tan, a friend and financial backer of Estrada, obtained control of Philippine National Bank (PNB) on Estrada's watch with a government-endorsed rights issue that only Tan subscribed to. Tan then reneged on a promise to buy out the government's share in PNB because he already had control. Eduardo 'Danding' Cojuangco, another Marcos crony and Estrada pal, also prospered during the latter's presidency, regaining the chairmanship of San Miguel. In Indonesia, the main governance reforms were that requirements be introduced for more independent directors and the creation of audit committees. In Thailand there were similar, modest changes.

Plus ça change…

The previous section is not meant to suggest that the crisis was not an agent of change. Rather, the point is that change was at the margin and not fundamental in nature. This becomes clear as we return to a more anecdotal analysis of how our godfathers fared.

The Philippines, as has been mentioned, was less affected by the crisis than other south-east Asian states because it had undergone an economic near-meltdown in the last years of Marcos and the years following his flight into exile. The economy shed its crudest crony characteristics under IMF supervision and the presidencies of Cory Aquino and Fidel Ramos[55] and was not, in the mid 1990s, carrying an Asian-style debt load; this was assisted by the fact that chastened foreigners were unwilling to pour money into the Philippines in the period. None the less, the Philippines does provide a lead in to the post-crisis experience of its political cousin in the region, Thailand. In the 1998 Philippine presidential election, which followed the terms of Aquino and Ramos – both members of the traditional political élite[56] – Joseph 'Erap' Estrada won election with a media-savvy pitch to the urban and rural poor. His true background was that he was the middle-class delinquent son of a government contractor, who happened to grow up in a rough part of Manila, but Erap's self-characterisation as a man of the poor, and his B-movie career in which he specialised in 'poor hero' roles, saw him voted into office. Estrada was heavily backed by godfathers like Lucio Tan and Danding Cojuangco, as well as by owners of illegal gambling operations, all of whom stood to gain from his tenure. He lasted only two years before parliament started its first presidential impeachment proceedings over corruption allegations, and was forced out of office by a combination of street protests, the opposition of the armed forces and the manoeuvres of his (independently elected[57]) vice president, Gloria Macapagal-Arroyo, in January 2001. With Macapagal-Arroyo, the daughter of a former president, power was back in the hands of the establishment. But Estrada had pointed to the possibilities of a new, populist way to play the political game in the television age.

In Thailand, the same game was being explored not by a *parvenu* politician with godfather backing, but by a tycoon himself. Ever since the era of military juntas in Thailand began to fade in the 1970s, the number of businessmen elected to parliament has increased with each passing election. This is a long-term trend that began to blur the distinction between political and economic power. It was reinforced by the ongoing assimilation of ethnic Chinese Thais who dominate big business; by the 1990s the economic nationalism of the 1940s was forgotten and it was not a racial issue that part-Chinese businessmen constituted the majority of the members of parliament.[58] As a result, the stage was set for big business and politics to merge completely, and the vehicle for this was Thaksin Shinawatra. Thaksin came from a tax farming and business family based in Chiang Mai with a long history of involvement in regional politics. He was drawn into national politics because his wealth derived from telecommunications and broadcasting concessions,[59] which were the most politically fought-over rents that the state had to offer in the late 1980s and early 1990s. Other Thai telecom companies were arms-length backers of political parties in the quest for favour, but in 1994 Thaksin joined the cabinet of Chuan Leekpai as foreign minister. As Thaksin's biographers, Pasuk Phongpaichit and Chris Baker, note: 'He stepped across the line dividing business and politics.'[60] He never went back. Thaksin took over leadership of a small party called Phalang Tham (Moral Force) and served two short terms as deputy prime minister in coalitions before the crisis. When the baht's peg was broken, Thaksin had the only major telecommunications business whose foreign exchange debts were largely hedged against the devaluation. It was a provocative coincidence that Thanong Bidaya, the finance minister in the lead-up to the crisis and one of those who took the decision to float the currency, was Thaksin's former banker, employee and a director of some of his businesses.[61] Another person party to the decision to devalue, Bokhin Polakun, was subsequently accused in a parliamentary debate of being the channel through which information about the devaluation was passed to Thaksin; in 2004 he became Thaksin's minister of the interior.

The baht's loss of half its value against the dollar had nothing like the effect on Thaksin that it had on his rivals. But by the time of the crisis he had still accumulated huge debts and his entry into politics had not prevented the issuance of new telecoms licences and concessions to other tycoons who backed rival political factions. Moreover, after the IMF's intervention the government agreed to deregulate telecommunications and establish an independent regulator, beginning in October 1999. This was not good news for a godfather business. In July 1998, however, a year after the crisis broke, Thaksin took a decision that would see him become a cash billionaire: he formed the Thai Rak Thai (Thais Love Thais) party, based initially in his office building. Over the next twelve months, as Thaksin honed a false public image of a poor boy made good, and his populist agenda and telegenic manner appeared to resonate with voters, other godfathers lined up behind him. He was endorsed by his long-time rival Dhanin Chearavanont, from the CP Group, whose business and family would provide two cabinet members for Thaksin; [62] by the Bangkok Bank's Sophonpanich family; by decimated media tycoon Sondhi Limthongkun; and by several major real estate players. It was a coalition of godfathers, brought up on economic rents and shell-shocked by the crisis, with almost no involvement from the manufacturing economy. But, brilliantly and brazenly, Thaksin sold himself and Thai Rak Thai as the political representatives of entrepreneurial small business and the rural poor, with a strong nationalist (but non-racial) tone. Unlike previous political parties, Thai Rak Thai also articulated a number of clear policies, including an amnesty on rural debts, the provision of village credit and universal healthcare.

Thaksin was well-funded and well-organised and, as his momentum built in the run-up to national elections in 2001, around a hundred sitting MPs defected to stand under his banner. This is the Thai and Philippine tradition whenever politicians see that the wind is blowing from a new direction. Thaksin ensured much of the campaign was focused on his own cult of personality, assuring his ascendancy. There was a biography, serialised in the press and synopsised in campaign material, that expanded on his Horatio Alger fantasy: 'Brothers and sisters, I come from the countryside ... As a rural kid, the son of a coffee shop owner, I helped my father with his orchards, newspaper delivery, and mobile cinema ... Today, my friends range from hired motorcycle drivers to the presidents of great countries.'[63] In the election, Thai Rak Thai won an unprecedented 248 out of 500 seats.

Five major business supporters, including Dhanin Chearavanont's CP Group, were rewarded with cabinet posts. As Pasuk and Baker observe: 'Thaksin's rise was a logical extension of Thailand's business-dominated "money politics", but also a dramatic change of scale. It brought some of the wealthiest elements of domestic capital into the seat of power. It superseded "money politics" with "big money politics".' To the victor, spoils quickly began to flow. On his first day at work, Thaksin's minister of communications announced a review of a new state company-run mobile phone business, approved by the outgoing Chuan Leekpai government to increase competition, which put the company's launch on hold.[64] The Thaksin family's Shin Corporation – the premier and his wife, to meet constitutional requirements, had formally passed their shares to their children, relatives and employees – bought out another local mobile business and forced its foreign partner, Telekom Malaysia, to withdraw. Thaksin, meanwhile, publicly rubbished the competing technology standard of another operator and successfully supported the state Telephone Organisation of Thailand to maintain interconnection fees on rivals that were not charged to Shin businesses; (one of the rivals was controlled by Dhanin Chearavanont, an early warning to him that his new political partner would not look out for his interests).[65] The appointment of regulators at a new National Telecommunications Commission, which was supposed to lead deregulation efforts, was stonewalled. With competition limited, deregulation blocked and economic recovery fed by more expansive economic policy, Shin's core cash flow from its Advanced Info Service (AIS) mobile phone unit ballooned. Profits from the business increased from less than THB4 billion in 2001 to more than THB18 billion in 2003. Shin diversified into financial services with Singapore's state-run DBS bank (granted various licences), into an airline joint venture with Malaysian low-cost carrier AirAsia (granted Thai landing rights and a 50 per cent discount on landing fees),[66] and bought control of independent television channel iTV (granted a reduction in the licence fee it paid the government and an increase in the amount of low-cost entertainment it was allowed to broadcast). When the Thai stock market staged a recovery in 2003, doubling its much-reduced capitalisation, the value of Shin's five listed businesses tripled.

Thaksin was not unduly short-termist. While Shin prospered, he delivered on his major campaign promises, particularly with respect to farmers. He promoted growth by encouraging the expansion of household debt and using quasi-fiscal financing arrangements to increase public expenditure without a short-term blow-out in public borrowing. Thai Rak Thai absorbed three more political parties after the election and, in February 2005, secured a second term with three-quarters of the seats in parliament – giving Thaksin sufficient votes to change the constitution and to block censure motions. He spoke of a quarter century in power. Unfortunately, Thaksin made two miscalculations:

he failed to keep his fellow godfathers happy and he paid too little heed to middle class opposition in Bangkok. This opened the way for the military to step in.

In the best tradition of the so-called 'bamboo network', Thaksin forgot about his tycoon backers the moment he was elected. Not a bank owner himself, he showed no interest in defending the old banking cartel, which had to trade equity – and in some cases control[67] – for infusions of foreign capital. Bangkok Bank's Sophonpanich family, which was forced to reduce its stake to under 20 per cent after the crisis, pulled away from Thaksin during his first term. Dhanin Chearavanont, the top godfather before the crisis, supplied funds and cabinet ministers to Thaksin, but found him unwilling to provide the kind of political support for CP Group's telecom businesses that he did for his own.[68] When bird flu hit Thailand, Thaksin let the Cheara-vanonts manage their own response in their vast poultry-processing opera-tion – without the intervention of public health officials – but then he did not have a chicken business. When members and employees of the Sophonpanich and Chearavanont families were interviewed for this book in 2005 and early 2006, they were visceral in their loathing of Thaksin.[69] It was a bad case of godfather jealousy and a harbinger of problems to come for the premier. Sondhi Limthongkun, the failed media tycoon who evangelised Thaksin early on, was to become the leader of the popular protests against him.

The trigger for Thaksin's ouster was the sale of Shin Corp. to the Singapore government's Temasek Holdings in January 2006. The sale was smoothed by stock market exemptions; the cabinet had approved an attractive new tax deal for the AIS mobile unit weeks before the sale; and an increase in the maximum equity ownership allowed to foreign investors in telecommunica-tions companies came into effect one day before the deal was done. More-over, US$1.9-billion proceeds – because they came from a share transaction – were tax free.[70]

To his godfather enemies, Thaksin added middle-class Bangkok, outraged both by the manoeuvres that had led to his cash windfall and by a sale to the widely despised Singaporeans.[71] Street protests, drawing tens of thousands of people, occurred throughout the spring. In April Thaksin, sure that his rural support would deliver another victory at the polls, called an election as a referendum on his leadership. The opposition boycotted it. Thaksin tried other manoeuvres, including temporarily stepping down from the leadership. By summer it was apparent to Thaksin's opponents in the old political and business élites that intervention by the army was unlikely to spark the kind of popular reaction in the capital seen in 1992 when people took to the streets in opposition to military intervention in politics. Former three-time military premier – and now adviser to the king – General Prem Tinsulanonda sounded out support among the old élite for a coup. This duly took place on the night of 19 September, while Thaksin was abroad, forcing him into exile.

The coup almost certainly signalled a return to the traditional division of labour between political and tycoon groups. It was proof, if proof were needed, that the godfathers are incapable of sustained co-operation. Thaksin brought the tycoons together for the Thai Rak Thai adventure, but when it became clear that he would be the major beneficiary, the arrangement fell apart.

This is not to say, however, that Thaksin actively impeded the post-crisis recovery of his peers. The banking families suffered considerably, as market forces in the financial sector were allowed to play out. But Dhanin Chearavanont, with constant cash flow from his agribusinesses, was able to sell off non-core companies, including brewing and motorcycle manufacturing interests in China and his Lotus supermarkets in Thailand, settle some of his debts and renegotiate others. By 2006, the CP Group was expanding again, opening scores of supermarkets in China and, with Thaksin gone, Dhanin was once more vying for the top godfather spot. He had competition from Charoen Siriwattanapakdi, another erstwhile Thaksin backer. Charoen's revenues from his Thai whiskey and brewing franchises held up as well as those of any godfather during the crisis[72] and he acquired many new businesses at a discount. By 2006, *Forbes* ranked him the richest man in Thailand, with net worth of US$3 billion. A paper by researchers at Hitotsubashi University in Tokyo in 2004 found the share of stock market capitalisation accounted for by the top thirty family conglomerates in 2000 was the same as it had been before the crisis.[73]

After the coup against Thaksin, the new military government launched several investigations founded on suspicions the former premier was guilty of corruption, but there was no question of raking over the affairs of other godfathers. The Thai Rak Thai party began to fall apart as soon as Thaksin disappeared, with scores of its members of parliament renouncing their affiliation. They waited to see what political incarnation elections promised by the military government would recommend. Whatever the answer, there was little doubt they would be looking once again for tycoon patronage.

The Doctor will See You Now

In Malaysia, the grip exercised by the United Malays National Organisation on political life meant there was no likelihood of a change in the relationship between political and economic power. The political response to the crisis played out within UMNO and godfathers dealt with the consequences. The group of proto-tycoons brought on by Anwar Ibrahim in the 1990s – such as banker and broker Rashid Hussain and Tong Kooi Ong, who put together a large banking, brokerage and real estate business[74] – provided fodder for a government-led corporate consolidation exercise after Anwar was jailed. Daim Zainuddin's would-be *bumiputra* godfathers were cast adrift when Daim was let go from government in 2001. As Mahathir crushed his political challengers within UMNO, and won a 1999 general election with support from ethnic Chinese voters afraid of big gains by Islamic parties, godfather well-being came down to relations with the good doctor. The big boys were all marked out by the fact that their rapport with him was carefully maintained.

Quek Leng Chan suffered a shock when his Hong Leong bank was not on the initial list of core institutions that would be allowed to survive bank consolidation; but after some intensive lobbying, his business was added to the list. Ananda Krishnan was saddled with vast foreign exchange-denominated debts because of purchases of imported telecommunications, broadcasting and satellite equipment. But he had unrivalled access to Mahathir. State oil and gas company Petronas came to Krishnan's aid, buying out most of his interest in the mammoth Petronas Twin Towers and Kuala Lumpur City Centre real estate project. Deep-pocketed Petronas, it will be remembered, had already put up the cash to fund the project's development. Krishnan had dug himself a big debt hole, but with Petronas – of which he was a founding director in the 1970s – acting more like a captive bank than an oil company, and constant cash flows from his gaming and broadcasting monopolies, as well as shares in de facto power generation and mobile telephony cartels, he was able to clamber out. He sold a third of his mobile telephone business to British Telecom in 1998 for cash, but managed to buy it back in 2001.[75] As the economy recovered, Krishnan listed his telephony, broadcasting and satellite units and, together with the gaming and power plant business that was already quoted before the crisis, by 2004 he controlled public companies capitalised at more than US$10 billion. Among Malaysian godfathers he is an above-average manager (though not as good as he thinks), while the quality of the concessions he obtained from the state showed through.

Lim Goh Tong and son Kok Thay, with their casino monopoly, had little to worry about during the crisis. Malaysian punters kept gambling while gambling tourism – not least from China – was on the rise. The main issue was what to do with the cash. The Lims expanded into cruise ships, which also feature gaming tables, becoming the third-largest such business in the world by 2004.[76] But Hong Kong-listed Star Cruises, which faces global competition, has not yet produced healthy returns and its stock price has languished. Better news came for the Lims in 2006 when a consortium they organised won a bid to build a US$3.4 billion gaming complex on Singapore's Sentosa island. This led Macau's gambling king Stanley Ho to give the Lims the right to operate a casino in booming Macau in return for equity in Star Cruises and hence access to the Singapore deal. Unfortunately, the Lims, unused to working with Harry Lee, had not thought this trade through. The Singaporean government quickly made clear it would not have the unsavoury Stanley working on its turf and the deal had to be unwound. It was probably just as well for the Lims, since Stanley's attempts to work with other godfathers in the past – not to mention his sister Winnie – have been plagued by bitter acrimony and law suits. Separately, the Lim family acquired British betting chain Stanley Leisure in 2006, reinforcing a trend for the senior Malaysian tycoons to invest their economic rents in assets in the former colonial power.[77]

Like Ananda Krishnan, the Lims enjoy some additional guaranteed cash flow in Malaysia as independent power producers (IPPs). IPP contracts, given to the big godfathers without open tenders, run on subsidised gas from Petronas and produce electricity that state utility Tenaga is forced to buy.[78] The biggest beneficiary of the concessions, and the first to be granted one, was Francis Yeoh's YTL Corp., with nine power stations.[79] The conservatively managed business was a case study of how tycoons with monopoly core cash flows actually benefited from the crisis. In 1997, as the crisis struck, Yeoh had money on hand. He moved in on Taiping Consolidated, an indebted *bumiputra*-controlled real estate business with prime assets in Kuala Lumpur. For MYR332 million – around US$80 million at the time – he picked up the capital's prime shopping mall, a newer and more glitzy mall nearby, the five-star JW Marriot hotel and a 118-hectare urban land bank for development.[80] It was a politically sensitive move for an ethnic Chinese tycoon to make – Taiping was a *bumiputra* showcase from the early 1990s – but Yeoh kept the former owner in as a shareholder and company chairman,[81] and UMNO let the move go. Yeoh's cash continued to pile up, but there were no more deals so sweet to be had in Malaysia. So in 2002 he raised US$1.8 billion and bought the British regional utility Wessex Water from failing US energy company Enron. Three years later he moved on power generating assets in Indonesia. These were transactions in the best tradition of Malaysia's richest godfather, Robert Kuok. He too was quickly buying up assets – around the region and the rest of the world – during the crisis as his core cash flows remained intact. Kuok's decades-long near-monopoly on Malaysia's sugar industry, as mentioned earlier – based on an 85 per cent share of import quotas[82] – survived the financial crisis, despite lobbying by other godfathers.

That little had changed in the economic structure was demonstrated by Mahathir who, having dispensed with some of the businessmen connected with Anwar and Daim, found himself a new 'chosen one'. Syed Mokhtar al-Bukhary, a former cattle and rice trader (who, like Daim Zainuddin, was from the prime minister's home state of Kedah), obtained his first audience with Mahathir as the financial crisis was breaking. Mahathir soon decided that Syed Mokhtar, whose background was less elitist than those of men like Halim Saad and Tajudin Ramli, was a genuinely gifted *bumiputra* business-man. Within five years, Syed Mokhtar became the single biggest independent power producer in Malaysia, was given government financing to build a new container facility at Port of Tanjung Pelepas (PTP),[83] and had major interests in mining, plantations and hotels. Like Ananda Krishnan, who took Maha-thir on holiday and looked after his children while abroad, or Francis Yeoh, who poured money into Mahathir's beloved Langkawi island and other loss-leading but high-profile projects, Syed Mokhtar worked out how to press the premier's buttons. He built an Islamic arts centre in Kuala Lumpur, replete with onion-shaped domes, fountains and white marble; Mahathir frequently turned up on site to check the progress. Syed Mokhtar then followed time-honoured tradition by selling concessions he acquired through private com-panies to listed vehicles, where he controlled the board, at rich prices. PTP was sold in 2002 for US$500 million, and a private firm with the rights to build a 2,100-megawatt power plant in Johore state was sold in 2003 for US$220 million. In effect, he was stripping cash out of the long-term, capital-intensive concessions granted to him by the government. It was Syed Mokhtar who lobbied the state, unsuccessfully, to give him a substantial share of Robert Kuok's sugar monopoly;[84] in 2006 he was attempting to take over publicly quoted Bernas, which holds the monopoly for rice importation and distribu-tion. Along the way Syed Mokhtar also took on interests in failed govern-ment businesses – including an electrical appliances maker, Kuala Lumpur real estate developments and the dismal Proton national car project; contrary to Mahathir's view, he looked to many like a new Halim Saad.

In October 2003 the doctor finally stepped down, after twenty-two years in power. His latest deputy, Abdullah Badawi, took over and, in May 2004, won a resounding national election victory. In the months before the election, Abdullah had launched a handful of corruption investigations against middle-ranking businessmen and cancelled some high-profile state projects associ-ated with Mahathir – including, pointedly, a couple of concessions granted to Syed Mokhtar. Many Malaysians hailed a new political beginning. With the National Front coalition holding 198 out of 219 parliamentary seats, however, this was naïve. UMNO was more powerful than ever, and a rising generation of political aspirants – including the children of former premiers and ministers[85] – jostled for power in the post-Mahathir environment. They demanded a fresh round of pro-*bumiputra* positive discrimination policy, traditionally the code for what Abdullah had condemned before the election as hand-outs to 'greedy Malay rent-seekers'. The fervour for anti-corruption prosecutions and deregulation soon dissipated, big government projects were restarted, and the godfathers carried on business as usual. There was a break from Mahathir – testified by the doctor's periodic public rants, sometimes to journalists summoned to his fishbowl office atop one of the Petronas towers, that Abdullah was not up to the job – but it was personal rather than systemic.

The Dark Arts

In Indonesia it is not possible to tell the post-crisis story of individual Indonesian godfathers with certainty because – as with most things in Indonesia – that story is extremely opaque. More than ever, tycoons who were at the heart of the region's worst economic meltdown have sought to conceal their activities from public view. As one top-tier godfather who profited handsomely from the Suharto years laments: 'You really don't know who owns anything.'[86] In broad outline, however, several things are clear about godfathers' businesses after the crisis hit: they exported large sums of capital, particularly to Singapore, and managed to hang on to overseas assets; they handed over domestic assets of dubious quality to the Indonesian government in lieu of debts and then sought to buy back some of those assets for less than they had claimed they were worth; and, with respect to politics, the fall of Suharto was followed by a period of free-for-all corruption that even the old man would have blushed at. When the first family exited the presidency, incoming politicians' first instinct was to lay their hands on the bounty that thirty years of Suharto ascendancy had denied them. This situation began to cool down only under the presidency of Susilo Bambang Yudhoyono, elected in the country's first direct presidential election in 2004.

Sudono Salim – also known as Liem Sioe Liong – and son Anthony ran Indonesia's biggest crony conglomerate – largely funded by Indonesia's biggest private bank, Bank Central Asia (BCA) – at the time of the crisis. By some reckonings its consolidated turnover was equivalent to 5 per cent of GDP.[87] The Salims, who fled to Singapore well before mobs overran their family compound in north Jakarta in the early summer of 1998, set the tone for their peers in their efforts to salvage as much as possible of their empire. When the dust settled, they owed the Indonesian Bank Restructuring Agency (IBRA) IDR53 trillion – US$6.6 billion at the average exchange rate in the five years from July 1997 – for credits that had been pumped into BCA by the central bank. In return for immunity from prosecution, the family handed over more than 100 domestic Indonesian businesses it said were worth IDR53 trillion. At the IMF's insistence, the Salims lost their most lucrative monopolies and control of BCA, but they hung on to some 400 companies, including their flour milling business Bogosari, and Indofood, the country's dominant noodle maker. In addition, the Salims retained control of their Hong Kong-based conglomerate First Pacific, which at the onset of the crisis accounted for 40 per cent of group revenues. IBRA slowly set about selling off the companies it had been given. When the agency finished its Salim disposals, it had raised just under IDR20 trillion, or about two-fifths of what it was owed. Despite this, there were no prosecutions, the government of Megawati Sukarnoputri announced the Salims had settled their debts and IBRA closed its doors in February 2004. The Salims' position was that the assets they handed over were fairly valued and subsequently only lost value because of the crisis in the Indonesian economy. By 2005 Anthony was living back in the refurbished family compound in north Jakarta – where the mob had painted 'Suharto's dog' on the gate. That was in reference to Daddy, who maintained his base at his house in Singapore.

The Salims were beneficiaries of relativity. Paying back two-fifths of the liquidity credits borrowed from the central bank in the last days of Suharto turned out to be well above average. The Indonesian government shelled out IDR650 trillion in bail-outs (of which temporary bank credits were a subset) – or about half of one year's economic output – but less than a quarter was recovered. Sjamsul Nursalim, whose bank received IDR27 trillion, handed over assets, including his famous shrimp farm, which allowed IBRA to recover about 10 per cent of what he owed. Basing himself in Singapore – and styling himself at different times with three variants of his Chinese name: Liem Tek Siong, Lim Tek Siong and Liem Tjen Ho – Nursalim carried on business as usual. He expanded the Singapore-listed real estate and printed circuit manufacturing companies he controls, Tuan Sing Holdings and Gul Tech, as well as Habitat Properties, another Singapore real estate firm controlled by his family, and he acquired other businesses in the island state.[88] He also extended his control of Grand Hotel Group, listed in Australia. Nursalim did not appear to want for cash, circumstantial evidence perhaps of the claim that godfathers used their central bank liquidity credits during the crisis to buy foreign exchange (thereby driving down the value of the rupiah) which was exported to Singapore and elsewhere. When, in 2003, IBRA sold two of Nursalim's Indonesian businesses – tyre maker Gajah Tunggal and GT Petrochem Industries – to Singapore-based Garibaldi Venture, many observers suggested that Nursalim was behind the purchase. The fact that Nursalim's son-in-law remains a director of Gajah Tunggal's fast-growing China operation, [89] which by 2004 claimed to be the country's biggest producer of replacement tyres with revenues of over US$1 billion, makes it clear the family is far from out of the picture. 'The structure of the recapitalisation allowed the big families to wiggle back in,' says Michael Chambers, head of the CLSA Asia-Pacific Markets office in Jakarta, and one of those who believes Nursalim controls Gajah Tunggal again. He says the ruse was common: 'The conversation goes: "Listen, Michael, don't tell anyone but I just bought it back for 5 cents on the dollar." It's outrageous.' [90]

The Riady family was another accused of surreptitiously buying back assets on the cheap. Unlike most of the big godfathers, the Riadys were not blacklisted from owning a bank again. They found some additional capital for their Bank Lippo during the crisis and, thanks to close relations with Suharto's immediate successor Habibie, secured most of a first tranche of state recapitalisation funds. The Riadys remained the largest private shareholders, with an official 9 per cent of the bank – the government held 52 per cent – and brought in ING-Baring as management advisers, in line with IMF requirements. From 2000 to 2003, however, the Riadys engaged in a series of infringements of stock exchange rules, including manipulation of the 2002 Bank Lippo annual report, that led to record fines by regulators and saw Bank Lippo's share price fall dramatically. There were also revised audits that contained large downward revaluations of collateral assets on the bank's books. Many people in Jakarta concluded that the Riadys were driving Bank Lippo's stock price down ahead of the government's sale of its equity. The curiosity was that the Riadys could have bid direct for those shares in 2004, but chose not to do so, despite their continuing involvement in Bank Lippo management and apparent desire to control the bank again. Instead, IBRA unilaterally narrowed down a group of bidders to just one, which bought the government's stake in January 2004. The consortium comprised Austrian bank Raiffeisen and three investment funds. Critics said the Riadys were hiding behind the investment funds, one of which, according to Michael Chambers, is 'run by Italian-Americans living above a shoe shop in Switzerland'. [91]

Reality is an elusive beast in Indonesia. Chambers' view is that post-crisis: 'Of the top ten families, nine of them are probably still top ten' if one considers the assets they hung on to offshore and those they still control through nominees in Indonesia. Other seasoned observers believe there has been greater change. Gene Galbraith, a veteran Jakarta-based stockbroker and entrepreneur who was brought in to run Bank Central Asia after it was sold to American investors and the Hartono tobacco family, contends: 'Almost all the old rascals are much reduced or frozen. They have retained much of their wealth, but their ability to operate is much reduced.'[92] There is some truth in this. A decade after the crisis there is an uneasy stand-off between the government of Susilo Bambang Yudhoyono and several big godfathers. Prajogo Pangestu, for instance, a leading timber baron who was in business with several Suharto family members, has more than once been threatened with prosecution for past abuse of reforestation funds and other alleged crimes. Prajogo is concerned enough to keep a very low profile, yet legal action never actually takes place. He has been forced to sell controlling interests in his pulp manufacturing subsidiary to Japan's Marubeni, and in his petrochemicals business to Singapore's Temasek. Yet Prajogo and his son remain in management control of his flagship, listed Barito Pacific Timber, despite the fact that almost all the equity belongs in theory to his creditors. It is indicative of a complex situation that the man identified by *Forbes* as the richest Indonesian in 2006 – worth an estimated US$2.8 billion – is another Suharto-era timber tycoon, Sukanto Tanoto, whom state bank Mandiri in 2006 listed as one of its six biggest delinquent debtors; he subsequently negotiated a repayment schedule and was taken off the list.[93] Tanoto is also under investigation for fraud at the bank he used to own.[94] Needless to say, his Asia Pacific Resources International Holdings Ltd (APRIL) is run from Singapore.

One reason why the Indonesian government does not move more aggressively against the godfathers is the belief that by working with them flight capital from the crisis will be repatriated. Michael Chambers, basing his views on information from banking sources, believes that up to US$200 billion of Indonesian money is sitting in Singapore alone. In 2005 Indonesian vice president Jusuf Kalla met with a group of godfathers including Prajogo Pangestu, Anthony Salim and Tanoto, who promised a gradual repatriation of funds stashed overseas.[95] The notion that negotiation between the state and godfathers is a substitute for the rule of law, however, is a dangerous one. It none the less typifies the way that Javanese political culture has always worked. The fully democratically elected government of Yudhoyono, which has brought back a measure of stability since 2004, is no stranger to this tradition. Jusuf Kalla and fellow cabinet minister Aburizal Bakrie are from major *pribumi* business dynasties that have long benefited from state concessions; one of the other people on Bank Mandiri's list of leading recalcitrant debtors in 2006 was Kalla's brother-in-law.[96] Yudhoyono himself is a former Suharto general.

The most remarkable post-crisis Indonesian godfather story – and one that shows that even if the country is moving in the right direction almost anything is still possible for the tycoons – is that of Eka Tjipta Widjaya. The polygamist Widjaya, whose prized possessions include a great deal of jade and a well-worn belt with 'Eka' inscribed on it in diamonds, created the Sinar Mas group, second only to the Salim empire before the crisis. The sprawling Sinar Mas conglomerate's biggest business is an integrated forestry, plywood, pulp and paper unit, many of whose assets are grouped under Singapore-based Asia Pulp & Paper (APP) and its numerous subsidiaries. The Widjayas are masters of the godfather arts of pyramiding listed companies and opaque interplay between private and public businesses. Before the crisis, they had their own bank, whose deposits they milked, and which fell into IBRA's hands. But a local piggy bank was insufficient for Eka Tjipta Widjaja's ambitions. In the 1980s and 1990s he became Indonesia's corporate bond king, selling foreign currency-denominated debt through a host of subsidiaries. Major bond sales in the three years before the crisis were facilitated by APP listing on the New York stock exchange, at the height of Asia fever, in 1995. Then came the Asian crisis, which was followed by a dip in the international wood pulp price in 2000. In 2001, APP units called a moratorium on payments of interest and principal.[97] It was then revealed that the group's consolidated debt was a stunning US$13.9 billion.

In a functioning legal system, that would have been the end of APP, as bondholders would have taken charge of its assets in the wake of default and liquidated them. But for Eka Tjipta Widjaja and his family in Indonesia, it was game on. The first move, within days of the default, was an APP announcement that it had lost US$220 million in foreign exchange dealings and that its financial statements for 1997–9 'should not be relied upon'. APP then said it was having trouble collecting US$1 billion in receivables from offshore trading companies. The company insisted the British Virgin Islands-registered firms were unconnected to it or the Widjayas, but the *Wall Street Journal* found APP staff worked at them.[98] Creditors condemned what appeared to be a move by the Widjayas to hide cash offshore. The view was reinforced when an outside auditor discovered that an APP unit had put US$200 million on deposit with a bank in the Cook Islands, in the south-west Pacific, that the Widjayas controlled. Two other Widjaya businesses that were not part of APP also had hundreds of millions of dollars on deposit.[99] In New York, APP's share price crashed to around 1 per cent of its peak, and in July 2001 the company was required to delist.[100] Thereafter it stopped producing consolidated, audited accounts, putting creditors almost completely in the dark about what was happening in the business.

All this began a decline in the price of APP bonds outstanding in the secondary market, because of the reduced likelihood they would be repaid in full. In public, the Widjayas said they wanted a debt workout, but they showed little interest in negotiating seriously with creditors, who were now being paid neither interest nor principal. Instead, in 2003, two APP units started legal action in the Indonesian courts alleging that bond issues they had made were illegal under local law and the result of misrepresentation by international investment banks. [101] Meanwhile, creditors casting a more careful eye over APP assets noted that the company's pulp processing operations were largely hostage to Indonesian forestry concessions held privately by the Widjayas; even if pulp and paper factories could be seized, they might be denied their raw material. The price of APP bonds in the secondary market sank lower still. In 2004, local courts found in favour of both the cases by the APP subsidiaries; in one instance US$500 million of bonds were declared null and void.

The results of these shenanigans were three-fold: first, the Widjayas almost certainly stashed large amounts of cash offshore and out of the reach of creditors; second, the family's hand in restructuring its overall debt load was greatly strengthened; and third, it became possible to buy up bonds that APP units had issued for pennies on the dollar. The family's underlying strategy, as far as can be seen, was to split off the debts of its Indonesian businesses from those of subsidiaries overseas. With domestic demand in Indonesia decimated, other operations had better near-term prospects. In particular China, which began a period of rapid economic expansion in 2003, was producing strong growth for local APP units, which were expanding.[102] The company also kept its repayments of Chinese bank loans fully up-to-date, despite its moratorium on bond debt. In 2003, the Widjayas proposed exchanging US$660 million of outstanding bond-based debt for 99 per cent of the equity of APP's China operation, controlled via a Bermuda company. In the offer document, the Widjayas were said to own about 23 per cent of the bonds via the bank they control in the Cook Islands;[103] three-quarters of the bonds by value would be required for approval. After what traders said was frenzied activity in the purchase and sale of bonds issued by the China unit, a vote was called in which bondholders representing 89 per cent of the value of bonds concerned, said they were in favour of the proposal. A Bermuda court approved the restructuring. The Widjayas had their deal. Unfortunately, there was then some rather negative publicity as the New York firm retained to run the vote tried to contact registered bondholders in order to send them shares in the China business. Around 150 bondholders, representing 19 per cent by value, were Taiwanese who submitted physical registration documents for the vote through Nomura Securities in Singapore, where APP is headquartered (institutional investors dealt with the registration electronically, which is now the norm). The Taiwanese all voted in favour of the restructuring; when the New York firm Bondholder Communications called the contact numbers given on their forms, some numbers did not exist, some were wrong and others were answered by people who refused to put the caller in touch with the named bondholder. Other respondents identified themselves as relatives of the bondholder, but said it was highly unlikely the person in question owned millions of dollars of investments – they were low-ranking employees of APP in Taiwan. In 2004 Bondholder Communications wrote to the Bermudan supreme court judge who approved the restructuring the year before to say it believed that up to one-third of registered bondholders by value may not have been the real beneficial owners; this was easily enough to make the difference between success and failure in the vote. APP did not deny that the registered bondholders were its employees but claimed in a written statement that, for cultural reasons, Asians do not like discussing financial matters with strangers and, by implication, the persons in question may not have wanted to admit to their large investments. Barring an unfavourable judicial review in Bermuda, which has not occurred as of May 2007, the Widjayas have their Chinese baby.

In Indonesia, the Widjayas secured an agreement in 2005 with respect to the US$6.7 billion of debt attributable to their Indonesian units. The terms looked pretty good from the family's perspective. Only US$1.2 billion would be repaid in full. The rest of the debt was converted into new bonds – after a significant write-down of unpaid interest – with maturities as long as twenty-two years. Most creditors decided they had to accept the deal, which achieved the necessary two-thirds support, although the US Import–Export Bank and some American bondholders continue to pursue APP in the US courts. The continuing power of the Widjayas in Indonesia, and their ability to move cash in and out of their businesses at will, wore creditors down. Deutsche Bank and BNP Paribas petitioned a court in Singapore to appoint an administrator to run locally based APP instead of the Widjayas, but the court would have none of it.[104] A March 2003 letter from the ambassadors of the US, Japan, Canada and eight European countries urging the Indonesian government to do something about APP's treatment of creditors, as well as interventions by several heads of state, were ignored in Jakarta. Indeed, creditors will be lucky if they are even paid out on the terms the Widjayas agreed in 2005. In November 2006, the supreme court in Jakarta upheld one of the 2004 district court rulings that US$500 million of bonds issued by an APP unit were illegal and therefore need not be repaid.[105]

The Widjayas are untouchable. Their involvement in illegal logging in Indonesia has been proven by journalists and environmental groups on numerous occasions, but the government does nothing. While the family fended off creditors of APP after 1998, and retained control of all their pulp and paper businesses, its separate, vast interests in plantations entered a period of breakneck growth by virtue of the recent global commodity boom. The Widjayas, Indonesia's leading international debtors at the time of the crisis, are today richer than ever. As Gene Galbraith puts it: 'They made out like bandits.'[106]

It should also be noted that Indonesia fits the post-crisis godfather pattern not only because some big boys were unscathed, while a few actually benefited. In addition, the political and economic system produced new godfathers. The most feared of these is Tommy Winata, a businessman with close links to the military, including former armed forces commanders Edi Sudradjat and Try Sutrisno, and, critics allege, the criminal underworld.[107] After the crisis, his Artha Graha conglomerate ballooned. 'He is a top three real estate developer from nothing, the rising star of the Indonesian economy,' says Philip Purnama, a senior executive working for Anthony Salim.[108] Winata received licences to move into shipping, coal, financial services and many other new businesses. Tommy, like his recently released namesake Tommy Suharto, is not a man to be messed with. When Indonesia's best-known news magazine, *Tempo*, aired a report in 2003 that apparent arson at a Jakarta market area that Winata was interested in redeveloping might be to his benefit, a large group of thugs with a police escort turned up at *Tempo*'s offices and proceeded to assault the chief editor.[109]

A less scary, but none the less mysterious, godfather on the rise since the crisis is Bambang Harry Iswanto Tanoesoedibjo, commonly known as Harry Tanoe. He bought control of the Bimantara conglomerate from Suharto's son Bambang Trihatmodjo in April 2002. He also acquired valuable licences during the presidency of Abdurrahman Wahid, with whom both he and his father have long-standing relationships. Apart from Bimantara, Harry Tanoe's major investment vehicles include PT Bhakti Investama. Inevitably, there is much speculation about how a businessman in his early forties acquired the financial heft to build up one of the largest business empires in the country in the past few years. Some say Harry Tanoe, an ethnic Chinese who converted to Islam (like Bob Hasan), is running on Salim cash, others that he is a new

Suharto front. As ever in Indonesia, there is no shortage of conspiracy theories, any one or none of which might be accurate.

Sunny places, Some Shady People

The tycoon experience in Singapore and Hong Kong following the financial crisis was a relatively passive one. The city states' domestic economies depend on growth in the regions around them, and the godfathers, whose wealth is rooted in banking and real estate, simply had to wait out the downturn. It was a long wait, but the local billionaires' core cash flows are such that not one of them faced a serious threat of insolvency.

In Singapore, the *dirigiste* government of the Lee family was relatively more proactive than the Hong Kong administration in making policy adjustments, almost all of which coincided with the godfathers' best interests. One decision was also of significance to the multinational-dominated export processing sector: the Singapore dollar was allowed to depreciate from 1.4 to the US dollar in early 1997 to a low of more than 1.8 after the crisis. This boosted the competitiveness of exports and limited the rise of unemployment. A quest for new sources of growth in the domestic economy – where tycoon concern is focused – turned up two bright ideas. The first, as mentioned previously, was to woo more international private banking business in a period when the European Union and the United States were trying to clamp down on tax evasion through other international financial centres, particularly Switzerland. After a series of regulatory changes that were crafted with the help of international private bankers, total funds under management in Singapore-based asset management firms increased from US$92 billion in 1998 to US$350 billion and rising at the start of 2005; of this latter total, more than a third was private banking money. The second change, also already discussed, was to licence two multi-billion-dollar casino resorts; one franchise went to Malaysia's Lim family, the other to the Las Vegas-based Sands group.

On the back of scores of billions of dollars of Indonesian capital flight into Singaporean banks and high-end real estate – the *Jakarta Post* claimed in 2007 that 18,000 of an estimated total of 55,000 'super-rich' living in Singapore were Indonesians[110] – these two moves were a significant boon to local godfathers, who own prime real estate and stakes in the Singapore bank cartel. The government also began to woo private banking and investment money from wealthy Indians, although in this task it faced stiff competition from Dubai.[111]

Banking families in Singapore had had little chance to ruin themselves prior to the crisis because the government there mandates reserves of capital relative to assets that are far in excess of international norms. The big three privately held banks – OCBC, OUB and UOB – were constrained in their expansion but remained strongly profitable thanks to their membership of the small and cosy cartel. The real estate downturn after 1997 was pronounced, with commercial property prices and rents falling by around 40 per cent. But the top-end office and residential sectors in which godfather interests predominate were the most resilient and, by 2006, had surpassed the peak price levels of the boom years. The likes of Kwek Leng Beng and Ng Teng Fong did not suffer unduly, and had cash on hand to buy up assets that became available in distress sales. The major Singaporean godfather families either maintained their net worth or increased it somewhat. Meanwhile, the government showed little embarrassment at the lengthening list of Indonesian godfathers camping out in Singapore – many of them wanted in Jakarta for questioning in civil and criminal investigations. In October 2006 Indonesia's *Tempo* magazine listed Sukanto Tanoto, Sjamsul Nursalim, Liem Sioe Liong and Eka Tjipta Widjaja – all major tycoons this book has dealt with – plus Bambang Sutrisno and Andrian Kiki Ariawan (both sentenced to life in prison by Indonesian courts for embezzling central bank funds),[112] Agus Anwar (wanted for embezzlement and granted Singaporean citizenship in 2003),[113] and several others as being holed up in the city state.[114] In a surprise move in April 2007, Singapore did agree to an extradition treaty with Indonesia – though at the time of writing it had not been ratified and it was impossible to know how it would work in practice.

In Hong Kong, like Singapore, the godfathers saw the values of their listed businesses and real estate holdings tumble during the crisis – property values dropped by more than 40 per cent on average – but, again like Singapore, much of their private wealth had been recycled into investments in the United States, Canada, Australia and Europe and was thus insulated from the turmoil. The main difference in Hong Kong was that 1997 witnessed a transition from colonial rule to government by tycoon, as the nice-but-dim shipping heir Tung Chee-hwa became the territory's first chief executive. Tung had been heavily backed by his fellow godfathers for the job – particularly Henry Fok and Li Ka-shing – and the plutocrats had high hopes for his administration. Perhaps conscious that he was seen by many as a tycoons' marionette, Tung made early policy pronouncements which were pointedly populist. He called for a large increase in the supply of residential housing units and more bank support for small and medium-sized businesses. But it was not long before the godfathers' interests were being met. In August 1998, the government sank US$15 billion of its foreign exchange reserves into equity investments to support the stock market; much of the money went on tycoon company shares. In 1999, Li Ka-shing's son Richard Li was granted untendered rights to develop an enormously valuable parcel of land on Hong Kong island, the so-called Cyberport project. After this, there followed a series of grandiose and controversial development projects whose main beneficiaries would be the godfather class. The government rolled out plans for a vast new exhibition centre, a logistics park on Lantau island and new harbour reclamations for development in the central and Wanchai areas of Hong Kong island. In 2004, with the bottom end of the property market in the doldrums but the top recovering, the Kwok brothers' Sun Hung Kai and Cheng Yu-tung's New World Group, which had built 2,000 government-subsidised public housing flats in line with Tung Chee-hwa's new housing policy, applied to tear them down and put up luxury condominiums instead.[115] There was a public outcry. More indignation ensued when the Tung government tried to privatise shopping and parking facilities in public housing estates without seeking approval in the Legislative Council.[116] The most contentious Tung project involved a plan to develop a vast site in west Kowloon which had long been promised as park land for the densely populated city. The administration said that instead of a park it would create a 'cultural centre'. To most observers the plans submit-ted by tycoons looked much like any other high-rise real estate development, with a few public buildings in the middle. But the godfathers insisted culture was close to their hearts. The Kwoks put up a 10 metre by 16 metre stage curtain designed by Picasso in their IFC tower in Central and had French presi-dent Jacques Chirac unveil it. Li Ka-shing's Cheung Kong took Hong Kong jour-nalists on a trip to the Louvre.[117] The public was unimpressed, and by Tung's second term, which began in 2002, popular indignation was palpable.

The Tung regime suffered the same two problems as Thaksin Shinawatra's godfather government in Thailand. First, it focused educated middle-class opinion on the nature of godfather economics as never before. It did not matter that the reality of colonial Hong Kong had been far removed from the official myth of a free market state presented by the British rulers. Once a tycoon was in charge – and in the midst of the worst economic downturn in a generation – questions of collusion between political and economic power were pushed to the forefront of public debate. The tycoons' representatives who hold industry-based (and not popularly elected) 'functional constitu-ency' seats in the Legislative Council did their best to present vast construc-tion projects as the rational answer to economic malaise, but their popularly elected peers in the council were increasingly adept at drawing attention to the self-serving nature of the business lobby.[118] Tung's second problem was that his ascendancy stoked the latent jealousy and bitterness that exists between godfathers around the region. Unlike Thaksin, Tung was not himself a big financial winner from gaining power, but his tycoon pals were soon consumed with neurotic fury that he was showing favouritism among them. The 1999 award of the Cyberport franchise to Richard Li brought about an unprecedented stream of public denouncements by rival godfathers. Ronnie Chan, Robert Ng and Gordon Wu all condemned the failure to follow an open tender procedure. The latter, a failing infrastructure and real estate billionaire who competes with Ronnie Chan to vilify democracy as the enemy of development, moaned to the *South China Morning Post* in 2005: 'Look at Cyberport and the West Kowloon cultural district project and you know only the mega companies would be qualified to play in Hong Kong ... The business environment in the past years has been very bad.'[119] By Tung's second term, the public did not like him and most of the godfathers did not like him either. He stumbled on for another eighteen months before resigning on the grounds of ill health on 10 March 2005. China fingered a British-trained civil servant, Donald Tsang, to replace him.

The appointment of Tsang took some of the heat of public resentment off the godfathers. He is more politically astute than Tung and canned the former's outstanding white elephant projects, notably the west Kowloon development.[120] Instead of telling the public that Hong Kong had no need of a competition and monopolies law, Tsang said he would think about one and – to tycoon relief – has already been thinking for two years. The godfathers lined up to support his formal 'election' by an 800-member group of notables, most of them sanctioned by Beijing, in March 2007 and he duly won. It will not, however, be possible to put all Tung's spilt milk back in the bottle. The politicisation of Hong Kong that occurred on his watch is deep-rooted and complex. As well as a rise in political consciousness among voters, the Tung years saw the blossoming of non-government pressure groups that are unprecedented in the region. Minority investor associations were organised to block many of the attempted tycoon privatisations described earlier and to put forward candidates for election to the board of the Hong Kong stock exchange.[121] Independent think tanks, most notably Civic Exchange, produce a steady stream of reports highlighting the case for greater competition in the domestic economy and the conflicts of interest inherent in functional constituency electoral arrangements. The godfathers have been stirred if not impoverished – something attested by their increasingly frequent statements about the dangers of political reform.[122] The big outstanding question, which is addressed in the final chapter, is whether the godfathers can hold the line until popular political momentum dissipates or whether the challenge to their way of life will increase further.

For now, the tycoons are in fine financial fettle. They were thrown some meaty bones by Tung Chee-hwa, while the trend of post-colonial government in Hong Kong is towards higher levels of capital expenditure – mostly on infrastructure – which will always benefit them. The local real estate market returned to 1997 price levels in 2006, and the stock market was at a record high in early 2007. Much of the time, the market still dances to the god-fathers' tune, even if they do face stiffer opposition from minorities. In 1999 and 2000, the leading real estate billionaires all spun out vapid dot.com subsidiaries in initial public offerings to take advantage of the US and European technology bubble. They were businesses without business, and soon on the skids. After the internet economy crash of 2001, the next fashion was listings of real estate investment trusts (REITs). The game here was for tycoons to sell low-grade property assets into new corporate entities, back-load the debt repayments of the purchaser and list them with the story that dividends in year one would be a guide to future earnings. As ever, K. S. Li was the ring-master-in-chief. His Cheung Kong Prosperity Reit in late 2005 raised HK$1.92 billion, offering an attractive yield of 5.3 per cent.[123] But Prosperity's debt structure was such that it paid no interest on its borrowings in year one. The listing followed the classic godfather curve. Sold at HK$2.16, the REIT's price spiked 20 per cent on day one before going into steady decline despite a rising market; by March 2007 it was trading at HK$1.78. In early 2004, Li and his investment bankers pulled a similar stunt with a Hutchison spin-off into a company called Vanda Systems and Communications, which also flew briefly, and crashed, before being taken back into private ownership for half the listing price.[124] Son Richard achieved perhaps the most savage drubbing of minority investors in Hong Kong history with his Pacific Century Cyber Works (PCCW) all-stock takeover of Hongkong Telecom during the internet bubble; the peak-to-trough drop in PCCW's share price was 97 per cent. For good measure, the young Li followed up with a back-door listing of PCCW's real estate assets that was also characterised by a big spike and crash in the stock price.[125] Reflecting on the behaviour of Li Ka-shing, former Morgan Stanley managing director Peter Churchouse comments: 'To me it is a totally cynical exploitation of a public that adores him but doesn't know better.'[126]

Why people do not know better is hard to fathom. The Prosperity REIT was a quintessential case study of the kind of godfather business not to buy into. Li Ka-shing's Cheung Kong retained an interest of only 18.6 per cent at listing, with Hutchison holding 10.4 per cent. This meant the boss himself would own only about 10 per cent of what he was selling, a powerful signal that the asset was overpriced. The few godfather businesses that have ever been worth buying into as a minority are the ones the big boss owns most of, because then he must share in any pain as well as any gain. It is not possible to protect small investors from their own poor judgement, but it is curious that more people have not grasped a simple rule such as this. Anson Chan, Hong Kong's chief secretary under Chris Patten, lambasts Li Ka-shing for more than just his capital markets antics after the crisis. On several occasions, she says, he made threats to government officials and in public that he would pull his money out of Hong Kong if regulators acted against what he deemed to be the best interests of 'business'. 'I have very little respect for most of the [big] business people in HK,' she huffs.[127] But Li's threats are nothing new. He made similar statements in 1990 when he needed special regulatory exemptions for Star Television, which he then controlled. Moreover, it is hardly plausible that Li is going to walk away from his dominant positions in the de facto real estate, power, retail and ports cartels in order to compete in more open markets. After Hutchison made a windfall profit of US$15 billion from the sale of its stake in the European Orange mobile telephony business in 1999, and immediately gambled the money back into a raft of 3G licences around the world, Li needed his Hong Kong cash flows once more to shore up a loss-making, capital-intensive business. If he had no such revenues, Li would quite possibly have had to write off his '3' business in recent years.[128]

Instead, Li entered 2007 with his empire intact and expanding, and his name at the top of the *Forbes* list of the richest people in Asia. He was also, as of the 2006 list, estimated to be the tenth richest person in the world. Li's personal fortune had increased by US$8.2 billion to US$18.8 billion since the last pre-Asian crisis rankings, in 1996. No other south-east Asian tycoon featured in the top twenty-five billionaires in 2006, and only two families – the Kwok brothers with US$11.6 billion and Lee Shau-kee with US$11 billion – were in the top fifty. (This, it will be remembered from the introduction, compares with eight godfathers in the global top twenty-five and thirteen in the top fifty in 1996.) The change, however, was not because the Asian godfathers had seen their wealth reduced. Rather, they have been overtaken by Europeans and Americans whose stock markets continued to prosper in the late 1990s and were only briefly set back by the worldwide bursting of the internet bubble in 2001.[129] Looked at in terms of simple net worth, of the eight south-east Asians in the top twenty-five in 1996 Li Ka-shing increased his wealth substantially despite the crisis, four tycoons maintained it, one died and had his money split among his heirs, and two lost.[130] The cumulative net worth of the top eight south-east Asian godfathers in 2006 was US$66.5 billion versus US$65.1 billion a decade earlier. Beyond the top eight in 2006, many other south-east Asian tycoons had increased their fortunes markedly through the crisis era. Among those featured in this book were Stanley Ho, whose gambling fortune increased to an estimated US$6.5 billion, and Malaysia's Ananda Krishnan, whose net worth rose to US$4.3 billion by 2006. From a godfather's standpoint, the Asian crisis – to put it mildly – could have been a lot worse.

7

Finale: The politics, stupid

'If we have done anything wrong, send your man to my man and they can fix it up.'

J. Pierpont Morgan to President Teddy Roosevelt,
after hearing news of a government anti-trust suit

*'I may have committed many sins in my life, but I can tell you that stealing is not
one of them.'*

Ferdinand Marcos, interviewed in exile by Ted Koppel on *ABC Nightline*, 4 April 1986

From a macro-economic perspective, the recovery of the south-east Asian economy in recent years boils down to two things: exports, and the boom in China that began in 2003. South-east Asia's manufactured exports, as we have seen, are driven by multinational companies outsourcing processing work, efficient but small-scale local contractors, and the quiet industriousness of Asian workers; the godfathers are only marginally involved. The extent to which exports rescued south-east Asia from the financial crisis has been little recognised. Readers of newspapers may be forgiven for thinking that all of the world's export processing activity has moved to China, and that this perceived change was a significant factor in the Asian crisis. In reality, south-east Asian exports since 1997 – after a brief pre-crisis and crisis dip – diverged little from their long-term average growth rate of the past thirty years.[1] Because they are globally competitive, export manufacturers managed to fund post-crisis growth from operating cash flows or – in the case of multinationals – through fresh investment from parent corporations. Lower valued-added processing work has migrated to China (and Vietnam, and Bangladesh) at a rapid clip, but this started well before the crisis and will continue. More specialised tasks, or ones requiring the kind of intellectual property protection unavailable in China, have continued to expand in south-east Asia. Semi-conductor exports from Malaysia and the Philippines, for instance, have rocketed in the past decade. At the same time, multinationals have reacted to the possibility of

US and European export constraints against China because of the country's ballooning trade surplus and artificially cheap currency[2] by identifying, and sometimes using, alternative suppliers around the region.[3] This is the same game as was played in the early 1990s, when the Clinton administration threatened China with sanctions over its human rights abuses; Nike, as one example, made half its sneakers in China and half in Indonesia, just in case. Exports were the south-east Asian pillar that did not crumble after the crisis. The one that did was domestic investment, much of which comes from the godfather companies that dominate local (as opposed to external) economies. When the crisis hit, regional banks – many of them controlled and manipulated by godfathers – were revealed to be insolvent and could no longer lend. Tycoons, awash in unsaleable real estate and other unproductive assets, were unable to borrow until politicians bailed them out or economies recovered sufficiently to ease their surfeit. The share of south-east Asian Gross Domestic Product accounted for by investment fell by more than ten percentage points after the crisis.[4] The result was that the contribution of net exports leapt. Nominal exports as proportion of GDP in the territories we are following increased from 45 per cent in 1997 to 65 per cent in 2006.[5] Governments, quite aware of what was coming to their rescue, bought up foreign exchange inflows to keep their currencies (and hence exports) cheap, resumed informal dollar pegs and piled up reserves.[6]

Many godfathers, though not active in processing of manufactures, were big beneficiaries of a second export resurgence after the crisis – commodities. This was driven by demand from China, a country which began a powerful investment-led boom in 2003 that saw growth spike up to more than 10 per cent a year, where it has remained ever since. To manufactured exports whose end-users are mostly in Europe, America and Japan, China's *dirigiste* industrialisation programme has added demand for south-east Asian soft and hard commodities – Malaysian gas, Thai rubber, Indonesian lumber, and so on. Unlike manufacturing, these are sectors in which godfathers are very active, because they depend on political concessions. South-east Asian tycoons who lost large sums of money in China during the 1990s in that decade's real estate boom and bust made back larger sums in recent years in the China commodities bonanza.[7] Typical beneficiaries include Robert Kuok and Eka Tjipta Widjaya with palm oil and other plantation commodities, and Ananda Krishnan, who has private oil and gas concessions. The Chinese engine also powered an explosion in Asian gambling, since casinos and most forms of betting are illegal in the People's Republic but cross-border travel for its citizens has been liberalised. The Lims' vast Genting Highlands casino complex near Kuala Lumpur began to specialise in cut-price junkets for Chinese punters, but the biggest beneficiary was Macau, since 1999 a Special Administrative Region (SAR) of China. The former Portuguese colony became an enormous money laundromat, providing costly diversion for the Chinese masses while cleansing the ill-gotten fortunes of many a Chinese government official and state enterprise manager. The expiry of Stanley Ho, Henry Fok and Cheng Yu-tung's casino monopoly in 2001 – and the arrival of competing US casino operators – turned out to be less important than the floodtide of new Chinese money into Macau. In 2006, the SAR overtook Las Vegas as the world's biggest gaming town by turnover.[8] The ageing Stanley Ho may be dribbling these days, but he is also smiling and richer than ever. What good fortune it was that the Second World War caused him to cross the Pearl River estuary from Hong Kong.

The Tab

If not the average godfather, who did pay the price for the Asian financial crisis, a malady so serious that south-east Asia's gross domestic product has only just returned to 1995 levels? The answer requires a detour into the lives of so-called ordinary people. In theory, it is possible to measure changes of wealth in different societies by calculations based on macro-economic data: economists try to calibrate both financial wealth – summing cash, bank deposits, stocks, bonds and investments overseas – and physical wealth – real estate, plant and equipment, inventories, and so on. By both measures, converted into US dollar terms, south-east Asians were still worse off at the start of 2007 than they were in 1995, despite the return of solid economic growth.[9] Macro-economic wealth measures, however, suffer from all kinds of methodological weaknesses and it is probably more instructive, when considering who suffered most from the crisis, to look at simpler indicators like real wages and poverty.

Beginning with the city states of Singapore and Hong Kong, it is hard to escape the conclusion that those who picked up the tab for the crisis were the people who had least to do with its creation and were least able to pay. This was partly the result of deflationary pressures unleashed after 1997 and partly the result of deliberate government policy. In Singapore, on the government's own data, real incomes of the poorest 40 per cent of the population fell between 2000 and 2005, even as strong economic growth resumed. The biggest losers were people over fifty who were made redundant from already poorly paid jobs and discovered that, for all its wealth, Singapore offers almost no state unemployment benefits. At the same time, the city's administration continued a long-standing policy of cutting income tax for the richest segment of the population – the highest level was cut from 28 per cent in 2000 to just 20 per cent today; the corporate profit tax rate was also shaved. In contrast to these moves, indirect taxes paid by everybody were increased in 2007 – local value-added tax was put up from 5 per cent to 7 per cent. Bizarrely, government ministers said this broad-based tax increase was necessary to provide a little extra support for the poor. Raffles Institution- and Cambridge-educated Harry Lee Kuan Yew, justifying tax policy, told journalists: 'This is a tough and competitive world.'[10] The local population acquiesced for the two usual reasons: people in neighbouring countries are relatively poorer and more mistreated, and Singaporeans are justifiably terrified of Harry's wrath. To the business traveller, confined to the Central Business District, it is difficult to imagine there are such things as poverty and an underclass in Singapore; but a short taxi ride into the city's public housing estates reveals just that.

In Hong Kong, the tab for the Asian crisis also fell squarely into the lap of those less able to pay it. Despite some increases in welfare provision under the administration of the last governor, Chris Patten, a trend to greater poverty in the city was apparent throughout the 1990s, and the crisis exacerbated this as many people's real wages fell. The benchmark for poverty in Hong Kong is normally given as the proportion of households living on less than half the median monthly household income, which is itself a remarkably low US$1,290.[11] By this measure, the poor increased from 11.2 per cent of the population in 1991 to 15 per cent in 1996 and 18.3 per cent in 2000.[12] Because most rich Hong Kongers send their children to private schools overseas, one quarter of children in Hong Kong schools are now from impoverished families, putting further pressure on a public education system that has traditionally been grossly underfunded. The crisis also hit the earnings of people who had considered themselves more middle class. By 2001, only 15.6 per cent of household income was going to the less well off half of the population.[13] The main difference between Hong Kong and Singapore in terms of the broad impact of the crisis was that the former retained its currency peg. This meant that deflationary pressure in Hong Kong was borne solely by the stock and property markets, and not the exchange rate. Tens of thousands of home owners – almost all from the richer half of the population – were pushed into negative equity for a decade until average residential prices began to approach 1997 levels in late 2006. This shock to the professional classes may have contributed to the remarkable politicisation of Hong Kong in recent years.

In Thailand, Malaysia and Indonesia, the urban middle class was also hit hard, but the real suffering fell to tens of millions of people pushed back under – or close to – the poverty line as real wages dropped, unemployment and under-employment increased, and the cost of daily necessities rose. Urban middle-class wealth was hit first, in 1997–8, as stock and real estate values collapsed, and real urban salaries fell. The impact on the less well off arrived more slowly, but five years later the crisis was undeniably severe. The crisis had a common geographic trait, where the initial impact hit big cities – especially the capitals – and then spread slowly but inexorably to the rest of the country. In Thailand, most estimates suggest that around 1 million people out of a population of 60 million were pushed back into poverty.[14] In Malaysia, where little domestic research on poverty has been conducted since the crisis, the proportional impact was likely similar. In Indonesia, where inflation eroded real wages by around 40 per cent, the poverty rate doubled during the crisis to 27 per cent of the population, or 54 million people.[15] Absolute poverty then receded somewhat before trending up again from 2005; some welfare groups estimated 80 million Indonesians were living in poverty in 2006.[16] An equally lamentable legacy of the crisis is the number of persons in south-east Asia living just above the poverty level. The World Bank's *2006 World Development Report*, whose theme was 'equity and development', showed the proportion of the population living on more than its indexed US$1-a-day poverty threshold, but on less than US$2 a day, was 52 per cent in Indonesia and 32 per cent in Thailand.[17] The comparable ratio in Argentina was 14 per cent and in Brazil 22 per cent.[18]

It is to be hoped that the Philippines, whose economic unravelling began in the last years of Marcos, does not provide a guide to future poverty and employment performance in the rest of the region. According to the *2006 World Development Report*, 15 per cent of Filipinos were living in absolute poverty, and 47 per cent subsisted on an income between US$1 and US$2 a day. Half the 12-million population of Manila lives in shanty towns that line the expressways, rail tracks and waterways of the metropolis. After twenty-five years of repeated economic crises, the Philippines' economy is now critically dependent on the overseas earnings of an estimated 10 million, mostly female workers – out of a population of 80 million – employed as child carers, nurses, and more in richer states around the world.[19] The working population continues to move abroad and no country is more dependent on remittances to keep itself afloat: US$12 billion sent back in 2006 amounted to some 15 per cent of the Philippines' gross domestic product.[20]

The Politics

There is little doubt that godfather economics have been the agent for much of the increased poverty and inequality in south-east Asia. The tens of billions of dollars of bank asset write-offs and corporate bail-outs for the businesses of the few were borne in the form of inflation, reduced welfare spending,[21] higher taxes and lower real wages for the many. None the less, the godfathers – so many of whom have recovered their fortunes – were only the agents of this calamity. Real responsibility rests with the politicians who allowed godfather economics to exist in the first place. In the introduction to this book it was stated that post-crisis south-east Asia finds itself at a crossroads at which it must make a political choice between a descent towards the levels of inequality and social alienation, and repetitious economic crises, associated with Latin America, or a higher road that leads to sustainable growth and greater social equity. This is not a rhetorical construct designed to shock the reader. Post-crisis, absolute poverty in the Philippines is worse, and in Indonesia as bad, as in South America, while the proportion of people in the Philippines, Indonesia and Thailand living on less than US$2 a day is significantly greater.[22] A poverty profile that compares unfavourably with Hugo Chavez's Venezuela is a serious matter. Inequality – as opposed to poverty – in the four major south-east Asian countries we have followed, as calibrated by the standard Gini coefficient,[23] remains less severe than in Latin America, but it is worsening.[24] In Hong Kong and Singapore, inequality has increased to such an extent in the past decade that the city states' Gini coefficients are now the same as that of urban Argentina.[25] Politics has a lot to answer for in south-east Asia, and it is with a contemporary political tour that we must conclude. For without political change, the region is likely to find itself stuck on a Latin American highway.

It was the Philippines that pioneered post-colonial political failure in south-east Asia, and developments there since the crisis have given little succour to optimists. The old political élite, restored by godfather progeny Corazon Aquino after Marcos's departure in 1986, appears as entrenched as ever. The current president, Gloria Macapagal-Arroyo – herself the daughter of a former president – spends much of her time fending off congressional attempts to impeach her because of the possibly unconstitutional manner in which she ousted her predecessor, Joseph Estrada, in 2001, and allegations of vote-rigging in her own election victory in 2004. In a development that has strong Latin American echoes, there has been a frightening increase in extrajudicial killings of government critics, including journalists, academics and social activists, on Ms Macapagal-Arroyo's watch, although she is not implicated personally. The Philippine police say there have been 110 political murders since 2001; Amnesty International has documented 240 cases; Kerapatan, a local human rights group, claims more than 700 – the latter tally would put the annual average toll in line with the 3,000 people who disappeared during Marcos's two decades. Philip Alston, a United Nations special rapporteur for extrajudicial killings despatched to Manila in early 2007, described the armed forces of the Philippines – units of which even government officials admit are responsible for many of the murders – as in 'a total state of denial'.[26] Ms Macapagal-Arroyo, who in February 2006 declared a state of emergency that allows warrantless arrests of alleged enemies of the state, blames the constitution for political instability. She says the Philippines needs to switch to a single-chamber parliamentary system: But while Ms Macapagal-Arroyo's arguments are not without merit, her efforts to secure constitutional change have shown little respect for democratic norms. In December 2006 she used her majority in congress to vote away the senate's veto; this led to widespread popular protests and a hasty retreat. Faith in the political process is falling, communist insurgency is present in most provinces, and the local élite remains the most selfish and self-serving in the region. The Philippines best-known living author, Francisco Sionil José, lamented in the *Far Eastern Economic Review* in December 2004: 'We are poor because our élites have no sense of nation. They collaborate with whoever rules – the Spaniards, the Japanese, the Americans and, in recent times, Marcos. Our élites imbibed the values of the colonizer.' The Philippines, in short, has never moved on from the colonial era and the patterns of amoral élite dominance that it created.

Thailand has long echoed the polity of the Philippines and today the similarities are more apparent than ever. From the 1980s, the Thai economic élite – by standing for and winning an increasing proportion of seats in parliament – began to overrun the political process and merge economic and political vested interests into a unified oligarchy. This development reached its apogee, post-crisis, with the rise of Thaksin Shinawatra, before the bitterness and jealousy that his rule engendered within the élite opened the door to another military coup. Life after the coup, which took place in September 2006, showed that politics in the south-east Asian country with the least colonial legacy continues to fail almost as badly as in the Philippines. The white man is not to blame for everything wrong with the region. Within months of his investiture, the military's new 'civilian' prime minister, General Surayud Chulanont, was at odds with the junta leader General Sonthi Boonyaratglin. Policy was a shambles, with the administration committing itself to an ill-defined 'sufficiency economy' dreamed up by King Bhumibol. Policy appeared to lean towards nationalism and protectionism, and led to hasty moves to impose limited exchange controls and to amend laws relating to foreign-owned businesses. The stock market and foreign investment went into a tailspin, the government back-tracked, and the finance minister – a minor member of the Thai royal family – resigned in February 2007. In the south, the government continued Thaksin's brutal campaign against a Muslim insurgency and the insurgency became worse. Meanwhile Thaksin, in exile with his billions intact, toured the world, giving interviews in which he presented himself as a humble saviour of the people undone by ruthless generals. In Bangkok, in a testament to Thai political hypocrisy, large cracks appeared in the runway of the new airport, Thaksin's flagship infrastructure project. It was a political comedy in which the joke, as ever, was on the Thai people. The military promised yet another new constitution, a referendum and elections by the end of 2007, but it was far from clear if the generals would bow out.

The Philippines, and to a lesser extent Thailand, are reference points for politicians like Lee Kuan Yew who argue that too much democracy is bad for development. But all these countries really prove is that democracy comes in many flavours and is only one component of a functioning liberal polity that requires an efficient, independent judiciary, police force, bureaucracy and central bank. In the absence of the latter institutions, the Philippine and Thai élites are able to assemble blocks of rural and urban working-class votes, operate in shifting coalitions that produce little real turnover in political power, and carry on as they please without fear that policemen, judges or central bankers will stand up to them. South-east Asia provides few lessons in the failings of democracy; it offers many in the complexities of making democracy work.

The Malaysia-Indonesia Variant

In Malaysia, the studied manipulation on ethnic lines of the country's nominal democracy presents another ugly picture as the fiftieth anniversary of independence approaches in 2007. The Malay aristocracy – and its *parvenu* successor Mahathir – have held unbroken power for half a century by combining the mainstream Malay vote with Chinese and Indian support fearful of the Islamic opposition. A vast patronage network, largely paid for by political contributions from Malaysia's godfathers, has grown up around the ruling National Front coalition and its United Malays National Organisation core. In 2004, voters granted Mahathir's successor, Abdullah Badawi, a general election landslide – 198 out of 218 seats – after he promised a fresh start, with economic deregulation, reforms to the sometimes brutal police force and a serious fight against corruption. But little has changed; the anti-corruption and police reform campaigns in particular went eerily quiet after victory was secured. Badawi talked for a while about curtailing Malaysia's costly positive discrimination policies, which created a generation of *bumiputra* rentier capitalists and contributed to widespread poverty among ethnic Indians, but has since reversed course.[27] He fears an UMNO rebellion if he challenges positive discrimination and, in 2006, announced a new MYR2 billion fund to help Malays buy real estate. This will not be enough for a new generation of UMNO leaders – many the sons of former leaders – who have grown up on a diet of hand-outs and want only more of the same. At UMNO's annual congress in November 2006, delegates made some of the most racially inflammatory speeches in living memory. One promised to 'bathe in blood' to defend the rights of the Muslim majority against the Chinese and Indian minorities. The Minister of Education brandished a traditional *keris* dagger to signify the strength of his passions, and was urged to use it. Many Malaysians say there is less interaction among the different racial groups in the country now than there was thirty years ago. Those who hope for a reversal of this trend, and a reduction in ubiquitous cronyism, took heart from the release from prison in 2004 of Mahathir's former deputy, Anwar Ibrahim. Anwar has attempted to unite opposition political parties on a common platform. His own party, Keadilan, is multi-racial. But given the way UMNO works, if Anwar ever becomes a serious political threat, the chances are that it will welcome him back into the fold with a senior government post; and it is quite possible, based on past performance, that Anwar will accept.[28] It is hard to imagine what will change Malaysia's political trajectory. Without change, waste and economic inefficiency will remain high and growth lower than it otherwise would be.

Indonesia is the one 'proper' country we have considered where there has been a measure of political progress since the financial crisis. This was far from a given when Suharto fell in 1998. The governments of Abdurrahman Wahid and Megawati Sukarnoputri, from 1999 to 2004, were characterised by frenzied regional power grabs, corruption on a par with or worse than the Suharto era and a descent into sectarian conflict in different parts of the archipelago. Susilo Bambang Yudhoyono, who became the first directly elected post-crisis president in 2004, did well to stabilise the situation. Unlike governments in the Philippines and Thailand, he dealt with insurgencies that are rooted in poverty and inequity as much as in ideological dissent by negotiation, as well as 'wars on terror'. A deal struck with rebels in Aceh in northern Sumatra, where more than 10,000 people have died in conflict with security forces since the late 1980s, brought disarmament and peace in 2005. Sectarian conflict in the eastern provinces of Maluku and Sulawesi, which claimed thousands of lives between 1999 and 2001, also eased. SBY, as the president is popularly known, does not represent a political watershed; he was a senior Suharto general and has a tendency to equivocate that is typical of Javanese political culture. But, despite rising poverty, most Indonesians consider him honest and a representative of broad community interests. SBY's approval rating in opinion polls in early 2007 was close to 70 per cent, well ahead of the vote share that brought him to power. Economic growth has returned to a level around 6 per cent, inflation is under control and the currency has appreciated. Meanwhile, the president has made some effort at institutional reform. He formed an executive team modelled on the West Wing of the White House in an attempt to force change in Indonesia's gargantuan bureaucracy. A greater share of tax revenues has been distributed to local authorities in the hope that devolution will make government more efficient. Fuel subsidies were slashed in order to balance the budget and tentative steps were taken to reduce the number of businesses controlled by the military and to subject its members to civilian courts. It would be unduly sanguine to say that progress on reform has been impressive – many undertakings have been half done or delayed – but change has been sufficient for retired army chiefs Try Sutrisno and Tyasno Sudarto to start railing in public that the new democratic arrangements are a recipe for 'chaos'. In Indonesia, these lamentations are probably a sign of progress. Despite the generals' condemnations of democracy, in the long struggle to reform Indonesia's venal judiciary and its powerful military–business structures, SBY faces less risk of a coup than exists in the Philippines or Thailand. The Indonesian military, though corrupt and greedy, is traditionally responsive to public opinion and SBY's popularity is undeniable. More of a threat is a challenge from deputy president Jusuf Kalla in the 2009 general election. Kalla, from a *pribumi* godfather family that grew rich on state concessions in the 1950s, has sometimes been a useful – and certainly more charismatic – adjunct to SBY in power. But the prospect of a local tycoon family holding the presidency is not an attractive one; it could lead Indonesia into the Philippine and Thai political morass. With luck, Indonesian voters will recognise this.

Predictable Singapore

About that favourite refuge of Indonesian scoundrels, Singapore, there is little to say of its politics in recent years. In 2006 the ruling People's Action Party (PAP) won its tenth successive election victory, with 67 per cent of the vote. The PAP deployed its vast political machinery, made the usual promises of additional housing funds for working-class constituencies that supported it and threats of grant denial for those that did not, and was reliably supported by the state-owned media. PAP lawyers also rolled out the traditional defamation suits against opposition politicians who said anything perceived to be defamatory, and most of them quickly grovelled rather than face Singapore's equally traditional outsize awards of damages.[29] The main opposition leader was briefly incarcerated before the poll – for questioning the judiciary's independence – and again after it, for speaking in public without a permit.[30] It was a first election victory for Lee Kuan Yew's son Lee Hsien Loong; the old man retains his cabinet seat with the preposterous title of Minister Mentor. Like UMNO, a big part of the PAP's success is that it appears unassailable and can therefore co-opt most politically ambitious newcomers; more than a fifth of its candidates in recent elections have been first-timers. None the less the PAP's support did fall in 2006 – from 75 per cent of the vote in the previous general election – and the government's post-crisis drive to woo offshore money with tax cuts, while balancing its budget with indirect tax increases, is producing stresses in society. Gross Domestic Product growth returned to a level around 8 per cent in 2006, but aggregate private consumption growth was at 3 per cent; in part this reflected much faster expansion in foreign-owned, as opposed to local, business. Similarly, a foreigner-driven boom in the luxury real estate market compares with local mortgage growth of just over 2 per cent. Singapore and Hong Kong, by most measures, are the two most unequal rich cities in the world and this is becoming increasingly noticeable. Those who wish to complain in Singapore, however, must consider that the government has lately tabled penalties for nineteen new public order offences and increases in the tariffs for nineteen existing ones – ranging from public gatherings to postings on the internet.[31] It is also worth recalling that tranquil Singapore maintains what is probably the highest rate of state executions in the world, well ahead of China or Saudi Arabia.[32] Political change is improbable before Harry Lee passes from the scene.

Hong Kong: Another Kind of Leadership from the Periphery?

Around south-east Asia, much of the political problem is that the main countries pass on (and pass off as 'normal') the same, bad lessons – that manipulated democracy is a valid substitute for a free market in politicians, that concession-based domestic economies are an alternative to real competition, and that high headline growth rates alone signify sustainable development. In this respect, the real political hope for south-east Asia in the next few years may be Hong Kong, a city on the geographic edge of the region. It is the one place that shows signs it might provide much-needed leadership. What social scientists call 'demonstration effects' are extremely important for developing countries: the model established by Japan, as will be outlined below, has been critical in influencing former colonies South Korea and Taiwan, and in helping them become very much richer than south-east Asian nations despite comparable post-war starting points;[33] in Europe, the demonstration effects of the European Union have provided a guide for the remarkable, and under-reported, economic and political progress of eastern European states since 1989. Although Hong Kong is at the periphery of the region, south-east Asia's business community does already look to the city for a lead in economic and business ideas. Hong Kong has the region's dominant capital market, an economy twice the size of Singapore's, and the most important indigenous industrial capitalists in a part of the world that is grossly over-dependent on multinational manufacturing investment. Going forward, it is just possible that Hong Kong can also provide the kind of political demonstration effects that south-east Asia needs.

The politicisation of the Hong Kong population in recent years has taken most people by surprise. In the colonial era, political development was repressed by two forces: the fact that until the 1990s most of the population was made up of first-generation immigrants with a limited sense of Hong Kong identity; and the determination of governors despatched by the British Foreign Office to stymie the rise of popular politics, a policy that was dressed up in the fanciful notion that people of Chinese descent are inherently 'apolitical'. The expression of a clear Hong Kong political identity was further delayed in the 1980s when a large proportion of more wealthy local people took out insurance against the resumption of Chinese sovereignty by applying for foreign citizenship. Opinion polls have consistently shown that those who hold foreign passports are less likely to concern themselves with politics, or to vote.[34] None the less, a latent desire for change was brewing by the 1990s, and it began to boil under the last governor, Chris Patten. By the time Patten was appointed by British premier John Major in 1992, after Major lost patience with the Foreign Office's obsequious and inept handling of the relationship with China, the majority of Hong Kong people were locally born and had a clear identification with the territory. Patten, a career politician with no knowledge of China, then made a cathartic determination – to handle Britain's last big colonial exit on the basis of political principle. He introduced substantial changes to Hong Kong's electoral arrangements – which were within the letter of formal handover agreements with China, though contrary to prior undertakings made by British officials to Chinese mandarins behind closed doors – and finessed the closest thing possible to fully democratic elections in 1995.[35] Pro-democracy politicians triumphed and gained in public stature. Patten defied Beijing to reverse the electoral changes when it resumed sovereignty in 1997. This is indeed what happened, but the genie of political pluralism in Hong Kong was already out of the bottle and has never been forced back in. Patten's baby-kissing, public walkabouts and his willingness to put himself before the legislature and debate with its members gave Hong Kong a taste of something new. He was, and remains, extremely popular in the city, despite the fact that he speaks no Chinese and arrived with minimal knowledge of Asian history.

The impact of Patten is impossible to unravel from other forces – the long-term rise of a distinct Hong Kong political identity, the maturation of local politicians, popular recognition that decades of growth had not made most people rich – but it was significant. On 1 July 2003, six years after Patten had departed, all the trends towards greater politicisation in Hong Kong became shockingly apparent in a single event. After the first chief executive, Tung Chee-hwa, tabled anti-subversion legislation that was sought by Beijing, more than half a million people – 10 per cent of the population – took to the streets to denounce both the attack on civil liberties and the tycoon's leadership. To anyone, like the author, who lived in the politically insipid Hong Kong of the early 1990s, the spectacle was amazing. The bottom-up, phlegmatic and non-revolutionary politics of ordinary people – as opposed to top-down management by élites – had arrived in Hong Kong, and by association in south-east Asia.

Little more has been heard about anti-subversion laws. Instead, the political agenda has switched to reform of Hong Kong's electoral arrangements. The pre-Patten colonial system restored by Beijing in 1997 means that small-franchise, business-based Functional Constituencies controlled by conservative professional and godfather interests – once beholden to Britain and now to China – hold the balance of power in the Legislative Council. In this respect, political reform is absolutely a tussle between the man on the street and the economic élite. Separately, there is the question of how to elect the chief executive, who is currently chosen by an 800-member Election Committee packed with supporters of Beijing. The struggle for democracy in Hong Kong has produced much the most interesting game of political chess in south-east Asia. On one side are big business, related vested interests and China, and on the other Hong Kong voters who – when allowed to in geographic constituency elections – show overwhelming support for pro-democracy and pro-economic deregulation candidates.

The most important piece on the board is Donald Tsang, a former senior colonial civil servant and the Beijing-endorsed replacement for failed tycoon leader Tung Chee-hwa. Tsang is an élitist and as naturally deferential to power in the form of China as he was to power in the form of the British Foreign Office (he retains the affectation of wearing bow ties from that era). But he is also smart enough to grasp the concept of public opinion. His first move, in 2005, was to propose marginal alterations to electoral arrangements for his own job in 2007, and Legislative Council elections in 2008. Unfortunately, he failed to understand just how much Hong Kong has changed or the scale of the popular demand for more responsive government. The measures could not secure the necessary two-thirds majority in the Legislative Council, because they had almost no mainstream support. Tsang then said there would be no changes in 2007 and 2008. This, however, only undermined his capacity to divide his opposition. The main political parties, and senior former civil servants such as Patten's chief secretary Anson Chan, coalesced around proposals for a staged transition to democracy in both legislative and chief executive elections between 2008 and 2016.[36]

In March 2007 Tsang was formally 'elected' by the unreformed, Beijing-dominated Election Committee. His victory was a foregone conclusion,[37] but the manner of Tsang's election campaign painted him into a corner that looked increasingly like Tung Chee-hwa's. He failed to build a political image based on popular aspirations and instead relied on the traditional, establishment support of the godfather class. His campaign chairman was the Bank of East Asia's Sir David Li, who also provided plush corporate offices as a campaign headquarters. Tsang's major donors were a *Who's Who* of vested tycoon interests. Almost every godfather in the territory, and in many cases godfather children and senior executives as well, put up a standard HK$100,000 donation suggested by the Tsang camp. Three major families – those of K. S. Li, Peter Woo and Stanley Ho – each contributed a total of HK$900,000. Tsang's plutocratic backers paid in seven times more money than he spent on the election; the balance was given away to charity.[38] Just as the original news that Tsang would take over from Tung Chee-hwa in March 2005 had become public because of remarks made to journalists by gambling godfather Stanley Ho, so the 2007 election reinforced the notion that the tycoons are at the centre of the Hong Kong political system. Tsang won, but the manner of his victory failed to provide any serious popular legitimacy. The campaign for political reform was probably strengthened by the fact that Tsang was unable to deliver the appearance of a broader political support base under existing electoral arrangements. If he does not accept the need for substantive reform, Tsang risks a drift towards Tung-like unpopularity. His higher risk – but, given the state of public opinion, more realistic – strategy is to go quietly and firmly to Beijing and say that without a timetable for political reform Hong Kong may become ungovernable. This would have to be backed by an implicit threat of resignation. Supplication or aggressive confrontation will yield nothing in China; a simple statement of facts, and the possibility of another change in chief executive, just might.

Most likely, of course, Tsang will gamble that he can get away with doing nothing serious on political reform, that economic growth will temper popular interest in politics and that China will not be foolish enough to provide another tipping point – like the anti-subversion legislation – that will bring people on to the streets. He may be right, but Hong Kong is the most interesting political story in south-east Asia precisely because he may also be wrong. The population has understood the élite's grip on politics and wants it unclasped. There is now unremitting political noise around the need for a competition law and deregulation of the domestic economy. The godfathers are under siege in a manner they have not been before. The Chinese-language print media is much more aggressive than a decade ago. And the old ruse of justifying restrictive economic and political practices on the basis of socio-logical and cultural differences rings ever more hollow. As Edmund Terence Gomez, the leading academic authority on political–business ties in south-east Asia, observes: 'The Asian crisis broke myths about authority.'[39] In this respect, an analogy with British history is not unreasonable. Hong Kong has left its Victorian era, where the mere trappings of authority were enough to secure deference to political and economic power, and entered an Edwardian one, where the expectations of the élite versus everybody else are misaligned. The godfathers and some civil servants carry on as if nothing has changed, insisting that the old ways are the best ways and that anyone who disagrees with them is a troublemaker. The bulk of the population, meanwhile, has much increased personal and political aspirations, and elected politicians are beginning to react to these, but it is far from clear how the political will of what Winston Churchill referred to in the 1910s as 'the left-out masses' will be accommodated. The upshot is a curious spectacle in which Hong Kong is in many ways much more sophisticated and cosmopolitan than it was in 1997 and yet at the same time is filled with billionaires and government leaders who express absurdly arcane and patronising political views without even a hint of irony.

It should be stressed that, while political reform in Hong Kong would cer-tainly lead to economic deregulation, it would not likely mean the end of the established godfathers. They have too much money already and, as the nephew of one of the richest men in south-east Asia puts it: 'In general, money makes more money.'[40] However, deregulation would be enormously important in raising the glass ceiling that is placed over younger, more innovative, and manufacturing- and technology-oriented corporations. At present, these companies occupy a parallel world, with their productive operations across the border in China. There is nothing for them to do in Hong Kong because all the economic space in the domestic economy is occupied by an entrenched élite. Hong Kong's leading industrial entrepreneurs, Michael Ying of clothing business Esprit and Patrick Wang of micro-motor maker Johnson Electric, have entered the ranks of the world's billionaires in recent years,[41] but by contrast with service sector tycoons they enjoy zero political and policy influence in Hong Kong. It is also indicative of where the easy money lies in Hong Kong that industrialists tend to sell down their equity once manufacturing-based enterprises have reached a certain scale and put money instead into passive investments like real estate.[42]

At a minimum, political and economic reform in Hong Kong would make the place fairer, and this is the best possible argument for change. Contrary to official spin, Hong Kong – like the rest of south-east Asia – is a very unfair place. The richest businessmen are rich because of cartels and monopolies, while everybody else pays artificially high prices and receives unnecessarily poor service, because of those same restrictive arrangements. A fabulously wealthy tycoon class which pays no tax because it takes its income in tax-free dividends stands in stark contrast to a working population that is almost unique among rich societies in being denied a minimum wage while having to pay inflated prices for food, electricity, gas, banking services, real estate and much more.[43] The lack of popular input into the political process also means that things that make life tolerable for the less well-off in other rich cities are absent in Hong Kong. There is almost no urban parkland (it takes up development space), there is minimal attention to environmental quality (pollution is becoming rapidly worse and tycoons, who spend much of their time overseas, appear not to care) and constant road building (approved by a wealthy minority that owns cars) further degrades the areas in which most people live. Hong Kong is an exercise in shared hard work and extremely unfairly distributed returns on that work. Increased political responsiveness and economic deregulation are rational, necessary and possible. In this respect Hong Kong is the one place that could show people throughout south-east Asia that a better life than most of them are accustomed to is entirely practicable.

The Model that Worked (Better)

If the above analysis of Hong Kong's political potential seems to be driven by wishful thinking, it is worth remembering that Asia does have an alternative, proven model of development that has made societies richer, more equal and freer than those in south-east Asia. The model is far from perfect, but it points up the dialectic weakness of those who argue, for instance, that because the poverty rate in a country like Thailand fell from two-thirds of the population in the 1960s to under 10 per cent today, south-east Asia can be adjudged to have done just fine. Such a line of thinking only works if one severely limits one's expectations. If, instead, a comparison with north-east Asia is undertaken, it becomes apparent just how important politics are to economic development. The north-east Asian model developed by Japan more than a century ago was based squarely on political choices; it remains the only model to have taken a significant non-white country from poverty to developed nation status. The fact that one of the two states to have followed the Japanese demonstration effect – Taiwan – is a Chinese society is a further indication that culture and race are actually rather marginal to economic development, despite the determination of south-east Asian leaders to try to prove the opposite. Taiwan is just as Chinese as Hong Kong or Singapore, but in economic terms it is much more like Japan, while the city states are thoroughly south-east Asian.

Three things set the north-east Asian model apart from the south-east Asian one, and they all come down to politics. The first is that Japan, South Korea and Taiwan each implemented land reform and thereby ensured they would enjoy a bottom-up development process in which almost everyone had a little bit of capital on which to build a better life. In south-east Asia, political élites avoided land reform. The most egregious case is the Philippines, which, as has been noted, boasts the most selfish and self-serving political class, based heavily in landed wealth. The ability of north-east Asian governments to force through land reform was complemented by a broader political commitment to social equity. The Gini coefficients of Japan, South Korea and Taiwan are 0.25, 0.32 and 0.24 respectively. In south-east Asia they begin at 0.34 in Indonesia and track quickly out to more than 0.5 in Hong Kong and Singapore.[44] Political inclusiveness in north-east Asia is also reflected in countries' toleration of organised labour in the form of trades unions. Politicians may not have liked the unions much but they did not, as in south-east Asia, set out to crush or emasculate them, or argue that independent worker representation would hinder development (which it obviously did not).

The second characteristic of the north-east Asian model is that when governments tried to pick economic winners – as all developing states are wont to do – they gave their backing to manufacturers and businesses with a demonstrated capacity to originate technologies. Almost all the favoured corporations in Japan, South Korea and Taiwan were family-based, and quite used to bribing politicians, but they were not firms whose activities were restricted to trading and services. As licences for economic rents in finance and utilities, and access to capital, were doled out, these valuable cash flows were therefore less likely to remain trapped with a narrow, unproductive business élite that could not compete globally. A Samsung or a Hyundai was a sprawling family conglomerate, but it was also a business some of whose subsidiaries produced branded, globally traded goods. The south-east Asian conglomerates, by contrast, were not disciplined by global markets and when granted a concession simply farmed out the technology requirements and much of the work to multinationals. The long-term implications of this 'technology-less industrialisation' – as Yoshihara termed it two decades ago – tended to be masked by high growth rates, gleaming urban skyscrapers and the fact that large-scale export capacity was being created in south-east Asia by foreign investors. It is controversial to say so, but there is a strong case to be made that the nature of this export-oriented industrialisation actually reinforced the lack of international competitiveness in south-east Asia, because it reduced the pressure for more effective domestic economic policy. Today, South Korea and Taiwan enjoy *per capita* GDP between three and twelve times higher than that prevailing in the four main south-east Asian countries.[45] In the early 1950s, the difference was negligible. South Korea and Taiwan – like Japan – have internationally successful, branded corporations; south-east Asia has almost none.

The third difference in the north-east Asian model is that political systems have always been taken more seriously, relative to south-east Asia, as drivers of development. When Japan began its modernisation in the late nineteenth century, there was a concerted, open-minded debate about what type of political institutions would best suit the country. After much investigation, Japan copied most of its constitution from Germany and moved beyond the largely sterile – and very old – debate about cultural exceptionalism that plagues the Asian region. In the post-Second World War era, when Japan repeated the rapid development trick under a constitution modified by Americans, South Korea and Taiwan both experienced long periods of military dictatorship. Nevertheless, as the limitations of authoritarian leadership became apparent in the 1980s, the countries showed considerable capacity to make political and institutional adjustments. South Korea and Taiwan undertook painful but determined transitions to democracy. When South Korea became much the most affected country in north-east Asia during the financial crisis, political maturity was again apparent. Kim Dae-jung, a long-time democracy and human rights activist, was elected president in 1997 and initiated the most effective reform process to have occurred in the main crisis countries. One measure of South Korea's relative success in addressing the financial meltdown is that its US dollar exchange rate in early 2007 was back where it was in 1996, while the dollar exchange rates of the major south-east Asian countries have not similarly recovered. South Korea has its problems, but its political, institutional and economic record since 1997 puts south-east Asia in the shade.

Saying No to a Free Lunch

The people of south-east Asia have been failed, more than anything, by their politicians. This is apparent not just in the historical failures of the post-independence political class, but in its inability to grasp opportunities for development that are readily available today. The most obvious of these is the benefits to be derived from an integrated ASEAN common market.

A theoretical ASEAN Economic Community, around which tortuous discussions on deregulation revolve, is a precise eponymous echo of the European Economic Community (EEC), set up by six disparate states in 1957. But there the similarities end. Fifty years ago, the European Union, as it is called today, was already characterised by robust political leadership. The founding members of the EEC – France, West Germany, Italy, Belgium, the Netherlands and Luxembourg – had been serious about market sharing for years, and in some respects moderated their aspirations to cut a deal in 1957. ASEAN, by contrast, has a tradition of much talk and little action. The group, now ten countries, supports a tiny, central secretariat based in Jakarta. Each member nation has a local secretariat, reflecting a political tradition of 'non-interference' in other members' affairs. In effect, ASEAN is a pleasant club for regional politicians that has never moved on from its inception in the 1960s as a US-led assembly of anti-communist allies.[46] Talk of a common market and deregulation has been voluble since the Asian crisis, but reality lags far behind. In 2003, ASEAN committed itself to free trade in goods, services and investment by 2020; in early 2007 the deadline was brought forward to 2015. However, there is no detailed timetable, no compliance mechanism and no charismatic regional leader, or leaders, driving the process forward. One measure of the state of affairs is the creation, in 2007, of an elder statesmen's Eminent Persons Group, headed by former Marcos acolyte Fidel Ramos, that pleads with ASEAN's current governments for enforcement of stated objectives.

The lack of utilitarian leadership, and the capacity to seize stasis from the jaws of progress, is depressing. In Europe, market integration produced three decades of rapid growth in small and diverse countries already much wealthier than south-east Asian ones. The French called it 'les trentes glorieuses'. Of course, much of the impetus for integration in Europe was provided by the Second World War, a cataclysm of which the Asian crisis is the palest imitation. None the less, south-east Asian economic imperatives are at least as strong as Europe's were. ASEAN boasts a population of 560 million, compared with a little over 300 million in the current 27-member European Union. It competes for capital and attention with both China and India, where Europe has to reckon only with the United States. In doing so, ASEAN faces a simple challenge: to match the reality of low-cost export processing with the promise of a large domestic market. This should not be so hard, given that average *per capita* incomes are well ahead of those of China and India. But, in ten small pieces, the ASEAN sales pitch will never work; the region is presently a retirement home for also-ran middle managers from multinational companies. Without a common market, it can never be front-page global news.

It is impossible to know how long south-east Asia can defy the gravity of economic logic. In the post-crisis era, Malaysia, an extraordinarily well-endowed small country of 27 million people, was instrumental in blocking free trade arrangements in a region with twenty times its population; the drivers were a desire to protect a tiny, inefficient automotive industry and vested interests in palm oil. Around the region, the cost of such deference to minority interests can be seen in the fact that, post-crisis, most reckonings suggest that genuine intra-regional trade has fallen. Nominal exports power ahead but, once the evolving parts and components business passing through China is stripped out, it is clear that south-east Asia is as much a slave to Europe and America as ever. It is not expanding intra-regional trade – currently around 20 per cent versus well over 50 per cent in the European Union – because ASEAN will not reform. If political application does not change this, external circumstance eventually will. In a decade, south-east Asia's post-war free ride from oil and gas and lumber reserves will start to exhaust. But change under these conditions, likely informed by popular political recrimination as the weakness of real, underlying economies is exposed, would be ugly.

And Finally, the Good News

If there is good news, post-financial crisis, in south-east Asia, it is this: that a traumatic experience has finally undermined the lie that the region's economic story is a racial rather than a class one; or, put simply, that immigrants, rather than élites, are the problem. Attempts by ethnic Thai politicians in the summer of 1997 to pin the blame for the breaking crisis on 'Chinese' business interests elicited almost no public support. Subsequent popular opposition to the government of Thaksin Shinawatra, after 2001, made – remarkably – no reference to his Chinese ethnicity, or that of so many of his cabinet ministers. In Indonesia, it is widely believed – though not conclusively proven – that the military was behind many of the violent attacks on the Indonesian-Chinese community in the spring of 1998. But this probable attempt to prime racial tensions failed to produce the kind of murderous popular explosions that the country witnessed in the 1960s and 1970s. On the contrary, post-Suharto governments lifted bans on the use of Chinese-language signs and the public celebration of Chinese New Year with barely a murmur of dissent. The notion that responsibility for the crisis could be laid at the door of persons of Chinese ancestry simply did not wash.

If anything, Chinese-ness is rather trendy in south-east Asia these days, sometimes bizarrely so. The theatres of Bangkok's original Chinatown are thriving, even though most of the players are now Laotian, the Chinese having moved on to better-paid work. Under Thaksin, most Thai Rak Thai election candidates made a point of putting their name in Chinese characters on their election posters. All this owes a lot to China's economic rise, and to a desire to be seen to be in tune with what is presently perceived as 'the future', but it also reflects a waning of the capacity of indigenous élites to divide and rule their subjects. Time – since the end of large-scale immigration before the Second World War – has been both a healer and an educator. In the Philippines, race is a non-issue. Hong Kong has become a far more culturally relaxed, mature and integrated society since the end of colonialism in 1997. The exceptions are Chinese-majority Singapore, where Harry Lee Kuan Yew will likely take his dreary eugenic theories to the grave, and Malaysia, where the still relatively even demographic balance between ethnic Chinese and *bumiputras* allows the indigenous (if this term is still meaningful) political élite to plunder the country in the name of positive discrimination. None the less, around the region, the race relations story is a very positive one.

It is not the remit of this book to discuss China's development, but there are profound lessons for the Asian giant – the source of so much of the south-east Asian immigrant population – in recent experience. Moreover, anything that concerns China will have certain implications for the rest of the region. Today, China is caught up, as it grows at annual rates that were familiar not long ago to south-east Asian countries, in its own fascination with cultural theories of development. It would do well to avoid them. Many senior Chinese government leaders, and a good many outside observers, have decided the country enjoys some cultural right to progress. The oft-stated analogue is Japan, another large, populous and culturally closely defined nation. Since Japan derived much early moral instruction from China, how could the latter not be better? This argument falls apart when one returns to the earlier discussion of contemporary political and economic systems. Set against the three things that define Japan and north-east Asia – land reform, the development of branded businesses that originate their own technology and compete globally, and an ability to adjust political structures – China actually looks, on balance, uncomfortably south-east Asian. Land reform did take place after 1979, allowing rural households to farm family plots as state tenants; but ownership of land has never been transferred, meaning that peasants cannot sell, lease or mortgage their fields; these things are the essence of real land reform. On the growth of global, technology-capable companies, the jury is out. China is a continent-size country, with a large domestic market that guarantees local manufacturers economies of scale unlike those in south-east Asia. Yet 60 per cent – and rising – of the country's exports are being made by foreign companies, mostly on the export processing model familiar to Thais or Malaysians. The number of Chinese businesses able to compete on brand and product development, rather than as suppliers to multinationals, is tiny. On the willingness to engage political development and institutional pluralism – a market in politicians, free press, independent judiciary, and so on – China is behind south-east Asia. The risk of a south-east Asian debacle could, on the above metrics, be greater than that of a north-east Asian ride to prosperity and freedom. But things may change.

In the meantime, south-east Asia, like Latin America, provides an object lesson in how to do development the hard way. The road to a couple of decades of brisk economic growth, in a globalised world, is not so very hard to find. But the challenges of constraining political and economic élites that are embedded by class and history is very much greater. And herein lies perhaps the biggest challenge of sustainable development. It is truly remarkable that, as noted, Japan should have tackled effectively political and institutional as well as economic tasks more than a century ago – and without much fuss until the rise of Japanese quasi-fascism in the 1930s. The origins of that latent cancer are complex and contentious, but there is no doubt it has obscured the brilliance of the original Japanese modernisation programme. Subsequently, the world has found it surprisingly hard to improve on the performance. For all our modern, global institutions – an International Monetary Fund, a World

Bank, global think tanks and business schools – we struggle as much as ever to understand how to make poor countries rich.

And It's Good Night to Them

The reader will have noticed that the godfathers have been almost entirely absent from this final chapter. That is an inevitable consequence of the structural sleight behind this book – using these colourful, obscenely rich and interesting people to tell a bigger story about history, economics and development. The godfathers are merely the products of south-east Asia's political environment and, ultimately, it is the environment itself that is the region's big problem.

None the less, we ought to bid farewell to the tycoons. Whether you live in south-east Asia, or merely visit, spare a thought for these, and other, enchanting plutocrats: Li Ka-shing and Lee Shau-kee, out for an early morning round *à deux* at the Hong Kong Golf Club next to Deep Water Bay; is it too early for a small wager? Stanley Ho, adjusting his tuxedo button-hole, as half a dozen bodyguards look on while he prepares to open another casino. Madame Kwok inspecting Hong Kong's tallest high-rise, the International Financial Centre, with her three middle-aged sons – Walter, Raymond and Thomas – in obedient tow. (Their wives are busy ordering another 5,000 bathrooms for a new estate on Kowloon side.) On the waterfront, a rather moody Simon Keswick attends a board meeting at the Tower of a Thousand Arseholes; damn those blood-sucking shareholders! The more relaxed Sir Adrian Swire and Sir William Purves, meanwhile, semi-retired to London, recline on corporate sofas in different parts of town and reflect on hospitality arrangements for Cheltenham and Ascot; (how the Asians do love horses). In Singapore, Ng Teng Fong picks up the phone and orders young Robert to take the afternoon flight from Hong Kong for a dinner with Harry Lee Kuan Yew. Up the road in Kuala Lumpur, Ananda Krishnan strolls across the city's golden triangle with the ever-loquacious Dr Mahathir at his side; Quek Leng Chan might be watching them from his penthouse office suite, grinning as he puffs on a big cigar. In Bangkok, Dhanin Chearavanont is not at home; he has gone to Shanghai to check on his racing pigeons and all those Lotus supermarkets. In Jakarta, Anthony Salim is in a bit of bait – no one quite takes him seriously any longer and Budi Bloody Hartono has bought his bank; still, there are always China projects. In Manila, Lucio Tan picks up a paper at the golf club and reads of politicians threatening another tax evasion case against him; will these silly people never learn?

It is all go in godfather land. Whatever one's opinion of them, the tycoons have led lives less ordinary – adjusting to colonialism, wars, independence and now, as several of them point out, the internet. It is not easy, which is part of the reason why immigrant, outsider families – with their hunger for success and recognition – are such a big part of the south-east Asian story. It is, however, a great shame that callow notions of racial and class superiority have been superimposed on this wonderful tale of human flexibility and enterprise. Some godfathers, and most of the region's key post-war political leaders, really do believe that they are superior by dint of birth and education. None the less, as was stated in the introduction to this book, there are also godfathers who know perfectly well where the economic wind blows from in south-east Asia. They recognise that post-war progress has been a collective endeavour of immigrants and indigenes, with fault and value on both sides. They also know that the immigrant contribution would amount to very little without the unsung efforts of ethnic Chinese, Indian, Sri Lankan and other shopkeepers, petty professionals and small-time manufacturers whose energy – added to that of local populations – is the real source of the economic power of the region. One of the very wealthiest godfathers, reaching for a parable to capture regional reality in a few sentences, offers a final anecdote:

In more youthful days, the tycoon in question had as a favourite recreation long fishing trips in the South China Sea. He and family and senior managers in his businesses would go off for days at a time. On these voyages, the putative godfather was much taken with a man who had a tiny shop on the beach of an island where he and his crew would stop for provisions. This person, an ethnic Chinese, worked all hours of the day and was regularly woken in the middle of the night by local fishermen wanting diesel and other necessities before they set out for the fishing grounds at dawn. Often the fishermen were without money and demanded credit, which was invariably given. The storekeeper was an individual of unrelenting personal generosity. He married a single mother (hardly the done thing), a Hainanese woman, and took on responsibility both for her and for the daughter she already had. Over the years, the godfather and this man became good friends. The only difference between them, the tycoon observes, was that he was already rich by birth and superbly educated and went on to be a multi-billionaire, while the storekeeper never made any money from his ceaseless endeavour and dropped dead at a young age. 'And that,' concludes the godfather matter-of-factly, 'is the real story of south-east Asia'. At this point he assumes the look of a man enjoying fond memories and proffers your correspondent a glass of very fine French wine.

Notes

Introduction

1. The exchange almost certainly never took place – Hemingway was a great *raconteur* who employed considerable licence. The lines 'Let me tell about the very rich. They are different from you and me' appear in Fitzgerald's 1926 short story 'The Rich Boy'.
2. World Bank Policy Research Report, *The East Asian Miracle* (1993).
3. The combined GDP of Vietnam, Cambodia, Laos, Myanmar and Brunei in 2005 was US$63 billion; that of Singapore was US$111 billion. The combined population of the former five states is 150 million; that of Singapore 4 million.
4. With respect to the five south-east Asian countries that are (largely) left out of this book, they are not omitted solely because they are small economies. Vietnam does have, by regional standards, a significant and fast-growing economy; but Vietnam, like Laos and Cambodia, is a country that experienced a communist revolution that proved a cathartic moment in its historical development and made contemporary Vietnam less readily comparable with the states we will be following. Myanmar, meanwhile, has been crippled by five decades of military rule, while prosperous Brunei – population 400,000 – is too small to follow closely and is referred to only in passing (like the tiny former Portuguese colony of Macau).
5. The *Forbes* list for 1996 of the twenty-five richest individuals in the world contained the following persons from south-east Asia as defined in this book:

World Rank	Name	Country/Territory	Estimated Net Worth
4	Lee Shau-kee	Hong Kong	US$12.7 billion
6	Kwok brothers	Hong Kong	US$11.2 billion
7	Li Ka-shing	Hong Kong	US$10.6 billion
16	Tan Yu	Philippines	US$7 billion
17	Wonowidjojo family	Indonesia	US$6.7 billion
22	Robert Kuok	Malaysia	US$5.7 billion
23	Kwek Leng Beng	Singapore	US$5.7 billion
24	Cheng Yu-tung	Hong Kong	US$5.5 billion

6. The term moral is used in its strict and narrow sense – from the Latin, meaning 'customs' or 'habits'. There is no suggestion of some universal morality to which Asian leaders must adhere.

7. For a compelling, detailed discussion of working relations between British colonial authorities, and subsequently Japanese occupiers, and Hong Kong triads at the time of the Second World War, see Philip Snow's magisterial tome, *The Fall of Hong Kong* (2003). The relationship between China's Communist Party and offshore Chinese triads has not been so well written about, but is reckoned by many Sinologists to be of some significance, particularly with respect to Hong Kong; the late paramount leader Deng Xiaoping once famously remarked that not all triads are bad, and indeed some are 'patriotic' – mainland code for 'good'. For a discussion of Suharto's approaches to and meetings with the notorious Indonesian underworld figure Yorrys Raweyai as he manoeuvred to protect his family's wealth and status in 1998, see Kevin O'Rourke's *Reformasi* (2002). There is some further discussion of historic links between British colonial administrations and triads in chapter 1.

8. Interview with Associated Press, 1996.

9. The poem of this name, published in 1899, was inspired by the United States' seizure of the Philippines. Some literary historians have claimed Kipling's poem was satirical, but that is not the consensus view and the poem is certainly not interpreted in this way by most people.

10. In 1993 Nomura Research Institute made estimates for ethnic Chinese equity ownership in each major bourse. The results are as follows, with the ethnic Chinese proportion of the relevant national population in brackets: Indonesia 73 per cent (3.5 per cent), Malaysia 61 per cent (29 per cent), Philippines 50 per cent (2 per cent), Singapore 81 per cent (77 per cent), Thailand 81 per cent (10 per cent).

11. Temario Campos Rivera, 'Class, the State and Foreign Capital: The Politics of Philippine Industrialization, 1950–1986' (1991). 'Politics, Business and Democratization in Indonesia' in *Political Business in East Asia*, Edmund Terence Gomez, ed. (2002), p. 223; as of 1993, the two conglomerates not controlled by ethnic Chinese were Bimantara Group and Humpuss Group, both businesses of Suharto children. 'Pathways to Recovery in Thailand' in *Chinese Enterprise, Transnationalism, and Identity*, Edmund Terence Gomez and Hsin-

Huang Michael Hsiao, eds. (2004), p. 241; as of 1995, the exception in Thailand was the brewing dynasty of the Bhirombhakdi family. Edmund Terence Gomez, *Chinese Business in Malaysia: Accumulation, Ascendance and Accommodation* (1999), pp. 4-5; most other large companies in Malaysia are state-owned.

12. See, for example, Kunio Yoshihara, *The Rise of Ersatz Capitalism in South-east Asia* (1988). Of late, the most prominent sceptic of the cultural determinism line is probably Edmund Terence Gomez. See the list of works questioning the cultural arguments in the selected bibliography.

13. Of the commercial godfathers who have dominated the domestic economy since the end of the Cold War, almost every one is Jewish. They operate entirely at the discretion (at the highest levels) of a non-Jewish political élite, whose whimsy has sent several to prison or exile. The World Bank has estimated that before Yukos was recently renationalised, twenty-two oligarchs controlled 40 per cent of the Russian economy. The only big Russian godfather who is not Jewish is Vladimir Potanin, who controls Norilsk Nickel. Meanwhile, the leading Jewish and half-Jewish businessmen are:

Roman Abramovich – Sibneft

Boris Berezovsky – Logo VAZ, ArtoVAZ; in exile in London; once extremely close to Boris Yeltsin, he opposes the Putin government which is trying, so far unsuccessfully, to extradite him.

Len Blavatnik – Access Renova (investments); TNK-BP (oil and gas)

Oleg Deripaska – Base Element; RUSAL (aluminium)

Mikhail Fridman – Alfa Group (banking); TNK-BP

Vladimir Gusinsky – Most Bank, NTV Television, print media; in exile in Israel

Mikhail Khodorkovsky – former head of Yukos; once close to Boris Yeltsin, he opposed the Putin government, and was arrested and sentenced in 2005 to nine years in a penal colony for alleged tax evasion and fraud.

Vikto Vekselberg – Access Renova (investments); TNK-BP

Anatoly Chubais – myriad private investments and CEO of UES, the national electric monopoly; it was Chubais who oversaw the implementation of much of the Russian privatisation process as a vice premier under Boris Yeltsin in the mid-1990s; he is half-Jewish and a popular hate figure in Russia.

14. Victor Purcell, *The Chinese in Malaya*, (1948).

15. George Windsor Earl, *The Eastern Seas, or Voyages and Discoveries in the Indian Archipelago, in 1832,'33,'34*. (1837).

16. Lynn Pan, *Sons of the Yellow Emperor* (1990), p. 74.

17. Matthew Josephson, *The Robber Barons* (1934).

18. Chronology: Theodore 'Teddy' Roosevelt was US president from 1901 to 1909; Federal Reserve Act (1913); Securities Act (1933); Glass–Steagall Act (1933).

19. Currently defined as a 2005 Gross National Income *per capita* of US$876–US$3,465.

20. 'Boom, Bust and Beyond' in *Thailand Beyond the Crisis*, Peter Warr, ed. (2005), p. 10.

21. A comparison with a more 'normal' economy – the United States – is provided in Figure 2 on p. 300.

22. From US$1.2 billion in 1960 to US$141 billion in 2005.

23. The current account surplus has risen even more since the Asian financial crisis; it was 26 per cent of GDP in 2004.

24. Thai exports rose 25 per cent in 1995 but fell 1.3 per cent in 1996.

25. Malaysian-owned Star Cruises (the world's third largest cruise operator), Singapore's Tiger Beer, and one or two others might claim otherwise; but these, the biggest south-east Asian brands, have at best patchy recognition in the rest of the world. Li Ka-shing's '3' mobile phone business is a more realistic claimant, but it is essentially a series of international licences he bought at auction, with no original technological or service structure input.

26. Kunio Yoshihara, *The Rise of Ersatz Capitalism in South-east Asia,* (1988), p. viii.

27. Krugman's famous attack on the south-east Asian economies came in 1994, at the height of the 1990s boom. Entitled 'The Myth of Asia's Miracle', it was published in the November–December issue of *Foreign Affairs*.

1. The Context

1. There are several reasons for this. One is that more work needs to be done by historians. Another is that since immigrants were almost all 'freelancers', they generated no state history on the part of the countries from which they came. China had imperial ambitions, but these were expressed, as in Russsia, by expansion at the geographical periphery rather than through the acquisition of overseas colonies.

2. The term 'feudal', which in medieval Europe denoted a specific set of economic and military obligations between lord and vassal, is used more loosely here. It is none the less broadly appropriate to the type of polity found in many parts of pre-modern south-east Asia.

3. Tej Bunnag, as one example of continuing influence, was until recently Thai ambassador to the United States; at the time he was only the most senior of several Bunnags to be serving as Thai ambassadors to various countries around the world. The mother of Seni Pramoj and younger brother Kukrit, minor members of the Thai royal family who served between them four times as prime minister in the 1970s, was also a Bunnag.

4. G. William Skinner, *Chinese Society in Thailand* (1957), p. 92. The author was writing about Thailand, but his points apply regionwide: 'The south Chinese peasant lived in a grimly Malthusian setting where thrift and industry were essential for survival … the Thai peasant … lived in an under-populated and fertile land where requirements for subsistence were modest and easily obtained.'

5. For instance, unskilled labour rates in Thailand in the 1870s were three times those in China.

6. The list is a long one: Gibraltar (as good as an island), Malta, Cyprus, Bombay (seven islands that were joined up), Penang, Singapore and Hong Kong formed a chain of island redoubts for the world's leading naval power that, with the opening of the Suez Canal, were a line of dots all the way from London to Shanghai. The economic legacy of these isands, and others in places like the Caribbean, as offshore trading and financial centres is insufficiently appraised.

7. Not having to wait on the wind made trade a year-round rather than a seasonal activity.

8. Indenture was a theoretically 'liberal' replacement for slavery from the mid-nineteenth century. But it turned out to be less liberal than its proponents claimed. Indentured workers around the world tended to be contained in barracks, denied education for their children and were frequently controlled by means of physical punishment. The British government in India stopped indentured labour in 1916; it was one of Gandhi's major causes during the period.

9. United Nations special report, *World Economic and Social Survey 2004: International Migration.*

10. The only real paper trail in China comes from the credit ticket system, which has led historians to focus too much attention on the suffering

of a minority of Chinese emigrants who were abused by credit ticket operators. In reality, the average Indian indentured labourer was much more downtrodden than the average Chinese imigrant, who had far greater control over his destiny. The UN report on migration published in 2004 (see note 9, above) concludes that most Chinese migrants had more in common with European migrants in the nineteenth and early twentieth centuries than with Indians.

11. Colonial data from Malaysia illustrate the point. Between 1786 and 1957, 4.2 million Indians went to Malaysia and 3 million returned. A high proportion of the difference was accounted for by death in transit and death by malaria, which was endemic in rural Malaysia. Real net migration – in terms of people who remained alive for more than a couple of years – and stayed in Malaysia is probably less than half the apparent net migration of 1.2 million.

12. See Michael R. Stenson, *Class, Race and Colonialism in Western Malaysia: The Indian Case* (1980), p. 16.

13. Equivalent to the Indonesian *peranakan* and Filipino *mestizo*. designations; the biggest concentrations were in Malacca and Penang.

14. Madame Wellington Koo, *No Feast Lasts Forever* (1975), p. 3.

15. See Author's Note, p. xxv.

16. K. Thamboosamy Pillay was from a wealthy Indian family based in Singapore. He was educated at the élite Raffles Institution and worked both in business and government with the first British Resident in Malaya, James Guthrie Davidson. He organised the importation of indentured labour under government auspices before entering various businesses as a moneylender, government contractor and miner. He and Loke Yew were partners in the New Tin Mining Company in Rawang; Pillay was also a founder of the Victoria Institution.

17. Andrew R. Wilson, *Ambition and Identity* (2004), p. 89. Wilson points out that the maintenance of multiple identities was not an easy task: 'The most successful of these colonial middlemen walked a fine line between their Chinese identity and their colonial masters,' he writes. In this game the purchase of Mandarin titles from Qing China and the right to wear the Mandarin's attire was '*de rigeur* for an élite whose Chinese identity was the foundation of their economic success'.

18. The bizarre architecture and furnishing of homes owned by Oei Tiong Ham, Aw Boon Haw and various Penang-based tycoons – among others – was commented on by numerous contemporary visitors. Eu Tong-sen, a tin mining godfather to rival Loke Yew, originally from

Penang but who died in Hong Kong in 1941, built three Gothic castles in the latter called Euston, Eucliffe and Sirmio; they were filled with statues of European nymphs.

19. (1859–1914). Grandson of an early Singapore government employee, son of the Reverend Ho Fuk (who doubled as a successful property speculator), Kai Ho-kai became a major tycoon and one of the first ethnic Chinese appointed to Hong Kong's Legislative Council, in 1890 (his brother in law, Ng Choy, was the first). He was a partner in the land reclamation that created the runway for Kai Tak airport (and took part of his name). Kai Ho-kai read law in England and was a key Chinese community leader for the British, though his English language skills were far ahead of his Chinese ones. Other anglicised Chinese appointed to Legco had the same problem, though they typically did their best to hide it. It was a knowledge of written Chinese in particular that the anglicised Chinese lacked.

20. The precise picture was inevitably a little more messy, but these broad generalisations are valid.

21. How non-colonial Thailand actually was is a matter for debate; British advisers employed by the government in Bangkok had considerable influence over economic policy.

22. James C. Ingram, *Economic change in Thailand 1850–1970* (1971), pp. 216-17.

23. Off the record interview, October 2004.

24. Akira Suehiro, *Capital Accumulation in Thailand* (1989), p. 130.

25. Suehiro, *Capital Accumulation in Thailand*, p. 133.

26. Suehiro, *Capital Accumulation in Thailand*, p. 172.

27. A substantial part of this section is based on the original notes of an interview Stanley Ho granted to the historian Philip Snow on 27 September 1995, for which the author is extremely grateful. Much of the information has not previously been published.

28. See Philip Snow, *The Fall of Hong Kong* (2003), p. 51. When Ho Tung returned to Hong Kong after the war his first acts were to make some conspicuous charitable donations and put up a new office building called 'Victory'.

29. Macau's population increased from 200,000 to 500,000 in the space of a few months.

30. Lobo made his first millions before the Second World War by operating the colonial Portuguese government's opium farm. During the war he was formally titled Director of the Economics Department,

with monopoly control of essential foodstuffs. His biggest cash flows
came from gold; given his dual government and commercial roles,
he collected tax on gold for the government and a larger mandatory
cut for his cartel. A busy man, Lobo also composed music, including
operettas. He is commemorated in Rua do Dr Pedro Jose Lobo in
downtown Macau. Lobo worked in partnership in various businesses,
including gold, with Ho Yin, father of current Macau chief executive
Edmund Ho and Lobo's successor as the top godfather in the 1960s.

31. Sawa was terrified of assassination – a dirty war between the British
and Japanese was ongoing in theoretically neutral Macau, which
claimed many lives. But Sawa was convinced to trust Stanley Ho
because he was the grand-nephew of Sir Robert Ho Tung, whose
business empire would have been in a lot of trouble without Japanese
support. Stanley Ho and Sawa used to meet at 6 a.m. and walk up
Macau's Zhongshan hill while practising English; Stanley was pleased
to note that the Japanese guards bowed to him as well as to Sawa.

32. Interview of 27 September 1995. Mr Snow recalls a smoke-filled
corridor, filled with lounging bodyguards, that led to Stanley's
penthouse office suite in Hong Kong's Shuntak Centre.

33. This was reinforced by an air and naval blockade by Nationalist
(Kuomintang) forces based on Taiwan.

34. Off the record interview with a long-time close family associate of the
Foks, 20 October 2004.

35. *Time*, 20 August 1951.

36. Interview, 8 February 2005. Cheung said the bed across the door
was the advice of a *feng shui* man, but he was living a very low-
profile existence for one so wealthy. Cheung's medicine trading was
well-known.

37. Quek's surname is spelt differently, according to the family, because of
a nurse's English language error on his birth certificate.

38. Off the record interview, 4 March 2005.

39. Twang Peck Yang, *The Chinese Business Élite in Indonesia and the
Transition to Independence, 1940–1950* (1998), p. 213.

40. See Kunio Yoshihara, *The Rise of Ersatz Capitalism in South-east Asia*
(1988), p. 215. Ko was from Palembang in Sumatra.

41. Lim Goh Tong, *My Story: Lim Goh Tong* (2004), p. 25.

42. See Snow, *The Fall of Hong Kong*, p. 284.

43. Akira Shehiro, *Capital Accumulation in Thailand, 1855–1985* (1989),
p. 154.

44. This remarkable story is told in Alfred W. McCoy, *The Politics of Heroin: CIA Complicity in the Global Drug Trade* (1991), p. 135, and, in a more tabloid form, in Sterling Seagrave, *Lords of the Rim* (1995).

45. Paul D. Hutchcroft, *Booty Capitalism: The Politics of Banking in the Philippines* (1998).

46. See Edmund Terence Gomez, *Chinese Business in Malaysia: Accumulation, Ascendance and Accommodation* (1994), p. 32.

47. Gomez, *Chinese Business in Malaysia* p. 33.

48. Suharto was instead transferred to the Army Staff College in Bandung, west Java.

49. Liem's Bogosari flour mills were able to impose a margin of about 30 per cent, which in the 1990s, the World Bank pointed out, was about six times mill margins in the United States. Control of flour in turn gave Liem the dominant position in downstream businesses like noodle making. In cement, the government fixed a domestic market price that was well above international levels. See Adam Schwarz, *A Nation in Waiting* (1999), p. 110.

50. Author interview, 11 March 2005.

51. Suehiro, *Capital accumulation in Thailand*, p. 231.

52. Temario C. Rivera, *Landlords and Capitalists: Class, Family and State in Philippine Manufacturing* (1994), p. 71.

53. Richard Robison, *Indonesia: the rise of capital* (1986), p. 45.

54. Schwarz, *A Nation in Waiting*, p. 55.

55. There were a few thousand people in Hong Kong island and Kowloon when the British took over, almost none in Singapore.

56. This is still the case. There is a brief discussion in W. G. Huff, *The Economic Growth of Singapore* (1994), p. 14.

57. See Frank Welsh, *A History of Hong Kong* (1997), p. 268. Jardine Matheson appealed to the home government in London to rein Hart in.

58. Author interview, 9 March 2005.

59. See Edward Taylor and Cris Prystay, 'Swiss Fight against Tax Cheats Aids Singapore's Banking Quest', *Asian Wall Street Journal*, 6 February 2006. Both Singapore and Hong Kong rejected European Union calls to provide information on suspected EU tax evaders in 2006; Singaporean officials refused even to discuss the issue. See Tom Mitchell, 'HK Set to Reject EU Savings Tax Demands', *Financial Times*, 12 October 2006.

60. The incident was widely report, including by Netty Ismail, Bloomberg, 5 October 2006.
61. Author interview, 28 March 2006.

2. How to be a Godfather, #1: Get in character

1. Author interview, 18 October 2004.
2. See Adam Schwarz, *A Nation in Waiting* (1999), p. 124.
3. Kevin O'Rourke, *Reformasi* (2002), p. 58 and p. 332. As of March 2001, the Indonesian government put Sinivasan's unpaid debts at IDR17 trillion, or just under US$2 billion based on the average exhange rate in the five years following the crisis.
4. See Paul D. Hutchcroft, *Booty Capitalism* (1998), p. 133.
5. At university in Singapore Mahathir was listed as an Indian.
6. See Harry Lee's entry in the Cast of Characters. The similarity between the logo of the People's Action Party and that of the British Union of Fascists is remarkable.
7. Philip Snow, *The Fall of Hong Kong* (2003), p. 278.
8. There were strikes and riots on occasion – as at the time of China's Cultural Revolution in 1966–7, but there was no serious structural threat to the way politics was run until the arrival of Chris Patten as governor in 1992.
9. Snow, *The Fall of Hong Kong*, p. 12.
10. Leo F. Goodstadt, *Uneasy Partners* (2005), p. 124.
11. The research was published in two books, which appeared in successive years: G. William Skinner, *Chinese Society in Thailand* (1957) and G. William Skinner, *Leadership and Power in the Chinese Community of Thailand* (1958).
12. Skinner, *Leadership and Power in the Chinese Community of Thailand*, p. 239.
13. Off the record interview, 13 November 2005.
14. Correspondence with Justin Doebele, *Forbes*, 30 September 2004.
15. Skinner, *Leadership and Power in the Chinese Community of Thailand*, p. 245.
16. Off the record interview, 15 March 2004. Separately, an investment banker recalls spending the weekend in Edinburgh with Stephen Riady during a promotional roadshow for his family's listed companies. On the Sunday Riady insisted he be taken to church, and rather upset a local congregation by marching directly to the front pew with his

party. All was forgiven, however, after he placed several hundred pounds on the collection plate; the vicar had him home for tea.

17. Almost always Christianity, but there are exceptions. Malaysia's Vincent Tan is a follower of the controversial south Indian evangelical mystic Sai Baba.

18. Author interview, 18 March 2004.

19. Author interview, 11 March 2005.

20. His grandfather, born in 1873, was already in the English stream of the colonial school system; Lee Kuan Yew himself was offered, and refused, Chinese tuition as a child.

21. Lynn Pan, *Sons of the Yellow Emperor* (1994), p. 260.

22. Pan, *Sons of the Yellow Emperor*, p. 264.

23. Pan, *Sons of the Yellow Emperor*, p. 265.

24. Pan, *Sons of the Yellow Emperor*, p. 273.

25. His time at university, like that of many contemporaries born in the early 1920s, was cut short by the start of the Pacific War.

26. Off the record interview, 13 February 2004.

27. G. William Skinner, *Leadership and Power in the Chinese Community of Thailand* (1958), p. 40.

28. He started, and runs, Amanresorts, Asia's leading luxury boutique hotel chain.

29. Author interview, 4 March 2005.

30. Author interview, 7 March 2005.

31. See Pasuk Phongpaichit and Chris Baker, *Thaksin: the Business of Politics in Thailand* (2004), p. 25 and p. 60.

32. Chung Nam remains a major manufacturing and retail concern, with 6,000 employees. Li Ka-shing's uncle, and Chung Nam founder, was Chong Ching Um.

33. K. S. Li and Amy were married in 1963. Off the record interview, 16 March 2005. The person has known Li Ka-shing for half a century.

34. The Koos were involved in many businesses, but among the most important was shipping. C. Y. Tung married Koo Lee Ching. In the course of research, the Tungs rebuffed all enquiries by the author about the relationship between C. Y. and the Koo family.

35. Off the record interview, 28 October 2004.

36. Off the record interview, February 2004.

37. Off the record interview, 8 February 2005.

38. Cited in Anthony B. Chan, *Li Ka-shing: Hong Kong's Elusive Billionaire* (1996), p. 3.

39. Author interview, 11 November 2005.
40. Off the record interview, 20 October 2004.
41. Off the record interview, 28 March 2006. The source knows the Ng family intimately.
42. Off the record interview, March 2005.
43. The reader may respond that unquestioned male dominance is typical of Asian families in general, and Chinese ones in particular. But the phenomenon is much amplified in godfather families by the presence and patriarchal control of huge amounts of money.
44. Author interview, 17 March 2005.
45. As heard by numerous K. S. Li executives and counter-parties.
46. Off the record interview, 8 February 2005.
47. Off the record interview, 28 March 2006.
48. Amy died on 1 January 1990. On the day Amy died, a call was placed to Hong Kong emergency services reporting that she may have taken an excessive amount of medicine, believed to be sleeping pills. She was taken to hospital in a family car, which was involved in an accident with a taxi; Amy died after admission. The Li family said the cause of death was a heart attack. The death certificate stated 'dissecting aneurysm'. The coroner refused to answer journalists' questions about a possible overdose. See *Next Magazine* 22 December 1995.
49. *Wo Shi Wo Zi Ji* (Eastern Publishing, 2004). The title means 'I am My Own Person', although the book was published with an official English title 'I am What I Do'.
50. Author interview, 20 October 2004.
51. Off the record interview, 14 October 2004.
52. Off the record interview, 13 February 2004.
53. Madame Wellington Koo, *No Feast Lasts Forever* (1975), chapter 3.
54. Off the record interview, 28 October 2004.
55. See Jonathan Friedland, 'Robert Kuok: Merchant Mandarin', *Far Eastern Economic Review*, 7 February 1991. Cultural reticence did not stop Kuok buying the *South China Morning Post* in 1993.
56. Ron Chernow, *The Death of the Banker* (1997), p. 99.
57. The *Far Eastern Economic Review* was Asia's publication of record, with a superb investigative tradition, until the early 1990s when Dow Jones took control and sent in senior managers who knew little about the region.

58. Author interview with Ben Kwok, writer of the *South China Morning Post*'s Lysee column, and *bête noire* of the K. S. Li empire, particularly Li's factotum Canning Fok. The information was confirmed off the record by senior management at the newspaper.

59. Anson Chan, Hong Kong chief secretary at the time, called Walter Kwok's two brothers – Raymond and Thomas – into her office at the time of the 1996 kidnap and demanded to know what was going on. They denied point blank that Walter had been kidnapped. The Lis were not summoned in the same way, but never publicly admitted that Victor had been taken. Off the record interviews, March 2005.

60. Details of the Walter Kwok and Victor Li kidnappings are based on numerous off the record interviews conducted in 2004, 2005 and 2006.

61. Author interview, 20 October 2004.

62. See Joe Studwell, 'Sweet and Sour Times for a Sugar King', *Asia Inc.*, December 1994.

63. Author interview, 17 March 2005.

64. Author interview, 17 March 2005.

65. Off the record interview, 14 March 2004.

66. Author interview, 16 March 2005.

67. Chan is a member of Hong Kong's Executive Council.

68. Off the record interview, 23 October 2004.

3. How to be a Godfather, #2: Core cash flow

1. In 2006 Macau became the biggest gambling city of all, turning over nearly US$7 billion.

2. Hong Kong's local supplies of sand suitable for construction were already insufficient by 1934, when the government passed a sand ordinance to make trade in local sand a monopoly, clamping down on what it called 'sand thieves'. Since that period, most of Hong Kong's construction sand has come from China, just as Singapore's has come from Indonesia. It is important to structural longevity that building sand does not contain sea salt.

3. The franchise is held by Pan Malaysian Pools, which in turn is owned by Krishnan's private holding company, Usaha Tegas.

4. See Paul D. Hutchcroft, *Booty Capitalism* (1998), p. 133.

5. Ricardo Manapat, *Some are Smarter than Others* (1991), p. 344.

6. *Wall Street Journal*, 8 July 1997.

7. See Annex 9 of the 1996 Hong Kong Consumer Council report.

8. Author interview, 8 February 2005.

9. Off the record interview, 14 October 2004.

10. There is a detailed discussion of textile quotas in Leo F. Goodstadt, *Uneasy Partners* (2005), including p. 127.

11. Hong Kong Shippers' Council data show terminal handling charges in Hong Kong are, for instance, more than twice those in Germany.

12. As more port business moved to mainland China, K. S. Li has managed to secure a leading position in the heavily protected Chinese ports sector. His subsidiaries are dominant in key container-handling facilities, including Yantian, in Guangdong province, and Shanghai.

13. Author interview, 15 March 2005. Admart was set up by maverick retail and publishing tycoon Jimmy Lai, the only Hong Kong billionaire to have campaigned for democracy in the territory. Simon says of K. S. Li's and Jardine's tactics towards Admart: 'If they were in the US they would be in jail.'

14. Author interview, February 2005. Murray was Group Managing Director.

15. For a detailed discussion, see Leo F. Goodstadt, *Uneasy Partners* (2005), p. 185.

16. Six operators entered the mobile market and drove charges down to some of the lowest levels in the world.

17. The *Standard*, Hong Kong, 15 July 2002.

18. The Hongkong Bank's small business centre at its Queen's Road headquarters, as the author knows from long experience as the editor of the *China Economic Quarterly*, can get away with making customers queue for up to two hours; the only way to avoid the wait is to befriend the queue managers, who keep a stash of tickets at their desks allowing the less patient to jump the queue. While people with cash balances of millions of Hong Kong dollars are stuck in the basement, tycoons are dealt with in a vast board room, and suite of private offices, on the top floor of Sir Norman Foster's splendid building.

19. Off the record interview, March 2004.

20. Off the record interview, 14 October 2004.

21. Bremridge told Legco: 'In these circumstances designation of more than one Hong Kong airline on any route would be considered only in circumstances where it was judged that more competition was needed in the public interest and the traffic was sufficient to sustain a substantial operation by more than one Hong Kong airline. At the

present time however the most heavily travelled routes to and from Hong Kong are already well served by several established operators. The Government has therefore decided that as a general rule, and subject to the existing arrangements in any given case, designation in respect of routes available to Hong Kong will be limited to one airline per route.' *Hong Kong Hansard*, 20 November 1985.

22. Mahathir won a vicious UMNO election, involving everything from death threats to massive bribery, by only 43 out of 1,479 votes. He then saw off various legal challenges by securing the removal of the judiciary's Lord President, Salleh Abbas and five supreme court justices. There followed a ruthless purge of politicians and businessmen linked to Razaleigh. See Edmund Terence Gomez, *Political Business in East Asia* (2002), p. 62.

23. The Indonesian equivalent of this phenomenon under Suharto was 'Ginanjar's boys', after Ginanjar Kartasasmita, the principal cabinet-level patron of *pribumi* tycoons.

24. All these men were born within two years of each other: Hussein Onn and Abdul Razak in 1922, Lee Kuan Yew and Robert Kuok in 1923.

25. This section is based on a mix of publicly available documents, private documents in the possession of the author and off the record interviews conducted in Malaysia in 2004.

26. A brochure for the project opined: 'The people of this harmonious multi-racial country have united in the pursuit of Vision 2020, Prime Minister Datuk Seri Dr Mahathir Mohamad's economic blueprint for Malaysia to achieve industrialised nation status by the year 2020.'

27. The Petronas Twin Towers were a direct replacement for Mahathir's first pet architectural project as premier – the 35-storey Kompleks Dayabumi, completed in 1984, and also featuring high-rise Islamic architecture. Petronas, the government's long-time milch cow, has been the core tenant of both projects. The Twin Towers, of course, are more than twice the height of Kompleks Dayabumi.

28. The architect, César Pelli, also designed the International Finance Centre 2 building in Hong Kong, the tallest in the city, completed in 2003.

29. See Joe Studwell, *The China Dream* (Profile Books, 2002), p. 72 and p. 149. Lee fumed to CNN: 'Obviously we are not happy because we are not getting the kind of attention [in Suzhou] we were assured [in Beijing] that we would get – special attention. Indeed, what we are getting now is competition.' It wouldn't happen in Singapore. The

Singaporean government sold out of the Suzhou project in 2001 and did not publish a profit and loss account.

30. Off the record interview, 28 January 2004. The stress on 'template' was his.

31. Off the record interview, 23 March 2006.

32. Pasuk Phongpaichit and Chris Baker, *Thaksin: The Business of Politics in Thailand* (2004), p. 42.

33. Author interview, 10 March 2005.

34. *Far Eastern Economic Review*, 1 August 2002.

35. In Hong Kong this led to the creation of the Independent Commission Against Corruption (ICAC), in 1974; the enthusiasm of imported British detectives who ran the ICAC led governor Sir Murray MacLehose to declare an amnesty for the entire civil service in 1977, with no further investigation of previous crimes unless they were 'heinous'; in 1977 officers from Hong Kong's thoroughly corrupt police force had attempted to storm ICAC headquarters as arrests of their members increased. Corruption was probably at its worst in Hong Kong under the governorship of Sir Alexander Grantham (1947–57), but remained widespread until the 1980s; needless to say, no senior government figures were ever prosecuted. In Singapore, anti-graft measures adopted by Lee Kuan Yew included the payment of the world's highest civil service and government salaries to reduce the incentive for bribe-taking; Hong Kong also has an extremely well remunerated civil service.

36. Author interview, 10 March 2005.

37. Off the record interview, 14 March 2004.

38. Author interview, 11 October 2004.

39. Author interview, 4 March 2005.

4. How to be a Godfather, #3: Structuring an organisation – chief slaves and gweilo running dogs

1. Off the record interview, 7 March 2005.

2. See Ricardo Manapat, *Some are Smarter than Others* (1991), p. 83.

3. The Cheung Kong centre is in fact majority-owned by Hutchison, and Cheung Kong has never paid for naming rights, something Hutchison shareholders ought to be miffed about. It is a good illustration of how godfathers treat their empires.

4. This paragraph is based on various off the record interviews.

5. Author interview, 21 February 2004.

6. Off the record interview, 29 February 2004.
7. Off the record interview, 13 February 2004.
8. Author interview, 7 March 2005.
9. Author interview, 9 March 2004.
10. Author interview, 8 February 2005.
11. Author interview, 8 February 2005.
12. Author interview, 15 March 2005.
13. Off the record interview, 14 March 2005.
14. See *Far Eastern Economic Review*, 10 October 1991.
15. To be fair to Tose, one of Carrian's key bankers – Hongkong Bank – was assuring the market that Tan's business was in good shape. Hongkong Bank was being run by Michael Sandberg, who features prominently in the next chapter.
16. Off the record interviews, 3 March 2004 and 14 March 2005.
17. Author interview 15 March 2005. When reminded of the event, Tose muttered something inaudible about the legal trials and persecution of former Citygroup boss Sandy Weill; he also said that 'seven years' of legal cases with the Hong Kong government had left him without money. That was the end of the interview.
18. See Henny Sender, 'Peregrine's Great Leap', *Far Eastern Economic Review*, 9 May 1996.
19. A line Mr Wood has used on many occasions.
20. This could easily have happened. Jardine, Matheson considered buying the stock, but Henry Keswick thought K. S. Li lacked staying power as a businessman. How wrong he was.
21. The tribunal's findings can be found at http://www.idt.gov.hk/english/doc/internation_city_report_vol1.pdf
22. As mentioned earlier, the Hutchison dividend was only paid on preference stock, so many minority shareholders did not receive it.
23. John Richardson, the Hutchison chief executive, made clear his personal anger about the dividend at a board meeting, but never went public.
24. Before hiring Murray, K. S. Li had been thinking of getting Philip Tose to run Hutchison, which could have been a very bad idea.
25. Author interview, 20 December 2005.
26. Hemlock's diary: http://www.geocities.com/hkhemlock/papers.html

5. How to be a Godfather, #4: Banks, piggy banks and the joy of capital markets

1. Another was Prasit Kanchanawat, Thammasat alumnus and long-time executive director and vice-chairman of Bangkok Bank, who succeeded Chin as chairman in 1984.
2. Three deputy prime ministers – Prapass Charusathiara, Major-general Pramarn Adireksarn and former bank president Boonchu Rojanasathien, plus two speakers of the Thai parliament – Major-general Siri Siriyodhin and Prasit Kanchanawat.
3. See *Far Eastern Economic Review*, 17 September 1973.
4. Off the record interview, 14 October 2004.
5. Off the record interview, 20 October 2004.
6. Off the record interview, 2005.
7. Leo F. Goodstadt, *Uneasy Partners* (2005), p. 192.
8. The absurdity of this situation was apparent in 1983 when Hongkong Bank, simultaneously quasi central bank and commercial bank, was at the heart of the decision to peg the Hong Kong dollar to the US dollar at a rate of 7.8. In the midst of the early 1980s financial crisis, the knowledge that a peg would be implemented, and at what rate, was of great commercial value. It is the understanding of the author that more than one godfather, and other related persons, were privy to the plan before it was implemented and were able to buy up Hong Kong dollars in anticipation. It should be remembered that many godfathers sat on Hongkong Bank's board. The episode echoes the 1946 decision to honour 'duress notes' issued by the Japanese, described in chapter 1, from which many godfathers, and doubtless some expatriates, made huge profits.
9. The business's different gas, tanker, dry bulk and offshore operations are gradually being rebranded as the BW Group. The Sohmen family bought out Bergesen, Norway's largest shipping line, in 2002. The combined BW fleet of 140 ships compares with just over 200 when Y. K. Pao's shipping business was at its peak; however total tonnage is similar, reflecting today's larger vessels.
10. Author interview, 17 March 2005.
11. Author interview, 17 March 2005.
12. HSBC still owns a minority stake in the consolidated Bergesen WorldWide group.
13. Interview with William Mellor of Bloomberg, 23 December 2002.
14. Off the record interview, 11 October 2004.

15. Off the record interviews with four persons present at the event, which was held in the Eagle's Nest restaurant. The Hilton has since been demolished to make way for K. S. Li's Cheung Kong centre. Sir William Purves, who succeeded Sandberg, was said by other senior Hongkong Bank staff to be extremely embarrassed, not to say angered, by the golden gift; he is a great defender of Hongkong Bank's reputation. In interviews with the author, Sir William appeared to suffer some memory loss with respect to the event at the Hilton hotel. He first recalled that Hang Seng bank, a Hongkong Bank subsidiary, gave a statue to its parent. Hang Seng did give a much smaller, and different, statue to the bank. Presented with additional evidence, he later commented: 'As far as I know, a model of the new building was given to the board, I think probably from K. S. It is still in the boardroom of the bank. I don't think, I don't know, that it is solid gold.' In reality Purves, along with everyone else at the leaving dinner, saw the golden statue presented by K. S. Li to Michael Sandberg. It was shipped to England. It is not in the Hongkong Bank boardroom in Hong Kong (the much smaller statue given by Hang Seng bank is).

16. Several bankers from several different banks were sentenced to jail terms for taking bribes from George Tan. In 2000, after a long period on the run, the former head of Hongkong Bank's investment banking unit, Ewan Launder, was sentenced to five years for accepting HK$43.95 million in preferments, discovered by chance in a different investigation in the late 1980s. The cynics who said a senior Hongkong Bank executive could never go to prison in Hong Kong, however, were subsequently vindicated when the Court of Final Appeal acquitted Launder, partly on the basis of a minor grammatical error in the charges laid against him.

17. Off the record interview, February 2005.

18. Sandberg's choice of tycoon friends appears systematically poor. Soon after retiring from Hongkong Bank he reappeared on the board of Polly Peck, the UK-based investment vehicle run by Asil Nadir who fled to northern Cyprus in 1993 to escape criminal charges involving theft of £34 million.

19. Off the record interview, February 2005.

20. Paul D. Hutchcroft, *Booty Capitalism* (1998), p. 81.

21. *Far Eastern Economic Review*, 7 April 1978.

22. Ferdinand E. Marcos, *The Democratic Revolution in the Philippines* (Prentice Hall International, 1979), p. 6.

23. Hutchcroft, *Booty Capitalism*, p. 133.
24. Hutchcroft, *Booty Capitalism*, p. 165.
25. Ricardo Manapat, *Some are Smarter than Others* (1991), p. 316.
26. A major crisis was precipitated in 1981 when Dewey Dee, an ethnic Chinese godfather who had funded his businesses by issuing commercial paper as well as bank borrowing, fled the country owing US$80million. This was not among the Philippines' bigger financial problems, but it sparked a general crisis. Among leading crony godfather groups pushed to the brink of insolvency in the panic surrounding Dee's flight were Herminio Disini's Herdis group, Ricardo Silverio's conglomerate and Rodolfo Cuenca's construction empire; each was a Marcos creation.
27. Hutchcroft, *Booty Capitalism*, p. 210.
28. Hutchcroft, *Booty Capitalism*, p. 213.
29. The non-performing loan (NPL) ratios of Indonesian state banks remained worse than those of private banks at the time of the Asian financial crisis, a reminder that there was a logic to the deregulation programme of the late 1980s.
30. Eugene Galbraith, current president commissioner of BCA, says the level would be over 90 per cent if loans to Suharto family companies were included; the Suharto children were minority shareholders in BCA. Author interview, 9 March 2005.
31. See Joe Studwell, 'Showdown at Summa-Astra', *Asia Inc.*, April 1993.
32. See Dominic Casserley *et al.*, *Banking in Asia* (1999), p. 266. The authors put unrecovered central bank loans to Summa in 1998 at US$180 million. In an email exchange with the author on 8 February 2007 Edwin Soeryadjaya, eldest son of William, said his father has repaid the outstanding debt to the central bank, since 1998, on Edward's behalf; he claims the last of several instalments was paid in October 2004. The author has seen no documentary proof, but the Soeryadjayas are more likely than most Indonesian tycoon families to have settled their obligations.
33. Author interview, 7 March 2005.
34. Kevin O'Rourke, *Reformasi* (2002), p. 325.
35. Bob Hasan's bank was Bank Umum Nasional, Usman Atmadjaya's was Bank Danamon. O'Rourke, p. 60, p. 365.
36. See Merton H. Miller, 'The Current South-east Asia Financial Crisis', *Pacific-Basin Finance Journal* 6 (3/4), p. 232.

37. For instance: Hong Kong Stock Exchange capitalisation increased from US$173 billion at the end of 1992 to US$386 billion at the end of 1993; Stock Exchange of Thailand capitalisation increased from US$58 billion to US$130 billion; Stock Exchange of Singapore capitalisation increased from US$62 billion to US$146 billion; Kuala Lumpur Stock Exchange capitalisation increased from US$95 billion to US$229 billion.

38. *Total Return Indices (Denominated in US Dollars with All Dividends Reinvested), Selected Countries and Regions*

	USA	UK	Eastern Europe and Middle East	Latin America	Hong Kong	Singapore	Malaysia	Thailand	Indonesia	Philippines
% return Jan 1993 to 2007*	314	314	721	568	270	128	58	-9	71	-10
% return Jan 1988 to 2007*	770	558	647	4792	1011	467	267	247	554	198

* as of 25 October 2006

Sources: MSCI Barra; author's calculations

39. US$100 earning the average federal funds rate of 4 per cent, 1993–2007, made a 73 per cent return, compared with 58 per cent in Malaysian equities and 71 per cent in Indonesian equities.

40. See table, above.

41. South Korea's total dollar returns of 247 per cent since 1993 and 327 per cent since 1988, and Taiwan's of 111 per cent since 1993 and 231 per cent since 1988, can be compared with those in the table above.

42. The market capitalisation of listed real estate developers in Hong Kong in 1996, near the peak of the market, was greater than that of listed real estate developers in the whole of the European Union.

43. The name changed to Swire in 1974.

44. Author interview, 8 February 2005.

45. Author interview, 7 February 2005.

46. Author interview, 7 February 2005.

47. Insider trading became a criminal offence in the UK in 1980. Collier was given a 12-month suspended sentence and was fined £25,000 – small beer compared with what he had probably earned from illicit trades over the years.

48. Peter Wong, a 20-year associate of Philip Tose and Peregrine's finance director, who former colleagues say was the one person who really knew the secrets of Tose's dealings with K. S. Li, was banned from being a Hong Kong company director along with Tose; he left for Australia. Carlton Poon, a Vickers director in the mid 1980s, was convicted in 2005 in Hong Kong, along with his wife, of insider trading that had occurred in 1997. Dickson Lai, another Vickers director of the mid 1980s, was investigated for insider activity by the Securities and Futures Commission after he moved to a Hongkong Bank investment banking subsidiary, James Capel, in the late 1980s; he reached an out of court settlement.

49. As noted previously, the different spellings of the surname Quek is attributed to a midwife's error at the time of the birth of Quek Leng Chan.

50. Singapore is the obvious exception.

51. Off the record interview, 10 November 2006.

52. The work was conducted by a Chinese University of Hong Kong team led by Larry Lang in conjunction with World Bank economists Stijn Claessens and Simeon Djankov. It gave rise to a series of academic papers published in different journals. The most prominent appeared in the *American Economic Review* of March 2001.

53. Sime Darby was a British plantation-based business already closely connected with the family of Lee Kong Chian (of Lee Rubber in Singapore, an investor) and former Malaysian finance minister and tycoon Tan Siew Sin before independence. In the 1970s the Malaysian government bought a controlling interest through purchases of mostly British-owned shares on the open market. Precise shareholdings today are opaque because of the use of nominees.

54. This information was deduced from several interviews. The six big Japanese conglomerates were Toyota–Mitsui, Mitsubishi/Meiji, Sumitomo, Yasuda–Fuji, Sanwa/Nippon Life and Dai–Ichi Kangyo Bank group. Ironically Larry Lang, the research project organiser who was particularly outspoken when the findings were released in 2000 and 2001, subsequently accepted a senior post at the Cheung Kong Graduate School of Business in Shanghai, controlled by Li Ka-shing. 'Larry is now in pretty thick with Li Ka-shing,' observes a former colleague. Mr Lang did not respond to the author's requests for an interview.

55. *American Economic Review*, March 2001.

56. See David Webb's synopsis, 'A Brief History of Tom', 21 February 2000, at www.webb-site.com. He shows that not only did Ms Chau become a paper billionaire, but rather than achieve that through investment she was actually paid to become one. Shrewd indeed.
57. Woo, Kwan, Lee & Lo is a significant locus of power in Hong Kong about which little is written. Another partner in the firm is the father-in-law of Francis Leung, Philip Tose's partner at Peregrine and another long-time K. S. Li associate. Francis Leung was in the news in 2006 because of a proposal by him to buy over Hong Kong telecoms assets from K. S. Li's son Richard, using a bridging loan from K. S. Ronald Arculli (see p. 115) started out at Woo, Kwan, Lee & Lo in the 1970s.
58. Off the record interview, February 2005.
59. Not a democratically elected one.
60. A key proponent of this case was Monetary Affairs Secretary David Nendick.
61. Off the record interview, 18 March 2005.
62. Spitzer brought numerous cases against US investment banks and corporations for malfeasance, fraud and breach of trust during his tenure as Attorney General from 1998–2006. He was elected New York governor in November 2006.
63. 'Restructuring Involving a Capital Restructuring and Subscription of Share Capital in Orient Overseas (International) Limited and Interim Results', notice to shareholders, 10 November 1986. The Tung family's understanding of corporate governance norms has not improved. When Orient Overseas (now run by C. H. Tung's brother) decided to put its ports division up for sale in 2006 it did so by posting a notice on its website on the morning of 25 July. By the time this hugely price-sensitive information was passed to the Hong Kong Stock Exchange's company announcements unit, as listing rules require, on the late evening of the same day, the stock price had risen almost 10 per cent. Neither the company nor the Tungs were censured. The ports sale was completed in November 2006. To be absolutely fair to C. H. Tung, it should be stated that the decline of OOHL, and Tung private companies, had started in the last years of his father's tenure, the result of unwarranted and excessive investment.
64. See Joe Studwell, 'Sweet and Sour times for a Sugar King', *Asia Inc.*, December 1994. PCL was listed in July 1990.
65. CIMB, Malaysia's leading merchant bank by business handled, is run by Nazir Razak, brother of Deputy Prime Minister Najib Razak; both

men are sons of Abdul Razak, Malaysia's second post-independence premier.

66. Lee Shau-kee made offers for Henderson Investment in 2002 and, separately, in 2005, for Henderson China. David Webb's calculations regarding the Wharf offer for retail subsidiary Lane Crawford can be found at http://www.webb-site.com/articles/lane.htm. The New World TMT case was complex; the company was on its knees because it was owed hundreds of millions of US dollars for investments in the US and mainland China; the price offered suggested this money would never be recouped, but some long-time followers of Cheng Yu-tung suspect otherwise. Richard Li's 2005 offer for Sunday Communications proposed to pay with cash and a promissory note in a connected transaction, and then distribute cash to minority shareholders, but only if they approved the delisting; it was in essence a threat to minority shareholders that if they did not go along with the deal they might end up owning untradeable shares in a delisted business.

67. Author interview, 11 November 2005.

68. Author interview, 11 October 2004.

69. Coull told the author he resigned from New World TMT when he noticed Cheng's son Henry – 'out of his depth' – making significant investment commitments without notifying the board.

70. Author interview, 27 October 2004.

71. Off the record, February 2004.

72. It is just possible that Jardine is changing. Since 2004 its share price has put in the best performance in thirty-five years. However, the Keswick family continues to fight efforts by minority investors to force it to unlock its cross-holding structure and open businesses up to the discipline of possible takeover bids.

73. Data as of the end of 2006.

74. The Philippines, true to form, has several mandatory provident funds with only patchy application. Government employees are subject to the Government Service Insurance System (GSIS), established in 1936. Private employees are subject to the Social Security System (SSS), established in 1954; but only about 10 per cent of employed Filipinos file income tax returns and are subject to contributions. Marcos created other forced savings funds: for housing (the Pag-Ibig Fund, or Home Mutual Development Fund), for military personnel (the Armed Forces of the Philippines–Retirement and Separation Benefits System), and for overseas workers (Overseas Workers Welfare Administration

Fund). The private employees provident fund and the military fund, in particular, are characterised by perennial shortfalls against what they are supposed to pay out. The SSS is currently forecast to be completely depleted by 2015. The Malaysian and Singaporean mandatory provident funds were started in the 1950s.

75. See Jon Hendricks, Hyunsook Yoon, Hyungsook Yoon, eds., *Handbook of Asian Aging*, (Baywood Publishing, 2005), p. 76, quoting Mukul G. Asher.

76. *Asian Wall Street Journal*, 12 July 2006. GIC officials, attending a press conference at which Lee Kuan Yew spoke, indicated that 40–45 per cent of current GIC assets were in the US, 20–25 per cent were in Europe and 8–10 per cent were in Japan.

6. The 1990s: Ecstasy and reckoning

1. This explains why export growth in Indonesia 1960–85 led the group, averaging 15.5 per cent per annum. At the peak of the commodities boom in the early 1970s, the nominal value of Indonesian exports increased 81 per cent in 1973, followed by 131 per cent in 1974.

2. Thailand led the way, with average growth of more than 23 per cent *per annum* from 1986 to 1995. Indonesia, which retained its relative over-dependence on commodity exports, is the only one of the six territories covered in this book whose average export growth rate fell in the period.

3. Recent research by World Bank economist Bert Hoffman shows that 19 per cent of the increase in *per capita* output in Indonesia between 1978 and 2005 came from human capital factors; 8 per cent was attributable to increased participation in the workforce, and 11 per cent to changes in the so-called dependency ratio – the proportion of people in work versus the proportion not in work. Returns would likely be similar in other countries covered by this book. The research will be published in the *Bulletin of Indonesian Economics and Statistics* in 2007.

4. This story has shifted to China in the past decade, although productivity gains have been relatively more important than changes in human capital factors compared with south-east Asia. Most women were already in employment in the 1970s in China, whereas they had a big impact on the participation rate of labour in the workforce in countries like Indonesia.

5. The administrative capital is called Putrajaya and needs to be seen to be believed. The Multimedia Super Corridor features Cyberjaya (Cyber City) and many other large white elephant projects within it.

6. Off the record interview with a senior manager at Putrajaya Holdings, who frequently dealt directly with Mahathir.

7. See Victor Mallet, *The Trouble with Tigers* (1999), p. 39. Mallet also points out how Lee has changed his tune over the years. Back when he wanted the British colonists out of Singapore, he was all for democracy and individual rights. Speaking in the Legislative Assembly on 27 April 1955, he told his British overlords: 'If you believe in democracy, you must believe in it unconditionally. If you believe that men should be free, then they should have the right of free association, of free speech, of free publication.' Once in charge of Singapore, however, Lee had second thoughts.

8. Off the record interview with someone who heard the line from Princess Anne, November 2005.

9. Real name Siti Hartinah; she died on 29 April 1996.

10. The US$800 million estimate came from the Thai Farmers' Bank Research Centre. It was one of, if not the, most corrupt elections in Thai history.

11. The best known of the reports, published nine months before Patten sailed for home, is *Competition Policy : The Key to Hong Kong's Future Economic Success* (November 1996). Patten rejects the notion that he lost the plot on economic reform, arguing that his political battle with Beijing was so consuming that he could not afford to fight a war on two fronts. Quoting the fulsome encouragement Sir Humphrey Appleby gave to his boss in the British sitcom *Yes, Minister*, Patten remarks that taking on the godfathers as well would have been 'a very brave thing to do'. (Interview, 20 December 2005.) He may have a point. But it is the conviction of the author that Patten, who arrived in Hong Kong in July 1992 with no previous Asia experience, did not comprehend the godfather stitch-up that is the domestic Hong Kong economy until it was too late to act. Of course the British Foreign Office and the Hong Kong civil service did little to point him in the right direction, and this criticism does not negate the importance of Patten's overall legacy.

12. See Joe Studwell, 'What Next for Vincent Tan?', *Asia Inc.*, July 1995.

13. See Edmund Terence Gomez, ed., *Political Business in East Asia*, (2002), p. 272.

14. To be fair, the report contains some solid, if one-sided analysis, and the preface by then World Bank president Lewis T. Preston points out that there has never been a single Asian model of development. But the title, the hype and claims such as one that the whole region is characterised by high levels of social equity were a terrible mistake.
15. See Adam Schwarz, *A Nation in Waiting* (1999), p. 314.
16. See Schwarz, *A Nation in Waiting*, p. 314.
17. See Schwarz, *A Nation in Waiting*, p. 316. Key parts of the internal review were subsequently leaked.
18. Post-crisis, the World Bank is trying to refocus its work on governance issues. This raises a whole other set of theoretical and operational problems that there is no space to discuss here. It is not intended to suggest that the World Bank's work is easy.
19. Author interview, 8 December 2006.
20. Author interview, 8 December 2006.
21. After the crisis, the IMF claimed it was first concerned about the sustainability of the Thai peg in 1993 and recommended abandoning it in consultations with the Thai government in 1994; however, the recommendation was not endorsed by the IMF board. None of the exchanges between the IMF and Thai authorities was made public and it was not until July 1996 that IMF chief Michel Camdessus wrote personally to the Thai foreign minister to request greater exchange rate flexibility.
22. To be fair to Friedman, he did concede this possibility. His full quotation was: 'It is not too much to say that had there been no IMF, there would have been no East Asia crisis, though countries might have had internal crises as with Japan, whose troubles cannot be blamed on the IMF.' Friedman was quoted in *The Times* in London and the *South China Morning Post*, 13 October 1998. The author maintains his difference with the great sage: the IMF cannot be held responsible for the fact that Asian countries had fixed exchange rates or for the fact that the international capital flows were massively greater in the 1990s than ever before.
23. Author interview, 12 March 2004.
24. These calculations are taken from Peter Warr, 'Boom, bust and beyond' in Peter Warr, ed., *Thailand Beyond the Crisis* (2005); in particular, see p. 12. Philippe Ries, *Asian Storm* (2000), p. 53 also contains some useful observations.

25. The mechanism was the Bangkok International Banking Facility, set up as an 'offshore' centre through which foreign banks could lend, and Thai banks could borrow, foreign exchange in a defined, Thai-run market.

26. 'When I was invited to speak at this World Bank and IMF gathering more than three months ago, things were going very smoothly indeed for Asia. There was much talk then of Asian dragons and tigers, and of course, the east Asian miracles. We were flattered. We thought they were admiring our strengths and skills ... We did not realise how close we were to a manipulated crisis.'

27. This was structured through the Indonesian Plywood Association (Apkindo), run by Hasan, which creamed off a large rent from the US$5-billion a year plywood export business.

28. Tommy inherited the clove import monopoly from Suharto's half-brother, Probosutedjo, who had held it since 1968. At the time of the crisis, Tommy's Clove Marketing and Bufferstock Agency was buying cloves at IDR2,500 a kilogramme and selling them on at IDR12,500 a kilogramme.

29. Bank Pacific, controlled by the family of Ibnu Sutowo, went bust in 1995, but was never shut down.

30. There was also a bomb that ripped through the top two floors of the central bank in December, killing fifteen people. Contemporary speculation was that Suharto's children were involved, although this was never proven. More likely is that the bombing was the work of the south-east Asian terrorist group Jemaah Islamiyah.

31. At least twenty-three dissident leaders were kidnapped; some were subsequently released and some were never seen again.

32. 17 March 1998.

33. Megawati was Wahid's vice-president; she took over from him in July 2001.

34. Joseph Yam, 'Causes of and Solutions to the Recent Financial Turmoil in the Asian Region', a speech given to Asian central bankers in Manila. Available at http://www.info.gov.hk/hkma/eng/speeches/speechs/joseph/speech_050199b.htm

35. UMNO was supposed to be getting out of business; in a famous 1988 gaffe, however, Halim Saad had already publicly admitted that his role was to hold vast corporate interests in trust for the party.

36. This took the form of a personal guarantee from Halim Saad.

37. Yohannes Yacob, Suharto's legal adviser, made barely veiled threats in the weeks following the president's resignation. In November 1998 he warned that any public enquiry into first family corruption 'will also drag down government officials, ex-officials and all the cronies. The legal process will be very long and tiring.' See Schwarz, *A Nation in Waiting*, p. 378.

38. In late 1998, in the face of public demands for action, the Habibie government published a list of land holdings belonging to first family-related companies. The list showed 9 million hectares of land holdings across 26 out of 27 provinces, amounting to 10 per cent of Indonesia's total area. Forestry concessions were the largest category.

39. There was unwelcome attention in spring 1999 when the British press identified three London properties owned by Suharto family members on the market for a combined £11million; Suharto's children educated many of their children at private British schools and also did a lot of shopping there. *Independent*, 16 March 1999.

40. This became known as the Goro-Bulog Case. A private firm of which Tommy was president-commissioner had swapped a piece of north Jakarta marshland for a valuable piece of downtown real estate owned by state logistics agency Bulog; Tommy's firm also received two Bulog-guaranteed bank loans. None of these transactions made any sense for Bulog, which was being milked in a typical act of first family corruption. The total loss to the state was put at IDR94 billion, tiny by Tommy's standards of expropriation, but the case was straightforward, easy to prosecute and limited in scope.

41. Between Tommy Suharto's indictment on 10 December 1998 and May 1999, five bomb blasts in Jakarta followed charges being laid, summonses of Tommy and Bambang to the Attorney-General's office, and appearances by Tommy in court. The September 2000 stock exchange bomb occurred the day before Tommy's father was supposed to make a court appearance. Subsequently, compelling evidence was unearthed that the stock exchange bomb was in fact the work of Jemaah Islamiyah. Responsibility for the other bombings remains a matter of conjecture. The main point here, however, is that at the time the possibility that Tommy – subsequently convicted of murder – and associates might be involved in terror seemed all too real.

42. See Kevin O'Rourke, *Reformasi* (2002), p. 413.

43. http://www.interpol.int/public/Data/Wanted/Notices/ Data/2006/84/2006_29984.asp

44. A summary list of the conditions agreed by Indonesia, running to four pages, can be found in Martin Feldstein, ed., *Economic and Financial Crises in Emerging Market Economies* (2003), p. 396. The Fund had never previously made so many demands on countries as it did in Asia after the crisis – around 140 items in Indonesia, 90 in South Korea and 70 in Thailand.

45. At the end of 2005, the top four banks in non-Hong Kong south-east Asia, and the only ones with assets over US$20 billion, were Singapore's DBS (much the biggest and state-owned), Malaysia's Maybank (state-owned), Thailand's Bangkok Bank (still controlled by the Sophonpanich family) and Indonesia's Bank Mandiri (state-owned). The largest bank in the Philippines was Metropolitan Bank & Trust, with assets of a little over US$10 billion.

46. DBS bank, the largest of the Singapore state banks, is much the biggest bank in the region outside Hong Kong. At the end of 2005 it had assets of US$108 billion, twice those of second-ranked Maybank of Malaysia. Singapore law requires capital to asset ratios for banks that are about 50 per cent more stringent than those recommended by the so-called central banks' central bank, the Bank for International Settlements.

47. The case concerned the failure to make 'adequate disclosure' during listing of eWorldSports.com in August 2000. UOB was fined SGD400,000 and five executives were forced to resign.

48. Curtailing, for instance, the ability of Hong Kong companies to undertake rights issues without consulting their shareholders, or ending the anomaly whereby the accounts of joint ventures of Hong Kong companies are not published.

49. 'Saints and sinners', *CLSA Emerging Markets*, April 2001.

50. Some of these privatisation attempts are discussed in chapter 5. That most of them were defeated is one of the strongest indications of rising minority investor power in Hong Kong.

51. Author interview, 13 October 2004.

52. Relating, among other things, to initial public offerings and disclosure. It is notable that in Hong Kong former Financial Secretary Hamish Macleod drew attention to the need for an overhaul of company law as long ago as 1994, yet no substantial revision has taken place; godfather interests oppose such a move.

53. Since, for example, every bank in Indonesia had broken regulations on related party lending before the crisis, every godfather was a theoretical target for prosecution – even if this was never likely to happen.

54. This was the BW Resources affair, a gaming company whose share price bounced around like a yoyo.

55. Aquino's 1986–92 presidency was characterised by political instability – there were seven coup attempts. General Fidel Ramos, a former adviser to Marcos, nicknamed 'Steady Eddie', was much more important in pushing through structural reform. He ended monopolies in civil aviation, telecommunications, power and water, pushed through tax reform, and allowed new foreign entrants into the banking system.

56. Aquino is from the Cojuangco family; Ramos is a cousin of Ferdinand Marcos.

57. It is a curiosity of the Philippine political system that the president and vice-president are elected separately and the president can therefore have a deputy who is not on his or her ticket.

58. Chavalit Yongchaiyudh, the premier when the financial crisis broke, made anti-Chinese remarks in a belated attempt to stir up anti-Chinese populism. His failure to rally support on racial grounds is indicative of how far the Chinese assimilation process has gone since large-scale immigration ceased in the late 1940s.

59. The government of Chatichai Choonhavan issued twenty-two telecom concessions between 1988 and 1991, of which Thaksin won seven, covering mobile phones, data networks and satellites.

60. Pasuk Phongpaichit and Chris Baker, *Thaksin: The Business of Politics in Thailand* (2004), p. 53.

61. Pasuk and Baker, *Thaksin* p. 57. Thanong was Thaksin's key financial adviser between 1989 and 1992; he reappeared after the crisis as a member of Thaksin's cabinet.

62. Pitak Intarawitayanunt, a long-time political ambassador of the CP Group, and Wattana Muang-suk, a son-in-law of Dhanin's brother. A son-in-law of Dhanin, Wirachai Wiramethikun, was a founding member of Thai Rak Thai.

63. Thai Rak Thai campaign material, 2001.

64. ACT Mobile. After protests, the business was started in November 2002, but on a shoestring budget that gave it little chance of competing successfully.

65. CP TelecomAsia. The other company paying the THB200 per subscriber per month fee was Ucom/TAC, the second incumbent in the original mobile telephony duopoly in Thailand.

66. The 50:50 joint venture is called Thai AirAsia.

67. The Sophonpanich, Rattanarak and Lamsam families retained management control of Bangkok Bank, Bank of Ayudhya and Thai Farmers Bank respectively, with reduced equity. But four family-controlled banks, including the Wanglee's Nakhongthon Bank which went to Standard Chartered, ended up with foreign equity and management. Five more banks, including the Taechaphaibun's Bangkok Metropolitan Bank, were nationalised.

68. Just before he formed Thai Rak Thai, in February 1998, Thaksin appeared to signal a willingness to work more closely with Dhanin Chearavanont when he sold his cable television interests to him. On Thaksin's side, however, there was a long-standing resentment that Dhanin had never shown gratitude for what Thaksin believed was his key role in helping CP Group secure a huge deal from the 1989–92 Chatichai Choonhavan government to instal three million landlines; see Pasuk and Baker, *Thaksin*, p. 45.

69. Off the record interviews.

70. Thanong Bidaya, former chief financial adviser to Thaksin, finance minister at the time of the crisis, and finance minister again under Thaksin at the time of the Shin Corp. sale, was on hand to tell the press that all aspects of the deal looked OK to him. See Amy Kazmin in the *Financial Times*, 1 February 2006.

71. It is an irony of contemporary Thailand that, while anti-Chinese racism has been taken out of domestic politics, the perceived 'blood-sucking' role of Chinese Singapore is a focal point of resurgent Thai nationalism.

72. Charoen's Thai Beverage Co. produces the country's best-selling Chang (elephant) brand beer, as well as local whiskies sold under the Mekong, Sangsom and Hongthong brands. He obtained licences when Thailand's Singha beer monopoly was opened up in the 1990s.

73. Piruna Polsiri and Yupana Wiwattanakantang, 'Business Groups in Thailand: Before and After the East Asian Financial Crisis', Centre for Economic Institutions working paper, Hitotsubashi University, 2004.

74. Phileo-Allied was the main company, with the usual feast of associate businesses spread around it.

75. When BT itself cut non-core investments in response to the bursting of the global information technology bubble.

76. Most of the growth came from the acquisition of Norwegian Cruise Holdings ASA in several tranches in 1999 and 2000. A small Singaporean operator, Sun Cruises, was also acquired in 2000. The fact that these deals occurred in the midst of the crisis is testament to Genting's casino cash flow.

77. Khoo Kay Peng controls retail chain Laura Ashley, the family of the late Lee Loy Seng controls retail chain Crabtree & Evelyn and, as noted in the next paragraph, Francis Yeoh controls the regional utility Wessex Water.

78. Gas makes up three-quarters of Malaysia's proven oil and gas reserves. Petronas' own data put the value of discounts to market price on gas supplied to IPPs of Ananda Krishnan, Syed Mokhtar Al-Bukhary, and the Lim and Yeoh families at MYR14 billion between 1997 and 2006. The discount to the international market price for gas averages around 50 per cent.

79. The first IPP deal, for two power plants and featuring a 21-year contract with Tenaga, was signed in 1992. The terms, from the IPP's perspective, were the best ever granted, with the price per kilowatt hour around 40 per cent higher than was subsequently achieved. Yeoh also secured power station sites that Tenaga had intended to develop itself, with gas pipes and electricity distribution lines already in place.

80. The shopping malls are Lot 10 at Kuala Lumpur's Bukit Bintang intersection, and the nearby Star Hill Shopping Complex. The land bank, in an area known as Sentul Raya, is sufficient for up to US$2 billion of property development.

81. Dato' Suleiman bin Abdul Manan.

82. Kuok imports raw sugar and refines it (he owns equity in all four Malaysian refiners and controls three of them). The importation of refined sugar is strictly limited, and minimal, while the government sets the retail price for sugar.

83. The money came from state-controlled investment fund Khazanah Nasional, which invested MYR600 million for a 40 per cent stake; Syed Mokhtar was unable to secure commercial credit for the project. Subsequently he bought out the government's equity and sold part of it to Maersk, which he brought in to manage the port.

84. Syed Mokhtar controls the 15 per cent slice of the sugar import quota that is not in Robert Kuok's hands.

85. For instance: Najib Tun Razak, Abdullah's deputy premier and son of former premier Abdul Razak; Hishammuddin Tun Hussein, Abdullah's education minister and son of former premier Hussein Onn.
Mukhriz, one of Mahathir's sons, is prominent in UMNO Youth, as is Jamaluddin, a son-in-law of Abdullah.

86. Off the record interview, March 2004.

87. See, among others, Schwarz, *A Nation in Waiting*, p. 110

88. Many Nursalim interests in Singapore are held through Nuri Holdings, control of which is in the hands of Nursalim's daughter Michelle Liem Mei Fung.

89. He is Tan Enk Ee, husband of Nursalim's daughter Michelle.

90. Author interview, 9 March 2005.

91. Author interview, 9 March 2005.

92. Author interview, 9 March 2005.

93. Mandiri, formed from four insolvent state banks in 1999, already had a non-performing loan ratio of 27 per cent by 2006. Tanoto owed Mandiri IDR5.4 trillion as of September 2006; at that point the bank said in a public statement that his companies 'lack good faith'.

94. Unibank, which IBRA said at the time of the crisis had made 51 per cent of its loans to Tanoto companies, versus a maximum legal limit for related party lending of 20 per cent.

95. See Indonesian press reports and Bill Guerin in *Asia Times*, 14 October 2006.

96. Aksa Mahmud, who owed IDR1.9 trillion, via his company Bosowa. See *Bisnis Indonesia*, 1 September 2006.

97. APP unit PT Pabrik Kertas Tjiwi Kimia failed to meet two bond interest payments totalling US$43 million in February 2001; the general moratorium followed less than a month later.

98. Sara Webb, 'Beleaguered Asia Pulp & Paper Seeks to Recover US$1 billion in Alleged Debts', *Wall Street Journal*, 28 August 2001. Reporters also found that the five firms shared the same post office box address in the British Virgin Islands; four of them registered offices in Singapore on the same date in 1998; all five closed their Singapore offices on the same date in 2001; at least one of the firms, on closing its Singapore office, left the APP headquarters and an APP employee as its forwarding address.

99. See Timothy Mapes, 'Asian Paper Giant Survives Debt Saga as Creditors Fume', *Wall Street Journal*, 15 August 2003.

100. The price of APP's American Depository Receipts was 12 cents, versus US$11 in 1995.
101. The units were PT Indah Kiat and PT Lontar Papyrus Pulp & Paper Industry.
102. In 2003 APP formed ventures to build two paper plants in China's Yunnan and Hainan provinces, in projects valued at US$2 billion and US$1.6 billion respectively.
103. BII Bank Ltd.
104. The action was brought in August 2002.
105. An appeal decision in the second case was pending in the supreme court.
106. Author interview, 9 March 2005.
107. The main allegation is that Winata runs illegal gambling dens in Jakarta and elsewhere.
108. Author interview, 10 March 2005.
109. Bambang Harymurti. The article was published on 3 March 2003. See Amnesty International for more detail: http://web.amnesty.org/library/Index/ENGASA210302004?open&of=ENG-2S3. Mr Harymurti and a *Tempo* reporter brought a case for assault, but none of the policemen accompanying the persons alleged to have attacked them would corroborate that they had been attacked; the case was dismissed.
110. Ardimas Sasdi, *Jakarta Post*, 26 February 2007.
111. Some very modest success is reflected in an increase, according to official Singapore data, in the number of properties purchased by Indian nationals from 104 in 2004 to 271 in 2005. Like Indonesians, who dominate the high-end Singapore real estate market, Indians' purchases are overwhelmingly concentrated on multi-million dollar properties.
112. Via Bank Surya, which they controlled.
113. The Indonesian government alleges that Agus Anwar stole US$376 million via a bank he controlled.
114. *Tempo*, 26 October 2006. It is impossible to know which, if any, of these people is wanted for questioning by the Indonesian attorney general because, as of June 2007, no list had been published.
115. The development is on Hong Kong's Hunghom peninsula.
116. The attempt was stopped by private court action.
117. The west Kowloon deal was so big that the Kwok and Li families, who famously loathe each other, joined forces to make a single bid.

118. As of the 2004 Legislative Council elections, 60 seats are split into 30 small-vote functional constituencies and 30 popularly elected geographical constituencies. Changes made by Chris Patten to massively enlarge the functional constituency voter base were immediately reversed when China resumed sovereignty in 1997.
119. *South China Morning Post*, 3 February 2005.
120. Tsang does, however, have his eye on a new civil service headquarters on the water front.
121. As of 2007, minority investor campaigner David Webb and Civic Exchange chief Christine Loh have both been elected to the stock exchange board.
122. A selection of comments: Ronnie Chan told the American Chamber of Commerce in a widely reported speech on 28 April 2004: 'A lot of us are pretty happy with the current system. Nothing major needs to be changed … I believe that, structurally speaking, the *status quo* is the best way to go.' Cheng Yu-tung's son Henry told the *South China Morning Post* on 1 May 2004 that a move to universal suffrage would bring 'chaos'. K. S. Li told the *Standard* in a rare public comment on 20 March 2004 that political reform must be 'gradual'. Peter Woo claimed in the *South China Morning Post* on 18 March 2004 that Hong Kong's Basic Law infers that business must never control less than one-quarter of the seats in the legislature.
123. K. S. Li listed two more REITs in Singapore. Prosperity was the first private sector REIT in Hong Kong; Li's godfather peers copied the template and created many more.
124. Hutchison swapped a fixed line telephone business and broadband service it controlled in Hong Kong for control of Vanda in January 2004, in what is termed a 'back-door listing'. Vanda was then renamed Hutchison Global Communications. On the day the back-door listing was announced, Vanda shares shot up 37 per cent to HK$1.52. But after the market closed, Vanda announced the issue of 2 billion new shares at a 41 per cent discount to the day's price, sending the stock into freefall. Hutchison re-acquired the company through another subsidiary in 2005 for 65 cents a share.
125. The back-door listing involved a takeover of already-listed Dong Feng Gas.
126. Author interview, 11 November 2005.
127. Author interview, 19 March 2005.

128. 3 was still losing a lot of money in 2006 but Hutchison, through which K. S. Li controls it, has managed to fund its losses through a mixture of operating cash flows and asset disposals. In the first half of 2006, for instance, on an operating cash flow basis the 3 business lost US$1.3 billion. Since 2004, Hutchison has made around US$8 billion of disposals, including a share in its Hong Kong port cartel, to cover 3 losses. None the less, in early 2007, there appeared to be light at the end of the tunnel for K. S. Li as Britain's Vodafone led a bidding war for his 3G subsidiary in India. Hutchison Essar, as the company is called, is only the number four mobile operator in India, but Vodafone's desperate quest for new growth markets suggested it might pay Hutchison as much as US$13 billion for its stake. This would be further testament to the importance of the godfathers' core cash flows. Most free market operators have long since written down the value of their 3G operations, but K. S. Li has been able to hang on for years until an acceptable deal came along. Still, the rest of his 3G subsidiaries do not have India's growth prospects and will continue to weigh on Hutchison's share price, which has long been in the doldrums.

129. The *Forbes* list is heavily based on holdings of equity in publicly listed companies, about which information is readily available. One of the reasons the list should always be treated with caution is that it can never fully account for assets held in private companies or, in the other direction, for debts and other liabilities held privately.

130. Li Ka-shing's estimated net worth rose to US$18.8 billion; that of the Kwoks (US$11.6 v. US$11.2 billion in 1996), Lee Shau-kee (US$11 v. US$12.7 billion), Robert Kuok (US$5 v. US$5.7 billion) and Cheng Yu-tung (US$5.1 v. US$5.5 billion) was little changed; the Philippines' Tan Yu died and his estate was divided; Indonesia' Gudang Garam Winowidjojo family dropped from US$6.7 billion to US$1.9 billion (it is worth remembering that this was mostly a function of the decline in the dollar value of the rupiah; without the collapse of the currency, the family's dollar worth would be little changed); and Singapore's Kwek Leng Beng dropped from US$5.7 billion to US$3.6 billion.

7. Finale: The politics, stupid

1. The average annual growth rate in the nominal value of exports in the six years 2000–2005 was 13.2 per cent in Singapore, 9.1 per cent in Hong Kong, 9.4 per cent in Malaysia, 11.7 per cent in Thailand, 10.6

per cent in Indonesia, and 3.2 per cent in the Philippines; the latter country's exports grew at an above-trend 19.5 per cent at the height of the crisis in 1997–9, reflecting a divergence from the regional cycle that has been apparent since the economic collapse at the end of the Marcos era.

2. This is not meant to single China out. All Asian countries, from Japan down, have used and do use central bank foreign exchange accumulation to keep their exchange rates artificially low. China simply gets more attention because it is bigger.

3. Currency devaluation in south-east Asia after the financial crisis also made local labour costs more competitive with China. CLSA estimated monthly factory labour costs in 2005, including social security contributions, at US$350 in Shanghai, US$250 in Shenzhen, US$200 in Manila, US$150 in Bangkok and US$120 in Batam, Indonesia. Chinese productivity is higher, and supply chains and logistics are generally better, but the potential attraction of south-east Asia is clear. Among the leading openers of new processing plants in Malaysia and Indonesia in recent years were Hong Kong contract manufacturers with long experience in China.

4. Across the territories we are discussing, from about 33 per cent to about 23 per cent.

5. Consumption, the third component of gross domestic product as measured by expenditure, was much more stable than is popularly believed, falling about three percentage points in south-east Asia after the crisis. A detailed analysis of the post-crisis macro story can be found in Jonathan Anderson's series of papers, 'The Return of Asia', published by UBS Investment Research, beginning 17 August 2006.

6. Some economists have dubbed this return to pegged exchange rates Bretton Woods II, referencing the global system of pegged exchange rates implemented at the end of the Second World War.

7. The 1990s adventure is recounted in the author's *The China Dream* (Profile/Grove Atlantic, 2002).

8. US$6.95 billion in Macau versus US$6.5 billion in Las Vegas; this compares with Macau gaming revenues in 2001 of US$2 billion.

9. For a full recounting of evidence about trends in financial and physical wealth, plus some background on problems associated with measuring these indicators, see the fourth part of Jonathan Anderson's series, 'The Return of Asia', published by UBS Investment Research, beginning 20 November 2006.

10. *Financial Times*, 30 January 2007.
11. This figure is for 2000 and is the US dollar equivalent of HK$10,000.
12. See Hong Kong Council of Social Sciences, 'Growing Seriousness in Poverty and Income Disparity', September 2004.
13. Hong Kong Council of Social Sciences, 'Growing Seriousness in Poverty and Income Disparity', September 2004.
14. See Isra Sarntisart, 'Socio-economic Consequences of the Crisis', in Peter Warr, ed., *Thailand Beyond the Crisis* (2005).
15. See Kevin O'Rourke, *Reformasi* (2002), p. 148, and contemporary World Bank reports from Indonesia.
16. The Indonesian government uses a calorific intake measure, which is lower than the World Bank's indexed US$1-a-day benchmark (it equates to about US$0.55 per day), to determine poverty. By the national measure, 18 per cent of Indonesians, or 39 million people, were living in poverty in 2006 – up by 4 million on 2005. Independent estimates of up to 80 million people living in poverty are based on the World Bank benchmark.
17. Indonesia data from 2002, Thailand from 2000. The World Bank was unable to give an up-to-date figure for Malaysia.
18. 2001 data.
19. The biggest populations are in the US (2.8 million), Saudi Arabia (1 million), Malaysia (820,000), Japan (430,000), Canada (390,000), Australia (210,000), United Arab Emirates (190,000) and Hong Kong (190,000).
20. This is only traceable/transfers through the financial system. Cash brought home by visiting migrant workers cannot be counted.
21. This includes reduced fuel subsidies which markedly increased poverty rates in the past couple of years in Indonesia and Malaysia.

22. *Poverty and Inequality Indicators, South-east Asia Versus South America*

	% Population below US$1 a day	% Population below US$2 a day	Survey year	Gini coefficient	Survey year	GDP per capita, US$, 2005
Argentina	3.3	14.3	2001	0.51*	2001	4,799
Brazil	8.2	22.4	2001	0.59	2001	4,320
Colombia	8.2	22.6	1999	0.54	1999	2,656
Venezuela	9.9	32.1	2000	0.42	2000	5,026

	% Population below US$1 a day	% Population below US$2 a day	Survey year	Gini coefficient	Survey year	GDP per capita, US$, 2005
Thailand	<2	32.5	2000	0.43	2002	2,659
Malaysia	na	na		0.49	1997	5,042
Indonesia	7.5	52	2002	0.34	2000	1,283
Philippines	15.5	47.5	2000	0.46	2000	1,168
Hong Kong	–	–	–	0.53	2001	25,493
Singapore	–	–	–	0.52	2005	26,836

* urban only

Sources: World Bank, IMF, Hong Kong and Singapore governments.

23 The Gini coefficient, named after its Italian originator Corrado Gini, measures deviation from perfect equality of income distribution, usually based on gross household income. In a graph of income distribution, a 45 degree line shows an equal distribution of income and the Gini coefficient measures the area of deviation from this. The Gini coefficient is not, as is often erroneously implied, a pure measure of income inequality. As well as extremes of income, a high concentration of, say, low-to-middle income relative to other income bands will push up the coefficient. None the less, Gini is the best and most readily available measure of inequality across states.

24. See table in Note 22.

25. See table in Note 22. In 2006 SingStat, the Singaporean statistics agency, made various changes to its calculation of the Gini Coefficient to include post-income government transfers to the poor. This methodology appears not to be consistent with standard international practice; it resulted in a very substantial reduction in the published 2006 Gini coefficient to 0.44.

26. See Donald Kirk, 'Fading People Power in the Philippines', *Asia Times*, 27 February 2007.

27. Ethnic Indians have been the big losers in Malaysia since independence, as the *bumiputra* majority, the beneficiaries of positive discrimination, forced them out of their colonial role in the civil service. Unlike the Chinese, the Indians had no broad-based commercial position in the economy to fall back on.

28. He has refused to rule out the possibility when interviewed. Remember that even Tunku Razaleigh Hamzah, after his near-mortal struggle with Mahathir, was brought back into UMNO in the 1990s.

29. One who failed to grovel was Hugo Restall, editor of the *Far Eastern Economic Review*, who was sued by Lee Kuan Yew and Lee Hsien Loong over an interview with Chee Soon Juan, leader of the Singapore Democratic Party. The Lees allege the article says they are corrupt, though it is difficult to find such an allegation in the text. Mr Restall and his magazine enjoyed an appetiser to their meal of Singaporean justice when, in a preliminary ruling in February 2007, their appointed counsel was denied the right to appear in court on the grounds that the lawyer had previously questioned the independence of the Singaporean judiciary. An interesting guide to the case, and the Chee Soon Juan interview, can be found at http://www.feer.com/articles1/2006/sing_banning/free/index.html. The Lees, and other senior PAP politicians, have brought dozens of defamation cases in Singapore and never lost.

30. Chee Soon Juan. He was given nine days inside in early 2006 for questioning the judiciary's independence, and another five weeks after the election for speaking in public without a permit. He was previously jailed in 1999 and 2002 for speaking without state permission, and declared bankrupt in 2006 after failing to pay SGD500,000 in libel damages relating to suits brought by the Lees and other members of the PAP.

31. See Shawn Donnan, 'Inconvenient Truths in Singapore', *Asia Times*, 1 December 2006.

32. The government declines to publish regular and full data on executions. Former premier Goh Chok Tong, questioned by the BBC about hangings in 2003, said he thought the number was around 70–80 that year. Asked why he did not know the precise figure, Goh replied: 'I've got more important things to worry about.' See http://web.amnesty.org/library/index/engasa360012004.

33. Gross domestic product *per capita*, at year-end exchange rates, in 2005 was US$16,308 in South Korea and US$15,203 in Taiwan, versus US$5,042 in Malaysia, US$2,659 in Thailand, US$1,283 in Indonesia and US$1,168 in the Philippines. In the early 1950s, GDP *per capita* in the Philippines was higher than in South Korea.

34. The best polls on this subject have been conducted by Hong Kong University. Many Hong Kong residents with foreign passports obtained them from the United States, Canada, Australia and New Zealand. Britain rejected the case for granting full British passports to Hong Kong citizens on the implausible grounds that large numbers of

Hong Kong people might move to the United Kingdom; instead, most inhabitants of the colony were fobbed off with British National Overseas (BNO) papers that do not grant rights of citizenship and diplomatic protection.

35. The root of the ruse was to massively expand the franchise in Hong Kong's functional constituencies – so that all those working in a particular sector of the economy could vote – without actually getting rid of the functional seats, which would have been contrary to public agreements with China. A side result of this was that many people had two votes in 1995, one for a geographic constituency and one for a functional one, but the polls were much the fairest and most democratic ones ever held in Hong Kong.

36. There are several different proposals but, on examination, the difference between the templates put forward by the most popular political parties and senior ex-civil servants is not that great.

37. The ballot was held on 25 March. Pro-democracy parties did, unexpectedly, manage to secure the 100 nominations from the Election Committee that were necessary to field a candidate, Alan Leong, a former chairman of the Bar Council. But his defeat was assured since almost half the Election Committee is comprised of Beijing loyalists who are appointed by virtue of their membership of bodies such as China's National People's Congress. In the ballot, Tsang garnered 649 votes and Leong 123.

38. The campaign raised HK$27.33 million, and spent HK$4.12 million.

39. Author interview, February 2004.

40. Off the record interview, 19 March 2004.

41. In the *Forbes* 2006 rich list, Michael Ying was shown with net worth of US$2.7 billion, and Patrick Wang with US$2.1 billion.

42. Esprit's Michael Ying has been selling down his shareholding – to around 16 per cent in 2006 – for several years. Another Hong Kong billionaire who made his money in textiles, Chen Din Hwa, took his capital out of manufacturing in the early 1990s and shifted much of it into the real estate cartel, principally by buying into the Ng family's Sino Land. This continued the pattern of Li Ka-shing, who bailed out of plastics manufacturing at the first opportunity.

43. The EU 15, the US, Canada and Japan all have minimum wages.

44. Figures from World Development Report 2006.

45. See note 33 above.

46. Even if new members, like Vietnam, are technically communist.

Cast of Characters

THE BUSINESSMEN/GODFATHERS

Thailand
The Bunnags

The most important of the Muslim Persian families to serve as senior administrators in Siam, as it then was, in the nineteenth century. Chuang Bunnag (1808–83), whose official title was Somdet Chao Phraya Borom Maha Si Suriyawongse, as one example, was minister of the interior – one of the four key ministries of Siam – and later became regent. The Bunnags ran the greater Bangkok region and, as allocators of tax farms, gave many to their own relatives; they controlled large shipping interests and innumerable other businesses. The family inter-married with Thai royalty and prominent Sino-Thai families; two twentieth century prime ministers of royal lineage, Seni Pramoj and his brother Kukrit, had a Bunnag mother. The Bunnag clan remains a significant force in both business and the civil service.

The Chearavanonts

Modern godfather Dhanin Chearavanont inherited the Sino-Thai agribusiness built up by his father, Chia Ek Chaw, and his uncle, in 1983. The Chearavanonts (as they now are) already had a successful seed business in China before 1949. Dhanin, born in 1939, built the CP (Charoen Pokphand) Group into the largest agribusiness, and before the financial crisis, the largest conglomerate, in Thailand. Politically astute, he made use of government import substitution initiatives for manufacturing, and was one of those financed by Chin *Sophonpanich's* Bangkok Bank, as well as by state banks. In the 1980s and 1990s, CP diversified both sectorally and geographically and became both a chickens-to-telecommunications empire and possibly the single biggest foreign investor in China. After the Asian financial crisis, CP was forced to sell many of its assets in China and Thailand.

Dhanin is assisted by an elder brother and three sons. In the 1990s he was a Thai senator and government adviser, but had to adjust to the ascendancy of *Thaksin Shinawatra* from 1998, placing a son-in-law in the new premier's cabinet; none the less, relations between the Chearavanont and Thaksin families are strained by the struggle for the top godfather spot.

Dhanin breeds fighting cocks and homing pigeons; the pigeons are now kept by a son on the roof of a building in Shanghai.

The Khaws

Khaw Soo Cheang was an early immigrant Chinese tycoon, born in 1797, who landed in Penang and made his fortune in tax farming and tin mining in southern Thailand. He also built up a shipping business in Penang. The next generation of Khaws, led by Khaw Sim Bee, formed successful tin mining joint ventures with Australian investors, but their Penang operations failed and thereafter the family went into decline.

The Sophonpanichs

Born in Bangkok in 1910, patriarch Chin Sophonpanich was sent back to Shantou, China, for schooling but returned to Thailand aged 17 when his father died. He was variously employed as a teacher and successful lumber trader. His big break came in 1952 when he was made general manager of the failing Bangkok Bank. His key political patron was General Phao Siryanon, director general of police. He brought in élite Thai Chinese, such as Prasit Kanchanawat and Boonchu Rojasthanien, to run the bank professionally. When Phao fell victim to the coup by General Sarit Thanarat in 1957, Chin put his lieutenants in charge and left for Hong Kong until Sarit died in 1963. During this period of self-imposed exile Chin focused on building up his foreign network and financed a generation of tycoons around the region. By the late 1980s Bangkok Bank was the biggest bank in non-Hong Kong south-east Asia and its associated conglomerate was the largest in Thailand. Having first convinced his state sponsors to provide the development capital for Bangkok Bank, Chin ended up with the controlling interest. He died in 1988.

Chin's eldest son, Robin, inherited the family's Hong Kong-based interests, while second son Chatri took over the core Thai assets. Bangkok Bank was hit hard by the Asian financial crisis, and reported accumulated losses of almost US$3 billion from 1998 to 1999, but the family retained control, albeit diluted, from a stake of around 33 per cent to one nearer 20 per cent, with a US$1 billion share placement. The biggest block of investors, comprising almost 50 per cent, is now foreign; Chatri's son Chartsiri is bank president.

Thaksin Shinawatra

Born to a wealthy Sino-Thai family based in Chiang Mai in 1949 (Thaksin's great grandfather was a tax farmer, his father a businessman and member of parliament), Thaksin has been at pains to deny his privileged roots. He attended university in the United States and followed a career characterised by rapid promotion in the Thai police force; he married the daughter of a police general. While working for the police, and later, Thaksin made many unsuccessful forays into business before making some money leasing computers and other equipment to the police, as well as with a paging company. In 1986 he was granted a 20-year, untendered mobile phone concession and in 1990 was licensed to run a domestic satellite service. After listing his Shinawatra (later renamed Shin) Corporation in 1990, Thaksin expanded into broadcasting and other telecommunications services.

In the mid 1990s, when telecommunications was the most politicised business in Thailand, Thaksin went into national politics. He was appointed foreign minister in 1994–5, deputy prime minister under part-Teochiu Banharn 'the walking ATM' Silpa-archa in 1995–6 and deputy prime minister again in the last days of General Chavalit Yongchaiydh's government in 1997. Under the latter, he was accused of benefiting from advance knowledge of the baht's July 1997 devaluation. In July 1998, in the depths of the Asian financial crisis and with his businesses heavily in debt, Thaksin formed the Thai Rak Thai (Thais Love Thais) party and campaigned on a mould-breaking populist agenda of universal healthcare, a debt moratorium for farmers and development funds for every village. He swept to power in 2001. Many of the policies were implemented, and poverty fell sharply, though critics alleged this was paid for with unsustainable debt financing. Thaksin also pursued a war on drugs and a battle against Muslim insurgents in the south that claimed thousands of lives. In 2005 he was re-elected in a landslide victory. However, Thaksin was deeply unpopular in Bangkok and was resented by interests ranging from the military to human rights groups. When his family sold out its controlling interest in Shin Corporation to Singapore's Temasek for a tax-free US$1.9 billion in January 2006, public protests broke out. Thaksin called fresh elections, which were boycotted by the opposition. After a summer of political bickering, a military coup took place in September while Thaksin was in New York and the army appointed *Surayud Chulanont* as premier.

Malaysia
Chang Ming Thien

Born in Penang in 1917, Chang made a lot of money during and after the Second World War smuggling rubber out of Malaysia. Charming and ruthless, he then set up banks in Hong Kong and Malaysia, and a finance company in

Thailand, as well as diversifying into numerous other businesses. In the 1970s Chang Ming Thien looked set to become a major regional godfather, but a life of sexual and alcoholic excess caught up with him. He died in 1982, choking on his own vomit after passing out in a room in the Merlin hotel in Kuala Lumpur. In 1985, Chang's Hong Kong Overseas Trust Bank (OTB) collapsed, having been systematically defrauded by its directors over many years; the Hong Kong government bailed out depositors with a US$256-million takeover.

Daim Zainuddin

Born in the same village in Kedah as Malaysian prime minister *Mahathir Mohamad*, Daim qualified in law in London and got his first break in business in real estate in Kuala Lumpur. He started to be given management control of government companies in the late 1970s when Mahathir was deputy premier; he took over the ruling United Malays National Organisation (UMNO) investment arm, Fleet Group, after Mahathir became premier in 1981 and served as UMNO's treasurer. Appointed finance minister in 1984–91, Daim nurtured a group of *bumiputra* businessmen – 'Daim's boys' – on a diet of untendered privatisations and state credit; they included *Halim Saad*, *Tajudin Ramli* and Wan Azmi Wan Hamzah. Daim was recalled to government by Mahathir at the time of the Asian financial crisis and organised bail-outs of various favoured companies. He fell out with Mahathir in 2001 – possibly in relation to the business interests of Mahathir's sons – and resigned. Dubbed by one long-time Asia correspondent as 'the cockroach capitalist' – because he could crawl out from under anything – Daim is generally reckoned to be the wealthiest *bumiputra* godfather.

Eu Tong-sen

Born to an immigrant Chinese father who had opened shops before going into tin mining, Eu (1877–1941) was given a cosmopolitan education in both Chinese and English institutions. He expanded the family business, becoming *Loke Yew*'s principal rival, and diversified into plantations, banking, real estate and trading. Towards the end of his life, Eu moved to Hong Kong, where he built three gothic castles and filled them with statues of nymphs.

Halim Saad

A *bumiputra* protégé of *Daim Zainuddin*, born in 1953 to a well-off family, Halim Saad used to run the Renong Group, a repository for some of the assets of the ruling United Malays National Organisation (UMNO) that prospered from major state infrastructure contracts, including the country's key North–South Highway. Despite this, Renong has been bailed out by the government on numerous occasions, most recently during the Asian financial crisis. Prior to the crisis Renong had eleven listed subsidiaries, but was subsequently forced to shed some assets. Halim Saad was removed from management in the wake of the crisis.

Rashid Hussain

Born in Singapore in 1946 to an Indian father and Malay mother (the same racial mix as *Mahathir Mohamad*), Hussain grew up in a wealthy anglicized family. After a stint of stockbroking in London, former deputy prime minister Ghafar Baba helped him obtain Malaysian citizenship, which put Hussain in line for a stockbroking licence under the government's affirmative action policy. Over the next fifteen years, he built up Malaysia's leading financial services conglomerate, Rashid Hussain Berhad (RHB). In the 1990s, however, Hussain allied himself too closely with deputy prime minister Anwar Ibrahim; when Mahathir canned Anwar in 1998, Hussain found himself without political cover in the midst of a financial crisis. He was also accused of short selling the ringgit during the crisis, thereby contributing to what Mahathir saw as an international conspiracy to ruin Malaysia. Hussain lost control of his business in a government-sponsored consolidation of the banking industry. He is married to a daughter of Robert *Kuok*, Sue.

Khoo Kay Peng

Born in Johore in 1938, Khoo started out in banking at Oversea-Chinese Banking Corporation (OCBC) and Malayan Banking before moving to Bank Bumiputra, set up in 1965 to provide credit to indigenous businessmen, under then chairman *Tengku Razaleigh Hamzah*. They formed a close relationship. When Razaleigh became finance minister in the mid 1970s, Khoo turned a small company, Malayan United Industries (MUI), into one of the largest listed businesses in the country, taking over companies involved in sugar, cement, finance, insurance, banking, hotels, real estate and manufacturing. Khoo was also close to other powerful UMNO politicians, including home affairs minister and parliamentary speaker Tan Sri Haji Mohamad Noah bin Omar, also from Johore. However, when Razaleigh challenged *Mahathir* for the UMNO leadership in 1987 and lost, Khoo discovered he had hitched his wagon too tightly to only one horse. His conglomerate has achieved little since. Khoo remains a close, if junior, associate of Robert *Kuok*, another native of Johore.

He is an evangelical Christian who has made several investments with American televangelist Pat Robertson. In 1998 Khoo took control of British fashion retailer Laura Ashley.

Ananda Krishnan

The son of a Tamil Sri Lankan civil servant, born on the eve of the Second World War, Krishnan obtained an MBA from Harvard and made his first millions in oil trading, leveraging Harvard Business School-derived friendships with the Saudi royal family as well as with Filipino politician Roberto Ongpin and doing business with the regimes of *Suharto* and *Ferdinand Marcos*. Krishnan, whose first jobs were with international consultancies, advised on the structuring of Malaysia's oil and gas industry and managed to forge lasting friendships with both *Tengku Razaleigh Hamzah* and his arch rival *Mahathir Mohamad*. Under Mahathir, Krishnan received a stream of valuable government concessions for horse-race and numbers betting, mobile telephony, broadcasting and satellites, and developed the vast Kuala Lumpur City Centre and Twin Towers project with financing from Petronas, the state oil company; Petronas pumped in more money when Krishnan needed cash during the financial crisis.

Krishnan received considerable publicity when he provided financial support for the 1985 Live Aid concerts. His children show no interest in his businesses; a son became a monk in Thailand, while a daughter works as a doctor in Britain.

The Kuoks

Patriarch Robert Kuok Hock Nian, the youngest of three brothers, was born in Johore in 1923 to a successful rice, flour and sugar trader. Educated at élite colonial schools in Johore, and Raffles College (one of the colonial precursors of the National University of Singapore), Kuok built up his business through soft commodity trading and import substitution deals after the end of the Second World War. In the 1970s he became known as the 'sugar king' for his huge sugar trading deals and astute manoeuvres in the London-based futures market. He diversified into other regulated commodity businesses like flour and palm oil, as well as shipping, real estate, hotels, financial services and much more. Kuok also moved his base successively from Malaysia to Singapore to Hong Kong and operated more successfully across different south-east Asian territories than any of his peers. He has been doing business in China since the Korean War in the early 1950s.

Kuok's bookish middle brother chose a very different course in life. Rather than enter the family business, William joined the largely working-class Malayan Communist Party to fight British colonialism and was shot by British troops in Pahang in September 1953; he was known to friends for his ability to recite vast tracts of Shakespeare. Eldest brother Philip assisted in the family business before pursuing a career as a Malaysian ambassador.

Robert Kuok has eight children from two marriages. Sons Beau and Chye from his first marriage to Anglo-Chinese Joyce Cheah hold senior positions in his businesses, as do nephews Chye and Edward and neice Kaye (children of Philip); it is unclear what the terms of Robert Kuok's succession will be.

Lee Loy Seng

Lee was born in 1921 into a successful Hakka tin mining family. He continued in tin mining for a few years after the Second World War before switching his attention to plantations. Lee acquired acreage at low cost, first because of the British-declared 'Emergency' following the communist insurrection in 1948–60, later because European plantation companies sought to divest assets after independence and the start of pro-*bumiputra* economic policies. His KL Kepong became the largest private plantation and oleochemicals business in the country; outside Malaysia it owns the Crabtree & Evelyn retail chain. Lee died in 1993 and his sons now run the business.

The Lims

Lim Goh Tong was born in China's Fujian province in 1918 and travelled to Kuala Lumpur in the late 1930s to work for his uncle's construction business, which depended mainly on government contracts. Lim made money trading war surplus construction equipment after the Second World War – he was adept at bid-rigging – and set up his own construction company, which won major public works contracts. He also went into mining. After independence in 1957, Lim obtained the only casino licence in Malaysia and built the vast Genting Highlands resort, with 4,000 guest rooms, outside Kuala Lumpur; numerous members of the political élite are believed to be shareholders through nominees. Other Lim interests include plantations, real estate and electricity generation.

Son Lim Kok Thay, preferred by his father to an elder brother, now runs the family business. Kok Thay has used his gambling cash flows to expand into cruise lines (Star Cruises), taking over Norwegian Cruise Line (NCL) in 1999, and recently won a US$3.4-billion bid to build a gaming resort on Singapore's Sentosa island.

Loke Yew

A godfather original. Born in 1845 in Guangdong, Loke made his fortune in Larut in Malaysia working with the Ghee Hin triad to import and manage

Chinese mining labour. He also took on colonial government revenue farms, learned English, acquired English manners and entered several joint ventures with foreigners. Loke Yew died in 1917 and his urbane son, Loke Wan Tho, carried on the family business until he was killed in a plane crash in 1964.

Quek Leng Chan
See under **Singapore**, the Kweks.

Tajudin Ramli
Bumiputra businessman and former investment banker Tajudin was born in Kedah in 1946 and has close links with *Daim Zainuddin* and the ruling UMNO party. He worked for Daim in the 1980s and subsequently received an untendered licence to operate a mobile telephone network, Celcom. In 1994 his group took a controlling interest in Malaysian Airline System (MAS), the national carrier. Both businesses hit the skids in the Asian financial crisis and Tajudin's holding company Technology Resources Industry (TRI) defaulted on bond payments. After Daim left government in 2001, he lost control of the companies and was indicted for defrauding MAS through service contracts with private businesses in which he held undeclared stakes.

Tan Koon Swan
Tan worked as a junior civil servant and employee of oil multinational Esso before becoming general manager of *Lim* Goh Tong's Genting Highlands casino resort in the early 1970s. He then built up his own conglomerate before starting Multi-Purpose Holdings (MPH) as an investment vehicle for Malaysian Chinese investors; Tan became president of the Malaysian Chinese Association (MCA). He mixed his own business freely with that of the MCA and in 1986 was arrested in Singapore for fraud. Robert *Kuok* posted bail and answered the MCA's call to clean up Multi-Purpose, which was plagued by corruption and posted record corporate losses; Tan Koon Swan was sentenced to two years in jail. Multi-Purpose, under new ownership, went bust again in the financial crisis.

Vincent Tan Chee Yioun
Born in 1952, Tan typifies a group of younger godfathers who got ahead through untendered privatisations in the 1980s and early 1990s. His big break was the acquisition of the Sports Toto lottery from the Malaysian government in 1985. With this core cash flow, and other untendered privatisations, he

diversified into everything from infrastructure to newspapers to hotels. Tan enjoys a close relationship with *Mahathir*.

K. Thamboosamy Pillay

Born to a wealthy Tamil Indian family based in Singapore, Pillay was educated at the élite Raffles Institution and worked both in business and government with the first British Resident in Malaya, James Guthrie Davidson. He organised the importation of indentured labour under government auspices before entering various businesses as a money lender, government contractor and miner. He and *Loke Yew* were partners in the New Tin Mining Company in Rawang. Pillay, like Loke Yew, was a founder of the élite Victoria Institution in Kuala Lumpur; he died in 1902.

The Yeohs

Modern godfather Francis Yeoh Sock Ping is the anglicised scion of a three-generation Chinese family engaged in construction and manufacture of building materials. The family business, YTL, is named after Francis Yeoh's father, Yeoh Tiong Lay, who expanded it through early public works contracts in the post-independence era of the 1950s and 1960s. Under *Mahathir*, from 1981, YTL won major public sector contracts and lucrative electricity generation deals, becoming the country's first independent power producer. Among overseas assets, YTL owns Britain's Wessex Water utility. The business's core cash flow was such that during the Asian financial crisis it was able to buy up prime Kuala Lumpur hotels and real estate at knock-down prices. Francis Yeoh and his six brothers and sisters are evangelical Christians; Yeoh's Kuala Lumpur mansion is called 'Genesis'.

Indonesia
The Bakries

Father Achmad Bakrie built up Bakrie & Brothers from a southern Sumatra trading firm into one of the few large indigenous *pribumi* manufacturing groups. Achmad benefited from the Benteng Programme, brought in to support indigenous businessmen after independence was declared in 1945, and took over steel interests nationalised from the Dutch. Son Aburizal was running the biggest *pribumi* conglomerate – from telecommunications to plantations – by the time of the financial crisis, and was involved in business with several *Suharto* family members, but came close to bankruptcy in the late 1990s; he was forced into a US$1-billion debt restructuring in 2001. After Suharto's fall, Aburizal reinvented himself as a democratic politician and served in several cabinet roles. The value of family mining interests has bal-looned in the recent global commodities boom and in 2006 the Bakries sold their Borneo coal business for US$1.2 billion, marking a stunning comeback. Aburizal was minister of welfare at the time.

The Hartonos

Current big boss R. 'Budi' Hartono is from an old-established Chinese family in Kudus, Java, which controls P. T. Djarum Kudus, one of Indonesia's three major cigarette companies. Budi Hartono was preferred by his father to elder brother Michael Bambang Hartono to run the business, but they continue to work together. Budi attended Dutch school and does not speak a Chinese dialect; from the 1970s he diversified into electronics assembly, textiles, food processing and banking. His son Victor Rahmat Hartono is the heir apparent to the family business. After the financial crisis, the Hartonos bought a major stake in *Liem* Sioe Liong's former Bank Central Asia.

Mohammad 'Bob' Hasan (The Kian Seng)

Born in Semarang in 1931 to a Chinese tobacco trader, Hasan became the adopted son of General Gatot Subroto, who defended *Suharto* when he was being sanctioned by army commander Nasution in the late 1950s for his smuggling activities. Hasan, who partnered in the smuggling, eventually became Suharto's closest confidant. They developed businesses together after Suharto took over from Subroto as commander of the Diponegoro Division of the army in the mid 1950s, and when Suharto became president Bob Hasan amassed huge logging concessions, partnering with foreign com-panies like Georgia Pacific of the US. When Indonesia banned the export of raw logs in 1981, Hasan led the Indonesian plywood association, Apkindo, which collected hefty surcharges from the local wood milling industry. He diversified into shipping, real estate, banking and much more and held many companies in tandem with Suharto family members. After Suharto's fall in 1998, Hasan was charged over a relatively minor forest-mapping fraud in Java in the early 1990s and jailed in February 2001; he was allowed many special dispensations while in prison and was released under licence in February 2004.

Hashim Djojohadikusumo

Elder brother of General Prabowo Subianto, who married *Suharto*'s second daughter, *Siti Hedijanti Harijadi*, known as Titiek. Hashim went into several businesses with his sister-in-law and, in 1988, took over Indonesia's second-biggest cement maker. His debt-laden Tirtamas cement, mining and shipping empire was largely wiped out in the financial crisis.

The Kallas

Hadji Kalla, the father of current patriarch Jusuf Kalla, started a *pribumi* trading company in Sulawesi that benefited considerably from the Benteng Programme of the 1950s (see *The Bakries*). Under *Suharto*, Hadji diversified into construction, motor vehicle distribution, agricultural processing and more. Son Jusuf took over in 1967 and added new businesses, including telecoms. After the fall of Suharto, Jusuf passed the helm to brother Achmad and went into politics. He backed *Habibie*, then obtained a cabinet post under *Abdurrahman Wahid*, but was dismissed amid unproven corruption allegations. He re-emerged in the government of *Susilo Bambang Yudhoyono* as vice-president and leader of the Golkar party built up by Suharto.

The Liems

Born in Fuqing, Fujian province, in China in 1916, Liem Sioe Liong (Indonesian name: Sudono Salim) travelled to Java in his early twenties to work with an uncle. Liem built up relations with *Suharto* when the latter was stationed with the Diponegoro Division in central Java and was engaging in trading and smuggling activity. When Suharto came to power, Liem received a string of monopoly rights that catapulted him from small-time regional trader to the biggest godfather in Indonesia, by the 1990s accounting for an estimated 5 per cent of gross domestic product. Key businesses included banking (with the management assistance of Mochtar *Riady*), soft commodities (where Liem had partnerships with Robert *Kuok*), food processing, cement, steel and real estate. Liem brought Suharto relatives – such as the president's children or his cousin, Sudwikatmono – into companies like the Bogosari flour monopoly, Indocement and Bank Central Asia (BCA) as shareholders. Liem's main offshore vehicle is Hong Kong-listed First Pacific. In the Asian financial crisis BCA collapsed under a mountain of illegal related-party lending and Liem had to hand over many of his assets to the state to pay for the subsequent US$7-billion bail-out.

Third son Anthony Salim (known in the family as Anton) now runs the residual businesses, but it is far from clear how much cash and equity the family really has in different companies; it still controls First Pacific and some significant Singaporean assets.

The Nursalims

Born in 1942, ethnic Chinese Sjamsul Nursalim (also known as Liem Tjoen Ho and by various other Chinese aliases) expanded a number of family manufacturing businesses in tyres and paint, using Japanese partners to provide the technology. In 1980 he became a 50 per cent owner of Bank Dagang Nasional Indonesia (BDNI), the country's oldest private bank, originally controlled by the Sultan of Yogyakarta. With Nursalim involved, BDNI embarked on an orgy of related-party lending and was one of the biggest consumers of central bank liquidity credits during the Asian financial crisis. Nursalim, who often invested with the *Suhartos*, became infamous for the shrimp farm he offered to the state in part repayment of his debts at a valuation of US$1.8 billion; it was subsequently valued by government auditors at US$100 million. Since the financial crisis he has based himself in Singapore, from where he continues to run a large regional business.

The Oeis

Son of an established merchant based in Semarang, Java, Oei Tiong Ham was born in 1866 and built the biggest locally controlled business in south-east Asia prior to the Second World War; his trading operations had branches throughout the region, as well as in India, China and Britain. Major business lines included trading, sugar processing, shipping and real estate. Much of the cash for expansion came from opium and other revenue farms. In the early 1920s, Oei Tiong Ham relocated to Singapore, where he died in 1924. Thereafter, several Oei sons took over management, but in 1961 the family's Indonesian businesses were nationalised. Overseas operations, principally in Singapore, Malaysia and Thailand, were retained and one son, Oei Tjong Ie, also worked with *Khoo* Teck Puat in setting up Malayan Banking Corp. in the 1960s, becoming its first chairman.

Prajogo Pangestu

Son of a West Kalimantan ethnic Chinese rubber tapper, Prajogo obtained vast timber concessions under *Suharto* and emerged as the world's largest producer of tropical hardwood plywood in the 1990s. He also partnered Suharto's second son, *Bambang Trihatmodjo*, in a vast west Java petrochemical complex. Prajogo's Barito Pacific lumber corporation and other heavily leveraged businesses took a big hit in the financial crisis, but he remains in charge.

Probosutedjo

Half-brother of *Suharto*, Probosutedjo was given one of two licences to import cloves (the other went to *Liem* Sioe Liong) in the late 1960s, as well as logging concessions and various government contracts. Probosutedjo expanded into motor vehicle assembly, plantations, real estate and more. He was found guilty of graft and abusing reforestation programmes in 2003 and was then caught trying to bribe the supreme court to overturn his jail sentence. In 2005 he was finally dragged out of an executive suite in a private hospital in Jakarta and taken to jail to begin serving a 4-year term.

The Riadys

Patriarch Mochtar Riady was born in Malang in east Java in 1929. He pursued a career in banking, working for the newly formed Pan Indonesia (Panin) Bank – controlled by his wife's family – in the early 1970s before accepting an offer from *Liem* Sioe Liong to manage and become a 20 per cent partner in his Bank Central Asia (BCA). Mochtar Riady made BCA the largest private bank in the country, and later built up his own, smaller private bank, Bank Perniagaan Indonesia, which was merged with another bank to form Bank Lippo. The Lippo Group subsequently diversified into manufacturing assembly work for Japanese conglomerate Mitsubishi, real estate and other financial services. Mochtar Riady lost control of his bank to the Indonesian government at the time of the Asian financial crisis, but is widely rumoured to have regained control through nominees when it was subsequently auctioned off by the Indonesian Bank Restructuring Agency (IBRA).

Mochtar's son James now runs the family business in Indonesia, while son Stephen takes care of interests managed from Hong Kong. The family are evangelical Christians. The Riadys hit the headlines in the United States in 1996 because of their long association with President Bill Clinton – they bought control of Worthen Bank in Clinton's political base of Little Rock, Arkansas – and because of the allegation that they made illegal donations to the Democratic party via a former Riady employee who worked for the Clinton administration.

Sudarpo Sastrosatomo

The son of an indigenous colonial civil servant, Sastrosatomo joined the republican revolution. After independence he worked at the United Nations and at the Indonesian embassy in Washington; his brother ran the Partai Sosialis Indonesia. Sudarpo Sastrosatomo went into business in the 1950s, taking advantage of the Benteng Programme. He then bought into a Dutch shipping company and gradually built up Sumudera, Indonesia's largest shipping group, listed in Singapore. The family also became involved in banking and other businesses.

Marimutu Sinivasan

Ethnic Tamil godfather and *Suharto* stooge Sinivasan obtained, with the president's authority, nearly US$1 billion of Indonesia's foreign exchange reserves during the financial crisis. He headed the Texmaco group but is currently on the run from the Indonesian police, who say they intend to pursue undefined 'financial irregularities', and is wanted by Interpol.

The Soeryadjayas

William Soeryadjaya (Tjia Kian Liong), born in 1923 in west Java, and his brothers built up the Astra Group, the second largest conglomerate in Indonesia until the early 1990s. Astra's core business was as the local partner of Toyota and affiliates in Indonesia, as well as Honda and Komatsu, making it much the largest automotive firm. From the 1970s the Soeryadjayas diversified into financial services, plantations, real estate and more. In 1993, however, the family had to sell its controlling interest in Astra to bail out Bank Summa, which had been taken over and expanded at breakneck speed by William's youngest son, Edward. An elder brother, Edwin, who was a senior executive at Astra, has subsequently forged a growing business empire centred on mining, but the family's net worth is a fraction of what it was. The Soeryadjayas are evangelical Christians.

Ibnu Sutowo

Sutowo, the son of a high-born Javanese official, joined the revolution and in 1957 was made head of what was to become the state oil company Pertamina. There he became a major source of patronage – that links him to numerous indigenous godfathers – while taking his own family into businesses from hotels to banking to shipbuilding to real estate. Sutowo authorised an orgy of investment at Pertamina, particularly when the oil price spiked in 1973–4. He left the company in 1976 with US$10.5 billion in debts – equivalent to 30 per cent of contemporary Indonesian gross domestic product. His family remains powerful.

Harry Tanoesoedibjo

Harry Tanoe, as he is known, is a rising tycoon who in 2002, in the wake of the financial crisis, bought control of *Bambang Trihatmodjo*'s Bimantara conglomerate. There is endless speculation about whose money (if anyone's) Harry Tanoe is fronting.

Sukanto Tanoto

Listed by *Forbes* magazine as the richest Indonesian in 2006 – with an estimated net worth of US$2.8 billion – Tanoto was originally a little-known Suharto-era timber tycoon who hung on to his assets and expanded through the financial crisis. He has hundreds of millions of dollars of delinquent loans with state bank Mandiri and is under investigation for fraud at the bank he used to control; none of this appears to impinge on his prosperity. Tanoto's Asia Pacific Resources International Holdings Ltd (APRIL) is based in Singapore.

The Thios

Born in 1840, Thio Thiau Siat was a highly flexible and successful nineteenth-century godfather. He developed his first businesses in Java and then followed the Dutch military as it moved into Sumatra, acting as the army's main provisioner for fighting in Aceh. Thio obtained tax farms both in Indonesia and in Malaysia, and invested in plantations, shipping and real estate. His business empire encompassed Indonesia, Penang and Singapore and, late in his life, he became an active investor in China. He died in 1916.

Thio's cousins, Tjong A Fie and Tjong Yong Hian, were also successful tycoons, based in Medan, Sumatra. They owned large plantations and started the first Chinese bank in Indonesia, Deli Bank.

The Widjayas

Eka Tjipta Widjaya (Oei Ek Tjhong) was born in 1922 in China's Fujian province, the son of a Sulawesi-based trader, and built up the Sinar Mas group, engaged in plantations, pulp and paper, shipping, real estate and more. Eka Tjipta Widjaya started out as a trader during the Second World War, moved into palm oil when it took off in the 1960s, and then acquired logging concessions under *Suharto* in the 1970s.

By the 1980s Eka Tjipta Widjaya was well enough hooked in to the political and economic élite to be heading Bimoli, Indonesia's leading supplier of cooking oil, in a joint venture with *Liem* Sioe Liong. In the 1990s he listed two pulp and paper businesses in Jakarta, as well as Asia Pulp & Paper in New York in 1995. He acquired a controlling interest in Bank Internasional Indonesia, and expanded his stock of plantation, real estate, hotel and financial services investments, within Indonesia and elsewhere in Asia. Sinar Mas also controls Singapore's largest food company, Asia Food & Properties. During the

Asian financial crisis Sinar Mas lost its banking and some other assets, while Asia Pulp & Paper managed a record emerging markets debt default of nearly US$14 billion in 2001; despite this, the resourceful Widjayas retained control of their businesses. Eka Tjipta Widjaya has numerous wives (seven is the most frequently quoted number – the family will not provide an accounting) and around 40 children. Four sons by his first wife Trini Dewi Lasuki – Teguh, Indra, Muktar and Franky – are the main managers of the family businesses today. Another son, Oei Hong Leong, was formerly involved in business with Harry *Lee* Kuan Yew's brother Lee Kim Yew and has been backed by Hong Kong's *Li Ka-shing*.

Tommy Winata

Military-linked businessman Winata has seen his Artha Graha conglomerate go from strength to strength since the financial crisis. Some regard him as the country's new top godfather.

The Wonowidjojos

The Wonowidjojos are the ethnic Chinese family behind Gudang Garam, Indonesia's largest clove cigarette business. Founder Tjoa Jien Hwie built the business up under *Suharto* and died in 1985. His eldest son Rachman Halim (Tjoa To Hing) took over and diversified wildly in the 1990s – he was reckoned the richest man in Indonesia by *Forbes* on the eve of the financial crisis – before many debts were called in after the crisis. The core cash flow from cigarettes, however, ensures the family's billionaire status.

Philippines
The Aboitizs

Basque Spanish family the Aboitizs emigrated to the Philippines in the late nineteenth century and started trading hemp, abaca and copra. The activity led to an inter-island shipping business and then further diversification under import substitution industrialisation (ISI) policies into flour milling, banking, real estate and more. Family interests are centred on the province of Cebu; the current patriarch is third-generation Luis M. Aboitiz.

Roberto Benedicto

Fellow law student and university contemporary of *Ferdinand Marcos*, from the mid 1960s Benedicto was a key Marcos crony. He was appointed to numerous government posts, including leadership of the Philippine Sugar Commission, which had a monopoly on sugar trade.

The Cojuangcos

The leading godfather family from Tarlac, the Cojuangcos are heavily involved in politics, and split into several factions. The original Cojuangco arrived from China in the 1860s; the family is now thoroughly mixed Chinese-Filipino. One line of the family had close ties to *Marcos*, and Eduardo 'Danding' Cojuangco Jr operated a monopoly in coconut oil production and headed food and brewery giant San Miguel. He fled with Marcos in 1986, only to return in 1989 and back the successful presidential run of film star *Joseph 'Erap' Estrada* in 1998. Two days after Estrada assumed the presidency, Danding resumed the chairmanship of San Miguel; however he did not regain overwhelming equity control since the Philippine courts determined that many shares his businesses acquired in San Miguel under Marcos were 'ill-gotten wealth'. Danding has other interests in shipping, mining, agribusiness and beverage distribution.

A second family faction is headed by Antonio 'Tony Boy' Cojuangco, who was chief executive and chairman of Philippine Long Distance Telephone (PLDT) until the late 1990s and who teamed up with *Lucio Tan* to privatise Philippine Airlines (PAL). A third group includes *Corazon 'Cory' Aquino*, who overthrew Marcos in the people power movement of 1986, and her elder brother Pedro 'Pete' Cojuangco, who led the family's purchase of its vast sugar estate and refinery in Tarlac in the 1950s; another brother, Jose 'Peping' Cojuangco, is a congressman.

Rodolfo Cuenca

Marcos crony and political contributor, Cuenca had a construction conglomerate which relied on government contracts and mushroomed into one of the Philippines' largest corporations. Bad enough at business to go bust even while Marcos was still in power.

Dewey Dee

A Filipino Chinese who inherited a family manufacturing business, Dee was a big speculator – in equity and commodity markets, and on the gaming tables. He issued commercial paper to cover his losses before, in January 1981, he was forced to flee the country with US$80 million in debts; this was the trigger for a major crisis in Philippine financial markets.

Herminio Disini

Marcos crony and political contributor Disini, of Italian extraction, married a cousin of Imelda Marcos. From the mid 1970s he monopolised the cigarette filter market because he was allowed to pay a 10 per cent import duty on raw materials while competitors paid 100 per cent. Disini was all but bust even before Marcos fled.

The Gokongweis

Patriarch John Gokongwei was born to a wealthy, pure Chinese shipping family based in Cebu in 1927. He began his career during the Second World War trading second-hand clothing, scrap metal and rice; later he expanded into food processing and mining. Gokongwei obtained large government loans in the *Marcos* martial law era. His family conglomerate is J G Summit, which has interests in food processing, retailing, telecommunications, petrochemicals, real estate, shipping and the airline Cebu Pacific Airways; in recent years J G Summit sold out its banking interests. Son John Jr, known as Lance, now runs the business day to day. Gokongwei lost a son-in-law to a shoot-out during a botched kidnapping in 1997.

The Lopezes

Long-time sugar godfathers of Negros, descended from Spanish gentry, the Lopezes diversified into electricity generation, media and much more to become the biggest business family of the early 1960s. Heavily involved in politics, the family fell out with *Marcos* in the early 1970s and was dispossessed. Some of its corporate assets were returned by the *Aquino* government after 1986 when Eugenio 'Geny' Lopez Jr returned to the Philippines from exile. He died in 1999 and his son Eugenio 'Gabby' Lopez III continued to rebuild the family's Benpres conglomerate. The family's key assets are media business ABS–CBN Broadcasting, the country's main television service, and Manila Electric (Meralco), its biggest utility.

The Palancas

Carlos Palanca Chen Qianshan was the Philippines' best-known nineteenth-century Chinese immigrant godfather. Born in Fujian in 1869, Palanca positioned himself halfway between imperial China and the colonial Philippines, running businesses from coolie trafficking to alcohol production. He died in 1901. His businesses were taken over by son Carlos Palanca Jr and subsequent heirs, but the family's power and wealth gradually dissipated. The Carlos Palanca Foundation is still active.

The Romualdezs

The Romualdezs are a small-time godfather family, long active in politics, that produced Imelda Marcos. Her younger brother Benjamin was assisted by *Ferdinand Marcos* to become governor of Leyte province and ambassador to the United States, and was given control of many large businesses, including ones confiscated from the Lopezs. Another brother, Alfredo, operated a casino monopoly in major cities. A sister, Alita, worked at the central bank while running a conglomerate with her husband.

The Tans (Lucio Tan group)

Lucio Tan (Tan Ing Chai), a first-generation Chinese immigrant born in Xiamen in 1934, was catapulted into the big time by *Ferdinand Marcos*. He came to dominate the tobacco industry, was handed control of a major bank and was allowed to open Asia Brewery Inc. to compete with the San Miguel beer monopoly; several younger brothers work with him. Post-Marcos administrations have for two decades tried to make graft and tax evasion cases against Tan stick, but without success. In 1992 Tan popped up with *Antonio 'Tony Boy' Cojuangco*, cousin of *Cory Aquino* who had replaced Marcos, in a deal that privatised the national airline, Philippine Airlines (PAL); PAL was then bailed out by the government after the financial crisis.

Only one of Tan's many companies is publicly traded – putting him in the same secrecy league as Henry *Fok*. Employees and counter-parties know Tan as 'El Kapitan'. His major companies include Fortune Tobacco, Asia Brewery, PAL and Allied Bank. In 2000 he became the biggest shareholder in Philippine National Bank (PNB) – which, for the umpteenth time, was in dire financial straits – during the administration of friend *Joseph Estrada*. In the 1990s, Tan expanded into China, Hong Kong and elsewhere in the region. His daughter Cherry married a son of China-born Philippine banking tycoon George Ty (Metrobank group).

The Tans (Asiaworld group)

Late patriarch Tan Yu was born to an ethnic Chinese copra trading family in Luzon in 1935. Together with elder brother Jesus, he expanded the trading and built a textile manufacturing business after the Second World War before setting up a finance company, A I C Development, which backed another local finance company, Bancom, and invested in real estate around the region, especially in Taiwan. Tan Yu became well enough connected in Taiwan to have his local business bailed out by the Taiwanese government in 1982. His key Philippine real estate asset, acquired after *Marcos* fled, was 200 hectares of prime land around Manila Bay, valued at the peak of the 1990s market at as much as US$7 billion. He also created a large portfolio of real estate investments in Vancouver and Texas. None of the Tan Yu companies is listed. Tan died in 2002, leaving fourteen children. Daughter Emilia 'Bien-bien' Roxas-Yang, preferred to eldest son Elton, now runs his Asiaworld group.

The Yuchengcos

Enrique Yuchengco was a wealthy, second-generation Chinese lumber merchant who went on to found China Insurance and Surety in 1930, later renamed Malayan Insurance Co. Son Alfonso, born in 1923 and a graduate of Columbia University, moved into banking, turning Rizal Commercial Bank into a major player. He also became principal shareholder in – and, until the mid 1990s, chairman of – the Philippine Long Distance Telephone (PLDT) company, expanding into everything from infrastructure to pharmaceuticals. Alfonso is an extremely urbane individual who partnered with Japanese companies in many of his ventures. He served under *Cory Aquino* as ambassador to China and was ambassador to Japan from 1995. Several of his children work in the family businesses; Alfonso 'Tito' Yuchengco III, the youngest child, is the most prominent.

The Zobel de Ayalas

This major godfather dynasty – the oldest one of its scale in the Philippines – derived from the union of the Spanish Zobels and the Ayalas, of German-Jewish origin. The family is also related to the Roxases and Sorianos. The Ayalas started out in estate agriculture in the first half of the nineteenth century; the Zobels became prominent as insurers in the early twentieth century; the Zobel de Ayalas have run the combined Ayala Corporation since 1914.

After the Second World War, the Zobel de Ayalas made a fortune transforming their Makati *hacienda* into the financial district of Manila, and diversified into banking, hotels, telecommunications, manufacturing and more. The family controlled the brewer San Miguel before selling out to the *Cojuangcos* in 1983. Its Bank of the Philippine Islands is one of the largest (of the many small banks) in the country.

The Zobel de Ayalas have the typically cosmopolitan credentials that have defined many of the biggest, multi-generation godfather families. It was a Scottish in-law, Joseph McMicking, who drove the development of Makati. Antonio Melian, a Latin-American Zobel in-law, took the family into insurance. Jaime Zobel de Ayala, born in 1934, currently heads the family, though the business is run day-to-day by his sons Jaime Augusto and Fernando.

Hong Kong

Ronnie Chan (Chan Chi-chung)

Born in 1950, Chan inherited a substantial Hong Kong property portfolio. Flagship listed businesses are Hang Lung Development and Amoy Properties, but Ronnie Chan spends much of his time on his private vehicle, Morningside Springfield. He has been a director of the Hong Kong Securities and Futures Commission (as well as Enron) and is known for his slavish pandering to the Chinese government. Chan is small of stature – barely five feet tall – and an evangelical Christian.

The Chengs

Born in Guangdong province in 1925, patriarch Cheng Yu-tung moved to Macau as a teenager at the start of the Second World War and began working as a salesman at Chow Tai Fook, the jewellery business of his father-in-law-to-be, Chow Chi-yuan, who was also a friend of Cheng's father. Cheng married Chow's daughter in 1943 and, after the war ended, moved to Hong Kong to help expand Chow Tai Fook's business, first in gold jewellery and later in diamonds. After the death of his father-in-law, Chow Tai Fook became Cheng's key private holding company and diversified into much more than jewellery. In the 1960s, Cheng bought a small but lucrative stake in *Stanley Ho* and Henry *Fok*'s Macau gambling monopoly, and proved to be a savvy real estate speculator in Hong Kong. His New World Development became a major player in the British colony's real estate market. From the late 1980s, however, Cheng Yu-tung pulled back from day-to-day management of his businesses and his son, Henry Cheng Kar-shing, took over. This was not good for the listed New World companies' business and they have struggled to recover after the Asian financial crisis. The family's best assets, however, are kept in its private companies.

The Foks

Born in 1922 in Hong Kong the son of a stevedore, Henry Fok Ying-tung won a scholarship to an élite colonial school. By the end of the Second World War he was already active in business, buying military surplus goods at auction. During and after the Korean War of 1950–53 he smuggled medicines, petroleum products and weapons into China in breach of the United Nations embargo, making both a fortune and invaluable contacts with the Chinese military and communist party that would serve him for the rest of his career. He was rewarded in the 1950s with a monopoly on the importation of Chinese sand into Hong Kong, and went into real estate development as the colony's population burgeoned.

In 1962 Fok was the major financier of a successful bid by *Stanley Ho* for the Macau gaming monopoly, and remained the largest shareholder in their company. Over the years, Fok and Ho had many quarrels over the division of spoils in Macau – it was Ho alone who managed the business day to day. After the start of China's reform era in 1979, Fok undertook several bellwether construction projects on the mainland, including the White Swan hotel in Guangzhou and the Beijing hotel in the capital. In 1985 Fok organised a US$120-million bail-out of the *Tung* family's shipping business, including a loan from the Bank of China, and subsequently backed Tung Chee-hwa to become Hong Kong's first chief executive.

Fok was made a vice chairman of the Chinese People's Political Consultative Conference in 1993. He had two official wives and several sons; the eldest, Timothy, was bypassed in favour of Ian to take over Fok's business when he died in 2006. Thomas Fok, long believed to be a son by Henry Fok's second wife, was jailed for five months in the United States in 1991 for conspiracy to ship 15,000 assault rifles to Croatia without a licence; in the wake of the scandal, Henry Fok said Thomas was not in fact his son.

Kai Ho-kai

Sir Kai Ho-kai was born in 1859, the grandson of an early Singapore colonial government employee, and son of the Reverend Ho Fuk (who was simultaneously a successful Hong Kong property speculator). Kai became a major tycoon and one of the first ethnic Chinese appointed to Hong Kong's Legislative Council, in 1890. (His brother-in-law, Ng Choy, was the first.) He was a partner in the land reclamation that created the runway for Hong Kong's original Kai Tak airport (which took part of his name). Kai Ho-kai read medicine and law at university in England and was a key Chinese community leader for the British, though his English language skills were far ahead of his Chinese ones. He died in 1914.

The Hos/Ho Tungs

Casino magnate Stanley Ho Hung-sun is a great nephew of Hong Kong's original Eurasian godfather, Sir Robert Ho Tung (father Dutch Jewish, mother Chinese). Stanley Ho was born in Hong Kong in 1921 and attended the élite Queen's College. Stanley's father lost most of his money in stocks while he was at school and the son worked hard to win a scholarship to Hong Kong University. Like his uncle Sir Robert, Stanley headed for neutral Macau during the Second World War and made his first fortune smuggling consumer and luxury goods across the Chinese border and operating a kerosene factory. He carried on his cross-border trading through the Korean War, expanded into real estate and other businesses, and in 1962 put together a consortium, including Henry *Fok*, that unexpectedly won the bid for the Macau gaming monopoly.

Ho thereafter modernised and expanded the casino business and constructed a vertically integrated group encompassing hotels and marine and air transport that dominated the Macau economy, contributing between a third and a half of local government revenues. In 2001, Ho and Fok's Sociedade de Turismo e Diversões de Macau (STDM) lost its monopoly as licences were granted to competing casinos. But a boom in the Chinese economy from 2003 more than made up for this and Macau outstripped Las Vegas as the world's biggest gambling centre in 2006.

Ho's first wife was the late Clementina Leitao, the daughter of a wealthy Portuguese businessman who provided Ho's political entrée into the (extremely corrupt) Portuguese colonial élite. He subsequently took three more wives and sired at least seventeen children. Stanley Ho is involved in protracted litigation with one of his sisters, Winnie, who was closely involved in the development of STDM and claims she has been cheated out of her share of the business.

Hongkong Bank/HSBC

Hongkong Bank, or the Hongkong and Shanghai Banking Corporation, is the local Hong Kong subsidiary and founding member of the HSBC group, now one of the largest banking businesses in the world. Started in 1865 by British merchant houses in Hong Kong, 'the bank' – as it is known locally – has always been widely owned. It enjoyed numerous special privileges in Hong Kong, making it a quasi-central as well as a commercial bank, and has dominated the financial life of the former British colony. Key chief managers during Hongkong Bank's expansion after the Second World War were: Arthur Morse, who built up business in Hong Kong following the communist takeover of China in 1949; Jake Saunders, who developed early relationships with ethnic Chinese tycoons like Y. K. *Pao* and took over Hang Seng bank; Michael Sandberg, a controversial figure with controversial friends; and William Purves, who transferred the bank's headquarters from Hong Kong to London in 1993 after the takeover of the UK's Midland Bank. Like his predecessors, Purves wielded considerable political power in Hong Kong, sitting on the Executive Council from 1987 to 1993.

The Kadoories

The Kadoories are Iraqi Jews who settled in Shanghai in the 1880s and developed close ties to the British colonial establishment. The original patriarch was Sir Elly Kadoorie (knighted in 1926), followed by sons Lord Lawrence and Sir Horace Kadoorie, and today's family head Michael Kadoorie. The family was heavily involved in textiles; it set up the Hong Kong electricity generator China Light & Power in 1901; it has a hotel group best known for the Peninsula hotel on Hong Kong's Kowloon waterfront.

The Keswicks

Distant relatives and successors to Dr William Jardine (1784–1843), the Scottish ship's-surgeon-turned-opium-smuggler who, with James Matheson, formed Jardine, Matheson in the 1820s. William Jardine, a bachelor, was succeeded by various nephews, one of whom was William Keswick (1834–1912). The Keswicks bought out the Matheson family's interest in the business in 1912, but the name Jardine, Matheson was retained. The Keswicks, and other relatives, have managed the business ever since.

Jardine, Matheson was made a public company in 1961, but over the next forty years its minority investors received shockingly poor returns. Although the company has many attractive cartel positions in Hong Kong, the Keswick family, which has been able to control management with less than 10 per cent of issued equity, has rarely acted to maximise profits. Rising Chinese tycoons, including *Li Ka-shing*, positioned themselves for hostile takeovers in the 1980s, but failed to complete; the Keswicks then established a system of cross-shareholdings between different listed vehicles that made their control unassailable – it was a masterclass in godfather governance. Brothers Henry and Simon Keswick, not much liked by their ethnic Chinese tycoon peers, are the current patriarchs.

The Kwoks

Kwok Tak-seng was one of the original partners – known as the 'three musketeers' – in the 1960s Sun Hung Kai real estate partnership, together with *Lee* Shau-kee and Fung King-hey. After the three men went their separate ways, Kwok retained the Sun Hung Kai real estate business; he died in 1990. Subsequently, Sun Hung Kai has been run by British-educated sons Walter, the eldest, and Raymond and Thomas, although their mother, Kwong Chiu-hing (known in the business as Old Madam Kwok), remains a powerful influence. In 1997 Walter was kidnapped by 'Big Spender' Cheung Tze-keung's group (the same gang that held *Li Ka-shing*'s son Victor), and was ransomed for US$77 million having been kept in a large box for several days; the family never admitted the kidnapping. Raymond and Thomas are evangelical Christians.

The Lees (of Henderson)

Patriarch Lee Shau-kee was born in 1928 in China's Guangdong province, the son of a wealthy banker and gold trader; the family managed to export some of its money before the communist takeover in 1949. In 1963 Lee Shau-kee set up Sun Hung Kai properties with *Kwok* Tak-seng and Fung King-hey. In 1976, he broke out on his own, establishing Henderson Land, of which he now holds around 68 per cent. He controls other, smaller listed real estate companies, as well as Hong Kong's main gas supplier and Miramar hotels and still has a significant stake in Sun Hung Kai properties; the sons of the late Kwok Tak-seng address him as 'uncle'. Lee has five children.

The Lees (of Hysan Development)

The Lees are a four-generation tycoon family that was close to the British establishment in the late colonial era, and whose wealth is based in property. Current patriarch is Lee Hon-chiu, born in 1929 and a graduate of both Massachussetts Institute of Technology and Stanford University. Hong Kong rumour linked the family to smuggling during and after the Second World War – the original Lee Hysan was a Hong Kong bank clerk turned opium trader assassinated in Central in 1928 – but its establishment credentials in the 1990s were reflected in directorships at Hang Seng and Hongkong banks, at the Securities and Futures Commission, as well as in numerous joint ventures over the years with the Swire group.

Li Ka-shing (K. S. Li)

Born in 1928, Li started out working for his wealthy father-in-law and built a successful plastics business before diversifying into real estate with his own company, Cheung Kong. Li was catapulted into the top rank of Hong Kong tycoons when Hongkong Bank sold to him, untendered, the controlling interest it held in former British trading house Hutchison Whampoa. Li Ka-shing remained close to Hongkong Bank and became its deputy chairman.

In the 1980s and 1990s Li built on Hutchison's dominant positions in the local port handling and retail cartels, and acquired Hongkong Electric, half of the electricity duopoly. In 1999 Li booked a US$15-billion profit when he sold his Orange mobile phone business to Germany's Mannesmann near the peak of that decade's technology bubble; however, he subsequently invested even more money in third-generation mobile networks, a move that has not yet paid off. He prides himself on accepting only nominal salaries from his businesses but, under Hong Kong law, collects hundreds of millions of dollars a year in untaxed dividends.

The Li Ka-shing empire will be inherited in equal thirds by his eponymous foundation, and sons Victor and Richard. Relations with the latter are strained. Richard runs the Pacific Century group, which was controversially awarded the Hong Kong Cyberport development without tender in 1999 and whose shareholders suffered huge losses in the 2001 stock market crash. Victor was a victim of the Chinese kidnap gang led by Cheung Tze-keung in 1996. The family never acknowledged the kidnapping and Victor was released after payment of a HK$1-billion ransom.

The Lis (of Bank of East Asia)

Perhaps the only ethnic Chinese 'dynasty' in Hong Kong to rival the British *Swire* and *Keswick* families for longevity and sustained wealth. The Lis, already prosperous, left China's Guangdong province for Hong Kong in the 1850s. The family built up shipping and trading businesses and became *compradors* to European firms. At the end of the First World War, they set up the Bank of East Asia. In the twentieth century the Lis produced leading government officials and civil servants – including Executive Councillors F. S. Li, Aubrey Li and Li Fook-kow and vice-president of the Court of Appeal Simon Li – as well as tycoons. The family also has its share of black sheep, including former billionaire stock exchange boss Ronald Li, who was jailed for four years for corruption in 1990. Dickson Poon, owner of Harvey Nichols in Britain who has been criticised for abuse of minority shareholders, is an in-law of current family patriarch David Li. The Lis are an anglicised, establishment family, although the preferential treatment enjoyed by British-run Hongkong Bank has long riled them.

The Los

Lo Ying-shek arrived in Hong Kong in the 1930s from Guangdong and began the family's Great Eagle real estate empire. His eldest son Lo Ka-shui (known as K. S. Lo), born in 1947, trained as a cardiologist in Canada and the United States but returned to take over the business in 1980. The company expanded into hotels and infrastructure and bought properties overseas. K. S. Lo's economic establishment credentials were demonstrated when, like *Y. K. Pao*, *Li Ka-shing* and other senior tycoons, he was brought on to the board of Hongkong Bank. His younger brother, Vincent Lo, built up his own successful real estate business, Shui On, in mainland China.

The Paos

Pao Yue-kong, known as Sir Y. K. Pao, was born to a prosperous family in Ningbo in 1918; among other interests, his father had a shoe manufacturing business. Pao went into insurance and banking in China before moving to Hong Kong with his family in 1949, having managed to get most of his money out of China. In Hong Kong Y. K. Pao started a small trading firm which grew quickly during the Korean War boom. In 1955 he purchased his first freight ship, and soon after, British managers he was friendly with at Hongkong Bank agreed to finance a second. In the 1960s, Pao applied his banker's mind to the commissioning of ship construction in Japan, developing an almost risk-free system whereby necessary credit was secured against long-term charters guaranteed by Japanese banks. Hongkong Bank became his co-investor and, by 1979, Y. K. Pao was the biggest ship owner in the world. In the 1980s he bought control of two British *hongs* (trading companies): the Hong Kong and Kowloon Wharf and Godown Company, now known as Wharf, and Wheelock Marden (now known as Wheelock). Y. K. Pao died in 1991, leaving four daughters; his sons-in-law took over different parts of his empire.

The Shaws

Runme Shaw (born in 1901), his younger brother Sir Run Run (born 1907) and five other children were born to a wealthy textile family in Zhejiang province, near Shanghai, and educated at foreign-run schools. They built an Asian entertainment empire, starting in Singapore in the late 1920s with a group of cinemas and moved into Chinese language film production. They developed close relations with the British in Singapore, and subsequently with Harry *Lee* Kuan Yew as well as the colonial authorities in Hong Kong, to where they expanded in the late 1950s. In Hong Kong the Shaws were allowed to develop the main local television broadcaster, TVB, from 1972 and remain its controlling shareholder. Sir Run Run's closeness to the British establishment was reflected in his being awarded a knighthood, in 1977. From films and entertainment, the brothers diversified into banking, hotels and real estate. Runme died in 1985; his businesses in Singapore and Malaysia were thereafter controlled by brother Vee Meng Shaw.

Helmut Sohmen

Born in 1939, Sohmen is an Austrian lawyer who was working as a banker in north America when he met Y. K. *Pao*'s eldest daughter, Anna. They married, a fact that initially discomfited both families. Pao, however, warmed to Sohmen and in 1970 convinced him to ditch his banking job and join the family business. He worked at Pao's World Wide Shipping, becoming group chairman in 1988 and taking over the business after his father-in-law's death. In the 1990s, World Wide bought out Norway's Bergesen marine transportation line and is today the biggest privately controlled shipping business in the world. In the 1990s, Sohmen condemned moves to democratise Hong Kong, but has since become receptive to the case for political reform. He has observed to friends that he can never be head of the Pao family because he is not Chinese.

The Swires

John Swire (1793–1847) was a Liverpool-based trader whose successors started a joint venture, Butterfield and Swire, to trade with China in the 1860s. The group, which reverted to the name John Swire & Sons in 1974, has been run by the Swire family ever since. Its businesses encompass major property interests in Hong Kong, Cathay Pacific and Dragonair airlines, shipping and marine services, bottling operations in Hong Kong and China, and trading. Like the Keswicks at Jardines, the Swires were hard-wired into the colonial establishment in Hong Kong and could rely on protection of their monopoly interests, particularly Cathay Pacific. None the less, since the Second World War, the Swire family has run its business with greater concern for its investors than was shown by Jardine, Matheson. The current patriarch is Sir Adrian Swire, born in 1932.

The Tungs

Patriarch C. Y. Tung was from a wealthy family in Ningbo, near Shanghai, and married into the wealthier Koo family. From the 1940s he built on his in-laws' shipping interests, developing a fleet based in Shanghai and Hong Kong and, after 1949, in Taiwan. C. Y. retired in 1979 leaving a highly-leveraged business, and, by the mid 1980s, eldest son *Tung* Chee-hwa brought the family's Orient Overseas business close to insolvency, partly by extending huge loans from the main listed vehicle to private family firms. A bail-out was organised by Henry *Fok* with cash from communist Chinese state banks. In the 1990s, Fok and *Li Ka-shing* backed Tung Chee-hwa for the role of Hong Kong's first chief executive, for which he was endorsed by Beijing. However Tung quickly alienated public opinion, especially during the Asian financial crisis, and resigned the post early in his second term in 2005.

Patrick Wang

Born in 1951, Wang is the richest industrialist in Hong Kong. His company,

Johnson Electric Holdings, was founded by his father in 1959 and manufactures micro-motors used in everything from car windows to cameras. *Forbes* magazine put his net worth at US$2.1 billion in 2006, far short of the big non-manufacturing godfathers.

Peter Woo

Born to a wealthy family in Shanghai in 1946, Woo married Y. K. *Pao*'s second daughter, Bessie; he was a banker in the United States before his marriage. After Y. K.'s death, he took over real estate and holding company Wheelock & Co., which in turn controls the diversified real estate business Wharf, with other interests in telecommunications, infrastructure and container ports. Woo attempted various high-profile manoeuvres to take Wharf into new areas of business, including media and a raft of projects in the Chinese city of Wuhan, but most proved to be cul-de-sacs. In 1996 he ran against *Tung Chee-hwa* in the China-managed 'election' for Hong Kong's first chief executive and was roundly beaten.

Macau
The Hos/Ho Tungs
See under **Hong Kong**.

Ho Yin

Ho was a Cantonese tycoon outstanding among the post-war pro-China godfathers known in Macau as the 'red fat cats'; he was famous for his uncontrolled obscene language. Ho Yin set up Tai Fung Bank in 1941, Macau's first locally incorporated bank. (A brother was involved in the setting-up of Hang Seng bank in Hong Kong.) His core cash flow came from his prominent role in the gold trading monopoly run by Pedro *Lobo* under the auspices of the corrupt Portuguese colonial administration. In the 1960s, when Ho Yin replaced Pedro Lobo as Macau's leading businessman, *Stanley Ho* tried to obtain the gold trading monopoly by offering the Portuguese a bigger cut, but they stuck with Ho Yin, who also became the key political conduit for dialogue between the Portuguese colonists and mainland Chinese leaders. The Portuguese also relied on Ho Yin to keep triad violence off the streets; he died in 1983. Ho Yin had various business dealings with Hong Kong-based godfathers Henry *Fok* and *Cheng Yu-tung*. His key business interests were taken over by fifth son Edmund Ho Hau-wah. With Macau's 1999 return to Chinese sovereignty there was no surprise when Edmund Ho was appointed the territory's first chief executive.

The Lobos

Pedro Jose Lobo, born in the 1890s of Chinese–Portuguese–Dutch–Malay lineage in Portuguese East Timor, from where his family transferred to Macau, was the dominant godfather of the Second World War and Korean War era. A consummate cultural chameleon, he doubled as Macau's chief economic minister. The root of much of Lobo's wealth was his leading position in the local gold trading monopoly. This was particularly valuable because Macau was not part of the 1944 Bretton Woods fixed exchange rate pact that circumscribed international gold trading – somehow the territory was left off the Portuguese government's list of dependent territories. Hence Macau became the Asian centre of gold trading and the place from which the precious metal was smuggled to India, China, Hong Kong and the rest of south-east Asia, having been imported from war-torn Europe and elsewhere. Until the anomaly was corrected under international pressure in the early 1970s, gold trading eclipsed gambling as Macau's leading business. Among Pedro Lobo's partners in the gold trading business was *Ho Yin*, who succeeded him in the 1960s as Macau's top godfather. Lobo's son Rogerio took over the family empire, but its fortunes have gradually waned in the absence of Pedro's connections.

Singapore
The Aws

Aw Boon Haw was born in 1882 in Rangoon, the son of a Hakka pharmacist. Aw built up the family business in Burma with his younger brother, Aw Boon Par, and they became famous for their Tiger Balm liniment, a bestseller throughout Asia. In the mid 1920s they relocated to Singapore and began to invest in newspapers in China and south-east Asia. Boon Haw also started the first Hakka bank, Chung Khiaw Bank, in 1950; he died in 1954. Most of the major businesses failed in the next generation. Haw Par International was bought out by the British investment firm Slater, Walker, which became embroiled in a celebrated fraud case in Singapore.

The Khoos

Khoo Teck Puat, the son of a wealthy Singapore family involved in rice trading and banking, was born in 1917. Khoo started out at OCBC, in which his family was a major shareholder, becoming deputy general manager. In 1960 he decided to set up his own bank, Malayan Banking, in Malaysia. It grew fast until a run in 1966, precipitated by rumours that Khoo was channelling funds to his own companies; he lost control. Khoo then set up the National Bank of Brunei, with the involvement of the local royal family, and used that to finance his other businesses, mostly in real estate. In 1986 a new sultan exposed massive insider lending at the bank and seized control of it. Khoo still died a very wealthy man in 2004, having made some sound investments; one of the best was to acquire 13.5 per cent of Britain's Standard Chartered bank.

The Kweks

Kwek Hong Png, a Hakka born in China in the early 1910s who died in 1994, developed the family fortune through trade in construction materials beginning in the Second World War; he and his brothers were also engaged in smuggling commodities such as rubber from Indonesia and trading with the Japanese. The Kweks built up a substantial Singapore land bank during the war era and moved into real estate before expanding into financial services in the 1960s. The Singapore end of the family business is today run by Kwek Hong Png's son Kwek Leng Beng, while the Malaysian interests are managed by Kwek Hong Png's nephew Quek Leng Chan (and two of his brothers); the two key cousins are both London-trained lawyers. The family's best-known companies are: City Developments and Singapore Cement in Singapore, Millenium & Copthorne Hotels, with properties in London, New York, Hong Kong and elsewhere; and the Hong Leong group and Hume Industries in Malaysia. The Singapore and Kuala Lumpur branches of the family do not always get on, but do manage to do a lot of business together.

The Lees

Patriarch Lee Kong Chian, who was a Hokkien born in China in 1894 to a well-off family, trained as a civil engineer. He became one of *Tan Kah Kee*'s most able lieutenants, married Tan's daughter and worked as his treasurer. Lee built up a hugely successful rubber business in his own right, acquiring plantations during the 1930s depression that later made Lee Rubber the largest plantation company in south-east Asia. Lee helped negotiate the merger that created OCBC Bank and became its first vice-chairman, and later chairman. After the Second World War he became OCBC's largest shareholder. When Lee Kong Chian died in 1967 he was succeeded by his youngest son, Lee Seng Wee. The younger Lee is the current chairman of OCBC (the number two Singapore bank after the state-owned DBS; the Lee family holds about 15 per cent) and also manages the family's interests in food processing, plantations, insurance, brewing and trading. The Lee Rubber Lees enjoy reasonable relations with Lee Kuan Yew.

The Ngs

Patriarch Ng Teng Fong, born in 1928, is the biggest private real estate owner in Singapore. His better known properties include the Fullerton and Orchard Parade hotels. Son Robert Ng Chee-siong, born in 1953, built up the family's Hong Kong real estate business under the direction of his father. Robert Ng was often the most aggressive bidder at Hong Kong land auctions in the 1990s; in 1987 he escaped prosecution and full payment of his debts after he made huge and misguided bets in the Hong Kong futures market which police suspected were illegally structured. Ng Teng Fong's second son, Philip, works with his father in Singapore. The family's main listed vehicles are Orchard Parade Holdings and Yeo Hiap Seng (a food and beverage business) in Singapore, and Sino Land in Hong Kong. The Ngs have enjoyed a close relationship with Harry *Lee* Kuan Yew.

George Tan

There is no definitive account of Tan's background. He was born in Malaysia, probably in Sarawak, around 1933, and moved to Singapore in his twenties. In the early 1970s he migrated to Hong Kong and, with backing from south-east Asian tycoons including *Chang Ming Thien*, went into property development. By the late 1970s he secured a large credit line from the Hong Kong subsidiary of Malaysia's Bank Bumiputra which he used to finance a series of huge property deals. International lenders such as Hongkong Bank, under then chairman Michael Sandberg, also started to lend to him. In 1982 the Hong Kong property market went into recession as difficult negotiations began for the resumption of Chinese sovereignty, due in 1997. George Tan's Carrian Group became insolvent in 1983 and its collapse revealed a web of corruption and bribe giving.

Tan Kah Kee

A Hokkien born in 1874, Tan built the biggest local business in Malaysia and Singapore before the Second World War. His father was an established trader and processor of rice and pineapple who had been granted British citizenship; the son moved into rubber with fortuitous timing. Tan Kah Kee was unusual in several respects. He sought to build manufacturing enterprises – for tyres, shoes, children's toys – and so forth on the back of his commodities businesses and he also sought to compete directly with Japanese, European and American manufacturers. With zero tariff protection in local markets, this was a tough challenge which left Tan dangerously exposed to the global recession of the early 1930s; most of his businesses were liquidated in 1934.

Tan retained considerable personal wealth and, again unusually, became a political idealist as well as a tycoon (despite having grown up in a pro-establishment family). After 1949 he accepted an offer to move to the People's Republic of China, where he died in 1961. Significant employees of Tan Kah Kee, who went on to be tycoons in their own right, include *Lee* Kong Chian (who married Tan's daughter) and Tan Lark Sye.

The Wees

Patriarch Wee Cho Yaw, born in 1929, was educated in Singapore and England. Wee's father, Wee Kheng Chiang, traded pepper and rubber from Sarawak to Singapore and also operated an informal bank in Kuching. In 1935, Wee Kheng Chiang set up United Chinese Bank in Singapore; he brought his son into management in the late 1950s and Wee Cho Yaw quickly took over most of the day-to-day operations. The bank grew rapidly in the 1960s and 1970s and changed its name to United Overseas Bank (UOB) in 1965; Wee Cho Yaw also expanded into insurance, real estate and hotels, and took over Chung Khiaw Bank, which had been set up by Aw Boon Haw, as well as Industrial and Commercial Bank. The Wee family today owns around 20 per cent of UOB; it has enjoyed cordial relations with *Lee* Kuan Yew, with Wee Cho Yaw serving on various government boards. UOB is the third-biggest bank in Singapore and acquired a Thai bank during the Asian financial crisis.

THE POLITICIANS

Thailand

Between 1932, when a revolution overthrew an absolute monarchy, and 2007, Thailand has had thirty-three prime ministers. Only a small number of these, and a few other less conspicuous political players, were of real significance. The following list highlights the major characters.

General Phraya Phahol Pholphayuhasena (1933–8)

Overthrew his predecessor, Phraya Manopakorn Nititada, who had lasted only seven months.

Field Marshal Plaek Phibunsongkhram (1938–44 and 1948–57)

From the military wing of the People's Party which ended absolute monarchy in 1932. As prime minister he pursued nationalist policies and created a semi-fascist state, legislating against ethnic Chinese Thais and becoming an ally of Japan during the Second World War. He changed the country's name from Siam to Thailand in 1939. After the war Phibunsongkhram escaped prosecution for war crimes by the allies and, following a 1947 coup in which he was prominent, returned to the premiership in 1948. Phibunsongkhram's flirtation with fascism was quickly forgotten when he took Thailand into the Korean War on the US side, and American aid money began to pour into the country as a perceived bulwark against regional communism; he continued his anti-Chinese policies.

In 1951, Phibunsongkhram was the victim of one of Thailand's more entertaining coup attempts, led by *Field Marshal Phin Choonhavan*. Attending a ceremony on board the battleship *Sri Ayutthaya*, he was taken hostage by a group of naval officers who put various demands before the government in Bangkok. Negotiations broke down, however, and the Thai air force, siding with the ruling army faction, bombed and sank the prime minister's battleship; he survived by swimming to shore and continued his premiership. Eventually, in 1957, Phibunsongkhram was overthrown in a coup by his most 'loyal' lieutenant, *Field Marshal Sarit Thanarat*; he went into exile in Japan and died there in 1964.

Field Marshal Sarit Thanarat (1958–63)

Staged a coup in 1957, but did not take the premiership for himself until late 1958, after two other short-lived incumbents. Sarit increased the role of the Thai monarchy – following post-1932 repression – and he promoted economic technocrats, welcomed foreign investment, invested in rural development and ended persecution of ethnic Chinese Thais. Sarit died in office in 1963, but his policies were maintained by his associates General Thanom Kittikachorn (prime minister, 1963–73) and Praphas Charusathian (Thanom's deputy prime minister). Thanom was overthrown by a popular anti-military uprising in October 1973. Three years later, the army (officially) killed forty-six people during the Thammasat University massacre of October 1976 and military rule returned.

General Prem Tinsulanonda (1980–88)

A key figure among the military leaders of the late 1970s and 1980s, Prem went on to be chief adviser to the king of Thailand and resurfaced in the September 2006 coup that ousted *Thaksin Shinawatra*. Prem was instrumental in the appointment of his former army subordinate *Surayud Chulanont* to replace Thaksin. As prime minister in the 1980s, Prem succeeded General Kriangsak Chomanan, who came to power in a coup and ruled for three years from 1977.

Prem won three, typically Thai elections – with lots of vote buying and some coercion – as a member of shifting political coalitions. He was succeeded in 1988 by Chatichai Choonhavan, the only son of *Field Marshal Phin Choonhavan*. Chatichai's brand of rather dilettante rule did not go down well in the army and he was ousted in a February 1991 coup led by generals Sunthorn Kongsompong and Suchinda Kraprayoon. The latter was briefly prime minister in 1992 when troops killed around 250 protesters in Bangkok in May; he resigned.

Chuan Leekpai, (1992–5 and 1997–2001)

Came to power following General Suchinda Kraprayoon's abortive coup of May 1992, and was Thailand's first premier not to come from an aristocratic or military background. Hailed by some as a clean broom, Chuan none the less had a younger brother who had already fled the country over embezzlement allegations at Thai Farmers Bank where he worked, and Chuan's first government fell in a scandal relating to the distribution of land titles in Phuket. Chuan was followed by the more traditionally corrupt regimes of Banharn Silpa-archa and General Chavalit Yongchaiyudh between 1995 and 1997 before returning to the premiership in the midst of the financial crisis in November 1997. He oversaw a programme of economic austerity; his second government was also plagued by corruption scandals before it was swept aside in 2001 by the advent of *Thaksin Shinawatra*'s Thai Rak Thai party.

Thaksin Shinawatra, (2001–2006)

See entry under **businessmen/godfathers**.

Surayud Chulanont (2006–)

Appointed premier by the military following the coup which ousted *Thaksin Shinawatra*.

Others
Field Marshal Phin Choonhavan

A key military leader who was behind several coups, including the one that sank the battleship with premier *Phibunsongkhram* on it in 1951 (the coup gained Phin's son a cabinet post). During the Second World War he was made military governor of the Shan states, which Thailand (an ally of Japan) occupied during the Burma campaign; this began a long and lucrative association with the drug industry. His son Chatichai Choonhavan was Thai premier in the late 1980s until he himself was ousted in a coup.

Phao Sriyanonda

Married Khun Ying Udomlak, daughter of *Field Marshal Phin Choonhavan*. Phao became deputy director-general of police after a military coup in 1947, and director-general in 1951. He used Central Intelligence Agency (CIA)-supplied military hardware to establish a police air force and maritime and armoured units that in the course of the 1950s became the biggest opium smuggling syndicate in the country. Phao and Phin were close associates of *Chin Sophonpanich*, the developer of Bangkok Bank.

Malaysia

Prime ministers since independence in 1957 (all from the United Malays National Organisation (UMNO)):

Tunku Abdul Rahman, known as 'the Tunku' ('prince') (1957–70)

Abdul Rahman was born in 1903, the son of the Sultan of Kedah, and educated at Cambridge University before studying law at London's Inner Temple. In 1951 he succeeded Datuk Onn Jaafar, UMNO's founder, as president, and in 1955 he became Malaya's first chief minister under the British. The Tunku married at least four times – twice to ethnic Chinese Malay women and once to a former English landlady. During his retirement he was not on good terms with *Mahathir*; he died in 1990.

Tun Abdul Razak (1970–6)

Born in 1922, Abdul Razak was a Malay aristocrat who became deputy prime minister to *Tunku Abdul Rahman*, whom he succeeded. Razak was a contemporary of Harry *Lee* Kuan Yew and Robert *Kuok* at Raffles College in Singapore, before qualifying as a barrister at London's Lincoln's Inn. He forced the Tunku out of the premiership after race riots in 1969 and launched the affirmative action strategy known as the 'New Economic Policy'. Tun Razak died of cancer in 1976. His successor, *Tun Hussein Onn*, was also his brother-in-law. Razak's family are of Bugis descent; his eldest son, Najib Razak, is currently deputy prime minister under *Abdullah Badawi*, while a second son, Nazir Razak, heads Malaysia's leading investment bank, CIMB.

Tun Hussein Onn (1976–81)

Born in 1922 the son of one of UMNO's founders and Johore aristocrat Dato Onn Jaafar, Hussein Onn, who was one-quarter Turkish, qualified as a lawyer at Lincoln's Inn. He worked in Malaya's civil service before entering politics, and took over from *Abdul Razak* when he died. Hussein Onn himself resigned in 1981, citing health reasons, and later fell out with his successor, *Mahathir*; his son, Hishammuddin Bin Tun Hussein, is currently education minister under *Abdullah Badawi*. Hussein Onn died in 1990.

Tun Dr Mahathir Mohamad (1981–2003)

Half-Indian (on his father's side), Mahathir was born in Kedah in 1925 and trained as a doctor in Singapore. He joined UMNO soon after its formation in 1946 and was first elected a member of parliament in 1964. However, he was thrown out of the party in 1969 after criticising *Tunku Abdul Rahman* in an open letter and wrote *The Malay Dilemma* (1970), setting out his rather bigoted racial views; the book was banned in Malaysia. After the Tunku's ousting, he rejoined UMNO in 1972, became education minister in 1974 and deputy prime minister in 1978. Mahathir succeeded *Hussein Onn* as premier in 1981 and remained in the post until October 2003.

Mahathir's premiership was associated with high growth, expanded affirmative action policies, monumental infrastructure projects and widespread cronyism. Mahathir was a ruthless master in UMNO's political struggles, seeing off an attempt by *Tengku Razaleigh Hamzah* to challenge for leadership of the organisation in 1987 and having his penultimate deputy, Anwar Ibrahim, sent to prison. Mahathir quarrelled with his predecessors as premier, his political contemporaries and is now lambasting his chosen successor, *Abdullah Badawi*; curiously, one of his criticisms of Badawi is that he has turned Malaysia into a 'police state' that curtails Mahathir's freedom of speech.

During his premiership, Mahathir's children went into business. Eldest son Mirzan created a diversified conglomerate that was heavily in debt by the time of the financial crisis; Anwar Ibrahim's opposition to a state bail-out of one of Mirzan's companies was critical to his falling-out with the premier. Second son Mokhzani created conglomerate Tongkah Holdings, with businesses in property, rubber, stockbroking and manufacturing; state concessions included a major waste disposal and laundry contract for hospitals. Third son Mukhriz also has substantial business interests.

Dato Seri Abdullah Ahmad Badawi (2003–)

Born in 1939 into a political family active in UMNO in Penang, Badawi was chosen by *Mahathir* to replace Anwar Ibrahim as his deputy in 1998, and successor in 2003. Initially Badawi launched high-profile anti-corruption investigations that set him apart from Mahathir but, having won a landslide election victory in 2004, he has since soft-pedalled on the anti-graft front. Meanwhile, Mahathir has attacked him publicly for doing too little to protect his pet projects – such as the Proton car programme – from international competition.

Others
Daim Zainuddin
See **Godfathers**.

Tan Sri Tengku Razaleigh Hamzah

Born in 1937 into the Kelantan royal family, Razaleigh rose to the senior ranks of UMNO and was appointed finance minister under the premiership of *Hussein Onn*. He was kept on under *Mahathir* from 1981 and continued to patronise a clique of rising non-*bumiputra* tycoons, such as *Khoo Kay Peng*. In 1987, however, Razaleigh challenged Mahathir for the leadership of UMNO, triggering the closest – and one of the dirtiest – elections in the party's history. UMNO split after Mahathir narrowly retained his position, Razaleigh resigned from the government and his business and political followers were purged.

Tun Tan Siew Sin

Born in 1916, the scion of a multi-generation Malaysian political and business dynasty that arrived in Malacca from China in the late eighteenth century, Tan was the son of early twentieth-century tycoon Tan Cheng Lock and great-grandson of nineteenth-century godfather Tan Choon Bock. He was minister of finance from 1959 to 1969 and head of the Malaysian Chinese Association (MCA) from 1961 to 1974. Family business interests included shipping and estate agriculture. Tan Siew Sin died in 1988.

Indonesia

Leaders since independence:

Sukarno (1945–67)

Born in 1901 the son of a schoolteacher from Surabaya, Sukarno was educated in élite Dutch schools. He became a member of the Partai Nasional Indonesia (PNI) when it was founded in 1927, and was arrested and jailed several times by the Dutch colonialists. Sukarno co-operated with the Japanese during the Second World War as a means to oust the Dutch, and declared Indonesian independence on 17 August 1945; there followed a conflict with Dutch forces attempting to reoccupy Indonesia, which lasted until 1950. Sukarno was a nationalist versed in Marxist theory running a large, newly independent state that was inherently unstable. He became increasingly autocratic, oscillating his affections between the military and the Communist Party of Indonesia (PKI).

In 1957 Sukarno nationalised 246 Dutch companies and soon after passed laws discriminating against the ethnic Chinese population. The CIA made several attempts to oust Sukarno, and he was the victim of numerous assassination attempts. His political demise came in 1965 in circumstances that have never been explained. On 30 September, six anti-communist generals were murdered. Some blamed the PKI and others blamed Sukarno's supporters. The result was an anti-PKI pogrom in which some 500,000 people were killed (with the US embassy helping to identify a small number of targets), and Suharto's rise to power. Sukarno died in 1970. He had expensive tastes and nine wives.

Suharto (1967–98)

Suharto's background and childhood are shrouded in considerable mystery, a state of affairs the former president has done nothing to change. It has been claimed that Suharto, born in 1921, was the child of landless peasants, but it is more likely that his family were small-time Javanese aristocracy fallen on hard times. There is no doubt, however, that Suharto's family was dysfunctional (his parents divorced soon after he was born), that he was passed around various relatives, and that his early education was only in the vernacular.

In 1940 Suharto joined the Dutch colonial army and attended military academy. At the end of the war he played a not insignificant part in the resistance against both Japanese and Dutch troops in Indonesia and was placed in command of a regiment of the Diponegoro Division based at Yogyakarta, his home area. It was in 1946 that he was first reported to be engaging in smuggling activities to support his army budget, working in particular with opium smugglers. He married Siti Hartinah, from an aristocratic family with its own cash flow problems, around this time; they went on to have six children.

By the time hostilities with the Dutch ended in 1949, Suharto had established his military credentials and went on to command the Diponegoro Division, headquartered in Semarang, holding sway over much of central Java. In this period his monopoly trading and smuggling activities, in league with future godfathers such as *Bob Hasan* and *Liem* Sioe Liong, expanded. Suharto faced a possible court martial for smuggling in 1959, but was instead – with the support of Bob Hasan's adoptive father, General Gatot Subroto – transferred to the Army Staff College in Bandung, west Java. He became strongly identified with the anti-communist wing of the military and, between 1965 and 1967, rose to dominance in the group that wrested power from Sukarno. For the next three decades he ran an authoritarian state that was friendly to the West and delivered high growth rates but also generated increasing debt levels and corruption.

Forced from office in May 1998, Suharto told the attorney general's office in December that his assets comprised about US$3 million cash in banks, his Jakarta home, a second Jakarta property, a 750-hectare ranch and 'several hundred thousand' hectares of land in Kalimantan. Michael Backman, an Indonesia specialist, has published research to show that the Suharto family had equity in at least 1,247 companies in Indonesia and, probably, considerable assets offshore. Much of the Suharto family's cash was collected through seven charitable foundations, or *yayasan*, to which civil servants and businessmen contributed; the post-Suharto government took over these foundations in November 1998. A *Time* magazine investigation in 1999 put Suharto family wealth at US$15 billion. Suharto was briefly placed under house arrest in 2000, but all attempts to prosecute him for corruption have been blocked with claims that he is medically unfit to stand trial. Legal proceedings against him were formally dropped in May 2006.

Bacharudin Jusuf Habibie, Known as Rudy or 'BJ' (May 1998–October 1999)

The Habibie family were friends of *Suharto* since their son was a teenager. From 1953, the family went to Germany, where Habibie, who was born in 1936, studied engineering and worked for Messerschmitt. In 1974 Suharto brought Habibie back to Indonesia to become his long-standing Minister of Technology and Research, in charge of investment-led attempts to leapfrog into high-tech industries. In the midst of the Asian financial crisis, Suharto made Habibie his vice-president and he took over the presidency when Suharto was ousted in May 1998. He hoped to hang on to the presidency, but stepped down in 1999, having failed to win Golkar party support.

Abdurrahman Wahid, Known as Gus Dur (1999–2001)

Grandson of the founder of Java's largest Muslim organisation, Nahdlatul Ulama (NU), and son of a Minister of Religious Affairs, Wahid was born in 1940. He became chairman of NU in the mid 1980s, severing its links with political Islam and forging a working relationship with *Suharto*. In the 1990s, Wahid developed an alliance with *Sukarno*'s daughter *Megawati Sukarnoputri* before patching up relations with Suharto. When the Asian financial crisis struck, he again tilted towards Megawati, but later won support from Suharto's Golkar party for his successful presidential bid. Wahid, in short, was thoughtful but opportunistic and power-hungry; he took Megawati as his vice-president. His short-lived presidency was characterised by much foreign travel and curious scandals.

Megawati Sukarnoputri (July 2001–2004)

The eldest daughter of *Sukarno*, who succeeded *Abdurrahman Wahid* as president without winning an election, Megawati was allowed to enter politics by *Suharto* in the 1980s as part of his charade of multi-party democracy. She is no intellectual, but by the mid 1990s had become the focus for opposition to Suharto. As president, she oversaw an amendment of the constitution that allowed for direct presidential elections, but otherwise failed to stem corruption or provide direction in economic policy. Her (third) husband, businessman Taufik Kiemas, was widely accused of profiting from his wife's position. Megawati lost the 2004 presidential race.

Susilo Bambang Yudhoyono, known as SBY (2004–)

Born in 1949, Indonesia's first directly elected president was a career soldier who attained the rank of general under *Suharto*. Formerly close to army commander Wiranto; Yudhoyono served several tours in East Timor and, like Wiranto, has been accused of human rights abuses, though on a lesser scale. He went into politics in 2000 as a minister under *Wahid*; under *Megawati* he held the security portfolio and pleased the US government with his tough stand on the 'war against terror'. In 2004 Yudhoyono ran for president. Far more articulate than Megawati, he proposed clear policies and won an easy victory. The economy has picked up since Yudhoyono's election, and he remains popular, but he does not represent a fundamental break with the Indonesian political establishment.

Others
Suharto's Children

Sigit Harjojudanto

Eldest son Sigit was born in 1951. He has found it hard to keep his eye on the business ball and has had frequent run-ins with Suharto including, allegedly, over a serious gambling habit. He often started businesses based on monopoly licences with Suharto cronies *Liem Sioe Liong* and *Bob Hasan* (with whom, for instance, he had a monopoly on the import of tin plate). Sigit also has equity in *Tommy Suharto*'s Humpuss Group and had a 17.5 per cent stake in Bank Central Asia, run by Liem Sioe Liong until its collapse in 1998. In 1996,

Sigit was hired as a consultant to Canadian mining firm Bre-X, while sister *Siti Hardijanti Rukmana* (known as 'Tutut') partnered Barrick Gold during the infamous Busang gold scam.

Bambang Trihatmodjo

Middle son Bambang, born in 1953, formed the Bimantara Group in 1981 with his brother-in-law Indra Rukmana (married to Tutut) and other friends. Bimantara went into shipping, trading (including various petrochemical monopolies), oil (with allocations from state oil company Pertamina), broadcasting, telecommunications and satellites, automotive (assembly of Hyundai cars), power generation and much more. Bambang lost some assets in the Asian financial crisis and sold his interest in Bimantara to *Harry Tanoesoedibjo*. He is believed to be worth hundreds of millions of dollars.

Hutomo Mandala Putra, known as Tommy

Youngest son Tommy, born in 1962, only got into business in the mid 1980s with his Humpus Group, which had monopolies on the distribution of terephthalic acid (used to make polyester fibre) and methanol produced by Pertamina. He subsequently picked up other big contracts from Pertamina and diversified into whatever took his fancy (including a Formula One racetrack outside Jakarta and the takeover of Italian car maker Lamborghini). He formed a joint venture with South Korea's Kia for car assembly (the 'Timor'). After the Asian financial crisis, the Indonesian Bank Restructuring Agency said Tommy's companies owed it US$1 billion. He was the only member of the Suharto family to be tried for corruption, initially sentenced to eighteen months in jail in September 2000 for a land-related fraud and then to fifteen years for offences including ordering the successful assassination of the judge who condemned him in the earlier trial. However the murder penalty was reduced on appeal and Tommy was released from prison on licence in October 2006.

Siti Hardijanti Rukmana, known as Tutut

Suharto's eldest daughter (and eldest child) Tutut was born in 1949. She married Indra Rukmana and developed various businesses with him, including toll roads, oil, petrochemicals, financial services, agribusiness and television, based on state concessions. Her father-in-law, Eddi Kowara, also built P T Teknik Umum into one of the largest companies in Indonesia under Suharto, engaged in construction, engineering and general trading. Tutut acquired a 17.5 per cent interest in *Liem* Sioe Liong's Bank Central Asia. She was on the board of taxi company Steady Safe in 1998 when it defaulted on a bridging loan from

Hong Kong investment bank Peregrine, precipitating the collapse of the latter. Tutut was social affairs minister in her father's last cabinet, from March to May 1998. After the Asian financial crisis, she and her husband managed to hang on to assets worth hundreds of millions of dollars, including offshore businesses; two younger sisters, *Titiek* and *Mamie*, have stakes in Tutuk's businesses.

Siti Hedijanti Harijadi, known as Titiek

Suharto's second daughter Titiek, born in 1959, married Prabowo Subianto, former head of special forces and the strategic reserve, dismissed after Suharto's fall for abduction and torture of political activists. Titiek partnered Tutut in various businesses in the 1990s, as well as Prabowo's elder brother, *Hashim Djojohadikusumo*.

Siti Hutami Endang Adiningsih, known as Mamie or Mimiek

Youngest daughter Mamie, born in 1964, has various companies involved in plantations, transport and more.

Philippines

Official Philippine history records fourteen presidents to 2007, the first being Emilio Aguinaldo, who led the rebellion against Spain before accepting American rule in 1901; his presidency was never recognised by foreign governments. The other presidents are:

Manuel L. Quezon (1935–44)

Ethnic Filipino–Spanish–Chinese who was president in the last period of American rule. He died in the United States in 1944 while running a government in exile. Qualified as a lawyer.

Jose Laurel (1943–5)

Instructed by President *Quezon* to remain in Manila during the Second World War, Laurel became president of the short-lived, Japanese-sponsored Republic of the Philippines until 1945. He later ran for president in the 1949 election – which set a new standard for bribery – and lost. Qualified as a lawyer.

Sergio Osmeña (1944–6)

Quezon's vice-president-in-exile, who was briefly president on his return to the Philippines before losing the presidential election of 1946. Of Chinese–Filipino extraction, he was from a hugely powerful godfather dynasty based in Cebu; his sons and grandsons went on to be senators and governors and the family is as influential today on its home turf as ever. Qualified as a lawyer.

Manuel Roxas (1946–8)

First president of the independent republic, who died in office. Qualified as a lawyer.

Elpidio Quirino (1948–53)

Vice-president who succeeded *Roxas* and won his own election in 1949. His term was characterised by economic growth, corruption and a rising communist insurgency. Qualified as a lawyer.

Ramon Magsaysay (1953–7)

The first Philippine president of humble origins, and also the first not to qualify as a lawyer (though he did start a law course). He waged a successful campaign against communist insurgents and died in a plane crash.

Carlos P. Garcia (1957–61)

Magsaysay's vice-president who took over when he died. Garcia ran a nationalist, sectarian agenda, shortening US military base leases and legislating to force ethnic Chinese Filipinos who were not citizens out of the retail trade. Qualified as a lawyer.

Diosdado Macapagal (1961–5)

Vice-president to *Garcia*, Macapagal was elected on an anti-corruption ticket. In 1961 he allowed the peso to trade freely against other currencies, leading to a major devaluation and a boost for exporters. Most of his other economic reform measures were blocked by congress. Father of current Philippine president, *Gloria Macapagal Arroyo*. Qualified as a lawyer.

Ferdinand Marcos (1965–86)

Born in 1917 to a political family in Ilocos Norte, of mixed Chinese, Japanese and Filipino ancestry. He was convicted of the murder of one of his father's political rivals in 1939 but successfully argued his own appeal before the supreme court and was acquitted. In 1954 Marcos married Imelda *Romualdez*, from a small-time godfather family; they produced three children and adopted one more; Marcos has additionally been linked to at least seventeen alleged illegitimate children.

He claimed to have been a key anti-Japanese resistance leader and US liaison during the Second World War, personally killing scores of Japanese and enduring torture; declassified US documents have subsequently shown that most of his claims were imaginary. Marcos touted his war record throughout his successful 1965 presidential bid. In office he promoted investment-led growth, promised to reign in regional oligarchs, and became a staunch ally of the United States (sending troops to Vietnam); he was re-elected in 1969. Early in his second term, however, the communist insurgency picked up and the economy weakened. In September 1972, Marcos declared martial law and proselytised what he called a 'new society movement' (it became the name of his party); this echoed *Suharto*'s New Order regime in Indonesia (and in turn Chiang Kai-shek's 'new society' movement in pre-1949 China). In practice, Marcos dispossessed some oligarchs he did not like and redistributed their assets to his cronies.

In 1981 Marcos lifted martial law, ran in an election in which no major party except his fielded a candidate, and was re-elected with 91 per cent of the vote. The economy, however, was headed for meltdown. Foreign debt increased almost thirty times under Marcos, and the country tipped into a severe recession in 1984. Foreign investors were additionally put off by the 1983 assassination of Marcos' main political opponent, Benigno Aquino. The US government began to withdraw support for Marcos and, with the army turning against him, he fled into American exile in 1986. Marcos' legacy was hundreds of extra-judicial killings, billions of dollars of looted public funds, and many godfathers who built fortunes from concessions he handed them. Marcos qualified as a lawyer.

Maria Corazon Cojuangco-Aquino (1986–92)

Known as Cory Aquino, she was the wife of opposition leader Benigno 'Ninoy' Aquino who was assassinated at Manila airport in 1983 on his return from exile in the United States. Cory Aquino is from the powerful *Cojuangco* Chinese-Mestizo family, based in Tarlac, one wing of which was allied with *Marcos*. Her presidency faced seven coup attempts and she decided not to run for re-election in 1992. Aquino started but did not finish a law degree.

Fidel V. Ramos (1992–8)

Marcos's chief of staff and the man who declared martial law in 1972; his defection was critical to the dictator's overthrow. Ramos served as defence secretary to *Cory Aquino* and was backed by her for the presidency. His running mate, Cebu godfather Emilio Mario Osmeña, lost out in the election to *Joseph*

Estrada who became Ramos's vice-president. Neither a lawyer nor a Roman Catholic, Ramos had followed a military career before entering politics and his presidency restored some stability in the Philippines. Known as 'Steady Eddie', he implemented some of the deregulation and anti-monopoly measures that had eluded Cory Aquino.

Joseph Estrada (1998–2001)

Son of a government contractor and local politician, Estrada was thrown out of university and became a successful B-movie actor. In 1992 he was the running mate of *Marcos* crony (and *Cory Aquino* relation) *Eduardo 'Danding' Cojuangco* in the presidential race against *Fidel Ramos*; Danding lost, but Estrada won. His vice-presidency set him up for the top job in 1998, when he ran a savvy television campaign based around the fictitious notion of himself as poor boy made good. His backers included veteran godfathers like *Lucio Tan* and Danding Cojuangco. Estrada's running mate was defeated and *Gloria Macapagal Arroyo* won the vice presidency. Estrada was dogged by allegations of corruption – mainly relating to alleged involvement in illegal gambling businesses – from his first day in office, and became the first president to face impeachment proceedings, in 2000. The president's trial was never completed but he was forced from office by a combination of political manoeuvring and street protests.

Gloria Macapagal Arroyo (2001–)

The daughter of 1960s president *Diosdado Macapagal*, Macapagal Arroyo succeeded *Joseph Estrada* in 2001. She was re-elected in 2004. She trained as an economist and worked as an academic before entering politics in the 1990s. *Macapagal Arroyo* has enjoyed some success in increasing tax revenue but insurgency movements and extra-judicial killings by state forces have increased on her watch (she is not implicated personally in the latter).

Hong Kong

From 1843 to 1997, Hong Kong was ruled most of the time by a succession of twenty-eight British governors. Most recent governors were professional diplomats from the British Foreign Office and natural conservatives with respect to Hong Kong's political and economic arrangements. The last governor, politician Chris Patten, was somewhat different. Arriving in 1992, Patten introduced major reforms to the Legislative Council by vastly expanding the franchise in its business-dominated 'functional' constituencies. The result, in 1995 elections, was to return Legislative Council members who were far more representative of the popular Hong Kong will than at any time previously. Patten also introduced some important social policy changes and deregulated telecommunications. In 1997, China immediately reversed Patten's democratic reforms, but could not reverse the general politicisation of Hong Kong.

Tung Chee-hwa

China's shoo-in selection as Hong Kong's first chief executive, tycoon sibling Tung Chee-hwa proved increasingly unpopular with the public. He was accused of favouring fellow godfathers with large public works projects. In 2003, an unprecedented half a million people took to the streets when Tung's government attempted to pass an anti-subversion bill requested by Beijing. Tung resigned in 2005, citing ill health.

Donald Tsang Yam-kuen

The replacement for discredited godfather chief executive *Tung Chee-hwa*, Tsang is a career civil servant nurtured by the British. He was 'elected' by a Beijing-controlled Election Committee in March 2007. Tsang has promised to confront Hong Kong's two main political issues – democratisation and the deregulation of the domestic economy – but it remains to be seen if he has the political courage to deliver his people's aspirations.

Macau

Following reversion to Chinese sovereignty in 1999, the first chief executive of Macau was Edmund Ho Hau-wah, son of *Ho Yin*.

Singapore
The Lees

Harry Lee Kuan Yew is a fourth-generation Singaporean, born in 1923, who was given a thoroughly English education by his family. He attended Raffles Institution, Raffles College and also did a law degree at Cambridge University. During the Second World War he began to study Chinese and Japanese and translated for Japanese forces. Lee's early political experience included work as a legal adviser to student and trades unions. In 1954 Lee and various friends set up the People's Action Party (PAP) in a marriage of convenience with pro-communist trades unions. Lee was secretary-general, elected to parliament in 1955; he was gratified when the last colonial chief minister, Lim Yew Hock, arrested many of the communist leaders in his party.

The PAP won elections in 1959 and Lee became prime minister. He campaigned for a union with Malaya, crushing pro-communist opposition to such a move, and led Singapore in joining the Federation of Malaysia in September 1963. His desire to be part of a larger political unit probably reflected a failure to understand the economics of a city state; Singapore, like Hong Kong, would always be better off on its own, handling regional trade and licit and illicit money flows. The egos and vested interests of the PAP and United Malays National Organisation could never be reconciled and, following fatal race riots in 1964, Singapore was pushed out of the union in 1965.

As premier, Lee became known as a micromanager, both of the economy and of his population; there were campaigns to learn English, then Mandarin Chinese, to have fewer children, then more; there were lots of by-laws about flushing toilets and closing curtains; and a Social Development Unit to help the intelligentsia find mates. Lee's racial views are similar to those of a section of the English upper classes in the late Victorian and Edwardian eras who joined organisations like the Primrose League and the Eugenics Society; the PAP logo bears an uncanny resemblance to that of Oswald Mosley's British Union of Fascists and must have been influenced by it. In 1990, after seven election victories, Lee stood down as prime minister and was styled Senior Minister.

In August 2004 Lee Hsien Loong, the elder of Lee's two sons, became Singapore's third prime minister and Harry is now known as Minister Mentor. Hsien Loong's most notable act has been to legalise gambling – long reviled by censorious Singapore – and licence two huge casino resorts. He says the city state needs the money.

Hsien Loong's wife is Ho Ching, a National University- and Stanford-trained electrical engineer who first joined Singapore's Ministry of Defence and then the state-owned Singapore Technologies Group, becoming its managing director in 1995; she is currently head of the opaque state investment agency Temasek. Ho Ching has served on numerous government boards, including the Economic Development Board, Singapore's productivity council and the science and technology council.

Lee Hsien Yang, Harry's younger son is a Cambridge engineering graduate who joined the state-owned Singapore Telecom (SingTel) in 1994 and quickly became its chief executive, while still in his thirties. In the mid 1990s, SingTel accounted for as much as half the Singapore stock exchange's capitalisation. Lee began an international acquisition programme whose latest purchase, the telecom business of ousted Thai godfather *Thaksin Shinawatra*, was showing an enormous paper loss at the end of 2006.

Lee Kuan Yew's daughter Lee Wei Ling runs Singapore's National Neuroscience Institute. The Lees guard their reputations jealously and have not lost a single defamation case in Singapore's courts.

Selected Bibliography

While most books are grouped geographically, the first two sections highlight works on both sides of the debate about the importance of race and culture in south-east Asia.

Proponents of Race- and Culture-based Interpretations of Development in Asia

Michael Backman, *Overseas Chinese Business Networks in Asia* (East Asia Analytical Unit, Department of Foreign Affairs and Trade, Australia, 1995)

Joel Kotkin, *Tribes: How Race, Religion and Identity Determine Success in the New Global Economy* (Random House, 1992)

S. Gordon Redding, *The Spirit of Chinese Capitalism* (W. de Gruyter, 1990)

Sterling Seagrave, *Lords of the Rim* (Bantam Press, 1995)

World Bank Policy Research Report, *The East Asian Miracle: Economic Growth and Public Policy* (Oxford University Press, 1993). There is no explicit enunciation of a cultural or racial view of development in this famous report, but in the author's view that is the unmistakeable subtext.

Sceptical of Race- and Culture-based Interpretations of Development in Asia

Economist Intelligence Unit, *Beyond the Bamboo Network: Successful Strategies for Change in Asia* (EIU, 2000)

Edmund Terence Gomez, *Chinese Business in Malaysia: Accumulation, Ascendance, Accommodation* (Curzon Press, 1999)

Edmund Terence Gomez, ed., *Political Business in East Asia* (Routledge 2002)

Edmund Terence Gomez and Hsin-Huang Michael Hsiao eds., *Chinese Enterprise, Transnationalism, and Identity* (RoutledgeCurzon 2004)

Rupert Hodder, *Merchant Princes of the East: Cultural Delusions, Economic Success and the Overseas Chinese in South-east Asia* (John Wiley, 1996). A curate's egg.

Kunio Yoshihara, *The Rise of Ersatz Capitalism in South-east Asia* (Oxford University Press, 1988)

Chinese Emigration

Lynn Pan, *Sons of the Yellow Emperor: A History of the Chinese Diaspora*, (Kodansha International, 1994). Wide-ranging and highly readable.

Wang Gungwu, *Don't Leave Home: Migration and the Chinese* (Times Academic Press, 2003). One of Professor Wang's many books on the subject.

Wang Sing-wu, *The Organization of Chinese Emigration, 1848–88* (Australian National University, 1969; revised and expanded edition, Chinese Materials Center, 1978). An early study, rich in detail.

Regional

William S. Borden, *The Pacific Alliance: United States Foreign Policy and Japanese Trade Recovery, 1947–55* (University of Wisconsin Press, 1984). The Japanese dimension in post-war south-east Asia.

John Butcher and Howard Dick, eds., *The Rise and Fall of Revenue Farming: Business élites and the emergence of the Modern State in South-east Asia* (Macmillan, 1993)

Dominic Casserley, Greg Gibb and the Financial Institutions Team, *Banking in Asia: The End of Entitlement* (John Wiley, 1999)

James Clad, *Behind the Myth: Business, Money and Power in South-east Asia* (Grafton, 1991). Ruminations of a former *Far Eastern Economic Review* correspondent that do not quite live up to the promise of the title.

Martin Feldstein, ed., *Economic and Financial Crises in Emerging Market Economies* (University of Chicago Press, 2003). A collection of essays by the great and the good with special reference to the Asian crisis and the performance of the IMF and the World Bank.

Kevin Hewison, Richard Robison, Garry Rodan, eds., *South-east Asia in the 1990s: Authoritarianism, Democracy and Capitalism* (Allen & Unwin, 1993)

Ruth McVey, ed., *South-east Asian Capitalists* (Cornell University South-east Asia Programme, 1992)

Victor Mallet, *The Trouble with Tigers: The Rise and Fall of South-east Asia* (HarperCollins, 1999). Country-by-country survey from a *Financial Times* correspondent.

David Northrup, *Indentured Labor in the Age of Imperialism, 1834–1922* (Cambridge University Press, 1995). A global survey.

Philippe Riès, *Asian storm: Asia's Economic Crisis Examined* (Tuttle, 2000). Good account of how the crisis broke by an Agence France Presse reporter.

Thailand

James C. Ingram, *Economic Change in Thailand, 1850–1970* (Stanford University Press, 1971).

Alfred W. McCoy, *The Politics of Heroin: CIA Complicity in the Global Drug Trade* (Lawrence Hill Books, 1991). Thai political power, US Cold War foreign policy and one or two godfathers.

Pasuk Phongpaichit and Chris Baker, *Thailand: Economy and Politics* (Oxford University Press, 2002)

Fred Warren Riggs, *Thailand: The Modernization of a Bureaucratic Polity* (Honolulu: East–West Center Press, 1967). Riggs coined the phrase 'pariah capitalist', referencing the sect of Indian untouchables known as pariah, to define an outsider group – here the Thai Chinese – allowed economic opportunity only at the behest of indigenous political power.

Shu-chin Yang, *A Multiple Exchange Rate System: An Appraisal of Thailand's Experience 1946–55* (University of Wisconsin Press, 1957). A case study of the effects of exchange rate manipulation.

G. William Skinner, *Chinese Society in Thailand: An Analytical History* (Cornell University Press, 1957)

G. William Skinner, *Leadership and Power in the Chinese Community of Thailand* (Cornell University Press, 1958)

G. William Skinner, 'Creolized Chinese Societies in South-east Asia', in Anthony Reid, ed., *Sojourners and Settlers: Histories of South-east Asia and the Chinese* (Allen & Unwin, 1996) Skinner achieved extraordinary access to the Chinese élite of the period in Bangkok. His work is more thoroughly based on original interviews than that of any other commentator on the overseas Chinese. Rigorous, sceptical and sympathetic.

Akira Suehiro, *Capital Accumulation in Thailand, 1855–1985* (Centre for East Asian Cultural Studies, Tokyo, 1989). A key business and economic reference work for the period.

Peter Warr, ed., *Thailand Beyond the Crisis* (Routledge 2005). A good collection of essays about post-financial crisis Thailand.

Malaysia

M. Bakri Musa, *The Malay Dilemma Revisited: Race Dynamics in Modern Malaysia* (toExcel, 1999)

Chin Peng, *My Side of History* (Media Masters, 2003). Autobiography of a recipient of the Order of the British Empire who went on to be the leader of Malaysia's communist insurgency.

Edmund Terence Gomez, *Political Business: Corporate Involvement of Malaysian Political Parties* (James Cook University of North Queensland, 1994)

R. N. Jackson, *Immigrant Labour and the Development of Malaya, 1786–1920* (Government Printer, Kuala Lumpur, 1961). A survey of imported labour that starts with pre-colonial slavery and documents British co-operation with Chinese godfathers and triads, and Indian managers of indentured labour, to bring in hundreds of thousands of workers in the nineteenth century.

K. S. Jomo, *Privatising Malaysia: Rents, Rhetoric, Realities* (Westview Press, 1995)

Mahathir bin Mohamad, *The Malay Dilemma* (Asia Pacific Press, 1970). Not the doctor's only book, but his most famous one; writing in exile in London, he shares his racial theories with the world.

Victor Purcell, *The Chinese in Malaya* (Oxford University Press, 1948)

J. J. Puthucheary, *Ownership and Control in the Malayan Economy* (Singapore Eastern Universities Press, 1960). Written in Changi prison in Singapore in 1958–9, where this erudite ethnic Indian lawyer had been interned by the British. He set out to prove that the notion that the ethnic Chinese controlled the economy of colonial Malaya was a myth: 'The commonly held view that Chinese dominate the economy is false,' he wrote. 'The capital that dominates Malaya's economy is European.' The British colonial office did not like the sound of his arguments; Puthucheary was sustained by various liberal European, Chinese and Indian friends who ferried notes and source materials to and from Changi.

K. S. Sandhu, and A. Main, eds., *Indian Communities in South-east Asia, 1786–1957* (Times Academic Press, 1993) includes K. S. Sandhu, 'Indians in Malaya'. Some detail on the much under-researched role of Muslim Indian traders and entrepreneurs in south-east Asia from the early fifteenth century. The collection of essays details the history of unassisted, assisted and indentured labour migration from India, with some useful class analysis, and suggestions as to why Indian migration has been more transient than Chinese. Also shows how the role of Indians and Sri Lankans in the British colonial civil service set them up for a big fall when indigenous groups obtained political power after independence.

Peter Searle, *The Riddle of Malaysian Capitalism: Rent-seekers or Real Capitalists?* (Allen & Unwin, 1999). Limited original material.

Michael R. Stenson, *Class, Race and Colonialism in Western Malaysia: The Indian Case* (University of Queensland Press, 1980). The author argues that

British colonial rule was a highly effective exercise in racial manipulation and that, in the 1940s, this undermined a nascent working-class alliance that crossed the Indian–Chinese ethnic divide. There are plenty of unanswered questions, but the work is thought-provoking.

Indonesia

Howard Dick, *The Emergence of a National Economy: An Economic History of Indonesia, 1800–2000* (Allen & Unwin, 2002)

Jamie Mackie, 'Towkays and Tycoons: Chinese in Indonesian Economic Life in the 1920s and 1980s', in *The Role of the Indonesian Chinese in Shaping Modern Indonesian Life* (Cornell Southeast Asia Program, 1991). Good on the historical relationship between *totok* (first generation) and *peranakan* Chinese. Concludes that under Suharto there was a return to the 'nested relationships' typical of the nineteenth century *peranakan* and their political masters. James R. Rush's essay, 'Social Control and Influence in Nineteenth-century Indonesia: Opium Farms and the Chinese of Java', in the same volume, details the pseudo-military system by which the Dutch managed their Chinese tycoon allies.

Richard Robison, *Indonesia: The Rise of Capital* (Allen & Unwin, 1986)

Kevin O'Rourke, *Reformasi: The Struggle for Power in Post-Soeharto Indonesia* (Allen & Unwin, 2002). An excellent blow-by-blow account of the financial crisis as it was played out in Indonesia.

James R. Rush, *Opium to Java: Revenue Farming and Chinese Enterprise in Colonial Indonesia, 1860–1910* (Cornell University Press, 1990). Good case studies of nineteenth-century godfather Chinese in Java and their role in turning Dutch taxes, paid in kind, into cash.

Adam Schwarz, *A Nation in Waiting: Indonesia's Search for Stability* (Allen & Unwin, 1999). The Indonesia story from independence to the turn of the century, by a long-serving, respected Jakarta correspondent of the *Far Eastern Economic Review*.

Twang Peck Yang, *The Chinese Business Élite in Indonesia and the Transition to Independence, 1940–50* (Oxford University Press, 1998). How the *totok* Chinese took out the *peranakan* incumbents under Japanese rule; sadly, the author fails to produce compelling anecdotal colour for the smuggling that was at the heart of this process.

Philippines

Patricio N. Abinales, Donna J. Amoroso, *State and Society in the Philippines* (Rowman & Littlefield, 2005). Good on the origins of crony parliamentarianism in the 1920s and the phenomenon of party-swapping among politicians (which strongly echoes the Thai experience).

Hal Hill and Sisiya Jayasuriya, eds., *The Philippines: Growth, Debt and Crisis* (Australian National University, 1985). Attempts to address the conundrum of how the Philippines threw away the economic advantages it enjoyed at independence.

Amando Doronila, *The State, Economic Transformation and Political Change in the Philippines, 1946–72* (Oxford University Press, 1992). Argues that colonial US trade policy and the terms under which the Philippines gained independence shored up the ascendancy of a landed élite.

A. V. H. Hartendorp, ed., *Short History of Industry and Trade of the Philippines, from Pre-colonial Times to the End of the Roxas Administration* (American Chamber of Commerce of the Philippines, 1953)

Paul D. Hutchcroft, *Booty Capitalism: The Politics of Banking in the Philippines* (Cornell University Press, 1998). An excellent guide to bank robbery.

Ricardo Manapat, *Some are Smarter than Others: The History of Marcos' Crony Capitalism* (Aletheia Publications, 1991). Journalistic survey with biographies of different tycoons and families.

Norman G. Owen, *Prosperity without Progress: Manila Hemp and Material Life in the Colonial Philippines* (Ateneo de Manila University Press, 1984). Compares and contrasts Spanish and American colonial rule.

Temario C. Rivera, *Landlords and Capitalists: Class, Family and State in Philippine Manufacturing* (University of the Philippines Press, 1994). Interesting study that argues post-war Spanish and Chinese *mestizo* landed élites also dominated the move into manufacturing under import substitution industrialisation policy in the 1950s.

Edgar Wickberg, *The Chinese* Mestizo *in Philippine History* (Kaisa Para Sa Kaunlaran, 2001) and *The Chinese in Philippine Life, 1850–1898* (Yale University Press, 1965). The main studies of the *mestizo* phenomenon, unfortunately chronologically limited.

Andrew R. Wilson, *Ambition and Identity: Chinese Merchant Élites in Colonial Manila, 1880–1916* (University of Hawaii Press, 2004). As the title suggests, good on the multiple identity aspect of the godfather species, albeit in a narrow geographical and time frame.

Wong Kwok-chu, *The Chinese in the Philippine Economy, 1898–1941* (Ateneo de Manila University Press, 1999). No great surprises.

Hong Kong

James Clavell, *Tai-pan: A Novel of Hong Kong* (Michael Joseph, 1966). The bestselling historical novel.

Colin N. Crisswell, *The Taipans: Hong Kong's Merchant Princes* (Oxford University Press, 1991). Lacks focus.

Leo F. Goodstadt, *Uneasy Partners: The Conflict Between Public Interest and Private Profit in Hong Kong* (Hong Kong University Press, 2005). Reflections of a former journalist and Hong Kong government policy adviser.

Frank H. H. King, *The History of the Hongkong and Shanghai Banking Corporation* (Cambridge University Press, 1988) and, ed., *Eastern Banking: Essays in the History of the Hongkong and Shanghai Banking Corporation* (Athlone, 1983). The official bank biographer.

John Lanchester, *Fragrant Harbour* (Faber, 2002). Beautifully crafted novel that tells the reader more about colonial Hong Kong than many non-fiction works.

Roger Nissim, *Land Administration in Hong Kong* (Hong Kong University Press, 1998). Policy detail about where the money comes from.

Alice Poon, *Land and the Ruling Class in Hong Kong* (self-published, 2006). A few interesting snippets.

Kevin Rafferty, *City on the Rocks: Hong Kong's Uncertain Future* (Penguin, 1991). Fine reportage from a former *Financial Times* correspondent.

Philip Snow, *The Fall of Hong Kong: Britain, China and the Japanese Occupation* (Yale University Press, 2003). Beautifully written and exhaustively researched story of Hong Kong during the Second World War and the behaviour of its élites.

K. N. Vaid, *The Overseas Indian Community in Hong Kong* (University of Hong Kong, 1972)

Frank Welsh, *A History of Hong Kong* (HarperCollins, 1997). An excellent reference work.

Dick Wilson, *Hong Kong! Hong Kong!* (Unwin Hyman, 1990). Sympathetic, anecdotal reminiscences of a former editor of the *Far Eastern Economic Review*.

Singapore

Michael D. Barr, *Lee Kuan Yew: The Beliefs Behind the Man* (Curzon, 2000). Excellent compendium of the contrasting views that have been espoused by one man over the years.

T. J. S. George, *Lee Kuan Yew's Singapore* (Andre Deutsch, 1973)

W. G. Huff, *The Economic Growth of Singapore: Trade and Development in the Twentieth Century* (Cambridge University Press, 1994). A very solid economic history of the island state, which makes clear Singapore's dependence on Indonesian money and trade (rather than the more popularly perceived Malaysian link). Also, *Currency Boards and Chinese Banking Development in Pre-World War II South-east Asia: Malaya and the Philippines* (University of Glasgow, 2003)

Lee Kuan Yew, *From Third World to First: The Singapore Story, 1965–2000* (HarperCollins, 2000). The view from the humble Mr Lee.

Eric Tagliacozzo, *Secret Trades, Porous Borders: Smuggling and States along a South-east Asian Frontier, 1865–1915* (Yale University Press, 2005). An under-researched subject. Unfortunately Tagliacozzo fails to break much ground in terms of either content or analysis.

Godfather Biographies and Autobiographies

E. C. Batalla, *Growth and Survival for Generations: The Case of the Ayala Group of the Philippines, 1834–1996* (forthcoming).

Irene Cheng, *Clara Ho Tung: A Hong Kong Lady, Her family and Her Times* (Chinese University of Hong Kong, 1976). A sanitised story of one of Sir Robert Ho Tung's two wives.

Frank Ching, *The Li Dynasty: Hong Kong Aristocrats* (Oxford University Press, 1999). The Lis of Bank of East Asia are unusual in being a genuine multi-generation success story; Ching is clearly a fan.

Jean Gittins, *Eastern Windows, Western Skies* (South China Morning Post, 1969). The autobiography of a daughter of Sir Robert Ho Tung; some interesting personal details but very much the official view – Daddy, for instance, 'by a stroke of good fortune, had been resting in Macau at the outbreak of war' rather than (the reality) being tipped off by the Japanese consul that he should flee.

Geoff Hiscock, *Asia's New Wealth Club: Who's Really Who in Twenty-first Century Business: The Top 100 Billionaires in Asia* (Nicholas Brealey, 2000). Biographical sketches of contemporary tycoons.

Robin Hutcheon, *First Sea Lord: the Life and Work of Sir Y. K. Pao* (Chinese University Press, 1990)

Stanley Jackson, *The Sassoons: Portrait of a Dynasty* (William Heinemann, 1989). Engaging portrait of 'the Rothschilds of the East'.

Madame Wellington Koo, *No Feast Lasts Forever* (Quadrangle, 1975). Ghost-written autobiography of one of Oei Tiong Ham's daughters.

Sam King, *Tiger Balm King:The Life and Times of Aw Boon Haw* (Times Books International, 1992). The Haw Par story.

Pasuk Phongpaichit and Chris Baker, *Thaksin: The Business of Politics in Thailand* (Nordic Institute of Asian Studies, 2004). An excellent treatment.

C. F. Yong, *Tan Kah-kee: The Making of an Overseas Chinese Legend* (Oxford University Press, 1987)

Hagiographies

Anthony B. Chan, *Li Ka-shing: Hong Kong's Elusive Billionaire* (Oxford University Press, 1996). A fawning collection of newspaper clippings.

Mike MacBeth, *Quiet Achiever: The Life and Times of Tan Sri Dr Tan Chin Tuan* (Times Editions, 2003)

Lim Goh Tong, *My Story: Lim Goh Tong* (Pelanduk Publications, 2004). Butter would not melt.

Other

Ron Chernow, *The Death of the Banker: The Decline and Fall of the Great Financial Dynasties and the Triumph of the Small Investor* (Pimlico, 1997). A short synthesis of some of the ideas of this excellent business historian, who has written biographies of the Morgans, the Rockefellers and the Warburgs.

Matthew Josephson, *The Robber Barons: The Great American Capitalists, 1861–1901* (Harcourt, Brace, 1934). The book that gave rise to the expression.

Lytton Strachey, *Eminent Victorians* (Bloomsbury, 1988; first published, 1918). A deconstruction of Victorian Britain, but also high-quality historical narrative.

Appendix

Figure 1 **The correlation between export growth and GDP growth in south-east Asia over the past forty years**

Year-on-year growth of nominal export value versus year-on-year growth of nominal GDP, ASEAN Five countries*, %

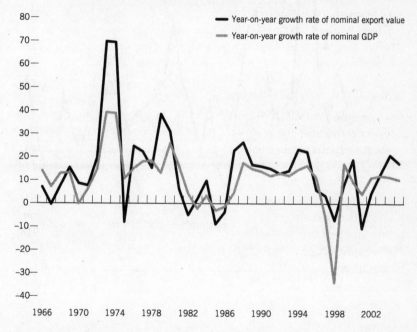

* Singapore, Thailand, Malaysia, Indonesia, Philippines. Hong Kong is excluded because it is not possible to separate out re-exports by mainland Chinese and China-based foreign companies via Hong Kong from local export data
Source: National accounts, author calculations

Figure 2 **The absence of such close correlation between export growth and GDP growth in a more balanced economy, such as the United States**

Year-on-year growth of nominal export value versus year-on-year growth of nominal GDP, United States, %

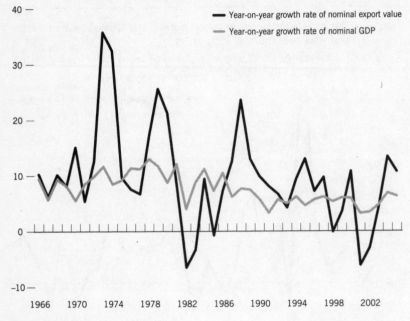

Source: US national accounts, author calculations

Figure 3 **The contribution of investment to growth in south-east Asia since 1977***

Gross domestic investment as a share of GDP in the ASEAN five countries and Hong Kong, and crude average across all states†, %

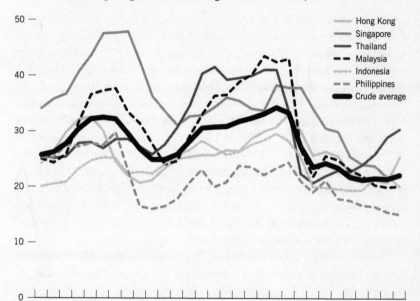

*The first year for which a full data set is available.
†This treats the six states as if their economies are the same size, which they are not. But the sizes are similar enough for a crude average to be instructive. If the Philippines, whose investment rate peaked in 1983 before falling substantially through a series of Marcos-inspired crises, is excluded, the peak average investment rate of the other five states, in 1996, is 36.5 per cent.
Source: National accounts, author calculations

Acknowledgments

A thousand thanks are due, of which only a small proportion can be honoured here. First and foremost, thanks to my beautiful wife, Tiffany Bown, who helped me through a 'difficult second album' period during the writing of this book in 2006. Mike Montesano and Arthur Kroeber also provided essential encouragement. My UK-based editors, Penny Daniel and Sally Holloway, showed extraordinary commitment to the publication of *Asian Godfathers* and faced down many trials with calm professionalism; thank you. The book was expertly read for libel in London by Richard Munden, supported by Stephen Brough, and both maintained good humour during a tortuous struggle to agree final text. Arthur Kroeber, Stephen Brown and Tiffany Bown provided important structural, content and proofing input during the editing stages. James Nunn created the cover, which was a lot of work. *Asian Godfathers* was commissioned by Andrew Franklin at Profile Books in London and by Morgan Entrekin at Grove, Atlantic in New York.

There is no way this book could have been written without the friends who provided free lodging during the research process. Those who can be thanked here are: Tom Mitchell, Simon and Miho Cartledge, and Micah and Rachel Katz in Hong Kong; Josh and Lorien Holland in Kuala Lumpur; Ruth Hill in Singapore; and Lincoln and Jacqui McMahon and Ivo and Tracy Philipps in London. Special mention also goes to Michelle Garnaud who provided occasional free victuals at her very fine restaurant in Hong Kong. When push came to shove, the author did shell out for hotels.

Much of the macro-economic framework for this book was drawn out of conversations and arguments with Jonathan Anderson, an old friend and a very fine economist. It should be stressed that Jon agrees with only some of what I have written. Data for graphs, as well as complex stock price information going back nearly forty years, were mined by Joe Man, a phlegmatic and relentlessly helpful analyst. Clare Alexander, my agent, provided comfort and support throughout.

Some people who assisted with this book prefer to remain anonymous. Those who can be thanked publicly are: Eric Batalla, Philip Bowring, Siew Nyoke Chow, Justin Doebele, Richard Elman, Mara Faccio, Edmund Terence

Gomez, Leo Goodstadt, Howard Gorges, Manggi Habir, Steve Hagger, Mark Hanusz, Hemlock, Kevin Hewison, Yopie Hidayat, Paul Hutchcroft, Ben Kwok, Kay Lee Ka-man, Keith Lee, Li Hoi-ying, Lim Kean Chye, Leslie Lopez, Paul Mackenzie, Camy Man, John McBeth, Ruth McVey, Francis Moriarty, Russell Napier, Peter Nightingale, Ross O'Brien, Kevin O'Rourke, Raphael Pura, Alanis Qin Jing, Gordon Redding, Hugo Restall, Rita Sim, Mark Simon (apologies for all that archival work), G. William Skinner, Philip Snow, Michael Vatikiotis, Sarasin Viraphol, Wang Gungwu, David Webb, and Chris Wood. MGG Pillai, a principled Malaysian journalist and an accomplished gossip, passed away while this book was being written: he is missed by many – perhaps even by those his writings so infuriated.

Index